Unshakable Life

*Living a Life of Purpose, Abundance,
and Eternal Impact*

Bradley Hawkins

Unshakable Life:

Living a Life of Purpose, Abundance, and Eternal Impact

Copyright © Bradley Hawkins (2025)

Unless otherwise noted, all scripture quotations in this publication are taken from The Holy Bible, English Standard Version. Copyright © 2001 by Crossway, a publishing ministry of Good News Publishers.

Scriptures marked KJV are taken from
The Holy Bible, King James Version, 1972.

Scriptures marked NIV are taken with permission from The Holy Bible, New International Version® [NIV] Copyright © 1973, 1978, 1984, 2011 by Biblica, Inc. All rights reserved worldwide.

Published by:

Table of Contents

Chapter 4

Journey 2

Chapter 5

Chapter 6

Chapter 7

Chapter 8

Journey 3

Chapter 9

Chapter 10

The Importance of Scripture **119**

Chapter 11

The Love of God **129**

Chapter 12

Lord and Savior **133**

Chapter 13

God's Will and Our Wealth...**142**

Chapter 14

Unlocking the Blessings of Tithing:

Chapter 15

Breaking Free: What the Bible Teaches About Debt and Financial

Chapter 16

True Riches: Unlocking God's Purpose for Wealth and Eternal

Chapter 17

Chapter 23

Chapter 24

Chapter 25

Journey 5

Dedication

I lovingly dedicate this book to my wife, Latisha, and our four incredible children: Chelsea, David, Benjamin, and Brittany. This book was born at a poignant moment in my life, sitting at my computer just after the last unmarried child in our family announced his engagement. With all four of our children stepping into the next chapter of their lives and beginning their own families, I felt compelled to share the deeper, more intricate details of our life story, the "behind the scenes version," if you will and how God worked miracles in our lives. My hope is that this book provides you with a richer understanding of the legacy you carry within our family.

This book has grown into a testament to how God provides for and prepares each of us for the unique journeys He lays out, weaving them together into an extraordinary tapestry. Thank you to each of you for the gift you are in my life and for your willingness to participate in this journey. My prayer is that this book will not only bless you individually but also inspire you to be a blessing to others as you carry forward your part of this story.

Latisha, your wisdom, encouragement, and endless patience in writing this book and more importantly living this life with me have been a priceless gift throughout this journey. Together, we have uncovered both the beauty and the challenges of our past, bravely revisiting difficult moments while celebrating God's unwavering faithfulness in our lives. I cannot imagine what the outcome of this life could have been without you. This book is as much a testament to what God has done as it is a testament to the faithfulness of you and our kids. You are all truly amazing, and I am grateful for the blessing each of you are in my life.

Stepping Into a Life Beyond Your Wildest Dreams

What if I told you that God has prepared a life for you so grand, so overflowing with joy, peace, and purpose that it surpasses anything you could ever imagine? A life where your dreams align with His promises, where your relationships are deeply fulfilling, your purpose is crystal clear, and your provision is abundant in every way. Imagine living in a flow of God's goodness, where victory over challenges is your norm and the impact of your life ripples into eternity. This isn't just a fantasy—it's the reality God desires for you, right here and right now.

But let's get real for a moment. Does this describe your life today? Or are you stuck in survival mode, trying to piece together a sense of peace and purpose amid the chaos? Maybe you've prayed for a breakthrough, for more joy, more provision, and more meaning, but it feels like those prayers hit a wall. Maybe you've read the promises in God's Word but wonder why they seem out of reach. I've been there, and I know what it's like to wrestle with the gap between what God says is possible and what life looks like today.

I want to tell you a story—a story that changed everything for me.

The Breakthrough Moment: From Surviving to Thriving

It was a season when life felt heavy. Bills were piling up, relationships were strained, and the sense of purpose I once had seemed to vanish. I was doing all the "right things"—praying, going to church, serving others—but I felt stuck. I kept wondering, "Is this really all there is? Where's the abundant life Jesus promised?" I knew the scriptures about God's blessings, His plans for prosperity, and the promises of living in victory, but none of that felt real in my life. I was surviving but definitely not thriving.

One night, after another exhausting day, I found myself on my knees, pouring my heart out to God. I didn't have polished words or even a clear prayer—I just needed answers. And in that raw moment, something inside me shifted. It wasn't an immediate solution to my problems, but it was a deep realization— I'd been focusing on what I wanted from God instead of truly aligning my life with Him. I was trying to create my own version of what I thought peace and abundance were. I sensed God gently saying, "You've been striving for what you think is abundance, but true abundance comes when you're fully aligned with Me; when you're living out the fullness of My kingdom promises."

That realization set me on a journey that transformed everything. It wasn't about chasing blessings anymore—it was about stepping into the grand, fruitful, and overflowing life God had designed, a life rooted in intimacy with Him, guided by His will, and flowing with His endless provision.

This is where the truth gets real: life didn't suddenly become problem-free. The challenges didn't disappear, and the enemy didn't stop throwing obstacles in my way. What did change was how I faced those battles. Walking side by side with my heavenly Father, I learned that victory wasn't about avoiding difficulties but overcoming them through His strength, wisdom, and unshakable love.

God's plan for your life isn't a quick fix or a magic bullet. Life is tough, and the enemy will always try to make it tougher. But God's incredible plan teaches us how to stand firm, how to flourish even when life gets hard, and how to experience victory and abundance right in the middle of it all. When you walk hand in hand with your heavenly Father, not only will you have a breakthrough—you'll learn how to thrive in the face of adversity and live in the overflow that God has always planned for you.

The Invitation to Live in Abundance

This book is your invitation to experience that kind of life—a life that's grand, richly fruitful, and overflowing in every sense. It's about shifting from survival mode into a life of victory, influence, and fulfillment that radiates God's glory. It's about understanding that God's abundance isn't just about material wealth, but about every area of life being touched by His favor—your relationships, your work, your health, your joy, and yes, even your finances.

God's desire for you isn't just to get by; it's for you to thrive so that your life becomes a beacon of His goodness. Aligned with His will, His blessings flow freely and naturally, even in the face of challenges. And you're not just building a successful life here—you're storing up treasures in Heaven that you'll one day offer back to Jesus in a moment of pure worship. Your life will echo into eternity, leaving a legacy that reveals God's love, power, and grace to everyone around you.

A Story of Abundance in Action

Picture this: Tim and Robin, newly married, struggling to make ends meet, yet passionate about their faith. They had dreams of starting a business, raising a family, and living a life that reflected God's goodness, but obstacles kept mounting. Debt was crushing them, unexpected health issues arose, and they found themselves barely able to stay afloat. They prayed, they fasted, they sought counsel, but it felt like every door remained closed.

One day, Tim said to Robin, "What if we've been focusing on the wrong thing, chasing our dreams instead of surrendering to God's plan for us?" They took a step back, and committed their business, their finances, and their future entirely into God's hands. Most importantly, they committed to pursue Him above all else. They didn't just ask for blessings—they asked to be aligned with His heart, His will, and His kingdom's purposes.

That simple shift changed everything. As they deepened their intimacy with God, they received ideas and strategies beyond their own wisdom. Doors opened that no human effort could have forced. Their businesses took off and became platforms for ministering to others. Their finances multiplied. Their health improved, their relationships flourished, and they found themselves living in an overflow they had only dreamed of. Challenges still came, and the enemy didn't stop trying to derail their progress. But they had learned the secret: walking in step with their heavenly Father, they were equipped to deal with every challenge and still flourish in the abundance God had planned for them. What had been survival mode became a life of grand, abundant, kingdom impact.

This is the story God wants to write in your life too.

Stepping Boldly onto the Path of Your Grand Abundant Life

Journey 1 serves as the starting block for a life grounded in God's promises, offering you a foundational understanding of living with purpose, abundance, and eternal impact. This is not a conclusion but an invitation to exploring these topics, which will be developed further in the following chapters. I aim to lay out these ideas so you can think deeply about them, allowing you to connect the dots as you progress through the journey.

The heart of Journey 1 is this: you are called to live a life of purpose and impact, but the depth of that calling unfolds as you delve deeper into God's promises. By considering concepts such as spiritual authority, free will, and abundance, you'll grasp how they might shape your life. And while we're laying a foundation here, the bigger picture will come into focus as you continue through the coming topics.

I invite you to join me in this pursuit. Let's explore what it means to live abundantly, not just in material wealth, but in every aspect of life. Together, let's seek the fullness that God has for us.

CHAPTER 1

Journey to Abundance: Discovering True Wealth, Including and Beyond Material Riches

God's plan for you is bigger, richer, and more glorious than anything you could ever imagine. But it's not about striving for more it's about aligning with Him, stepping into the flow of His kingdom, and living in the fullness of His promises. This journey is about building a legacy that impacts the world now and echoes into eternity. It's not a quick fix, and it doesn't mean life becomes problem-free. The enemy is real, and life can be tough, but walking hand in hand with your heavenly Father equips you to face those battles head-on and still thrive. Walking with God gives you an unshakable life.

God is ready to lead you into a life that's more vibrant, powerful, and impactful than anything you've experienced before. The choice is yours. Are you ready to step into the abundance He's prepared for you—even when life gets tough?

Understanding Eternity

To have an unshakable life you must know what this life is all about. Living with an eternal perspective not only fills each day with exhilarating purpose but also brings an incredible sense of peace, even in the face of life's toughest challenges. When we anchor our hearts in the grander purpose and the glorious future God has promised, the difficulties we face here lose their weight. It's as if the struggles and pain of this life fade into the background, overshadowed by the brilliant light of eternity. God reveals more and more about our true destiny, and in that revelation, we find strength, hope, and an unshakable joy that carries us through anything this world throws our way. It's not just about surviving the storms—it's about thriving with the confidence that our real future is far beyond anything we can imagine, and it's secure in His hands.

When we focus on eternity, our life of abundance naturally increases because we prioritize what truly matters—our relationship with God, our impact on others, and our alignment with His will.

So, let's lift our eyes above the temporary and fix them on the eternal.

Understanding Life's Purpose

Many people find it challenging to live according to the Bible's teachings due to a variety of factors, including the pursuit of personal happiness and success, cultural shifts toward individualism, and skepticism toward religious authority. The fast-paced, materialistic nature of modern life often prioritizes self-gratification over self-sacrifice, making it difficult to focus on spiritual growth, community service, and religious principles. Additionally, the prevalence of moral relativism and a decline in traditional religious beliefs contribute to a reluctance to embrace the biblical purpose of life.

Living according to the Bible's teachings offers profound blessings and avoids the pitfalls of worldly motivations. Jesus promises, "I have come that they may have life, and have it abundantly" (John 10:10), highlighting the abundant life found in following Him. Pursuing selfish desires and materialism leads to emptiness and loss, while a life dedicated to God brings peace, purpose, and fulfillment. As Proverbs 3:5–6 assures, "Trust in the Lord with all your heart and lean not on your own understanding; in all your ways submit to him, and he will make your paths straight." By embracing God's guidance and wisdom, we experience true joy, community, and eternal rewards, avoiding the fleeting and ultimately unsatisfying rewards of a self-centered life.

Biblical Perspective on Life's Purpose

The Bible offers a definite perspective on life's purpose and the source of true fulfillment. According to scripture, we are here to know God, to love Him, and to make His love known to others. Ecclesiastes 12:13 sums it up well: "Fear God and keep his commandments, for this is the duty of all mankind." Jesus also teaches that the greatest commandments are to love God with all our heart, soul, and mind and to love our neighbor as ourselves (Matthew 22:37–39). We are called to fulfill the Great Commission by making disciples of all nations. We are to honor God by living a holy and obedient life, serving others, and doing good works. Additionally, we are to steward God's creation responsibly. By following these principles, we live a life that honors God and prepares us for eternity with Him in Heaven.

The Choice Between Worldly Distractions and God's Abundance

Opportunities are often overlooked because of a desire for immediate gratification. And we can be deluded. We know what is offered in this world by pursuing what TV and movies show or what some of our friends talk about when we are hanging out, enticing us away from what we have known from our lives going to church. We have gotten distracted from all the earthly pursuits that seem so fun and so enticing. We see others "getting away with mediocrity" and think dabbling with what the world offers is not so bad. We have accepted Christ as our Savior and will be going to Heaven anyway. Isn't God a forgiving God?

The reality is that what the world offers is a cheap substitute for what God is offering us. He wants us to live an incredibly abundant life to the fullest. He is the one who has created wealth and abundance, and the enemy has created a cheap substitute. He is the one who has created love, and the enemy has created a cheap substitute. He is the one who has created joy and peace, and the enemy has created multiple cheap substitutes. This book encourages you to take the time to go through it with an open mind to what God might be offering you. Go through this book in neutral leaving your predetermined opinions off the table until you have completed it and given it a try. What do you have to lose?

The distractions of the world are designed to pull us away from the path of righteousness and the abundant life that God promises. When we see others seemingly enjoying a life of mediocrity, consider the deeper purpose and fulfillment that God has intended for you. Reflect on how earthly distractions have diverted your focus from your faith and the abundant life that God has promised. Embrace the opportunity to rediscover the true essence of a life lived fully in accordance with God's principles. By setting aside preconceived notions and approaching this book with an open heart, you may find yourself uncovering a more profound and meaningful connection to your faith, leading to a life that is truly rich in every sense of the word.

Living with a Focus on the Big Picture

The Importance of Vision and Direction

In almost everything I do, whether being a part of my family, starting and running different businesses, or my spiritual walk, I find it extremely helpful to have a vision and a direction in place. For example, when I am driving and my wife is giving me directions, she might say, "Go two miles down this road until we get to a different road, and turn right."

Frustration arises in me when I don't understand the big picture. I say, "You have to give me more than that. What town are we driving to? Will we be driving for an hour or five minutes? Am I headed to the highway, or am I headed to some back roads?"

My wife says, "I have this, don't worry."

God wants to tell us step by step how we are to go. Psalm 119:105 says, "Your word is a lamp to my feet and a light to my path." He does not say He is the beacon of light at your destination, nor does He say He is the spotlight down the path. He says, "I am the light unto your feet," telling us that He will show us our next step. To be honest, that is not easy for me. I always like seeing the big picture, but if He shows me the big picture right up front, I tend to say, "Okay, I got this. Step aside, God, I will take it from here." He wants me to rely on His every Word so that I don't miss any blessing He has as I walk step by step with Him.

On the other hand, He is also giving me the big picture—one that I cannot take into my own hands, but He shows us in all the details that He wants our focus to be on His big picture. Heaven is mentioned in more than 800 Bible verses, which means to me that it is important to our understanding of our Christian Walk. I want to understand as much as I can about what Heaven is and how it should play into my Christian Walk.

To be honest, I had not given Heaven a lot of focus in my past. It didn't seem fun to me the way others had described it. I have heard people say that I would spend eternity on a cloud playing a harp, singing. I don't know about you, but that does not sound like fun to do for eternity. Maybe an hour or two, but not for eternity. That cannot be the plan. Through my abiding (which you will learn in detail in this book), I have learned a lot about Heaven and am excited to be there one day once I fulfill all that God has for me to do while I am here on earth.

Being able to see the real big picture of my life and purpose on earth excites me for my life. I don't mind the step-by-step directions knowing what my end destination is going to be and why they are necessary. I find that trusting and obeying Him is far easier than if I don't know what my end destination is going to look like.

The Promises of Heaven

Let's look in a little more detail at what our heavenly destination is all about. The Bible gives us glimpses of Heaven that are meant to inspire and encourage us. Revelation 21:4 promises, "He will wipe every tear from their eyes. There will be no more death or mourning or crying or pain, for the old order of things has passed away." This verse alone offers a powerful vision of a place where suffering and sorrow are no more.

Additionally, John 14:2–3, where Jesus says, "My Father's house has many rooms; if that were not so, would I have told you that I am going there to prepare a place for you? And if I go and prepare a place for you, I will come back and take you to be with me so that you also may be where I am," reassures us that Heaven is a prepared place of personal and communal joy.

A Life of Purpose and Eternal Impact

By understanding these promises, we can appreciate the true nature of Heaven—a place of endless discovery, boundless love, and infinite joy in the presence of God. This perspective helps us live our earthly lives with a sense of purpose and anticipation, knowing that the steps we take now are leading us toward an eternal adventure with the Creator. Understanding how to live an unshakable, abundant life is foundational to stepping boldly onto the path of your grand, God-given journey. It's about embracing the promises and provisions of the Father with confidence, knowing that His plans for you are more magnificent than anything you could design on your own. This journey is not just about abundance in the earthly sense, but about a life so deeply rooted in faith and eternity that no storm can shake it. As we align ourselves with God's vision, focusing on eternal truths and living in the fullness of His promises, we tap into a life of unyielding purpose, overflowing joy, and abundant grace. The time to step boldly into this grand life is now, trusting that He's guiding you every step of the way and that the life of abundance He offers will impact not only your today but also your forever.

Let's delve deeper into this heavenly destination and see how it shapes our faith, our actions, and our ultimate hope.

CHAPTER 2

The Reality of Heaven for Our Eternity

The Bible assures us that Heaven is real, and for those who believe in Jesus, it is our eternal home. In Heaven, we won't be idle. Revelation 22:3 says, "His servants will serve him." This service won't be burdensome, and we'll experience unending joy in serving God and one another. Heaven is a place of complete contentment and satisfaction, where our deepest desires and longings are fully met in the presence of God. Our true fulfillment comes from a relationship with God, which continues into eternity. As we live out this truth, we find a purpose that transcends the fleeting nature of earthly life and leads us to eternal happiness.

Earthly Life as Preparation for Heaven

Seeing our earthly lives as preparation for Heaven shifts our view of earthly life. What we do now takes on meaning. Knowing that our ultimate destiny is either Heaven or hell based on our relationship with Jesus gives weight to all our choices. It is crucial to seek and understand the truth about God and His purpose for our lives—so we can align with them. The stakes are indeed high, and guessing wrong has eternal consequences. Understanding life on earth versus eternity is fundamental to grasping the biblical perspective on our existence. Life on earth is temporary and finite, characterized by growth, challenges, relationships, and learning. "There is a time for everything, and a season for every activity under the Heavens" (Eccl. 3:1). Earthly life includes growth and learning from childhood to adulthood, marked by education, career pursuits, and personal development. Relationships with family, friends, and colleagues bring joy and support, though sometimes conflict arises. Challenges and suffering, such as illness and loss, are part of life, yet James 1:2–3 encourages believers to view trials as opportunities for growth. Our moral and spiritual choices shape our character and spiritual destiny, with the Bible emphasizing righteous living and seeking God's will (Micah 6:8).

Do You Think About What Our Eternity Will Be?

The Bible describes eternity as an infinite state beyond time and space in which the soul continues after physical death. Eternity can be understood in two primary ways: eternal life with God or eternal separation from Him.

Eternal life with God, or Heaven, is a place of perfect peace, joy, and communion with God. Revelation 21:4 says, "He will wipe every tear from their eyes. There will be no more death or mourning or crying or pain, for the old order of things has passed away." Believers will experience God's presence fully (1 Cor. 2:9), receive glorified bodies free from decay (1 Cor. 15:42–44), and gain perfect knowledge and understanding (1 Cor. 13:12). Conversely, eternal separation from God, or hell, is a place of eternal suffering (Matt. 25:41–46), a consequence for those who reject God and His salvation (2 Thess. 1:9).

Eternal life is described as an existence of unparalleled joy, peace, and fulfillment, with Jesus calling it "life to the full" (John 10:10). Our deepest experiences of joy, love, and peace on earth are mere shadows of the greater joy, love, and peace in God's presence. For instance, the joy of a wedding or the birth of a child can be seen as a glimpse of the greater joy in Heaven.

Understanding eternity is challenging because our earthly experiences are bound by time and space. However, the Bible offers metaphors to help us grasp this concept. Second Peter 3:8 explains, "With the Lord a day is like a thousand years, and a thousand years are like a day," illustrating that God exists outside our perception of time.

While suffering is part of earthly life, it is temporary compared to the eternal glory that awaits (Rom. 8:18). Paul writes in 2 Corinthians 4:17–18, "For our light and momentary troubles are achieving for us an eternal glory that far outweighs them all. So, we fix our eyes not on what is seen, but on what is unseen, since what is seen is temporary, but what is unseen is eternal."

Understanding eternity requires trust in God's promises.

Story Time: Jacob and Eternity

Occasionally, I will create a fictional story in this book to illustrate a point I am trying to make. These stories are not perfectly aligned with scriptures, but they are how I imagine things after reading and studying scriptures. I will let Jacob clarify this point for you.

Jacob was known for his kind heart, dedication to his family, and unwavering faith in God. He spent his days working in the fields, raising his children, and teaching them the importance of living a righteous life according to the scriptures. Jacob often spoke to his children about eternity, explaining how the short span of their earthly lives was just the beginning of a much grander existence.

One evening, as the sun dipped below the horizon and painted the sky in hues of orange and purple, Jacob gathered his children around the fire. He wanted to share a story that would help them understand the significance of living according to God's will and the immense value of eternity.

"Imagine," Jacob began, "a timeline that stretches endlessly in both directions, with no beginning and no end. Our lives on earth are but a tiny dot on this infinite line. This dot represents our ninety years or so that we may live, filled with joys, sorrows, challenges, and triumphs. Now, think of eternity as the rest of that line, continuing forever, beyond what we can see or comprehend."

His children listened intently, their eyes reflecting the flickering flames of the fire. Jacob continued, "Our time on earth is a trial period, a test of our faith and our willingness to obey God's commandments. It is short, fleeting, and temporary, yet it holds great significance because the choices we make here determine our place in eternity. Heaven, the place of eternal life with God, is described in the Bible as a place of unparalleled joy, peace, and fulfillment."

He picked up a small pebble from the ground and held it up. "This pebble," he said, "represents our earthly life. It is small and insignificant compared to the vast ocean, representing eternity. Just as this pebble is nothing compared to the ocean, our earthly struggles and hardships are nothing compared to the eternal glory that awaits us in Heaven."

Jacob's children looked thoughtful. "But Father, what about those who do not live according to God's will? What happens to them?"

Jacob's expression grew somber. "The Bible also speaks of eternal separation from God, a place called hell. It is a place of suffering and regret, reserved for those who reject God and His commandments. The choices we make on earth have eternal consequences. That is why it is so important to live according to the scriptures, to love God and our neighbors, and to seek His will in all that we do."

He paused, letting his words sink in. "Our time on earth is short, but it is precious. It is our opportunity to build rewards in Heaven by living a life of faith, obedience, and love. As Jesus said in Matthew 6:19–20, "Do not store up for yourselves treasures on earth, where moths and vermin destroy, and where thieves break in and steal. But store up for yourselves treasures in Heaven, where moths and vermin do not destroy, and where thieves do not break in and steal.""

Jacob's children nodded, understanding the weight of his words. They realized that their actions, choices, and faithfulness on earth would echo into eternity, shaping their eternal destiny. The concept of eternity began to take root in their hearts, guiding them to live lives that honored God and reflected His love.

As the night grew darker and the stars began to twinkle in the sky, Jacob's family sat in silence, contemplating the vastness of eternity and the immense value of their short time on earth. They were filled with a renewed sense of purpose, knowing that every moment, every decision, and every act of faithfulness was an investment in their eternal home with God. They said, "Dad, can you tell us what we must do to have a great eternity?"

"Living on this earth with meaning and purpose is crucial to maximizing our eternity. By aligning our lives with God's will, seeking His kingdom first, and prioritizing love, faith, and obedience, we set the foundation for eternal rewards and everlasting joy in His presence. God, as a loving and just King, uses our actions and choices on earth as a basis for the rewards and roles we will receive in Heaven, recognizing our faithfulness (Matt. 16:27, 1 Cor. 3:14). In Heaven, He will reward us according to our dedication, giving us responsibilities and joys that reflect our earthly lives' impact. Let us not squander this precious opportunity by being swayed by the world's fleeting attractions. Instead, let's live with the awareness that our actions today echo into eternity, shaping our ultimate destiny and the fullness of life in His kingdom." We'll look at this more deeply in Chapter 25.

While living solely for our pleasures and neglecting God's will may not preclude us from Heaven—since salvation is by grace through faith in Jesus Christ (Ephesians 2:8–9)—it does affect the treasures and rewards we build up. Jesus urges us in Matthew 6:19–21 to store up treasures in Heaven, where they are safe from decay and theft. Living a self-centered life might result in a lack of eternal rewards, as our focus is diverted from God's purposes to our temporary desires. We will analyze this in more detail later in the book.

Our Inheritance as Believers in Christ—Some Definitions

- **Inheritance:** Believers are described as heirs of God and co-heirs with Christ (Rom. 8:17). This inheritance includes sharing in His authority and glory.

- **Priesthood of Believers:** 1 Peter 2:9 speaks of believers as a "royal priesthood," indicating a role that combines both priestly service and kingly authority. See also Revelation 5:10.

- **Kingdom Participation:** Believers are often referred to as citizens of Heaven (Phil.3:20) and participants in the Kingdom of God (Col. 1:13). This implies an active role in God's Kingdom both now and in the future. The Old Testament gets in on the concept as well. "But the holy people of the Most High will receive the kingdom and will possess it forever—yes, forever and ever. ... Then the sovereignty, power and greatness of all the kingdoms under Heaven will be handed over to the holy people of the Most High. His kingdom will be an everlasting kingdom, and all rulers will worship and obey him" (Dan. 7:18, 27).

The theme of believers reigning with Christ is woven throughout the scriptures, presenting a vision of a future where we share in Christ's authority and glory. This hope is meant to encourage and motivate believers to live faithfully and serve diligently, knowing that their ultimate reward is to participate in the eternal Kingdom of God. For those who are obedient to His will, ruling and reigning with Jesus in Heaven is part of the magnificent promise of eternal life, where we will find our true fulfillment in serving and glorifying God forever. If we endure in our faith, we will certainly reign with Christ" (2 Tim. 2:12). But if we disown Him, He will disown us.

Strength and Reward for Faithfulness

Second Chronicles 15:7 encourages believers to remain strong and courageous, reminding us that there is a reward for our labor. This reinforces the biblical principle that enduring trials and remaining steadfast in the faith will result in eternal rewards.

The Promise of Reigning in the Millennial Kingdom

Revelation 20:4–6 gives a vivid picture of the saints reigning with Christ for a thousand years. Those who remain faithful, even to the point of martyrdom, will be resurrected to reign in the millennial kingdom. This passage shows that their perseverance through suffering leads to a glorious future where they won't experience the "second death" but will reign as priests of God and Christ.

Believers Judging the World and Angels

First Corinthians 6:2–3 reveals the astonishing authority given to believers, as Paul teaches that the Lord's people will judge the world and even angels. This passage illustrates the significant responsibility that believers will have in God's Kingdom, implying that their current lives should reflect the wisdom and righteousness required for such authority.

By weaving together these scriptures, we see a cohesive vision of the future for believers: enduring in faith leads to sharing in Christ's reign, authority, and glory. These promises inspire us to live with strength, purpose, and anticipation for the eternal rewards awaiting those who remain faithful. Although we will get much deeper into this concept of rewards in Heaven in future chapters of this book, it is important to understand what our destination will look like as we build a case that our focus should be on eternity.

Criteria for Reigning with Christ

The Bible outlines several key principles for determining who will reign with Christ in His eternal kingdom. These criteria include faithfulness, stewardship, obedience, and humble service.

In the "Parable of the Talents" (Matt. 25) and the "Parable of the Minas" (Luke 19), Jesus teaches that those who are faithful with small responsibilities will be entrusted with greater authority. In Matthew 20:25–28, Jesus emphasizes obedience and humble service and explains that true greatness comes from serving others.

Believers will be judged and rewarded based on the quality of their work for God's Kingdom, as described in 1 Corinthians 3:12–15 and 2 Corinthians 5:10. Those whose work endures will receive eternal rewards and responsibilities.

As we continue into Journey 3 of this book, we will explore these criteria more deeply, understanding how our faithfulness and service now prepare us for reigning with Christ in the future.

Story Time: Tom's Faithful Life

Once upon a time, in a small village in the hills, lived a man named Tom. Tom was a humble farmer known for his kindness, integrity, and unwavering faith in God. Despite the hardships he faced, Tom always remained steadfast in his devotion, helping those in need and spreading love and compassion wherever he went.

Tom's life was marked by numerous challenges. The crops sometimes failed, and he had to work tirelessly to provide for his family. The winters were harsh, and the summers could be unforgivingly hot. Despite the struggles, Tom never lost hope. There were times when he felt overwhelmed, but he would retreat to a quiet place and pour out his heart to God. In those moments, he found solace and strength through prayer and the scriptures.

One particularly difficult year, a devastating storm destroyed much of Tom's harvest. The financial strain put his family at risk of losing their home. Desperate and disheartened, Tom knelt by his bedside and prayed fervently for God's help. In his darkest hour, he felt a gentle reassurance, a reminder of God's promise in Philippians 4:19, "And my God will meet all your needs according to the riches of his glory in Christ Jesus."

Tom remembered the story of Job and how he remained faithful despite immense suffering. Inspired by Job's perseverance, Tom decided to trust in God's provision. Soon after, the community rallied around him, offering help and support. Neighbors shared their resources, and a fellow farmer offered Tom work to make ends meet. This experience deepened Tom's faith and reinforced the importance of community and God's grace.

Tom's life was not only about enduring hardship but also about celebrating God's grace and forgiveness. He was known as a peacemaker in his village, often stepping in to mediate disputes. His words of wisdom were always seasoned with grace, reminding others of Jesus's teaching on forgiveness and reconciliation. He would often say, "Forgive as the Lord forgave you" (Col. 3:13), and his life exemplified this principle.

One day, a young man named Jacob, who had wronged Tom in the past, came seeking forgiveness. Jacob had stolen from Tom's farm during a time of personal crisis. Instead of harboring resentment, Tom forgave him and even helped him find a job. Jacob's life was transformed by this act of grace, and he became a devoted follower of Christ, spreading the message of forgiveness he had received.

In his village, Tom was known for his open fields and welcoming home. He would often host gatherings where people from all walks of life would come together to share a meal, sing hymns, and listen to Tom's stories of God's faithfulness. His hospitality and love created a strong sense of community, drawing many to seek the God he so faithfully served.

One day, after many years of faithful service, Tom's time on earth came to an end. His eyes closed in peaceful slumber, and he was gently carried by angels into the presence of God. As he arrived in Heaven, Tom was overwhelmed by the beauty and majesty surrounding him. The streets were paved with gold, and the air was filled with the sweetest melodies of worship.

He was greeted by Jesus, who welcomed him with open arms, saying, "Well done, good and faithful servant. You have been faithful with a few things; I will put you in charge of many things. Come and share your master's happiness" (Matt. 25:21).

Tom found himself in a grand assembly hall filled with countless saints who had gone before him. Each person was radiant with the glory of God, their faces shining with joy and peace. In the center of the hall stood a magnificent throne, and upon it sat the King of Kings, surrounded by a heavenly host.

The Lord spoke, His voice like the sound of rushing waters, "Welcome, my beloved children. You have run the race and kept the faith. Now, it is time for your reward."

God began to call each saint by name, revealing the roles they would play in His eternal kingdom. Those who had been faithful stewards on earth were given positions of authority. They were to rule and reign with Christ, overseeing the new Heavens and the new earth. Each assignment was given based on the faithfulness, obedience, and love shown during their earthly lives.

When it was Tom's turn, God said, "Tom, your life was a testament to My love. You served with humility, loved without condition, and remained faithful through every trial. Because of your faithfulness, I appoint you to govern over a region in My kingdom, where you will continue to guide and nurture, just as you did on earth."

Tom's heart swelled with gratitude and awe. He was led to a beautiful land, lush and vibrant, where he would oversee the growth of God's creation and care for the souls entrusted to him. His role was not just one of authority but of continued service, embodying the servant leadership that Jesus had exemplified.

As Tom walked through his new home, he felt a profound sense of peace and fulfillment. Eternity stretched before him, a boundless expanse of time that made his earthly life seem like a fleeting moment. The love and joy he experienced were immeasurable, far surpassing anything he had known on earth. Relationships in Heaven were deep and perfect, free from misunderstandings and pain. He was reunited with loved ones and met countless others who had been touched by his life.

Tom found that in this new role, the rewards were far greater than he could have imagined. There was a profound joy in serving alongside Christ, a deep peace in knowing he was fulfilling God's eternal purpose, and an overwhelming love that flowed from the throne of God to every corner of the kingdom.

He saw the impact of his earthly life in ways he had never known: lives he had touched, seeds of faith he had planted, and acts of kindness that had ripple effects throughout eternity. The rewards of Heaven were not just positions of authority but the eternal fruits of a life lived in faithful service to God.

Tom's story is a powerful reminder of the rewards awaiting those who live according to God's will. The promise of ruling and reigning with Christ is not just about power but about continuing the work of God's Kingdom in eternity. It is a call to live with purpose, love with abandon, and serve with humility.

For all who follow this path, the words of Jesus ring true: "To the one who is victorious and does my will to the end, I will give authority over the nations" (Revelation 2:26). The journey may be challenging, but the rewards are eternal and infinitely greater than we can imagine. Live faithfully, serve diligently, and look forward to the day when you will hear, "Well done, good and faithful servant."

CHAPTER 3

Origins of Conflict: Unveiling the Spiritual Struggle Behind Life's Challenges

To gain a deeper understanding of the big picture, we must delve into what is happening behind the scenes in the world. This involves exploring fundamental questions: How did the world of conflict begin? Why is the world filled with so much conflict? Let's examine the origins of conflict as described in the Bible.

According to the Bible, the struggle began with humanity's disobedience to God's commands, leading to the fall of man. This disobedience was a sin and introduced discord into what had originally been a harmonious creation. The story of Adam and Eve in the Garden of Eden illustrates the first instance of conflict, where temptation and the choice to stray from divine guidance set the stage for a world rife with challenges.

The narrative suggests conflict is not a random occurrence but is deeply rooted in the spiritual and moral dimensions of existence.

This raises more critical questions: Where are we headed? Why is the path so challenging before we reach our final destination of Heaven for eternity?

The Beginning of the Struggle

By looking at the beginning of conflict, we can better comprehend the struggles we face and the purpose behind our journey.

The Fall or the Beginning of Conflict

In the beginning, before time and creation, God had a divine plan that encompassed all of existence. Central to this plan was humanity, created to live in a state of perfect shalom—complete peace, harmony, and wholeness. The Garden of Eden was a paradise where Adam and Eve, the first humans, were placed. Here, they enjoyed intimate fellowship with God, living in a world free from pain, suffering, and death. God's ultimate desire was for humanity to love Him and walk in His ways out of a genuine, voluntary choice.

God, in His omnipotence, could have created beings who were programmed to love Him, but He knew forced love is not true love. True love requires choice. Therefore, God gave humans the freedom to choose Him or to turn away. This freedom was symbolized in the garden by the Tree of the Knowledge of Good and Evil. God commanded Adam and Eve not to eat from this tree, offering them the choice to trust Him or to seek knowledge and autonomy apart from Him.

The narrative of Lucifer's rebellion and transformation into Satan, the adversary, further underscores the importance of free will. Lucifer, a glorious archangel adorned with beauty and wisdom, chose to rebel against God out of pride (Isaiah 14:12–14). He wanted to elevate himself above God and became consumed with envy and anger. He was cast out of Heaven along with a third of the angels who followed him (Revelation 12:3–9). Satan's fall illustrates that even in the heavenly realms, God maintained the principle of free will, allowing His creatures the freedom to choose their paths.

The Accuser's (Satan) Authority

Satan's role as the accuser is evident in the story of Job, a man described as blameless and upright. Satan presented himself before God, questioning Job's faithfulness and suggesting Job's devotion was merely a result of the blessings and protection God provided (Job 1:6–12). God permitted Satan to test Job, allowing him to strip Job of his wealth, children, and health. However, God set boundaries, forbidding Satan from taking Job's life. This divine permission highlights that Satan's authority is limited and subject to God's sovereign control.

The story of Job also emphasizes the continued presence of free will. Job had the choice to curse God and abandon his faith or to remain steadfast. Despite his immense suffering, Job chose to trust in God, showcasing the resilience of faith that is freely chosen rather than coerced. This narrative demonstrates that God values free will so highly that He allows even His most faithful servants to experience trials, knowing their genuine love and trust in Him will be revealed and refined through adversity.

The Bible describes Satan, sometimes called the Devil, as a malevolent being with a clear agenda to harm humanity. In John 10:10, Jesus outlines the Devil's intentions, stating, "The thief comes only to steal and kill and destroy; I have come that they may have life, and have it to the full." This verse emphasizes the Devil's destructive goals. The Devil seeks to *steal* by taking away what is valuable, whether it be material possessions, peace, joy, or spiritual well-being, often tempting people to stray from their faith or prioritize worldly matters over spiritual truths. Additionally, the Devil aims to *kill*, leading to physical harm, spiritual death, or separation from God. This can manifest in various forms, such as promoting violence and hatred, or encouraging self-destructive behaviors. Furthermore, the Devil seeks to *destroy* lives, relationships, and even entire societies, often fostering division, spreading false teachings, and promoting moral and spiritual decay. While the Bible presents the Devil as a powerful adversary, it also reassures believers that through faith in Jesus Christ, they can resist Satan or the Devil's schemes and live a life filled with abundance and purpose.

The Schemes of the Adversary

Satan's strategies are rooted in deception and the manipulation of free will. His primary goal is to undermine God's plan by leading humanity away from Him. In the Garden of Eden, Satan took the form of a serpent and approached Eve, sowing seeds of doubt about God's goodness and commands (Gen. 3:1–6). He twisted God's words, suggesting God was withholding something beneficial from them. By appealing to Eve's desire for wisdom and autonomy, Satan tempted her to use her free will to disobey God. Adam followed suit, leading to the fall of humanity and the introduction of sin and death into the world.

Satan's deception extends beyond outright lies; he often mixes truth with falsehood, making his lies more convincing. In the wilderness, he tempted Jesus with physical sustenance, miraculous protection, and worldly power (Matt. 4:1–11). Each temptation was an attempt to sway Jesus's free will away from

God's will. However, Jesus resisted, using the truth of scripture to counteract Satan's lies. This encounter illustrates even the Son of God was subject to the exercise of free will, choosing to remain obedient to the Father.

Satan's ultimate motivation is to oppose God and assert his own dominion. He aims to corrupt God's creation, knowing that by leading humans into sin, he can create a rift between them and their Creator. Satan's strategies include planting doubt, promoting false teachings, fostering division, and blinding the minds of unbelievers to prevent them from seeing the truth of the gospel (2 Cor.4:4). He masquerades as an angel of light, deceiving even those within the church (2 Cor. 11:14). His goal is to manipulate human free will to his advantage, hoping to gain followers and disrupt God's plan.

The Authority of Believers

Despite Satan's influence, believers are endowed with the authority to resist him. Through Jesus Christ's death and resurrection, the powers of darkness have been defeated, and believers have been granted authority over evil (Col. 2:15). This victory empowers believers to choose to follow God's will and to resist the Devil's schemes.

Believers are equipped with spiritual armor, as described in Ephesians 6:10–18. This armor includes the belt of truth, the breastplate of righteousness, the shoes of the gospel of peace, the shield of faith, the helmet of salvation, and the sword of the Spirit, which is the Word of God. Each piece represents a conscious choice to live in alignment with God's truth and resist the enemy's lies. The armor of God symbolizes the active role believers must take in exercising their free will to stand firm in their faith.

Prayer and vigilance are essential components of this spiritual armor, connecting believers to God's power and guidance. The Holy Spirit, who dwells within them, empowers them to discern truth from falsehood and to make choices that align with God's will. Believers are called to use their free will to remain steadfast in their faith, resist the Devil, and submit to God's authority (James 4:7). This resistance is not a passive stance but an active engagement in spiritual warfare, rooted in the conscious choice to follow Christ.

Understanding how to live an unshakable life and embrace the abundance God offers is essential for navigating life's challenges with faith and trust. By stepping boldly onto the path of your grand, abundant life, you equip yourself with the strength to endure difficulties while keeping your eyes on the eternal promises of God. Even in the face of uncertainties, you can maintain a deep sense of peace, knowing God's plan is greater than any adversity. As you align your choices with His will, you experience His blessings on earth and prepare for the fullness of joy and purpose He has reserved for you in eternity.

CHAPTER 4

Jesus's Unshakable Victory: An Introduction

The Promise of Victory

The Bible promises us ultimate victory over Satan and his forces. God has assured believers that He will soon crush Satan under their feet (Rom. 16:20). After a thousand years of being bound, he will be released briefly, only to be defeated and cast into the lake of fire, where he will face eternal torment (Rev. 20:1–3, 7–10). This final judgment marks the end of Satan's reign of deception and destruction.

Until that day, God calls believers to exercise their free will to remain faithful to Him, knowing their struggle is not against flesh and blood but against spiritual forces of evil (Eph. 6:12). The trials and tribulations they face serve to refine their faith and strengthen their character. These sufferings are not in vain but work to develop a deep and abiding hope in God's promises (Rom. 5:3–5). The present sufferings we endure are temporary and not worth comparing with the glory that will be revealed in them (Rom. 8:18).

The Conflict: The Eternal Hope

The narrative of Satan's rebellion and the ensuing spiritual warfare is also a story of hope and redemption. In Jesus Christ, believers have a great High Priest who sympathizes with their weaknesses and intercedes for them at the right hand of God (Heb. 4:14–16). Through Jesus's sacrifice, they are forgiven, cleansed, and reconciled to God—a testament to the power of free will. It is the result of Jesus's willingness to lay down His life and the believer's choice to accept His gift of salvation.

The hope of the gospel is the assurance of a future where there will be no more death, mourning, crying, or pain (Rev. 21:1–4). God will dwell with His people in a new Heaven and a new earth, where the former things will pass away, and all things will be made new. This hope sustains believers as they navigate the challenges and uncertainties of this world, knowing that the choices they make in alignment with God's will are part of a greater, eternal plan.

This final state is the fulfillment of God's original design for creation, a return to the perfect shalom that was present in the Garden of Eden. In this place of perfect peace, harmony, and wholeness, humanity will once again experience intimate fellowship with God, ruling and reigning with Him over a restored creation.

Story Time: The Tale of Redemption—A Family's Journey through Struggle and Triumph

The Beginning of the Storm

In a quaint town surrounded by rolling hills, there lived a man named Daniel, his wife Rachel, and their two teenage children, Lily and Samuel. They were a family known for their warmth and unity, a beacon of love and faith in their community. Daniel, a skilled carpenter, took pride in his work, while Rachel managed the household and nurtured their children's dreams. Their home was filled with laughter, shared meals, and a sense of belonging.

But life has a way of shifting, and the winds of change began to blow against their once-stable foundation. Daniel unexpectedly lost his job, a blow that sent ripples of anxiety through the family. The financial strain quickly became apparent, and the once tight-knit family began to fray. Rachel, who had always been the pillar of calm and optimism, felt the weight of their situation bearing down on her.

Rachel had dreams of traveling, of seeing their children go to college, and of growing old with Daniel in comfort and peace. But with the sudden loss of income, those dreams felt like distant fantasies. The plans they had made, the life they had envisioned, seemed to crumble before her eyes. The security she had always felt in Daniel's steady job and their shared goals was gone. She felt as though the future was slipping through her fingers and, with it, her sense of purpose and hope.

The children's response to the family's turmoil was equally distressing. Lily and Samuel, both in their late teens, began to seek solace outside the family. Lily, once a bright and cheerful girl, withdrew into her room, spending hours on social media and finding comfort in the validation of strangers. Samuel, who had been a model student and athlete, started skipping classes and hanging out with a new group of friends who encouraged risky behavior. The family's bond, once their greatest strength, seemed to be unraveling.

The Enemy's Triumph and Realization

As the family's struggles deepened, Satan observed with a sinister delight. He reveled in the seeds of discord he had sown. The despair in Rachel's eyes, the detachment of their children, and the strain in Daniel's voice were like music to his ears. He whispered lies into Rachel's mind, telling her that she was powerless, that her dreams were dead, and that her family would never recover. He convinced her that their future was lost, leaving her paralyzed with fear and uncertainty.

Satan's twisted excitement only grew as he watched Lily and Samuel drift further from their parents. He knew that the cracks in the family unit made them vulnerable to his influence. He fed on their insecurities, making them believe that they could only find security and acceptance outside their family. He saw the potential to pull them further into a world of superficial validation and dangerous distractions, away from the love and support they truly needed.

The enemy's strategy seemed to be working. The once vibrant and hopeful family was now a shadow of its former self. But amidst the chaos and darkness, a small flicker of hope remained. One night, as Daniel sat alone in his workshop, he felt a deep sense of despair. He thought about the future that seemed so uncertain and the weight of the responsibilities he felt he had failed to uphold. But then, a memory surfaced—a memory of the stories of faith and God's unwavering love from his childhood.

Daniel realized that the enemy's greatest weapon was not the circumstances they faced but the lies they had believed. He understood that their struggles were not just a result of lost income or changed circumstances but a spiritual battle for their hearts and minds. With a heavy heart and newfound clarity, Daniel fell to his knees and prayed. He asked God for strength, wisdom, and for the courage to lead his family back to the light. At that moment, he felt a sense of peace and reassurance, a reminder that they were not alone and that they had the power to choose their path.

The Turning Point: Embracing God's Armor

Daniel shared his revelation with Rachel. They talked openly about their feelings of failure and the lies they had allowed to take root in their hearts. Rachel wept. But as they spoke, they also found a shared resolve to fight back against the despair that had taken hold of their family.

They turned to the Bible, seeking comfort and guidance in God's Word. They found strength in scriptures that spoke of God's love and the power of faith. Together, they began to pray, inviting God's presence back into their home. They reminded each other of the armor of God—the belt of truth, the breastplate of righteousness, the shield of faith, shoes of the readiness of the gospel of peace, the helmet of salvation, and the sword of the Spirit (Eph. 6:10–18). They chose to embrace these spiritual tools, using them to combat the lies and fears that had taken hold.

The couple also reached out to Lily and Samuel. They had heartfelt conversations with their children, acknowledging the struggles they had been facing and the impact they had on the family. Daniel and Rachel apologized for their own shortcomings and reassured their children of their love and commitment to their family. They encouraged Lily and Samuel to open up about their feelings and the pressures they faced. It was a difficult process, filled with tears and raw emotions, but it was also a necessary step toward healing.

Lily slowly began to disconnect from the virtual world that had become her refuge. She reconnected with old friends and started participating in family activities again. Samuel, with his parents' support, distanced himself from the negative influences in his life and focused on his studies and sports. The family's unity, once fractured, began to mend. They learned to lean on each other and on God, finding strength in their renewed faith.

The Enemy's Defeat and Rage

As the family grew stronger, Satan's frustration boiled over. He watched in fury as the family's faith and love for one another blossomed once more. The lies he had planted were uprooted and replaced by the truth of God's Word. His tactics had failed, and the joy he had felt at their suffering turned to rage. He saw that his strategies were powerless against a family united in faith and love. His plans to destroy their unity and faith had backfired, leaving him seething with anger.

Satan's rage was a testament to his impotence in the face of God's power. He had underestimated the strength of a family rooted in Christ, a family that chose to exercise their free will to seek God and His peace. The shalom that Satan had tried to shatter was being restored, and there was nothing he could do to stop it.

The Restoration of Shalom

In the end, the family's journey brought them full circle to God's original plan for creation. They experienced a taste of the perfect shalom that God intended—a state of complete peace, harmony, and wholeness. They rediscovered their role as stewards of God's creation, caring for their home and each other with love and respect. The authority they had been given over their lives was reclaimed as they chose to walk in God's ways.

The Garden of Eden had been a place of perfect unity with God, a place where humanity was meant to live in harmony with creation, ruling and reigning with God. Though their choices had led them away from that original design, God's redemptive plan had always been at work, offering them the opportunity to return to Him. Through their struggles, the family learned the importance of free will and the power of choosing God amidst adversity.

As they stood together, stronger and more united than before, they knew that the shalom they experienced was a foretaste of the eternal peace they would one day share with God. In this place of perfect peace and joy, they would dwell with their Creator, free from the pain and struggles of this world. The enemy's attempts to destroy them had failed, and in their victory, they found not only peace but a deeper understanding of God's love and the power of faith.

Thus, the family's story came full circle, returning to God's original intention—a life of shalom, where love, faith, and unity reigned. They had navigated the trials of life, faced the enemy's deceptions, and emerged victorious by choosing to trust in God. Their journey was a testament to the enduring power of faith and the beauty of a family united in love and purpose.

The Assurance of Triumph

Scripture assures believers of ultimate triumph over the forces of darkness. In 1 Corinthians 15:57, Paul proclaims, "But thanks be to God! He gives us the victory through our Lord Jesus Christ." This victory, won by Christ, guarantees the powers of evil won't have the final say. In Colossians 2:15, it is written that Christ "disarmed the powers and authorities, making a public spectacle of them, triumphing over them by the cross." This victory is a present reality, empowering believers to live boldly and confidently.

Believers are called to stand firm, knowing their battle is part of a larger spiritual conflict. Second Corinthians 10:4 reminds us: "The weapons we fight with are not the weapons of the world. On the contrary, they have divine power to demolish strongholds." This spiritual warfare strengthens our faith and character, as James 1:2–4 encourages believers to "consider it pure joy whenever you face trials of many kinds because you know that the testing of your faith produces perseverance."

The Promise of Eternal Restoration

The story of redemption is one of restoration and hope. Jesus Christ, our Mediator, stands at the right hand of God, interceding on our behalf (1 Tim. 2:5). Through His sacrifice, we are reconciled to God, no longer bound by sin, and are now children of God (John 1:12). This reconciliation is a powerful demonstration of God's love, and it invites us to live in the freedom and peace Christ has provided.

The promise of eternal restoration is highlighted in 1 Peter 5:10, which says, "And the God of all grace, who called you to his eternal glory in Christ, after you have suffered a little while, will himself restore you and make you strong, firm, and steadfast." This promise assures believers the struggles of this life are temporary and God Himself will restore everything, making all things new.

The battle against evil is ultimately a journey of everlasting victory and joy. Despite the efforts of the enemy, God's plan is unstoppable. This final victory will usher in a new era of perfect peace, where humanity will once again walk in intimate fellowship with God, as it was meant to be from the beginning (Rev. 22:5).

This triumph is not just a future hope but a present reality that empowers believers to live fully surrendered lives (Rom. 8:37). This serves as a foundational exploration, preparing us to dive deeper into the victories Christ has secured on the cross and encouraging us to embrace the incomparable triumph that is ours in Him.

Before We Move into the Next Journey

It is crucial to recognize we are engaged in a spiritual battle, one we can't avoid or ignore, for it comes from God's enemy, who seeks to do everything in his power to prevent us from reaching our glorious destination in Heaven. However, we need not fear or be anxious about this conflict. The victory has already been secured by Christ, who defeated the enemy on the cross.

Living an unshakable and abundant life is rooted in surrendering fully to God's will and trusting in His promises—even in the face of life's challenges. As we step boldly onto the path of our grand, abundant life, we embrace the victory Christ has already secured for us on the cross.

Takeaway Message: Journey 1 sets the stage for you to reflect on living a victorious and abundant life through Christ. It challenges you to see beyond life's struggles and to consider what it means to live in God's abundance and purpose, knowing this is just the beginning of an eternal journey. As you move forward, you'll discover how these foundational truths connect and lead you toward a deeper understanding of God's plan for your life and how He can rebuild even what seems beyond repair.

The Challenge: As you walk through Journey 1, we encourage you to embrace this early stage of exploration. Are you ready to open your heart and mind to the fullness of God's promises? Can you commit to thinking beyond survival and considering how your choices today lay the groundwork for eternal impact? The challenge here is to ask yourself these questions as you prepare for the deeper truths that lie ahead.

God is ready to show up for you. This is about building a foundation of faith that's unshakable, and you're invited to be a part of it. So, don't just sit back and read—*engage*. Bring your questions, bring your struggles, and get ready to experience something transformational. This journey is for you, and I believe God has something incredible waiting on the other side.

The Journey of Tenacity: Trusting God's Path to a Life Overflowing with Blessings

One of the hardest things I've encountered in life is continuing when everything and everyone around me seems to be against me. *Tenacity* is a word I didn't fully grasp at the beginning of this journey. It's easy to quit when things don't go well. Sometimes quitting feels like the simplest option, but other times, it's the most difficult. And then there are moments when moving forward feels easier than quitting, yet in reality, it's the hardest thing to do. The true challenge lies in knowing the difference between when to quit and when to press on.

Needing Guidance

We often find ourselves in a place of confusion, wondering what we are supposed to do and how to discern the best course of action. The answers can feel elusive, but trust me, they are there. The problem often lies in the way we seek them. We tend to create our own vision of how things should unfold in our lives, shaping outcomes based on our desires and expectations—usually without seeking God's input. When these outcomes don't materialize, we feel frustrated and assume life isn't working as it should. We pray, asking God for guidance, but if He doesn't align His response with our preconceived notions of what is best, we mistakenly believe He isn't answering our prayers.

In these moments, it's easy to fall into the trap of comparison, looking at others and thinking God is favoring them while neglecting us. But the truth is, we're often asking God to fulfill our plans rather than surrendering to the grand master plan He is orchestrating. God's wisdom far exceeds our understanding, and His plans are woven with eternal significance. What we see as a lack of response from God may actually be His loving guidance, steering us away from paths that lead to lesser things and guiding us toward His greater purpose. The key is not to force our plans onto God but to seek His will, trusting He knows what is truly best for us. When we align our hearts with His, we see His answers clearly and realize He has been leading us all along, often in ways we never expected.

Does God Have a Great Master Plan for Me?

I used to say, "Life sucks, and then you die." At the time, that's genuinely how I saw things. But that doesn't mean it was the truth. Life is incredibly complex, interwoven with countless stories. And God is at work in every single one of those stories. He loves each person involved in those millions of stories, and He is working out a plan that is the absolute best for each individual.

Do I trust He is working things out for me and my family in the best way possible? Sometimes yes, and sometimes no. But do I know He is? Yes, I do. I know His plan for me will always be better than my plan for myself. What I need is tenacity—the stick-to-itiveness, the perseverance to push through the difficulties to reach the great rewards on the other side.

Does this mean life will suck until I die? No, it doesn't. God wants to give us an abundant life, but He also wants to partner with us on a journey. He has a path planned for us, one that is overflowing with blessings. If we trust Him and allow Him to guide us step by step on that path, our lives will indeed be dripping with blessings.

CHAPTER 5

Tenacity in Faithfulness: Building a Story of Faithfulness

Everyone is building a story of faithfulness or unfaithfulness to God's plan. Sometimes, you clearly know you're on His path, and other times, His plan feels like a complete mystery. But the secret to truly fulfilling His plan is to never give up. Never quit. You will get off His path at times, but if you continue to seek Him and follow His directives, He will always guide you back. The key is to remember getting off course isn't failure—stopping is. The Bible shows us God's plan is always forward, always leading toward His best. So, give yourself grace when you stumble and keep moving forward. His path is marked with divine grace, second chances, and endless love.

Perseverance and Alignment with God's Will

Perseverance and unwavering commitment to keep going, even after setbacks, are the true marks of a heart aligned with His will. Through faith and obedience, we align ourselves with His purpose and store up eternal treasures. Every step we take in obedience prepares us for the incredible responsibilities we will joyfully embrace in Heaven.

Biblical perseverance is steadfast faithfulness to God and His purpose, even in the face of trials and challenges. It means trusting God's promises and relying on His strength, knowing He is working all things for good. As James 1:2-4 says, "Count it all joy, my brothers, when you meet trials of various kinds, for you know that the testing of your faith produces steadfastness. And let steadfastness have its full effect, that you may be perfect and complete, lacking in nothing." Following the example of Jesus, who endured the cross for the joy set before Him (Hebrews 12:1-2), perseverance shapes our character, strengthens our hope, and reminds us that faithfulness leads to eternal rewards far greater than any earthly hardship.

The key to staying on God's path is to never give up. In Galatians 6:9, Paul encourages us, "Let us not become weary in doing good, for at the proper time we will reap a harvest if we do not give up." This verse reminds us perseverance is essential. Even when we get off track, God's grace is sufficient to guide us back. Proverbs 24:16 says, "For though the righteous fall seven times, they rise again." This emphasizes falling is not the end; rising again and moving forward is what matters.

James 1:12 says: "Blessed [happy, spiritually prosperous, favored by God] is the man who is steadfast under trial and perseveres when tempted; for when he has passed the test and been approved, he will receive the [victor's] crown of life which the Lord has promised to those who love Him" (AMP).

Biblical Examples of Perseverance

Throughout scripture, we see examples of those who experienced both clarity and mystery in following God's plan. Abraham, for instance, was called by God to leave his home and go to a land God would show him (Gen. 12:1). Abraham didn't know the exact destination, but he trusted God's promise and moved forward in faith. Despite moments of doubt and deviation, such as when he went to Egypt during a famine or when he had a child with Hagar, Abraham remained faithful. God reiterated His promises to Abraham, and he eventually became the father of many nations.

Similarly, Joseph's life is a testament to perseverance and faithfulness amid mystery and hardship. Sold into slavery by his brothers, falsely accused, and imprisoned, Joseph seemed far from God's plan (Gen. 37–50). Yet, through it all, Joseph remained faithful. In Genesis 50:20, he told his brothers, "You intended to harm me, but God intended it for good to accomplish what is now being done, the saving of many lives." Joseph's story illustrates that even in difficult times, God is working behind the scenes to fulfill His purposes.

Hard Times Are Not a Sign of Being Out of God's Will

Sometimes, it will be hard, and sometimes it will be easy. We may hear from other believers that if our life is not going well, we must be out of God's will. However, the Bible shows us that hard times are not necessarily a sign of being out of God's will. We've already seen that Job, a man described as blameless and upright, faced immense suffering, not because he was out of God's will, but as part of a divine plan (Job 1–2). His story shows trials can be a part of God's plan to test and strengthen our faith.

Moreover, the New Testament is filled with examples of the early Christians facing persecution and hardship. Paul himself faced numerous trials, including shipwrecks, beatings, and imprisonment (2 Cor. 11:23–27). Yet, he remained steadfast in his mission, understanding these sufferings were part of his journey of faith and service to God. He wrote in Romans 8:28: "And we know that in all things God works for the good of those who love him, who have been called according to his purpose."

His Path Dripping with Blessings

God's path is dripping with blessings. When we recognize and follow His guidance, we discover true fulfillment, serving and glorifying Him in ways we never imagined. Psalm 65:11 declares: "You crown the year with your bounty, and your carts overflow with abundance." When we get off His path, God will use various means to direct us back to it. He uses Bible verses, circumstances, friends, and that still, small voice to guide us. All He is doing is trying to get us back on His path, dripping with His blessings. I don't know about you, but based on Psalm 65, I know the path I want to live on all the time. Imagine me looking around and not finding the time to pick up all the blessings that are around me?

Story Time: His Path Dripping with Blessings

The sun shone brightly as Sarah stood at the crossroads of her life, overwhelmed by the choices before her. She felt the weight of uncertainty pressing on her shoulders, her mind racing with thoughts of missed opportunities, wrong turns, and the fear that maybe—just maybe—she had strayed too far from God's path. But in that moment, a gentle breeze swept over her, whispering through the trees as if calling her name. She paused, closed her eyes, and breathed in deeply. Then, like a spark of light piercing through the clouds, the words of Psalm 65:11 flooded her heart: "You crown the year with your bounty, and your carts overflow with abundance."

Overflow with abundance. The words ignited something deep inside her. She could suddenly see it—the path God had laid out, not barren or filled with struggle but dripping with blessings! His path wasn't just a dry road to walk; it was an overflowing river of goodness, treasures, and joy, all waiting to be discovered. *Was it really true?* Sarah's pulse quickened. Could life really be this good, this full of blessings, if she just followed His way?

Excitement surged through her as she imagined what it would be like to live that way, day after day. In her mind's eye, she saw herself walking along a golden path, where every step was met with fresh, new blessings. Laughter bubbled up within her as she pictured blessings falling like rain from the Heavens—so many that she couldn't even gather them all! Blessings in her relationships, blessings in her work, in her health, in her spirit. Her hands would be full, her heart overflowing, her life radiant with joy she could barely contain.

"Yes!" she shouted aloud, her voice echoing in the stillness. She wanted that life! She wanted to walk God's path, the one that was dripping with His abundance. She had tasted enough of wandering, of walking her own way, and she was done with scarcity. It was time to return to Him, to the path He had carefully crafted for her, the path that led to overflowing carts of blessings.

Sarah began to move with purpose, fueled by the excitement of what was waiting for her. She knew that God would use everything—His Word, her circumstances, even the whispers of friends and the stirrings in her heart—to direct her back to His way. And with each step she took, she could feel it: that still, small voice leading her, the scripture lighting her way, and His love wrapping her like a warm embrace.

As she walked, she began to notice the blessings springing up around her, just as she had imagined. The more she walked, the more her path was filled with them—friendships rekindled, opportunities opening, her heart swelling with peace. It wasn't just a picture in her mind anymore. It was real, tangible, and gloriously abundant. Blessings were falling all around her, and she couldn't gather them fast enough.

With tears of joy streaming down her face, Sarah laughed again, this time from the depths of her soul. This was the life God had always meant for her—a life overflowing with His goodness, a life walking His path dripping with blessings.

And she never wanted to leave it again.

Recognizing God's Blessings

It's important to recognize the blessings He is giving us. Sometimes, we have preconceived ideas of what His blessings should look like, and because of this, we may miss the actual blessings He provides. James 1:17 reminds us: "Every good and perfect gift is from above, coming down from the Father of the heavenly lights, who does not change like shifting shadows." We need to stand back and look around to realize the immense blessings He is giving us.

Blessings in the Middle of Difficulties

Even in difficult times, God's blessings are present. The Israelites, wandering in the desert, often failed to recognize God's provision. Despite their grumbling, God provided manna from Heaven, water from a rock, and protection from their enemies (Ex. 16–17). Likewise, we need to trust that God is working for our good, even when His blessings come in ways we don't expect.

The Grace of Returning to God's Path

Jesus's parable of the prodigal son (Luke 15:11–32) is a powerful reminder of God's grace and readiness to welcome us back when we stray. The son squandered his inheritance on reckless living but was welcomed back with open arms by his father. This story illustrates that no matter how far we veer off course, God's love and forgiveness are always available, encouraging us to return to Him and continue forward on His path.

Trusting God's Path of Blessings

Living an unshakable and abundant life requires tenacity—faith that perseveres even when the path is unclear or difficult. God's path is always dripping with blessings, even when challenges arise. True faith involves trusting God's plan over our own, embracing His guidance, and allowing Him to lead us step by step, especially when the way forward seems uncertain. As we stay faithful, refusing to give up, we will experience the richness of His blessings and the victory He has already secured for us. This journey may not always be easy, but the rewards of trusting in God's perfect plan will overflow into a life filled with purpose, joy, and eternal reward.

CHAPTER 6

My Life: Standing Firm When Life's Plans Crumble

I'd Like to Share My Own Journey

I'd spent most of my life striving for success in every area, from nurturing my family to establishing multiple businesses. Yet, amid the beautiful life I'd created, a great tragedy struck. Whether this tragedy was a trial from God, His discipline, or an attack from the enemy akin to Job's suffering, I cannot say. But I know that through this profound hardship, the Lord has brought my family into a daily walk with His kingdom, bestowing upon us the greatest blessings we could ever receive.

First, let me say I hope God speaks to you through my story so you will see the significance of God moving and how He can move in your life, always bringing glory to Him.

I was a middle child in a family of five with an older sister and a younger brother. My mother often treated me as if I were her confidante and friend and a co-decision-maker for the family. Like all families, we had our struggles. But as I reflect now, I'm deeply grateful for the family I had, imperfections and all. It was a good life filled with love, lessons, and moments that shaped me into who I am today.

I struggled a lot in high school but didn't know why. One day, the principal pulled me into his office for a conversation. He said some people go to college, and others get a job in a factory and work their way up. According to him, I was a factory worker type of guy and should not bother with college. He thought that was helpful. I was so mad and embarrassed that I decided I would go to college no matter what.

After high school, I gritted my teeth and applied. When a school accepted me, first I was shocked. Then excited. Somehow, getting that acceptance letter, I felt a little more normal.

And I graduated with a degree in Theology!

After that, I took a two-month-long mission trip to several mission bases in Europe, where I assisted the directors with financial planning and helped them with their family finances. We created budgets and debt-elimination plans for their bases to match their organizations' visions. The day before I was going home, I sat on a pier in Spain, talking to God. For the first time in my life, I felt God speak to me, saying I needed to go back to school and get a degree in finance. When I made it home, I applied to a university in Denver. I completed a degree in Business and Finance. I learned a lot of tenacity and discovered I was severely dyslexic. It made learning much harder and took more time.

But looking back, I am grateful for dyslexia because it caused me to see life differently than others. I can't just read about something and learn it; I must see it and experience it to understand it and then become an expert at it. Now, mind you, at the time, I was devastated and confused and somewhat relieved to possibly put a name on, or, in some cases, an excuse for my struggles in school. Nevertheless, I have realized the gifts that dyslexia has given me. I am not limited to what others think and have experienced. God can show me more. The tenacity that my dyslexia has given me is nothing short of a God-given gift. I will always treasure this gift. One day, a friend asked why I don't pray for God to heal my dyslexia. I said if God gave me a choice to heal my dyslexia or not, I would choose not. I love the life it has opened for me. I can see life now, and I don't get trapped into seeing things from others' perspectives and experiences by reading about them. The Holy Spirit allows me to experience and see things in a new light all the time. It is truly a gift.

After graduating with my second degree, I also sent a copy of my certificate to my old principal. When he told me not to bother going to college, he'd made me angry. I struggled with forgiveness at the time, but realize now that he was only trying to help and give some guidance when he saw I had no idea what to do. It hurt, especially since this was a small school, and I really looked up to him. In some way, I just wanted someone to believe in me or see I was not as dumb as I felt sometimes. Unfortunately, I never got a response from my principal.

Getting Life Started

I took a job teaching English to automobile company executives in Japan. It was lucrative. In addition, I worked in a local church in Japan with the youth members. One month, my roommate and I took all the youth to China. The trip had two purposes: to show the Japanese youth what China was like and to smuggle several hundred Bibles into China. At the time, it was illegal to bring Bibles into China. The punishment was being kicked out of China for the first offense and going to jail for the second offense, as I understood it.

To ensure we would get some Bibles into the country, we took two separate flights. I had eleven Japanese high school girls in tow, and my friend John was coming later with the rest of the kids. We hid all our Bibles in our backpacks, as we were told they never go through the bags in customs. When we landed and got our luggage, we had to go through customs. I noticed they were going through each bag thoroughly. This was unfortunate and scary, as there was no way to get twelve of us through without getting caught. I prayed, and a man pushed through the line, almost knocking me over. He turned, smiled, and kept walking. I watched him walk to the end of the room, past all the investigators, and come back to the passport stamping line. I thought if he could do it, we could too. I told all the girls to put their backpacks on, and we walked single file around the investigators to the passport stamping line. They let us into the country without checking our luggage. To this day, I believe it was an angel showing me how to do it.

We had several experiences dropping off Bibles. At one stop, we gave a pastor one Bible. He brought several others from his church. He grabbed the Bible with vigor, held it up in thanks to God, and then proceeded to rip books out of it and give them to the others. He said they would pass the books around so each person could have a part of the Bible. What passion and love they had for God's Word.

On another occasion, I had to meet a pastor in the lobby of a hotel. I was told to sit in the lobby, and someone would identify themselves to me. I was also told to wait because the pastor was coming from a long way off, and transportation was not dependable. I sat there all day. No one came. There was an older man sitting in the lobby when I arrived. At about 7:00 p.m., he came over and apologized for not coming sooner. He said I was being followed and watched. The man following me left an hour ago, so he felt it was clear to come and get his "beautiful package." I remember finding it interesting when I had multiple Bibles on my shelf collecting dust at home.

After that experience, I had a new love for the Bible. I never looked at it the same way again. Just under a year of teaching English, I returned to the United States to get a job. I didn't have a plan, but I started applying for jobs. Interestingly, I was accepted into the FBI. I applied, made it through several tests, and was offered an entry-level job. At the time, my mom and girlfriend panicked. I didn't have the backbone to say I wanted to do this and was talked out of the opportunity. To this day, I don't know if it was God saying I should or should not have done it, but it would have been exciting for sure. God can take care of everything, but I often think about what path my life would have taken if I had accepted that position. Instead, I got a job with a nonprofit helping people get out of debt.

First Real Job, a Nonprofit

My job, with about two hundred other people, was to talk with our clients on the phone, teach people how to get out of debt and run financial seminars at a non-profit in the US. I quickly moved up to presenter in the education department and then to the director of education. I was responsible for about 800 financial seminars per year. This included managing people, going out to speak, and doing a lot of traveling and speaking myself. I enjoyed it a lot, although when I started the position, I had never spoken to a crowd before. One issue for my department was we didn't have an income strategy, though we had one of the largest draws on the company's finances not covered by one. It was a known problem in the company, so I took it upon myself to solve it.

Within a year, I reversed the entire problem, and we became one of the most profitable departments in the company per person. When I reported to the board what I had done, I expected great accolades and possibly a promotion or raise. Instead, I was demoted and almost fired for making a nonprofit a lot of money that the board was not anticipating. At the time, I didn't fully understand how nonprofits worked and quickly realized working in the nonprofit world was not something I was cut out to do.

Finding a New Church

During this time, I found a church I enjoyed being involved with. It was different from any church I had gone to, but the people were good. Most importantly, they had a college-and-career group I could get involved with. We did everything together on the weekends—hikes in the mountains and bowling in the evenings. A few of those friends started a band, so we had a lot of band practices, which turned into jam sessions in the evenings. Eventually, I was asked to be a leader of the college-and-career group with some other guys. This involved planning outings and speaking occasionally. I felt like I had found my people and truly enjoyed this time of my life.

Meeting My Wife

One winter, we had a retreat for the college-and-career group. We rented out a retreat center in the mountains and brought in speakers. One evening, after the speakers, an extremely cute girl came up to me and asked me one simple question: "What are you looking for in a wife?" I had never been asked that question before and was shocked she would ask so directly. She told me that all the girls in the girls' dorm were ranking all the guys to determine who was the most eligible bachelor. She was asking to help the girls know what interested me in a spouse, as my name came up on the list. I was oddly intrigued by this amazing girl who didn't seem like the others I had known. I produced an answer, but I honestly don't remember what I said. She later told me one of the things I said was they had to know how to work a budget. That does sound like something I would say! We ended up talking for almost the whole night. She was fascinating and could hold a conversation beyond anyone I had dated before. We talked and talked, went outside for a snowball fight, and then talked some more.

When we got home after the weekend, I found myself incredibly nervous about calling her for a date. This was very odd for me; I was surprised that I would be nervous. I sat on my bed for more than an hour, dialing the number several times and not finishing. Finally, I accidentally finished dialing, and it rang. We talked, and she said she would go out with me. We went to a movie, then out for a piece of pie, and talked all evening and night again. I had never been around anyone so enjoyable, and I didn't have to carry the conversation all the time. She was awesome. After dealing with some fears like "this cannot be real," "she cannot always be this great," or "she will eventually figure out that I am not particularly great and leave me," we finally married. Truly the best decision I had ever made. Now, more than thirty years later, Latisha is still fascinating, and her stories still captivate me. I love hearing her talk about her day and what she likes and dislikes. She has still not figured out I am not good enough for her.

Building a Career

After leaving the nonprofit, I found a job with a financial planner with a man from church. I loved the business of financial planning, however, the guy that I was working for struggled in the area of integrity. I found a new position serving as an economist with a company that sold financial strategies for economically struggling times. A major focus was selling or trading dollars for gold. The fun part was participating in hosting a radio show every day, discussing the economy and talking to callers about investment strategies. I enjoyed that role a lot. Unfortunately, the owner of that company also had a struggle with integrity as well.

Starting My Own Business

In my home life, I was incredibly happy. But in my career, I was frustrated. I couldn't find any business to work for that seemed to do fair, legal, profitable, and beneficial business in the financial arena. Tish and I decided to start our own investment management company in the basement of our 800 sq. ft. house.

I took on additional jobs while starting my investment-management company with Pony Express, delivering packages (drugs) to doctors' offices and hospitals. I was up at four every morning, loading my borrowed van and on the road by six. The route they gave me made no sense, but I drove it anyway. I got back to the hub to clock out at four every afternoon. I was so tired I didn't have much energy to work on my company in the evenings, so I had to produce a solution. I reworked my route, talking to all the doctors' offices and hospitals to adjust the delivery times. They all approved, and I started my newly designed route. I was able to complete my route by noon the next day. When I got back to the hub at 12:30, my bosses were furious. They didn't believe I had done it so fast and refused to let me go home. The next day, my direct boss said I should not come back until 4:00 tomorrow. So, I completed my route and went home, did four hours of work for my company, and returned to the hub to clock out.

After some time, I reworked the route again and was able to complete my full route by ten every morning, allowing me almost a full day of work for the investment company before needing to return to the hub. Once I got all the legal paperwork and licensing complete, I started to market and accumulate clients. I kept a suit in the back of my van, and sometimes, in the middle of my route, I stopped at a Starbucks, put on my suit, and had a meeting. Then I hopped back in the van, put my uniform back on, and finished the route. A few times, I had a couple of meetings in a day between deliveries. I left my suit on, and the hospitals and doctors' offices made a big deal about a delivery driver in a suit.

After getting some clients, I got a third job with a roofing company, giving roof-replacement estimates and selling the replacements, and another job with a stockbroker, selling by phone. I worked at Pony Express in the morning, then stock-brokering, then meetings for the investment company to build up clients. After about four years of this, I was able to end the craziness and focus solely on our investment company.

It was nice to sleep in until six. When I quit my Pony Express job, my boss asked if I would stay on as a manager to rework all the routes. I said I needed to work on my company. We laughed. He knew there was no way he would get me to stay. This all took so much time. Tish was an amazing wife who supported and encouraged me through this long, difficult, and frustrating process. I don't remember her ever complaining about all the time I was away trying to provide for our family. One of the biggest things God showed me was what an incredible blessing it was to have an encouraging, supportive wife. She was the strength behind the challenging work. She often worked a retail job in the evenings to help us make ends meet.

Building the investment company was strenuous, difficult, and fun all at once. I realized I could impact people's lives by helping them with their investments. I figured out our trading strategy while managing people's money. We created risk-tolerance questionnaires for every client to determine how much risk they wanted, which translated to returns. We managed our portfolios to five different risk strategies, essentially managing five portfolios and assigning clients to a portfolio that worked for their risk tolerance. We created a system where we only had trading authority on their personal accounts and couldn't touch the money for any other reason.

We got good at what we were doing, which attracted many clients. Our system was working so well that some other investment advisers wanted to build up their clients at our company and use our financial management system. Eventually, we hired a company to write software that would manage the portfolios in our own style. This ensured each account stayed perfectly balanced based on the strategy.

In 2008, the market crashed, as it does sometimes. Our system warned us of this potential several weeks prior to this historic event. We started a move out of the market into money markets. We followed the system and found it was dead on. Some clients were nervous about what we were doing but decided to stick with the system. After the market crashed, we looked like heroes. I saw it as God protecting our clients. After we computerized our process, I had more time and started our financial-life-coaching company, working with clients to build their investment portfolios by helping them accumulate more day-to-day money. This ended up being an amazing company. The Lord gave me amazing insights and financial connections between people's behavior and their money management. I wrote a book called *Money is the Smallest Part of Your Finances*, identifying that money was the smallest part of their finances. People make money decisions based on their emotional response to money, not what is best for their long-term benefit.

I worked with several hundred clients. Helping them out of debt allowed them to accumulate more wealth, but they would often find themselves back in debt. I helped them break the cycle and stay debt-free. By helping people work through life issues, they were able to automatically fix issues in their budgets and further their financial standing. It was interesting to see how God brought my past education from working for the nonprofit that I was definitely not the right fit for, full circle, back to helping people get their budgets working properly and helping them out of debt.

After a while, I had more clients than I could keep up with as the news of my clients' successes was getting out. I created a system for coaches to use while working with people, who started to accumulate exponentially more after they understood why they were doing the crazy financial things that caused them not to save or to save less than they could.

Although online training was not a thing back then, we created online courses to allow people to learn how to help themselves without having to use a coach. Truthfully, this didn't work as well as in-person coaching, but it did help to some degree. It was exciting work, helping people accumulate wealth at levels even they were surprised at. The most exciting part was the satisfaction and contentment our clients lived their lives in. They were not striving all the time, using up any extra money or sometimes borrowing money to somehow find satisfaction and contentment in what typically was a striving and unsatisfied life. I love to hear of the long-term successes that I sometimes hear even at this time of my life.

Successful Family and Successful Business, All is Good

Latisha and I had four kids by this point, and our home life was busy as well. We had moved from our small house, where I started the business in our basement, to a wonderful six-bedroom family home. I felt completely blessed and often said that the glory all goes to God for all He has blessed us with. We had two flourishing businesses, great friends, and respect in the community. Most people had heard of the success of our businesses even if they were not clients of at least one of them. I often had opportunities to speak in the community, often on the topic of *Money is the Smallest Part of Your Finances,* which was the name of my first book. It was more entertaining than a talk on investing or money management.

We were often stopped in restaurants, at church, or at our kids' activities by people wanting to talk with us. They had seen me speak somewhere, read my book, or heard about the interesting ways we were helping people find peace and satisfaction in their lives. We felt favored and blessed. This does not mean I didn't make a lot of mistakes, but I had a tremendous drive to prove to myself that I was worth something.

It was ironic that we were helping other people find peace and contentment, yet I hadn't found mine. I knew I was not like everyone else. The insecurities around dyslexia sometimes became significant, and I was always pretending I was just like others in this area. I always told myself that once I got my family financially secure and everything operating in a way that they didn't need me, I would work on myself to fix whatever was going on in my life that made me think I had to strive so much.

My Daughter's Medical Journey

At this time, my oldest daughter, Chelsea, had taken to ice skating. At one of the local ice-skating rinks, they were running a synchronized ice-skating team, which she got heavily involved with. She loved it at a young age. Tish got her into private ice-skating lessons, helping her pass test after test to qualify for the team. It was a big day at our home when she made the team! Tish volunteered as one of the team moms and traveled to all the competitions. Chelsea's team qualified for nationals for three or four years in a row, which was no small feat.

One day, we learned that Chelsea was taking way too many ibuprofen to help her deal with the pain. We assumed it was pain from the demands of ice skating, but after regulating the ibuprofen and seeing her pain increase exponentially, we decided to take her to the doctor.

To our surprise, she was diagnosed with rheumatoid arthritis.

Finding out that at the age of fifteen, she was struggling with an autoimmune disease was a devastating blow to the whole family. We tried everything to help her deal with the pain but we discovered there was no cure. It is a lifelong disease. We soon found out in some cases, the medicine is worse than the disease, as it slowly destroys the organs.

We found a treatment in Guatemala that would help Chelsea get off the drugs and create a different solution for the pain. We, as a family, moved to Guatemala for a few months for the treatment. I commuted back and forth as I had a larger company to manage. I had recently reconnected with an old friend from my college years who had also started his own investment management company, similarly structured to mine. We looked at merging our companies, but due to the regulations, it was too much work, so we kept the companies separate and shared office space, some of the expenses and some of the management of the employees. It was nice to share some of that responsibility at the time. Because he was in the office every day, I felt it was much easier for me to spend more time in Guatemala with my wife and kids. I don't know how I could have managed the situation if he was not in the office taking care of the day-to-day issues that always popped up.

Guatemala was an incredible experience for my family. My wife did an amazing job getting everyone involved in Spanish immersion classes, helping them all to be good at speaking Spanish. They also got involved in a great church where the kids made several friends in the youth group.

My oldest son started a coffee-import business with a Guatemalan friend from the youth group. He named the company Cobblestone Coffee because in Antigua, where we were living, the streets were all cobblestones. It was so fun to see how he learned so much about running a small business with that short-lived business. Just outside of the town were several impoverished villages where Tish took the kids and brought rice and beans sometimes. Other times, they brought the village kids some shoes. She also had our kids at the local hospital once a week, helping feed people who couldn't feed themselves. Tish did an amazing job making that adventure wonderful for all the kids.

Chelsea completed her full treatments, and thank the Lord, she was able to get off all the dangerous drugs that could have killed her. After returning to the States, there was a noticeable difference in our whole family. A definite change in focus and motivation. We will always be grateful for the family growth we experienced during that time.

When I got back into the swing of things at the office, I found I didn't have to be so busy. Everything seemed to be operating as I had hoped. I didn't have to make investment decisions. The software we designed and built was working as expected. The investment managers we hired were getting more clients. The financial-training company was working well and growing every month. Online training was working. Referrals were coming in regularly because of the news of our success in managing money and helping people manage their personal financial lives. The vision was operating, and the investment clients who had gone through the coaching company were increasing their managed assets dramatically. The whole company was doing well, so I didn't have to do much with running the company because my old friend seemed to have things fully under control overseeing the full operation.

New Ventures, Starting New Businesses

Being in this situation, I decided not to get fully back in and mess up the flow of things and just did the minimum I needed to do so I could look at other opportunities. One of my favorite things was to figure out a business model that would operate based on systems.

Since I was not needed for most of the day-to-day part of the other businesses, I wanted to work on a new one. Often, I had people come to me with great business ideas and thought if I could help them build a systemized business, it could assist them in being successful and give me another business that would be more diversification for our family's finances. My goal was to find other business plans where the business could run itself after the work is put in and the business was proven and stabilized.

I found a friend who wanted to start a medical-wellness company that would use doctors and their assistants to help people with basic health strategies. This included weight loss and energy-management strategies. I had no knowledge of this business but trusted that the people wanting to start it did. I didn't feel I needed to be an expert in the product, but an expert in the business. It took about a year to make the appropriate adjustments to the model to make it successful. This company didn't need additional financing because the margins were not large enough to support it, but the organic-growth strategy would work well.

There was another opportunity in the oxygen delivery business segment. This involved purchasing several oxygen concentrators and hiring drivers to deliver these concentrators to elderly people in nursing homes. Of course, there was more to this business, including regulations, licensing, real estate, human resources, partners, funding, etc., but it ended up putting the competition out of business in one year.

The business model was simple. The elderly are some of the loneliest people in our society. If you watch the competition, their business model is vulnerable. Get their drivers to drop off the equipment or a tank of oxygen as quickly as possible. This included not letting your delivery drivers take the time to get sucked into a conversation with an elderly person when they drop off an oxygen tank. I saw this firsthand when I visited an elderly friend and tried to have a conversation with the guy dropping oxygen off in his room. He was so rude that he didn't even acknowledge my attempt to be friendly. My friend said not to bother; he's always rude, and everyone in the nursing home knew it. I laughed and recognized a great opportunity.

If we hired friendly drivers who had to have at least a five-minute conversation with every elderly person, they would feel blessed that someone cared about them, and the news would spread. They each had to keep notes to share with other drivers, with the names of grandchildren and specific events they liked to talk about, so the next driver had ready questions for them as they dropped off the equipment. The news spread rapidly in the nursing homes as their biggest desire was to have a visitor. Of course, family was preferable, but a friendly delivery driver was a welcome surprise. Because of this, the elderly started to tell their doctors they wanted their oxygen delivered by our company and not by the rude competition. Everyone wanted one of our friendly delivery drivers and forced their doctors to prescribe our company.

Not every business was this easy to build and grow. One of the biggest and most difficult businesses was getting into the LED-light business when fluorescent lights were all the rage. I had a lighting engineer client who had an

LED light idea that would far surpass the fluorescent-light energy savings that everyone was excited about. Our society was moving away from incandescent light bulbs and buying a lot of curly cue lights. There were a lot of issues with these lights, including taking some time to warm up after you turn them on, but people loved the energy savings. My client's strategy would require about 96% less energy than the fluorescent lights being sold.

I had no idea about the technology and had to trust his invention would work, but I had known him for some time, and he had always been a straight shooter. We created a solution for him to prove his technology and see if he could truly get that kind of savings. There was a lot of work to get to this point, but the answer was *yes*. He could do it. We had an enormous potential opportunity and needed to build a company around this technology. The inventor had a lot of experience working in China, so we decided to start the company based out of Hong Kong. We built a small factory in China just over the border of Hong Kong in Shenzhen. We worked on getting the product patented, which encompassed several steps. The first step was to get Patent Pending while continuing to prove our patent with the patent office. Patent Pending protects you in the process. We got all the equipment in the factory and did several light runs to ensure the process worked.

The next step was to get our conversations with major light companies to contract level. Our sales strategy was twofold. Work with the major companies to license our technology to them and, while we wait for the licensing process to be complete, which sometimes can take years, sell direct to whoever would buy them, starting with office buildings. The reason for this strategy was we knew the time risk in getting under contract with the major lighting manufacturing companies and wanted to get to our break-even as quickly as possible. Therefore, we wanted to sell direct until we could let a major company pay us through our licensing agreement.

We were manufacturing some lights for display and small sales, but our goal was to get a large order and then make a larger manufacturing run. Amazingly, we made much faster progress with one of the major light companies than we'd expected. They had started engineering due diligence on the technology to determine if our light did what we said it would do. This was so exciting for us as we walked through the predetermined steps. It looked possible to get to our break-even under the licensing process and not the direct sales process. This was the direction I had hoped for and was much easier to accomplish.

There were several other businesses along the way, like a water-purification company, an oil-drilling company, a publishing company, and even flipping houses.

You get the idea.

One of the things I loved the most was being able to hire so many people, realizing we were having a significant impact on many personal economic worlds. I remember one time counting all the individuals, including families, who were relying on the economic successes of our businesses. Hundreds of mouths to feed every day. It was humbling and exciting, knowing we could create great businesses to help our customers and our employees provide for their families in a good way.

I thought I was extremely smart and believed I was almost bulletproof. Looking back, it was a Tower of Babel experience. I put myself in a place where I didn't think I even needed God, but I didn't realize it at the time.

One morning, Latisha had a horrible dream and woke up in a panic. In the dream, she had a bad car accident near a Starbucks. Her car was rear-ended by my old friend overseeing our investment company. On that corner were a Starbucks and two gas stations. She was shaken up in the dream after the accident, but no one was hurt.

In the dream, she looked up. All our friends and family were pouring out of Starbucks and piling into a large, white van. They were all our best friends, close friends, most of our family, and our church leaders, basically representing everyone meaningful in our life.

The van pulled out onto the street, and Tish said to herself that it was great. She was sure they were all coming to see if they could help. But the van got closer, and they were not stopping. Full speed, they ran over her, intentionally, as everyone in the van was messing around and having fun. Once they hit her, they just kept driving.

That morning, I comforted Tish. After that, I don't remember giving it a second thought.

But one day, not long after, I was sitting at my desk in the investment-company office when one of the asset managers came in, saying she couldn't access any of our clients' accounts on the brokerage-house website. Odd. I told her to contact them to see what was going on. Probably a technical issue. Turns out, she'd tried that and was told they were not allowed to talk to us. This made no sense.

Soon, several government-agency auditors arrived at our office for an annual audit. While an audit itself was not unusual, having more than one auditor was. I asked why they needed more than one person, but they didn't answer. Naively, I assumed they were just trying to get it done quickly. I was wrong. I reached out to my friend who oversaw the company, but he didn't respond for the first half of the day. By the end of the day, I was seriously concerned. I called our company attorney, who told me to come in the next morning to discuss what was happening. He didn't seem worried and didn't ask many questions.

The next day I was in his waiting room. Once the attorney came into the office, things started to take shape. The first thing he asked was for me to sign a release, allowing him to represent my friend and not me any longer. I said he would have to give me more information than that. He explained the government was coming after my friend for suspicions of a Ponzi scheme.

"Ridiculous", I said. We couldn't even access our clients' accounts to take money out of them to create a Ponzi scheme. That would be impossible based on how our business was set up. Nevertheless, he insisted I sign the document. I refused until I knew more about what was happening.

On my way out of his office, I reached out to a federal judge I knew to explain what had happened and get his thoughts. He said I was in for a long ride, and I'd better get a good lawyer. With his recommendation, I found a great attorney and began the process of figuring out what was happening.

CHAPTER 7

The Disaster

The Unraveling

After a couple of days, it became clear this was a first-class mess. Initially, I believed the authorities would realize their mistake and things would go back to normal. I was mistaken. Again. The government seized all my bank accounts, including those of my businesses. They shared their suspicions with the press. Most of my information came from the news.

It felt surreal, as if it was happening to someone else. I never imagined this could happen to me. Most of my days were spent reassuring clients their money was safe, and they hadn't lost anything, despite what the news suggested. When I wasn't talking to clients, I was speaking with employees and suppliers, explaining I had done nothing wrong and this would be over in a couple of weeks.

I had this timeline in my head because the audit team in my office said they were reviewing every client's file, which would take about two weeks. Then they said they needed to review every dollar I had made or spent in the last two years. Gathering all that information was difficult, but I knew I hadn't done anything that would cause them to shut me down, so I complied quickly. At this point, my outside businesses were losing faith in me due to the bleak news. I later learned that many believed I was headed to jail. I continued to reassure everyone there was nothing to worry about and that everything would return to normal once the audit was completed. I would regain access to the locked-up money and pay our vendors, and employees would get their payroll.

Once they completed the audit, they told my attorney they'd found nothing wrong. I assumed it was all over and breathed a sigh of relief. Unfortunately, the authorities didn't stop there. They insisted they knew I was guilty even though they had not found the evidence yet, so they added my name to the existing complaint against my friend, extending the audit to ten years.

At that point, I realized I couldn't save this mess. My CFO for the light company, a family member of my wife, and our corporate attorney escorted me out of the building, taking my keys as if I was being fired. It was an odd feeling, especially since I had hired my CFO as a favor to the family because he was commuting weekly to California while his wife was in Denver with a terminal disease. Being a family member, I expected he knew me well enough to believe I wouldn't do what was suspected. Mistaken again. He led a vote among investors and the board to eliminate me from the business. They feared my reputation would negatively impact the company's ability to finalize the license with the major light company. They assumed I was going to jail and wanted me out before that happened.

The Collapse

The other companies failed one by one. This essentially meant that everyone stopped working, and vendors started to sue. Additionally, auditors began to audit each remaining company. Within about three weeks, all the companies were shut down except the light company. I had lost all our income, and everyone I knew thought I was going to jail. I was so confused. I had no idea how all this had happened.

It became common for random people to serve me with lawsuits. I can't even remember how many I received. My attorney discovered that my friend, who had been running both my side of the business and his own, was being charged with multiple counts, including running a Ponzi scheme. However, he couldn't understand why I was being lumped in with him other than sharing the same office. None of my clients' funds were missing. There were a couple of joint clients who worked with both companies and had lost money, but the audit proved they didn't lose any money from my company; all the losses were from his side.

During this entire time, my old friend wouldn't respond to my calls, so I couldn't even get an answer to my big question: "Why?" I was overwhelmed with so many emotions I couldn't even identify them.

Even if the government dropped everything immediately and left me alone, the damage was too great to ever regain my clients' trust. The handwriting was on the wall. The business I had spent twenty years building, systematically managing investment accounts successfully, winning the trust of thousands of clients and helping people find contentment in their lives, was gone. It was so hard to imagine, but it was gone. There was nothing I could do to stop it. Everything I'd been so proud of accomplishing was blown away with unfounded accusations.

Descent into Despair

All I could do was shut things down. Following my attorney's advice, I ignored my phone and started selling office furniture, one Craigslist ad after another. A few loyal employees stayed until the end, selling everything they could. I will always appreciate that. They knew everything happening was unfounded because they had lived it with me.

Other than my wife, my kids, two loyal friends, and those loyal employees, there was no one else who maintained belief in my innocence. Some friends told me that no matter what I'd done, they would always be my friend, but that wasn't helpful at the time. "No matter what I'd done?" I was so mad, though I appreciate the gesture now. It's hard to hear good friends say they don't believe you didn't do anything but will still be your friend even if you did.

We found that our friends and most family didn't stand with us. They assumed what they heard on the news or the rumor mill was the truth. I heard some friends talking once, saying, "Where there's smoke, there's fire." Even if they weren't arresting me now, they probably would. I heard others say I was not being arrested because I had turned state's evidence to keep out of jail. What they were missing is that I had not even been charged with anything to be able to turn state's evidence on.

We realized we didn't have many devoted friends. We had people around us who wanted things from us—jobs, advice, influence, and even money—but not many faithful friends and relatives. My parents and siblings said they always wondered how I'd made so much money, that such money wasn't generally made in our family, so it must have been illegally gained. You don't know the pain of rejection until the people you love most abandon you and don't believe in you, like your mom and dad. My wife's family was supportive for a time, but as the situation continued and wasn't immediately rectified, most of them slowly exited the support circle. They weren't as overt, but they just stopped calling and inviting us to family events.

Trying to Survive

After I shut down the office and successfully closed each business, I simply sat on the couch and watched TV for weeks on end. Watching TV but not really watching, if you know the mental state required to do that. My wife stayed upstairs in our room until one of the kids needed help. We just survived in the ruins of what once had been an amazing life. I was so depressed I didn't recognize the depression my wife and kids were dealing with. There were times all I could do was sit for hours.

After weeks of living in depression, I realized I had to do something or I would just die. I got up, got ready as if I had somewhere to go, and left. I didn't know where I was going, but sulking on the couch was not my future. I drove to a park I used to take my kids to in the evenings and on weekends.

Across the pond at the park was a nursing home. I watched an old man struggle to feed himself. I couldn't believe no one from the nursing home was helping him, so I walked over and finished feeding him. He couldn't talk, and I don't think he could comprehend much, but I talked to him for quite some time, telling him all my woes. Somehow that was helpful, but I am not sure why. After someone came to get him, I went home feeling a little better. I remembered a chapter I'd once written in a book about doing things for others if you're struggling. I figured I should take my own advice and make that a focus.

The next day, I found myself in the same park, looking to see if my friend needed to be fed again. For more than a week, maybe longer, I was there feeding and talking with him, explaining how unfair life had been to me. No one knew where I was and probably didn't care, but somehow doing something for someone else in my depression helped me.

One day he didn't come out. I waited for some time, but he never came out. The next day he didn't come out again either. My time helping my new friend was over. I needed to find another way to fill my days and help me out of my depression.

Realizing we would deal with these lawsuits and legal issues for some time, I needed to find a job. All our money was locked up by our banks, so I didn't even have money to buy food for the family. I started calling everyone I knew who owned a business. Finally, after several no-return calls from people I had helped with their businesses for years, one of the owners called me back. He offered me a job in business development and operations for his auto repair company. We agreed to pay me a small stipend per month for food and necessities, and if I helped grow the business, he would pay me a bonus of a percentage of the growth beyond its past high-water mark.

I built relationships with all the insurance companies in the area, and the business grew substantially. At the end of that year, I was expecting a large bonus, close to six figures, which would have helped my family get back on our feet. He refused to pay anything other than my measly salary. He said he didn't care about the agreement and because I was tied up with legal issues, he knew I couldn't do anything about it. So, I quit.

During my time at the body shop, a family member of Tish asked if I would help look at an event venue, one he and a high school friend owned together. They had owned it for more than ten years, and it had never made any money. Almost every year they had to put money into it. I wrote a business plan and told him if he worked it, it would be successful. They reviewed it, but the business partner said it was a bad plan and would never work. Instead, we negotiated a buyout of the business partner and implemented the plan ourselves. The business grew from a small (under a couple hundred thousand per year) operation to a very nice business. It took a year longer than I had anticipated, but it has been good. It supports us and a few of my married kids.

During the growing phase of the event center, I reached out to a software company I had invested in during my past life. I wanted to know if the investment would pay out soon. They said the business was about to fail because the software didn't work. If I were willing to come in and help, they would pay me a little. I joined the company as COO and found that the software development company wasn't doing decent work. I fired them and found a new company to handle it. Once the software started to work, things got odd with the founders. They stopped talking to me in the office.

About a week later, they asked me to leave. I couldn't believe it. We had just gotten the software ready to go. The company was about to take off. I had never been let go before in all my life. After leaving, one of the founders told me there was some jealousy. One of the other founders had always wanted to be the big tech guy who built a big technology company, and everyone, including the board, was talking about how I saved the company. I had to go to ensure the other founder was seen as the hero in the story. I didn't care about the accolades; I just needed the money moving forward. It was frustrating trying to get back on my feet, as it seemed everything was against me. I can honestly say I wasn't handling it well emotionally.

Looking for Closure

My attorney had settled most of the lawsuits. I had to sit for several depositions, dealing with so many issues I can't even remember all of them. I just remember the mean and dishonest people in these depositions. They would intentionally lie, trying to get me to say things that weren't true. My attorney called for a recess often as I exposed the lies. He kept reminding me that my job was not to point out all the lies and manipulated strategies but simply to speak the truth. I often asked why I had to tell the truth if they were allowed to blatantly lie to lead up to a question. I'm sure they were excited when I left at the end of each day.

After all the forensic audits on my personal and business finances were completed, they said they couldn't find anything to pursue charges against me. However, they would leave me on the complaint with my old friend, meaning I would have to go to trial sitting next to him. We would then try to separate our cases and get the case against me dropped due to lack of evidence. Another year of miserable courtrooms and depositions loomed, along with legal expenses I couldn't afford. They gave me an out: if I agreed to give up my license to manage people's money and pay them $25,000 to cover some of their investigatory expenses, they would drop everything and remove my name from the complaint. I figured they had already destroyed my ability to restart my business by ruining my reputation, so agreeing not to restart it was no big deal. The money, however, was a different story. I had spent everything, including selling a vacation home to cover legal expenses.

An amazing family friend from our past came to me and said that God had told him to give me $25,000 to help with my problems. He didn't know anything specific other than I was being unjustly attacked by the government. It was the first sign I recognized that God was watching over me. Because of this, I was able to agree to their blackmail. When I went to my attorney's office to sign the document, I read it and saw it said all kinds of things that were not true to justify removing my license. I refused to sign it, saying I wouldn't agree to anything untrue. I hadn't lied throughout this entire process and wouldn't lie to make them go away. After a week of back and forth, I agreed to sign a document that said I did nothing wrong but was giving up my license. My attorney said there had never been a removal of a license in all of time that didn't explain what the person did wrong. I think they were embarrassed, but they deserved it after what they'd put me through for no reason. Shortly after that, my old friend went to court and was found guilty. He received a sentence of twenty-eight years.

Getting through that was a relief. The stress of trying to rebuild while dealing with legal issues was exhausting. I didn't realize the drain the legal issues were having on me. In the back of my mind, I knew they would never find anything I did was wrong, but I realized they weren't trying to find the truth. They wanted a notch on their belts. It didn't matter if I had done anything wrong; what mattered was the investigators had something to show their bosses. My attorney said we had to give them something, or they would never stop pursuing me. They couldn't go to their bosses with a final report saying they found nothing after spending two years investigating me. After all was said and done, they were able to take my license away. That was their great outcome. The rule of thumb is to never get in the crosshairs of regulatory people because they must justify their existence. The more they found nothing, the more they needed to dig to justify their hypothesis.

About eight years later, I received a letter from the federal regulators stating they needed to vacate one of the bans they placed on me. A court case unrelated to me caused them to review cases like mine and determine if they overstepped. They concluded they had overstepped and had to vacate one of the orders against me. It seemed like the way God works. I felt somewhat redeemed. It didn't tempt me to go back to get a license under their unjust ways and start an investment company again, but I was pleased to see them in a position where they had to vacate an order they'd fought hard to get.

What Looked Like a Glimmer of Hope

After the software company, another old family friend reached out and said I could work for his insurance company and help him grow it. I thought that would be easy, as I used to own an insurance company. This was a different kind of insurance, but the principles would remain the same. My job was simple, to set up systems to help the business grow efficiently. He didn't have the money to hire me but agreed to pay me a percentage of the increased profits. I thought I could do this while growing the event center and make enough to live on. My wife was not excited about him, as he wasn't known for his honesty. But I thought, *What could go wrong?*

We set up a sales system, hiring cold-calling experts, proposal experts, and closers, with regular staff handling ongoing issues. The company exploded with activity and sales. The home office sent people to see what was happening. Our old family friend won awards for beating past sales records. It was a lot of fun to see and experience, and I was happy for him. The agency grew so much he took over some failing agencies. The agreement was that he got paid quarterly from the home office. The first quarter, I wasn't to be paid because he needed reimbursement for expenses. The second quarter, I was to be paid.

You guessed it—my wife was right. He figured out a way to avoid paying us. He told the home office I was participating in selling insurance, not just operating the system, and because I didn't have a proper license to sell insurance, he couldn't pay me a commission. I had been careful to follow all the laws, never spoke to clients, and never sold a policy. The license is required to sell insurance, not to administratively set up business systems. He was aware of my situation. If he had told the home office I was a consultant overseeing a system and paid me a percentage of profits, it would have been legal. Instead, he wanted to keep the money. As a compromise I suggested he donate the money that he owed me to our church instead as this would not require a license and it is something that we both value. He said *no* because he wanted to keep the money. Another lesson learned.

Dream Realization

It took Tish and me a couple of years to realize how the Lord had warned us this would happen. One day, Tish remembered her dream, the one where she was in our Suburban and was rear-ended by my old friend from the investment company. All our friends and family piled into a large white van and ran over her. God was preparing us that most of our friends and family would do their best to destroy us. As I mentioned earlier, we found ourselves realizing we didn't have many devoted friends. People wanted things from us—jobs, advice, influence, money—but we didn't have many faithful friends and relatives.

Our friends, most of our family, our pastor, and our advisers all avoided us. Looking back, I understand what was happening, but at the time we were dying inside. We weren't invited to holiday parties or gatherings. People avoided us in public and quickly excused themselves if we tried to talk. At first, we thought we were imagining it. But it became more blatant. We loved our life and then we saw it all fall apart. I was asked to resign from all boards except one. That leader said God told him not to remove me. I did most of the financial training at our church and had a lot of influence, but the board removed me from all leadership positions without talking to me. They canceled my speaking engagements and rescinded my invitations. I was informed my volunteer assistance was not needed.

My pastor, who actually lived next door to us, avoided us. A few of our neighbors treated us like criminals. It was surreal. We never knew when the next issue would arise. In one of my kids' schools, a mom tried to get my daughter kicked out as a bad influence because of our family issues. Parents wouldn't let their kids play with mine. The YMCA across the street informed me our kids weren't welcome, making up a story to justify it. Everywhere we turned, we were cut out of relationships we had spent twenty-five years developing. It was a horrible time losing all our friends and influence in the community.

A Complete Restructuring of the Life I Knew

One completely random act will earmark this whole experience. My wife had always known she didn't know who her father was. Her mom got married shortly after Tish's birth, but the father-conversation was always elusive. During this time of abandonment from other family and friends, we thought it would be interesting to find out who her birth father was and meet new family members, hoping to recreate some family relationships. We had never talked about it, but we thought it might be good to see if she had any family members who would be more accepting and excited to meet their new daughter or sister. We had heard of remarkable success stories finding long-lost relationships. I had hope.

We ordered a kit from an online ancestry company to discover our DNA. My wife was nervous, so I ordered two sets to do one with her. I filled mine out first, so she could see what came back, but unfortunately, mine came back incorrect. I didn't recognize anyone in my ancestry lineage. I thought the company had mixed up my DNA with someone else. At dinner with an extended family member who had used the service, I told her about it. She asked to look at the results with me. The unfortunate reality was the company sent the correct DNA, and the results showed the dad I'd thought I'd had all my life was not my dad. My mom was correct, but my siblings became half-siblings.

My world turned upside down. In a few years, I went from being the son of an incredibly good man, a brother to siblings, a successful financial planner, an author, and a successful entrepreneur to not knowing who I was or where I belonged. Losing all my businesses, my reputation, our security, all our friends, my influence, my good name, to now losing my extended family nearly broke me. I thought I would soon lose my wife and have nothing left, as I was sure the kids would follow. I had no reason to think this, but I felt everything else was gone.

Conflict of My Belief

Where was God? Why did God do all this to me? Did God hate me? What did I do to deserve this? I wasn't perfect, but I didn't think I was worse than anyone else. I never intentionally tried to rip anyone off like some people did to me, and their lives were flourishing, while mine was a disaster. When would this stop?

A few days later, I had a meeting downtown. I was trying to sell an oil asset from past investments to help grow other companies and get our entrepreneurial life moving forward. It wasn't a lot of money, but it would help. I had been working on this deal for about six months, and it was finally coming together. I had to block out all the other issues and close this deal to have some money to work with. Thank God, the closing meeting had no issues. I signed everything and left as the principal of the buying company signed online from out of state.

Driving home, I got a call from the agent, saying the principal decided not to complete the deal.

I pulled off the road, crying and falling apart. I started yelling at God, asking why He hated me, why He was doing this to me, and what I did to deserve this. Hitting my steering wheel, I couldn't see how anything would work out. I told God in anger that I didn't care if He hated me. I knew His secrets. I knew what it took to get to Heaven, and despite His attempts to destroy me, I would be in Heaven. I told Him to prepare for me to be there despite His hatred. I yelled everything I felt from the past years, my anger at His unfair treatment, His failed promises, and His church's failure. I told Him everything, holding back nothing. Seven years of being life's punching bag came out. I yelled until I had no voice left. I laid my head on the steering wheel and fell asleep on the side of the road. When I woke up, my neck and head ached. I had nothing left. I finished the drive home and sat down, asking God what He wanted.

God Reminded Me Who He Is

As I sat there, several things came to mind. I realized God was sharing things with me. He reminded me that when we had no money for groceries, someone dropped off food on our front porch. He said, "That was Me." He reminded me that throughout the whole ordeal, we never lost our family home or our cars. He said, "That was Me." He reminded me that He kept our marriage together when all the odds were against us. He said, "That was Me." He reminded me that even under extreme pressure not to believe in me, my wife stood strong, knowing I hadn't done anything wrong. He said, "That was Me."

He reminded me that a godly man, who knew my wife and I were having an exceedingly tough time fighting all the dragons of the world, invited us to New York for several days. Although we knew him only a little, and we were not necessarily great friends, he and his wife paid for our airfare, our luxury hotel, all our meals on the street and in fancy restaurants. They introduced us to their friends, who are dear friends of ours even now. They simply loved this broken and worn-down couple. God said, "That was Me."

He then reminded me that the same couple invited us onto their small yacht in the Caribbean for a week of relaxation with a few other couples. They, of course, paid for everything for us and treated us like good people. It was a week of luxury and building great friendships with others they had invited. God said, "That was Me, as well."

He reminded me about a board meeting where God told the director not to let me go off the board. After the meeting, one of the board members pulled me aside and said he knew all about what we were dealing with. He said God told him to pay for all our kids' college expenses. Throughout my kids' college years, they sent him the bill, and he paid 100% of it. Even when two of my kids wanted to go on a Semester at Sea program, which involved studying on a cruise ship and visiting countries worldwide, he covered the extra expense. God said, "That was Me providing for your family." He also reminded me of a time when we didn't have money to pay for one of my son's senior year of high school at the school he had gone to all of his life. We were looking at having to make a change, which would have been extremely difficult for him, and a generous man walked into the school and paid for his entire year. We only found out about it after the fact. God said, "That was Me, as well."

When the government gave me an option to end the ridiculous process they were putting me through, God sent that man, who wanted to give me the money needed to help it all stop. God said, "That was Me." He reminded me that when a family member asked me to create a business plan for an event center, and the business partner couldn't see the vision and was willing to sell, God said, "That was Me." He reminded me that I had been invited with a group of successful businessmen to Nicaragua to speak at a Christian business conference, and He said, "That was Me, as well."

Not only that, but He said the group sent to Nicaragua was put together for His reasons, and He will use that group for years to come. He said, "I put you in that group for you and your family to fulfill my purposes." Those people have become faithful friends to my wife and me. He said, "That was My plan, and that was Me, as well."

He said, "These are the things I'm reminding you of today. But there are many things you don't know about. I will tell you some but not all. I was working in the background on things you didn't even know about. I was showing the government where they were wrong. I was working with your friends and family who were talking about things they didn't understand, and I was sharing the truth with them. Sometimes they listened, and sometimes they didn't, but that is always the case with my kids, including you. Everyone is on their own journey of knowing and hearing me. I was preparing a path forward, and even when you didn't take the path I had prepared, I made a new one. I was with you all along. I was there when you were sitting, staring at the TV, when you were feeding the old man, and when you thought the world no longer needed you. I provided for you in ways you will never see. I was with Latisha when she sat in your room for hours crying. I was with each of your children as they questioned me. I saw everything. I walked with you, Latisha, and each of your kids. I never left you. I cried with you when you were hurting, and I was angry at the injustices that happened to you, as you were. You were my constant thought and my constant companion. I never turned my face from you; I never took my eyes off you."

He also said, "I knew this was going to happen to you. I was fully aware. I prepared you for this day. I gave you a tenacity that few have. I taught you leadership so you could guide your family through this difficult time. I loved you and gave you scriptures to rely on during your struggles. I strengthened the unity in your family by sending you to Guatemala. Brad, this is hard, but I never promised life would be easy. What I did promise you was that I would never leave you—never in this life, and never in eternity. Brad, you are with me now and forever. Don't give up. You will finish this race."

I started to realize He didn't hate me, and He was taking care of us in this horrible situation. I began to understand I was looking at this situation wrongly, and God was not doing this to us, but He was working in the background, holding us up. He was providing for us in such a way that if I were not paying attention, I would miss it because He was not providing the way I had planned it in my head. I realized I was missing it all in my anger and frustration.

CHAPTER 8

Finding God: Realizing There Is More to Being a Christ Follower

A s I reflected on my journey, I realized my previous understanding of Christianity had been based on superficial practices rather than a deep, transformative relationship with God. The trials my family and I had faced made it clear that simply reading the Bible and being kind were not enough to shield us from life's challenges. Not only was I going to have to truly understand more about who God is and how His kingdom works, but I also needed to learn how to stand up against the enemy. It became evident I needed to dig deeper into the truths of God's love and His ways, not just as a checklist of actions but as a profound, living experience. I also needed to figure out how to lead my family out of this whirlwind of evil that continued to attack us. Only then could I hope to find true peace and protection in His presence. I wasn't in a place where I fully understood what was happening, but I knew there had to be more. I was still hurt and emotionally raw, but if I was going to lead our family out of this disaster, I had to pull myself together. Could I do it? I wasn't sure—but I knew I had to try.

Understanding My Old Strategy

Spending time with God and in his Word, I realized He showed me one of the things that was misleading me was also what I believed was one of my greatest accomplishments, finishing something.

My passion in life was to finish being a Christian. I went to Bible school and got a degree in theology, but I didn't wholeheartedly continue learning as life got busy, and I moved on to my next thing. It was not that I walked away from God, but I thought I had built a large foundation with God, and He and I had a good relationship already. I thought I would keep going to church, but my next job was to learn all I could about finance.

Next, it was to learn all I could about being married and raising kids. That is how I worked in my business life, as well. I finished one company and started the next. I seriously disliked leaving things unfinished. It never occurred to me that life was all integrated.

God participated in all my life, in every aspect, and not just the spiritual parts. I know that sounds silly because in the Christian world, we say that all the time, but we don't typically practice it. We go to church on Sundays and finish that, then move on to Monday and involve God little in our Monday through Saturday, except possibly reading a little of the Bible. But even that is limited. Are you on a read-the-Bible-in-a-year plan? Did you get your Bible read today? No? I will just read twice as much tomorrow to make up for it. Did you pray today? No? I will have to pray twice as long or twice as hard tomorrow to make up for it. There is truly little relationship with God, but more of a genie-in-a-bottle strategy. If I read the Bible every day and go to church every week, I assume God is going to keep me safe from the enemy, and we will prosper. If I do this, He will do that. If I don't do this, He will probably not do that. I was enormously mistaken.

My way of thinking is why I was so mad at Him. I had kept my end of the deal. I did all I thought I could. I'd gone to church all my life, I got a degree in theology—a step above most people, I thought. I sent my kids to Christian schools at great expense, showing God my priorities, I thought. I served on many Christian ministry boards, giving my time and money. We tithed to the church and to godly causes around the world. When I sinned, I asked God for His forgiveness. I prayed almost every day. I'd done the Christian thing my whole life, so why was all of this happening to me? I truly didn't know.

So, I had a choice: I had to either believe the God-and-Christian thing is not real, and it does not work, or figure out what God is all about and how to experience the amazing life the Bible told me about. I was done trying to create the great life that God talked about in the Bible on my own. If that great life was available, He was going to have to show me how to get it. I felt I completely understood the salvation thing—believing in God and asking Him to cover my sins with His sacrifice. It was everything after that I was unclear on. I needed to figure out what the truth was.

Starting My New Understanding of My Christian Walk

One day my friend told me he'd been to a weekend teaching, where participants were learning how to hear God's voice and walk the path God has planned for each of us. He called it Abiding with Christ.

What? Hear His voice?

In my past Bible studies, people always talked about this. Yes, some people say they hear from God, but in most cases, I thought, people use that to gain a one-up situation in a spiritual argument. Do I really believe this? How do people get others to do what they want on a board or a church committee? By saying, "God told me." How do you argue that point? But was that real? Does God really care to talk to us? If so, how do I know I really heard from Him?

I've also heard God has a plan for my life, but I couldn't help but wonder: was this really His plan? If this was his full plan for me, I do not believe it was a very good plan. I felt like a pawn in this whole scheme that was not planned out for my best but for someone else. If this was really his plan it hasn't been very nice, and I'm not sure I can trust His strategy. I do know He was there during our great disaster, though. I had a range of emotions, thinking about if this was His plan or whether I was walking my own plan. Did I somehow stray from His plan? How do I know if I'm following his path or my own? Honestly, if the planning is up to me, I'm not sure I can trust myself again. I was fairly confused about what had happened the first time. I needed to figure it out. These were all the questions I asked myself and my friend. It was the beginning of a journey.

What is Abiding?

Discovering Abiding

Just a few short weeks later, we found ourselves in the living room of a successful businessman, who had dedicated his life to helping other businessmen seek and find God's will for their lives. To be honest, that weekend was exceedingly difficult for me. He was reframing scriptures I had read for years to mean something different. He was actually reading the Bible like it was talking to him today for today's purposes and not merely as a historical account of how God had done things in the past.

He showed us in scripture how the Holy Spirit wants to speak to us, using scripture and sometimes other aspects of life, to help us walk a step-by-step life that God Himself has planned out for us. I had to adjust my thinking to a whole new way of life—a way of life believing God Himself truly had a full, detailed plan for my life, specifically for me, and He desperately wanted to share it with me. What made this so difficult was I loved finishing things, as I said. This meant that my spiritual life was not complete. I know this sounds odd at this point, but that's where I was. If I had not completed my learning and understanding of who God was and what I believed, the foundation of my life would get shaky. Well, my entire world had shaken, broken, and had fallen apart. Why not my spiritual walk?

A New Way of Trusting God

Did I believe God cared about me so much that He cared about the details of my life and not just its general direction? Did He really want to be involved in the day-to-day aspects of my life? I was not sure I could get myself there. And if I did get myself there, could I really trust that plan? Was it the plan best for me, or was it just best for God? Would His plan for my life be as good as or better than if I planned out my own life?

At the end of the weekend, I was asked if I would commit to what he called "Abiding," which came from two passages of scripture.

> Abide in me, and I will abide in you. Just as the branch cannot produce fruit by itself unless it abides in the vine, neither can you unless you abide in me. I am the vine; you are the branches. The one who abides in me while I abide in him produces much fruit, because apart from me you can do nothing (John 15:4–5).

> This is the confidence we have in approaching God: that if we ask anything according to His will, He hears us. And if we know that

He hears us—whatever we ask—we know that we have what we asked of Him (1 John 5:14--15).

If this was true, I needed to understand it. I didn't typically get any of my prayers answered, but was it because I was not asking according to God's will for my life? The reality was that I always prayed for "my plan" not "His plan." I didn't even realize there was another option. I might need to find God's will for my life. Rich's challenge was that I would abide once a day for at least fifteen minutes and write out what I was learning in a journal. I figured I could do that. It was a small commitment, and I might get the answers I was looking for.

I still didn't really believe it, however. The positive was that I might find a life-changing relationship with God I'd never known was there, and on the other side, I could say I did it and prove it was not as real as he said it was. I found myself in a whirlwind of emotions again, confusion, frustration, and anger that I couldn't fully explain or direct at any one thing. All my life, I thought I had the "God thing" figured out. I had the knowledge, the theology degree, and the hours of Bible reading. If anyone should have understood God, it was me. But now, I was standing on the edge of a dark, bottomless pit of uncertainty, questioning everything I thought I knew.

How did I end up here? Why was my life such a mess? I had tried to live in a way I thought God wanted—faithful, moral, and obedient. I prayed, went to church, and believed. And yet, here I was, broken and bewildered, looking at the wreckage of my life. If I had done everything I could to live as a believer, why did it feel like God had abandoned me? Or worse—had He betrayed me?

It was maddening. I began to question if I had ever really understood Christianity at all. Was it all a sham? Had I built my life around something that didn't even work? Maybe this whole "Christian thing" wasn't real, or maybe it was real but completely worthless when it came to giving me a good life. My mind spun in circles. Is God real? If He is, is He a God I can trust? Does He even care about my life—or anyone's life?

I was furious. But at who? Myself? God? The church? If God wasn't real, who was I angry at? If He *was* real, then why wasn't I outright angry with Him for letting all this happen? And if He's supposed to be Love—as I was always taught—then what in the world is love? Because whatever I thought love was, this didn't feel like it.

I couldn't stop wrestling with these questions. If God is sovereign, as I had always been told, doesn't that mean He's in charge of everything? And if He's in charge of everything, then doesn't that mean He *allowed* this—no, *caused* this? What kind of God does that? And if that's true, then what about the Devil? Does he exist? Is he real? How does the Devil factor into all this mess? If God is sovereign, how can the Devil have any power at all? The whole framework I had been taught felt like a tangled web of contradictions.

Was it the church's fault? Were the pastors who taught me all of this just as clueless as I was? Did they even believe half the things they said? Or were they just as confused, trying to make sense of it all while pretending they had the answers? I felt betrayed by the entire system. If God really did all this, then isn't *He* the evil one? The thought chilled me to the core.

I felt utterly lost like I was drowning in a sea of conflicting ideas and half-truths. And then, as if to rub salt in the wound, some businessman—a total stranger— had the nerve to suggest that the solution was simple: "Just read the Bible," he said. Really? Read the Bible? As if I hadn't already spent years of my life doing just that! How could I possibly figure out something that even pastors and theologians seem to stumble over? The arrogance of it infuriated me. What made him think he had it all figured out?

But then the challenge hit me differently. Was I really ready to give up on the idea of God altogether? Was I willing to walk away and say I was done with all of it? Or was there still a small part of me—angry, confused, and skeptical— that was willing to try one last time? Could I take this challenge, not to confirm what I already thought I knew, but to *prove it wrong*?

If this God thing wasn't real, I wanted to know. And if it *was* real, then surely there was more to it than what I had experienced. I decided I would take the challenge. I would spend time in God's Word every day—not because I expected to find answers, but because I needed to know if this whole Christian thing was worth holding onto. Was I willing to take the risk? To start over? To face the possibility that I might discover something I had been missing all along—or confirm that it was all a lie?

I wasn't sure if it was faith, desperation, or sheer stubbornness that drove me forward. But I was about to find out.

An Unexpected Experience

One day, my wife was out of town, and most of my kids were off to college, so I had the house to myself. These days were great to get projects done around the house, so I got an early start. My goal was to abide first, as was my practice, and then I would attack some neglected yard work. I grabbed a cup of coffee and headed out to the back porch. As I usually did, I asked God what He wanted to share with me today. I started out reading where I'd left off the day before and found some interesting truths.

At this point, I had been abiding for about two weeks and enjoyed it, but it was not necessarily life-changing. That day, God showed me some amazing things in scripture, things I had never noticed. It was fascinating and exciting. I didn't think I had ever been excited to read the Bible before, but this day it came alive. I was bouncing from scripture to scripture, wiping tears from my eyes as He was showing me some personal and meaningful insights.

He was even answering some of my lifelong questions about why some things happened to me in my life. He showed me how He'd made me different and special for what He had for my life. I went from scripture to scripture as God had a plan for what he wanted to share with me. It was like he finally had my attention, and he wanted to show me some amazing truths about who he was and what he really thought of me. I did not pay attention to anything other than reading, writing, and praying. I felt motivated and truly alive. I will never forget that time although these types of times with him have become more of the norm.

After a while, I struggled to see the Bible because the sun was directly in my eyes. Odd. When I had sat down, I positioned the Bible in my lap so my body would block the rising sun. Now I had the sun in my eyes. How long had I been sitting here? All day. Seriously?

One of the meaningful insights He showed me was in Psalm 23. I found my notes in my journal. Yes, it was in my sloppy and malty-colored handwriting, so I know I put it down. I have read this Psalm multiple times and always have gotten something out of it. This time, however, God showed me something specific.

> The Lord is my shepherd; I lack nothing. He makes me lie down in green pastures; He leads me beside quiet waters; He refreshes my soul.

> He guides me along the right paths for His name's sake. Even though I walk through the darkest valley, I will fear no evil, for You are with me; Your rod and Your staff, they comfort me. You prepare a table before me in the presence of my enemies. You anoint my head with oil, and my cup overflows. Surely, goodness and mercy will follow me all the days of my life, and I will dwell in the house of the Lord forever. (Psalm 23)

God showed me that He had me on this path. He was my Shepherd, and He always has been. Even when my original family was somewhat dysfunctional, He'd provided everything I needed. He'd provided amazing green pastures for me in the beginning of my life.

He made me lie down in those green pastures and helped me to relax in them for a while, fully enjoying the benefits of a great career. My soul was fully refreshed when I was able to help hundreds of people strengthen their souls in our financial life coaching program. Most of all, He refreshed my soul with one of the most spectacular wives I could have ever imagined, and He blessed me with an absolutely amazing family. He showed me that after every exhausting day, I came home to a family who truly refreshed my soul, provided by Him. My cup overflowed.

Upon the path He had me on, making me lie down in green pastures and refreshing my soul, He was preparing me to walk through the darkest valley. He knew the valley was coming, and He did walk me through it. He said, "My rod and staff comfort you."

I thought about what His rod and staff meant. The rod conveyed His authority. The enemy could come after me, but God's authority said, "Do not touch him." His staff represented long-suffering. As He walked me through the beginning of my life, if there was one thing He gave me the strength to do, it was to be long-suffering. It took a long time to deal with issues, to build companies, and to do it with dyslexia. He gave me the ability to be tenacious in challenging times.

He provided me with His staff all my life.

The biggest thing He showed me was that He was walking me along a path I had not seen before. He knew what was coming, and first, He prepared me for it, and then He comforted me in preparation to fight the battle of a lifetime. He didn't hate me. He didn't abandon me. He prepared me for the battle. The enemy took his best shot at me and my family, and the enemy failed. God then prepared a celebratory table in the presence of my enemies when He made the government rescind its ban.

God was all-powerful. I didn't understand that God Himself was walking me through the difficult times. This was just one of several amazing lessons He showed me that day as I went back into my journal to see what the day had been all about.

Refined by Trials: Trusting God's Path to Emerge as Gold

In that time on the patio, God also showed me a unique way of looking at the difficulties that we had been and were continuing to walk through. Job 23:10–11 reveals a profound expression of trust in God during times of testing. Job, amid his suffering, declares his confidence in God's wisdom and sovereignty, knowing even though Job cannot always perceive God's presence, God knows the path he is walking. This assurance underscores the belief that trials, though painful, serve a divine purpose. Just as gold is refined in the fire, Job understands that his faith will emerge purer and stronger from the refining process.

This refining drew us closer to God and prepared us for a greater impact on the world than we'd ever thought possible. As Romans 8:28 reminds us, "God works all things together for good for those who love Him and are called according to His purpose." The trial we faced, though intended for our destruction by the enemy, became the thing God used to transform us for His greater glory.

That day was a turning point in my journey—a day that transformed my understanding of who God is and how He sees me. Somehow, in the chaos and questions, I caught a glimpse of what God is truly about. It was like a window cracked open, and for the first time, I began to see pieces of His sovereignty, His love, and His purpose in ways I had never understood before.

I started to grasp, just faintly, the magnitude of who God is. He wasn't distant or indifferent; He was deeply engaged, both in the grand scope of the universe and in the details of my life. For the first time, I saw how the Devil works tirelessly to lead God's children astray, not just to harm them but to grieve the heart of God. The realization hit me hard—this wasn't just about me or my struggles. It was about something far greater: the battle between good and evil, and God's relentless love for His children, even in the midst of that battle.

I also began to see people differently. The wrongs they committed and the pain they caused wasn't the whole story. God loved them as much as He loved me. That truth was hard to swallow at first. How could He love people who hurt others? But slowly, I began to see them as He does—not just for their actions but for their worth, their brokenness, and their potential. It was humbling and overwhelming all at once.

Then came the most unexpected revelation: the Bible wasn't just a book anymore. It came alive. As I read and sought after Him, God began to reveal Himself to me through its pages. The stories, the words—they weren't just ancient texts or abstract teachings. They were a living dialogue between God and me. He was speaking, guiding, and showing me glimpses of who He is and who He created me to be.

I didn't suddenly have all the answers. I knew I wasn't figuring it all out perfectly, and I don't think I ever will. But after that day, I discovered something I hadn't truly understood before: God reveals new truths every day to those who seek Him. It's not always clear, and it's not always easy, but it's a journey path illuminated by His presence, even in the confusion.

I wasn't alone on this path, either. My friends who were studying His Word alongside me were on the same journey—from confusion to light, from questions to clarity. Together, we were learning to see new parts of God, new facets of His character, and new dimensions of His blessings. The blessings weren't always material or immediate. In fact, I started to realize that the blessings I had fought so hard for—success, comfort, achievement—paled in comparison to the spiritual blessings I discovered by walking closely with Jesus.

These spiritual blessings were beyond anything I could have imagined. They weren't things I could hold or measure. They were the peace that comes from knowing I am loved, the joy of seeing God's hand at work in my life, and the strength to face each day with hope. Walking with Him wasn't just about receiving blessings; it was about experiencing His presence in ways I never thought possible.

I also realized that without a personal, one-on-one relationship with God, I could never have understood any of this. I can talk about it, describe it, even try to explain it—but none of that compares to actually *walking in it*. The relationship makes all the difference. It's the foundation, the anchor, and the source of everything I've come to know and cherish about God.

That day wasn't the end of my journey, it was just the beginning. It was a day that marked a shift from striving to seeking, from confusion to trust, and from living for blessings to walking with the One who blesses. And every step since has been a reminder that while I may not see the whole picture, I am walking with the One who does.

Now let me share a small but powerful secret with you. The rest of this book is a collection of the journeys that have unfolded in my life—journeys revealed through scripture, drawn from the journals I've kept since the day everything changed for me. These pages are filled with thoughts, insights, and even secrets that God has shown me through His Word and His Spirit. But here's the coolest part: these revelations aren't just for me.

The truths about who God is, His character, His promises, and His love are available to anyone who seeks Him. What He's shown me isn't exclusive or hidden from you. If you seek Him with an open heart, He will reveal similar truths to you, just as He has to me. That's the incredible beauty of a relationship with God—it's deeply personal and yet universally available. He desires to meet each of us exactly where we are, and as we draw close to Him, He promises to draw close to us.

In Journey 4, I will dive deeper into what it means to spend time with God—how to abide in Him daily and allow His Word to come alive in your heart. I'll share the practical details about abiding, the methods I've learned, and how they've transformed my relationship with Him. This isn't about following a rigid formula but about discovering how to walk with God in a way that's real, meaningful, and life-changing.

As you continue reading, my hope is that you'll see this not just as my story but as an invitation to start your own journey. Because the truth is, the same God who revealed these things to me longs to reveal Himself to you, too. All you need to do is take the first step—seek Him, and you'll find Him. And as you abide, you'll discover more of His love, His truth, and His presence than you ever imagined possible.

The Revelation of God's Love

Ever since that day, I have been convinced of God's love for me, and now I have a deep desire to be in His presence always. He has shown me I had lived under His protection of salvation all my life. I believe in Him and look forward to eternity with Him in Heaven.

He also revealed salvation was just the beginning of what He had for me. I had never really committed to serving Him as my Lord. Since then, I have chosen to serve Him as Lord and have loved every minute of it.

Serving Him as Lord

This means knowing and accepting that His ways are better than my ways. (We will talk more about the difference between Lord and Savior in the coming chapters.) I want to know His plan for my life, and I only want to follow that plan.

My wife recently put a large sign up in our dining room that says, "God's Best and None Other," a great reminder that all we want to do is follow the plan

God has for us and not pursue any other paths. In my journey of discovery, I found being humble and asking God what to do was far more valuable and comforting than doing things that just made sense to me at the time.

Seeking God's Will in Every Aspect

In my life, I have proven I know what to do to make things good. I can start a business and run it. I can provide jobs for hundreds of people and do good work here on this earth. But I want to know what God says is best for me. That is where life is grand.

One of the new things God was teaching me was how to practically seek God's will for everyday things like managing a personal life or building a business. I was confused about following the Lord and seeking His will versus doing what made sense in my mind. And what if you're under a time constraint to make your decision, and you don't think you have heard any guidance from God? I had so much to learn. All I desired was that when I saw God for the first time, He'd say, "Well done."

Working with God, Not Just Waiting

One day I was reading stories about Jesus. I saw that God rarely does supernatural events when he does not partner with someone. Partnering means He does His part, and we do our part. He gives wisdom and guidance to those who listen to Him. When you read through the Bible, it is story after story of people obeying God, not God just acting and doing what He wanted. Even Jesus did this when he said in John 5:19, "Jesus gave them this answer: very truly I tell you, the Son can do nothing by himself; he can do only what he sees his Father doing, because whatever the Father does the Son also does."

In addition to this, I learned He was not just working things out mysteriously behind the scenes based on people's prayers (although sometimes He does this). He is mostly partnering with His beloved, doing what He does to pave the way for us to do what He tells us and finish His work. What an eye-opening experience to realize this.

A New Way to Pray

I've spent a lifetime praying for Him to do things in my life and not asking Him what I should be doing to walk in His will. He wants to work with us in a loving and caring way, with us hearing what He is saying and us trusting Him to do what He told us to do. That is "the trusting and obeying" that is so difficult.

My praying and sitting waiting for Him to act was not being helpful (unless that was part of my obedience—sitting because He told me to wait). I would pray that God would act on our behalf in a certain situation, waiting and watching and looking with the belief He would do what I said He should do. The key here is *Him* doing what *I* said He *should* do in my prayers. Again, the genie-in-the-bottle mentality.

Why do I think I have the best solution when I am talking to the Almighty God, the God who created and knows everything? What a silly idea. My prayers now are more, "God, what do You want me to do?" or "How do You want me to pray in this situation?" Show me Your ways and help me to set aside my selfish desires that won't get me to the place You want me to be.

I want only what You want for me because I completely trust that Your plan for my life and the plan for the ones I love are perfect. I can't improve on Your plans for our life, so I will trust You in Your plan for us. Now, Lord, please help me lay aside my plans for our lives.

A New Focus

This is now my journey, and in the rest of this book, I'd like to share with you the process I've gone through to find God's will for our lives and what I have learned in the process of finding and trusting His will.

I share this with you so you can understand the rest of the guidance in this book. My focus for you is to help you understand the genie-in-the-bottle strategy is never going to let you see the greatness and fullness of a real walk with God.

Seeking Shalom

Through seeking God's will for my life, I asked God why my world fell apart. Why did He allow such great destruction when I was doing such great things for my family and, frankly, for the world? God was simple. He said, "Shalom." You want Shalom.

So, I wanted to know what in the world shalom was. As far as I knew, shalom was a greeting that Jewish people said when they said *hello*. I asked a friend what he knew about the word, and he said he thought it meant peace, but he was not sure. I thought, I guess it is time to discover the real meaning of the word *shalom*.

After some research, I discovered that shalom is a Hebrew word that has a rich and complex meaning in the Bible and Jewish culture. Definitions include peace, completeness, wholeness, well-being, fullness, rest, harmony in all relationships, contentment, friendliness, and tranquility.

God was telling me that I was seeking the blessings of God, I was seeking shalom, but I was trying to accomplish it with my own efforts and plans—and not allowing God to give it to me the way He had planned. He didn't want bad things for me, but the way I was seeking shalom, I was building my world on a sandy foundation and not on the Rock, who is Jesus. I believe this is what every person in the world is seeking.

We use anything that we have accessible to accomplish this. Sometimes it is good for us, and other times it will harm us, but whatever it is, without God's involvement, it will never satisfy the desire to have shalom in our life.

The shalom I was trying to create without God, or at least His direct involvement, was a way to look at myself and say I was okay the way God made me. Instead, what I did was try to outdo anyone I had ever known. Create more businesses, hire more people, help more people, have someone say they believed in me. I know there was a lot more to this, but if someone told me that God provides shalom, I would say I will take it. I want complete peace, a world without conflict, wholeness, and complete contentment. I was just trying to do it by building an empire that everyone could look at and say they were grateful that Brad Hawkins had come into their world and helped them out.

Story Time: Isaac's Mysterious Peace, Seeking Shalom

Let me share with you a tale that beautifully illustrates this idea, as told by a man named Isaac.

Isaac was a figure well-known in his small village, renowned not for his wealth or power, but for his unwavering peace and contentment. In a world where many were consumed by their troubles, Isaac seemed to glide through life with an unshakable sense of joy and hope. He faced each day with a heart full of gratitude, even when the shadows of hardship loomed large. His response to adversity was marked by a calmness and wisdom that baffled those around him.

Isaac's demeanor was not born of ignorance to the harsh realities of life. On the contrary, he had faced his fair share of trials. Yet, while others would grumble about their misfortunes or lash out in anger, Isaac remained serene. His eyes shone with a quiet strength, a reflection of the deep well of peace he drew from God daily.

When people asked him how he maintained such tranquility amidst life's storms, Isaac smiled gently and explained, "The peace I have doesn't come from my circumstances. It comes from my relationship with God. Every morning, I choose to dwell in His presence, surrendering my worries and trusting in His mighty power. When adversity strikes, I don't focus on the storm but on the Faithful One who can redeem all suffering."

His words were simple, yet they carried the weight of profound truth. Still, not everyone understood or appreciated his perspective. Some mocked him, seeing his patience as a sign of weakness or complacency. They couldn't grasp how he could be so calm in the face of chaos. But Isaac bore their ridicule with grace, never retaliating or harboring resentment. Instead, he continued to love and care for them, praying for their well-being even when they hurt him.

There were times when tempers flared and men would confront Isaac with threats of violence, their anger boiling over in disputes. Yet, Isaac never met fire with fire. He responded with a quiet but firm reason, diffusing tensions without compromising the truth. His integrity was a shield that protected him, turning potential enemies into allies. His sincere and kind-hearted nature softened even the hardest hearts, and his gentle words often healed deep wounds.

As the years passed, Isaac's reputation grew. His wisdom became a beacon for the community, and even local leaders sought his counsel in resolving disputes. Merchants and neighbors, initially skeptical of his unyielding calm, found themselves drawn to the aura of wholeness and rest that surrounded him. In time, they came to understand the concept of shalom—the profound peace that comes from fully trusting the Almighty with one's life. People would ask him to join business enterprises and boards. They simply wanted to partner with him only to have his influence on their businesses and their lives, and of course share with him profits because of his Godly influence.

Isaac's life was a living testament to the power of faith and the beauty of a soul at rest. Through him, the village learned that true peace does not depend on the absence of trouble, but on the presence of a steadfast heart. And in their admiration for Isaac, they found a deeper respect for the God he so faithfully served.

Let's Be Real; Life Is Tough

We all face moments that push us to the edge. The question isn't if life is going to hit us—it absolutely will—the real question is, how will you respond when it does? I've been there. This journey is about learning to rely on God's strength, not our own.

This isn't just a story about how I survived—it's a guide to help you build an unshakable life. I want you to look at your own struggles and ask yourself: how do I respond when life gets hard? Do you react with anger, bitterness, or avoidance? Or are you willing to let God into the mess, to heal what's broken, and lead you to something greater?

Here's the truth: you have a choice. No matter what life throws at you— heartbreak, failure, betrayal—you can invite God into those places. You can trust Him to turn your pain into purpose and your struggles into strength. I'm asking you to stop pretending everything is fine when it's not. Take the discomfort to God, and let Him do the work He's been waiting to do.

So, here's the challenge: don't just read this—live it. Trust boldly that God has more for you than what you've been living. Step into His unshakable promises and see how He transforms your life. This is your story now. Are you ready to step in? Because God is waiting.

Let's Continue to Journey 3

Are you ready to go deeper? As we step into Journey 3, it's time to clear up all the confusion, the misconceptions, and the misunderstandings you've carried about God. We've all been through things that make us question—*Why did this happen? Where was God in all of it?* This part of the journey will help you see God's love even in the toughest times, the moments when you wondered if He was even there.

JOURNEY 3

Clarifying Misconceptions: Aligning with God's True Character

When you live the life of a believer for a long time, you inevitably gather a lot of input—some enlightening, some confusing. In the Christian world, if you've even attempted to walk the path for just a little while, you've likely searched for answers to many of life's most profound questions. Who is God? What does He do? Why does He give certain things to some people and withhold them from others? Who is really in charge of this world?

Sometimes, you find answers that bring peace or joy, while other times, the answers you've reached feel heavy, difficult, or even deeply unsettling. Yet, despite the emotions tied to them, these conclusions become part of what you believe about God and His ways.

Proverbs 23:7 reminds us, "For as [a person] thinks in his heart, so is he." Thoughts become emotions, emotions become behavior, and behavior becomes results. How we think is critical to understanding our lives and our understanding of God. This is why Philippians 4:8 instructs us, "Finally, brethren, whatever things are true, whatever things are noble, whatever things are just, whatever things are pure, whatever things are lovely, whatever things are of good report, if there is any virtue and if there is anything praiseworthy— meditate on these things."

Typically, our thoughts flow from what we believe, and what we believe is foundational to the life we end up living. If we believe in God, if we trust in the Bible, that belief steers our thoughts. And how we think steers how our emotions respond to the world around us. Our emotions, in turn, influence our behavior, and our behavior is how we show up in the world. Jesus says in Matthew 12:34, "For out of the abundance of the heart the mouth speaks." This is why our beliefs are so critically important.

But have you ever questioned where your beliefs come from? Proverbs 4:23 advises, "Above all else, guard your heart, for everything you do flows from it."

For most of us, our beliefs are shaped by an accumulation of life experiences—what we've done, what we've heard, and the people around us. But I'd like to challenge you to take a deeper look at your beliefs. Where did they originate? Is the source of your beliefs trustworthy? Will it provide you with the complete truth, giving your belief a solid foundation to stand on? Jesus Himself emphasizes the importance of building our lives on solid ground in Matthew 7:24–25, saying, "Therefore, whoever hears these sayings of Mine, and does them, I will liken him to a wise man who built his house on the rock: and the rain descended, the floods came, and the winds blew and beat on that house; and it did not fall, for it was founded on the rock."

Consider whether your beliefs are rooted in emotions from something good or bad that has happened to you. Are they based on the opinions of others? Or are they influenced by unknown outside sources? Colossians 2:8 warns us, "Beware lest anyone cheat you through philosophy and empty deceit, according to the tradition of men, according to the basic principles of the world, and not according to Christ." Can you go neutral in your beliefs, setting aside preconceptions, and search the scriptures—the true and infallible Word of God—and still wind up in the same place you started? Or are you holding onto beliefs that aren't based on scripture simply because they feel comfortable?

These are critical questions. By evaluating the foundation of our beliefs, we can ensure that we're building our lives on the solid rock of truth rather than the shifting sands of emotion, opinion, or convenience. As Psalm 119:105 declares, "Your word is a lamp to my feet and a light to my path." Let us, therefore, ensure that our beliefs are firmly rooted in God's Word, guiding us in truth and leading us to live lives that reflect His will and His ways.

When I began my abiding journey, I thought I had a clear picture of God—some aspects were spot on, others were slightly off, and yes, some were completely wrong. But as I spent significant time in the Word—the Word that God Himself authored through forty different people, partnering with them as He always does—my perspective began to shift.

The Word of God, proven true time and time again, has corrected many of my distorted views and clarified misconceptions. It has also strengthened my resolve on many things. I had to approach this journey with a neutral heart, willing to set aside my preconceived beliefs and allow God's Word to teach me what He wanted me to learn.

God guided me through a journey specifically designed for me, addressing my unique misconceptions. In His incredibly loving way, He revealed who He is and how, even when I strayed onto paths not meant for me, He continually redirected me. He provided multiple options to gently lead me back to a path rich with blessings.

I invite you to share this journey with me. In this part of the book, I will share what God has taught me through scripture—truths that were deeply meaningful to my walk with Him. Everything here is scripturally based and was tailored to what He wanted to teach me. When you are abiding, you might learn the same truths, but God, in His wisdom, will teach them in a way that fits your unique path and circumstances.

If something doesn't make sense to you as you journey through this book, know that God is ready to speak directly to you, answering your specific questions. He will guide you just as He guided me.

This part of the book will delve into how I learned to listen to God and align my life with His will. It's about understanding that our life choices are not just about making the right decision but about making decisions that align with God's plan for us. Through my journey, I hope to provide insights that will help you navigate your path with a greater sense of God's presence and guidance.

Life Choices and God's Will

Life is filled with choices, and every choice brings us down a potentially different path. Each path brings different opportunities and more different choices. Which is right? Which is wrong? How do we know? What does God want me to do? Many movies focus on time travel, and I personally love the mind-bending ideas that time travel brings—the opportunities to redo decisions that might be the wrong ones. Better yet, if I could know the outcome of each decision before I made it, what a great life that would be. No regrets, no bad decisions.

We know this is not reality, but we have a better opportunity than time travel to make the best decisions possible. We can make the right decision now before we must suffer through making the wrong one. If we surrender our will or desire for our lives to His will and plan, and we walk in the Spirit as He tells us to do, we can hear Him speak to us and lead us down the path He wants us to be on. I can trust that He has a plan for my life and follow that plan.

But how do I know if I follow His will that it will be the best for me? And if I do trust that His will is going to be the best for me, how do I know I heard correctly and am on the right path? Whatever I do in the future, I never want to go through the struggles I went through before. I also want to help save you from duplicating my past journey of managing my own life and guessing what God thought was best for me. I want to give you some ideas on how you might find God's will and plan for your life.

Learning from the Past

I don't know if my decisions led to the disasters our family went through. I cannot help but think that God was speaking to me, possibly daily, telling me how to avoid upcoming disasters. But if He was speaking, my business and not knowing how to hear His voice wouldn't have let me hear His warnings. I know there is a spiritual life that somehow, I missed—a closeness to my Father that I ignored for one reason or another. I have determined that my future will be different. I want my priorities to be in perfect alignment with my heavenly Father, so that I can know I am staying in His will.

My goal is to share the path I've traveled, moving from merely looking at God to truly abiding in Him. In this intimacy, God reveals profound spiritual truths and hidden treasures.

As you read, see this as an invitation to discover the great truths God has for you. What He offers me, He offers you too. The key is abiding in Him and spending time with the Holy Spirit. God loves you uniquely and wants to reveal the depths of His love and mysteries to you.

CHAPTER 9

My First Lesson in Abiding— Forgiveness

Y ou might guess one of the first and largest blessings up to this time was learning how to forgive. Honestly, it was one of the hardest things I had to do. God says that if I don't forgive others, He cannot forgive me. Wow. There would be nothing worse that I could think of than not being forgiven by God because I refused to forgive. Jesus teaches, "For if you forgive other people when they sin against you, your heavenly Father will also forgive you. But if you do not forgive others their sins, your Father will not forgive your sins" (Matt. 6:14–15).

As you might be able to guess, I was having a hard time forgiving some people. Somehow, I knew God was requiring me to forgive to move forward into His grand, abundant, loving life that He has planned for me. He showed me that if I forgave and gave up my right to harm the people who had harmed me, He would take care of both sides of the situation. He would help me to forgive, and God also says that vengeance is His.

"Do not take revenge, my dear friends, but leave room for God's wrath, for it is written: 'It is mine to avenge; I will repay,' says the Lord" (Rom. 12:19).

At first, I thought, since my not forgiving them was holding up God from being able to take godly vengeance against them, I would forgive so God's wrath could attack them. I know that is not forgiving, but that is where I started. I went through all the verses I could find about forgiveness and truly got to the point that I could forgive.

"Get rid of all bitterness, rage and anger, brawling and slander, along with every form of malice. Be kind and compassionate to one another, forgiving each other, just as in Christ God forgave you" (Eph. 4:31–32).

One of the great insights I came across is that everyone, not just the nice and godly people, but everyone, God created and loved. Just like He loved me. I felt that was a little mind stretching but I understood that when one of my kids messed up for one reason or another, I didn't stop loving them. So, why would I expect God to turn on one of His creations? I realized that I was hating someone God loves. Even when they have done so much harm to me, if I want to be like God and walk in the abundance that He has prepared for me, I must choose His path and not stay on my own. I can choose to forgive and walk toward love.

Forgiving nonbelievers was easier for me because they didn't claim to live by God's standards, but forgiving believers—especially those I'd trusted and respected—who hurt me or my family was far more difficult, particularly when they used God's name to justify their actions. This struggle became my nemesis, as I couldn't comprehend how people who professed faith could behave so hurtfully, but God gently reminded me that He loves them just as much as He loves me. Holding onto bitterness meant I was hating who God loves, and I realized I would rather be in alignment with Him, walking in peace and joy, than be stuck in unforgiveness. Though it took time, once this truth became part of my belief system, I was able to release the bitterness and walk in true forgiveness.

God's Love for Everyone

In John 3:16, we read, "For God so loved the world that He gave His one and only Son, that whoever believes in Him shall not perish but have eternal life." Notice that it says "the world"—meaning everyone, not just those who are already living in obedience to Him. This includes the people who hurt us, the ones we struggle to love. God's love is unrelenting and unconditional. Similarly, Romans 5:8 tells us, "But God demonstrates His own love for us in this: While we were still sinners, Christ died for us." This scripture emphasizes that God didn't wait for us to clean up our acts before He loved us—He loved us at our worst. In the same way, we are called to reflect that love, even toward those who have wronged us.

Our Call to Forgive and Walk in Love

When you realize you are "hating someone that God loves," it's a profound moment of conviction and alignment with God's heart. Matthew 5:44 says, "But I tell you, love your enemies and pray for those who persecute you, that you may be children of your Father in Heaven." This command isn't easy, but it's the path to becoming more like God. 1 John 4:20 also speaks to this: "Whoever claims to love God yet hates a brother or sister is a liar. For whoever does not love their brother and sister, whom they have seen, cannot love God, whom they have not seen." Holding onto hatred, even justified by our pain, creates a block between us and the fullness of God's love.

Forgiveness as a Path to Abundance

Forgiveness is one of the keys to unlocking God's abundance in our lives. Ephesians 4:31–32 urges us, "Get rid of all bitterness, rage and anger, brawling and slander, along with every form of malice. Be kind and compassionate to one another, forgiving each other, just as in Christ God forgave you." By forgiving, we free ourselves from the chains of bitterness that hinder us from experiencing the full measure of God's blessings.

A Father's Unconditional Love

The analogy of a parent loving their child, even when they mess up, is a perfect picture of God's heart toward us and others. Luke 15:11–32 (The Parable of the Prodigal Son) illustrates this beautifully. Despite the son's rebellion, the father's love remained steadfast, and he welcomed his son back with open arms. God does the same with us and with others, even when they have caused hurt or strayed far from Him. When we see others through this lens of grace, we step into God's perspective.

Walking Toward Love

Choosing to walk in God's love rather than holding onto resentment is a daily decision, but it is one that leads to life and peace. Colossians 3.13–14 encourages us, "Bear with each other and forgive one another if any of you has a grievance against someone. Forgive as the Lord forgave you. And over all these virtues put on love, which binds them all together in perfect unity."

Love brings unity, both with God and with others, and it aligns us with His will. By choosing God's path of forgiveness and love, you open yourself to walk in the abundance of His peace, joy, and provision. This is about stepping out of your own way and aligning with God's plan—a plan that always leads to life in its fullest expression. 1 John 4:20: "Whoever claims to love God yet hates a brother or sister is a liar. For whoever does not love their brother and sister, whom they have seen, cannot love God, whom they have not seen." "For my thoughts are not your thoughts, neither are your ways my ways," declares the Lord. "As the Heavens are higher than the earth, so are my ways higher than your ways and my thoughts than your thoughts" (Isaiah 55:8–9). This personal journey of forgiveness has taught me that God's ways are higher than my ways and His thoughts higher than my thoughts. Through His strength and guidance, I have learned to forgive, to release my right to revenge, and to trust Him with the outcomes.

The freedom He has given me through forgiveness is epic. I started to see amazing and meaningful aspects of God's love that I had never realized before. The bondage I was walking in, carrying all the anger and bitterness, kept me from an amazing understanding of God's love. When I was no longer wishing harm on so many people, I was able to see more about what God was doing. Now, does that mean that I never get angry or wish for justice to happen? Not at all. I fall into that trap all the time as I walk through this world. But as I recognize it, I can quickly adjust my thinking, ask for forgiveness, and turn the situation back over to God much faster than I was doing before. "Do not be anxious about anything, but in every situation, by prayer and petition, with thanksgiving, present your requests to God. And the peace of God, which transcends all understanding, will guard your hearts and your minds in Christ Jesus" (Phil. 4:6–7). "Trust in the Lord with all your heart and lean not on your own understanding; in all your ways submit to him, and he will make your paths straight" (Prov. 3:5–6).

Let's look at an example we find in scriptures. Matthew, a tax collector for the Roman Empire, was seen as a traitor by his fellow Jews in Capernaum. Yet, Jesus invited him to leave his job and become one of His disciples. This decision brought tension, especially with Peter, one of the first disciples. Peter likely held resentment against Matthew for his past actions, but Jesus did not immediately address the issue. Instead, He patiently waited for the right moment, allowing the tension to surface and both men to bring their struggles to Him.

When the time came, Jesus facilitated their reconciliation with wisdom, giving them the space to acknowledge their feelings while guiding them toward healing. Matthew courageously confessed his failures to Peter, not to manipulate forgiveness, but to genuinely repent. Peter, however, wrestled with granting forgiveness, which led him to seek Jesus' counsel. Jesus reminded him that forgiveness is a gift that reflects God's mercy and that forgiving others mirrors His image in us. Though forgiveness involves sacrifice, it also brings freedom and healing.

Jesus' teachings on forgiveness provide guidance in various situations:

1. **Unconditional Forgiveness:**

   Jesus taught us to forgive others unconditionally to guard our hearts against bitterness. "And whenever you stand praying, forgive, if you have anything against anyone, so that your Father also who is in Heaven may forgive you your trespasses" (Mark 11:25). This type of forgiveness frees us from resentment, which can poison our souls and harm other relationships.

2. **Forgiveness Leading to Reconciliation:**

   Jesus also spoke of forgiveness that restores relationships, requiring repentance from the offender. "If your brother sins, rebuke him, and if he repents, forgive him. And if he sins against you seven times in the day, and turns to you seven times, saying, 'I repent, you must forgive him" (Luke 17:3-4). This level of forgiveness may involve confrontation, confession, and sometimes restitution, as seen in Matthew and Peter's story.

3. **Seeking Reconciliation as the Offender:**

   Jesus emphasized the importance of taking initiative when we've wronged someone. "If you are offering your gift at the altar and there remember that your brother has something against you, leave your gift there before the altar and go. First be reconciled to your brother, and then come and offer your gift" (Matthew 5:23-24). Reconciliation begins with acknowledging our failure and seeking forgiveness, knowing our relationship with God is hindered until we make things right.

4. **Loving Those Closest to Us:**

The apostle John reminds us that love begins at home. "If anyone says, 'I love God,' and hates his brother, he is a liar; for he who does not love his brother whom he has seen cannot love God whom he has not seen" (1 John 4:20). True love for God is demonstrated in how we treat those around us.

These teachings call us to live out forgiveness and love authentically, starting with those closest to us. By tending to our own relationships, we can prevent ongoing offences and reflect God's mercy to the world. May we embrace the grace and courage to live out Jesus' and John's words, offering forgiveness as an act of worship and love.

Forgiveness and Reconciliation

When I was complaining that I wanted nothing to do with the people who had harmed me so much, God showed me they are not safe yet. I cannot restart doing life with some of these people until I understand that they are not going to harm me or my family anymore. God made it clear that there is a difference between forgiving and reconciliation.

God has offered forgiveness for everyone. It is a free gift to anyone who asks for it. Reconciliation is a different situation. God has offered forgiveness to everyone, but not everyone has chosen to accept His forgiveness and to be reconciled with Him. In my case, my job is to forgive, to give up my right of revenge and my desire to see them harmed like they have harmed me. I must turn it over to God and let Him deal with His creation, trusting that His justice is far greater than mine.

"Bear with each other and forgive one another if any of you has a grievance against someone. Forgive as the Lord forgave you" (Col. 3:13).

That does not mean that I must reconcile with the people who betrayed me immediately. I need to offer reconciliation or walk being willing to be reconciled. When they stop attempting harm to me or my family the relationship can start being rebuilt. This might take some time but when you are walking with forgiveness reconciliation is possible. I do, however, need to maintain a constant state of being willing to reconcile. That means I might need to reach out and make myself available for reconciliation, or it might mean that I need to wait for a bit, in forgiveness, as God works on the other parties, but reconciliation must be my goal. My job is to simply forgive and allow God to do the rest. If there is no possibility of reconciliation that is not an excuse for not forgiving.

In scripture, forgiveness and reconciliation are related but distinct concepts and understanding the difference between them is important for a healthy Christian life. While forgiveness is a command from God, reconciliation is the restoration of a relationship, which we are called to pursue and be available for, even though it may not always be fully realized because it will require two parties to do this as forgiveness is between you and your heavenly Father.

Forgiveness is the act of letting go of resentment or anger toward someone who has wronged you. It is a command given by God to all believers, regardless of whether the offender has apologized or sought forgiveness. Forgiveness is an individual act that frees the one who forgives from the burden of anger, bitterness, and hatred. It reflects God's nature, as He is quick to forgive us (Eph. 4:32). In Matthew 18:21–22, Peter asks Jesus how many times he should forgive someone who sins against him. Jesus responds, "I tell you, not seven times, but seventy-seven times," indicating that forgiveness should be unlimited and not conditional. This demonstrates that forgiveness is a constant, ongoing process, not dependent on the other person's actions.

Reconciliation goes a step further than forgiveness. It involves the restoration of a relationship that was broken due to wrongdoing. It requires genuine repentance from the offender and a willingness from both sides to rebuild trust and the relationship. While forgiveness is always required, reconciliation may not always be possible or advisable. However, the intent and pursuit of reconciliation should always be present, reflecting the heart of God.

Always Pursuing Reconciliation

Reconciliation can be a process and may not happen all at once. As believers, we are called to be available for reconciliation, always pursuing peace and restoration, even if it takes time and effort. In Matthew 5:23–24, Jesus teaches, "Therefore, if you are offering your gift at the altar and there remember that your brother or sister has something against you, leave your gift there in front of the altar. First go and be reconciled to them; then come and offer your gift." This shows the importance of pursuing reconciliation and taking the initiative to restore relationships. Even if full reconciliation is not immediately possible, pursuit and willingness to reconcile are essential but it is not a requirement for forgiveness.

Scripture encourages us to live in peace with others as much as possible. In Romans 12:18, Paul writes, "If it is possible, as far as it depends on you, live at peace with everyone." This verse emphasizes the believer's responsibility to pursue reconciliation and be open to it, even if the outcome is uncertain. Our role is to be agents of peace, always ready to forgive and seek the restoration of relationships, reflecting God's desire for unity and harmony among His people.

The Bible describes reconciliation as the restoration of broken relationships, grounded in forgiveness. God demonstrated this by forgiving our sins and reconciling us to Himself through Jesus Christ (2 Corinthians 5:18-19), removing the barrier of sin that separated us from Him. Similarly, we are called to seek reconciliation in our human relationships, prioritizing peace and unity. Forgiveness is the foundation of reconciliation, as it releases bitterness and opens the door for restored relationships, though reconciliation also requires mutual effort. Through forgiveness and reconciliation, we reflect God's love and His desire for unity among His people.

Key Differences

1. Obligation vs. Possibility: Forgiveness is a command and something we are obligated to do, regardless of the other person's actions. Reconciliation, however, depends on the actions and willingness of

both parties and may not always be possible, though the intent to reconcile should always be present.

2. Personal vs. Relational: Forgiveness is something you do within your heart before God. It's a personal decision. Reconciliation involves two people coming together to restore a broken relationship, which may involve time, healing, and rebuilding trust.

3. Immediate vs. Gradual: Forgiveness can be immediate, as it is a choice you make. Reconciliation, however, often takes time and may involve a process of healing and rebuilding the relationship. This process might lead to full reconciliation, or it may result in partial reconciliation, where some aspects of the relationship are restored while others remain not restored. For example, you might have an accountant who stole money from your company. You forgive them for the act of stealing. They might or might not restore you financially as God might tell you to work with them to restore the money back to your company or he might tell you to forgive the money; either way the restoration is led by God.

In addition to the money, you might not restore them back to the role of accountant of your company, ever. Still being led by God. The restoration process is always led by God. You have forgiven and you are not managing the restoration based on punishment or revenge but based on what God is saying is best for all people involved based on his great love for everyone. Your anger and bitterness do not get in the way of what God is doing because you have forgiven. Full restoration might not ever take place, but full forgiveness and reconciliation of the relationship is always pursued. Regardless, the pursuit of reconciliation should always be ongoing.

Forgiveness and reconciliation serve different purposes. While forgiveness is essential for the health of your own soul and your relationship with God, reconciliation is about restoring a relationship with another person. Reconciliation can be a journey with varying outcomes, from full restoration to partial healing, as both parties work together in the pursuit of a renewed relationship. The Bible teaches that we should always be ready and willing to pursue reconciliation, reflecting God's heart for peace and unity among His people. Even when reconciliation is not fully realized, the effort and intent to restore relationships are vital in our walk with Christ.

Story Time: Sarah's Forgiveness

Sarah sat in her small apartment, the weight of her past pressing down on her like a heavy stone. She stared out the window, watching the city bustle with life, but inside, she felt trapped, consumed by anger and bitterness. Her mind replayed scenes from her past—her sister Mary stealing her boyfriend, the one she thought she would marry, and her parents' shocking support of Mary's actions. They dismissed Sarah's pain, telling her to "move on" and "let it go." Just when she thought her heart couldn't break any more, her childhood friend Lisa, the one person she trusted implicitly, betrayed her by secretly applying for and getting the dream job Sarah had been aiming for. The pain and sense of betrayal were overwhelming, and it seemed impossible to let go.

The church bell tolled in the distance, and Sarah felt a tug in her heart. She had avoided church for years, fearing judgment and the painful process of confronting her wounds. But today, something was different. With a deep breath, she grabbed her coat and headed out the door, feeling an unfamiliar sense of urgency.

As she entered the church, she was met with the warmth of dimmed lights and the soft murmur of prayers. She found a seat in the back, hoping to remain unnoticed. The pastor's voice filled the room, speaking of forgiveness and grace.

"Matthew 6:14-15," the pastor read. "For if you forgive other people when they sin against you, your heavenly Father will also forgive you. But if you do not forgive others their sins, your Father will not forgive your sins."

The words struck Sarah like a thunderbolt. Tears welled up in her eyes as she realized the magnitude of her bitterness. The pain she carried was not just a burden—it was a barrier between her and God's love.

Sarah's anger had deep roots. It began with Mary, her sister. They were inseparable until the day Sarah discovered Mary had stolen her boyfriend.

Sarah had been planning a future with him, only to watch it crumble. When her parents sided with Mary, telling Sarah to "move on" and belittling her feelings, it felt like a betrayal from the people she trusted most. Just when she thought she couldn't hurt more, Lisa, her closest friend, applied for the job Sarah had her heart set on and got it. The betrayal cut deep. It wasn't just the job; it was the broken trust. Sarah felt her heart harden with each passing day, her anger growing like wildfire.

The pastor continued, "Romans 12:19: 'Do not take revenge, my dear friends, but leave room for God's wrath, for it is written: 'It is mine to avenge; I will repay,' says the Lord.'"

Sarah felt a flicker of hope. The idea of surrendering her right to vengeance was terrifying, but the thought of holding onto her anger forever was even more frightening. As the service ended, she approached the pastor, her heart pounding.

"I want to forgive, but I don't know how," she admitted, her voice trembling.

The pastor smiled gently. "Forgiveness is not easy, Sarah. But it is the key to freedom. Ephesians 4:31–32 tells us to 'Get rid of all bitterness, rage and anger, brawling and slander, along with every form of malice. Be kind and compassionate to one another, forgiving each other, just as in Christ God forgave you.' It's a journey, and God will walk with you every step of the way."

That night, Sarah knelt by her bed, tears streaming down her face as she poured out her heart to God. "Lord, help me forgive. I don't want to carry this pain anymore."

Days turned into weeks, and Sarah felt a change within her. She began reading the Bible more, finding solace in its words. She clung to 1 John 4:20: "Whoever claims to love God yet hates a brother or sister is a liar. For whoever does not love their brother and sister, whom they have seen, cannot love God, whom they have not seen."

One evening, as Sarah walked through the park, she saw a familiar face—Lisa. The betrayal rushed back, the anger boiling in her veins. But this time, something was different. She felt a sense of peace wash over her.

With trembling hands, Sarah approached Lisa. "I forgive you," she said, her voice steady. "I've been carrying this anger for too long, and I'm ready to let it go."

Lisa's eyes widened in surprise, then filled with tears. "I'm so sorry, Sarah. I never meant to hurt you. I was jealous and selfish."

In that moment, Sarah felt the chains of her past break free. She embraced Lisa, feeling a rush of relief and joy. She knew the journey of forgiveness was ongoing, but this was a powerful step.

As Sarah walked away, she felt a lightness in her spirit she hadn't felt in years. The freedom God had given her through forgiveness was epic. She started to see amazing and meaningful aspects of God's love that she had never realized before. The bondage she had walked in, carrying all the anger and bitterness, had kept her from an amazing understanding of God's love.

She was able to see more about what God was doing when she was not wishing harm on so many people. Now, does that mean that she never got angry or wished for justice to happen? Not at all. She fell into that trap all the time as she walked through this world. But as she recognized it, she could quickly adjust her thinking, ask for forgiveness, and turn the situation back over to God much faster than before.

Sarah's heart swelled with gratitude. She realized that the journey of forgiveness had not only freed her from the past but had also opened her heart to the depths of God's love and peace. She smiled, knowing that with God's help, she could face whatever came her way, armed with the power of forgiveness and the strength of His grace.

Understanding the significance of living an unshakable and abundant life is crucial for our spiritual growth and peace. As we embrace the truth of God's character, dispelling myths and misconceptions, we align ourselves with His redemptive power through forgiveness. The importance of scripture guides us to learn from the past and walk confidently in God's love, empowering us to navigate life's challenges with unwavering faith. By choosing to forgive, trusting in His will, and abiding in His Word, we open the door to an abundant life, rich in His peace, joy, and eternal purpose.

CHAPTER 10

The Importance of Scripture

Understanding the Journey Ahead

As you read this book, you might be at a different place in your spiritual walk. I'm sharing from a place where I fully believe in and accept Jesus as my Savior and my Lord. But I recognize that not everyone is on the same path, and that's okay. Before we dive into the heart of what I want to share, I'd like to take a moment to address some common questions about faith, so you can journey with us, no matter where you are.

This will also be valuable for those who already believe in Jesus as their Savior but may be struggling with the decision to fully trust Him as Lord over their lives. Accepting Jesus as the one who saves us from sin and death is one thing, but it's another to choose to let Him guide every part of our lives.

The Importance of the Bible

Throughout this book, you'll see that we are using scripture as our only guide. The Bible is God's Word, and it's through His Word that we understand His will, His character, and His deep love for us. It is the foundation for knowing who God is, what He desires for us, and how we can walk with Him every day.

As we go forward, we'll be exploring these truths and seeing how the Bible provides answers, guidance, and hope. Whether you're just beginning to seek God, or you've known Him for years but are struggling to fully surrender to His Lordship, the answers you're searching for can be found in His Word. He will reveal Himself to us as we seek Him.

The Power of Scripture

The scriptures are what this book is all about. We will be looking at what a lot of scriptures mean, but more importantly, we will end this journey by teaching you how to study this amazing Word of God yourself, so you can continue the journey of learning and following God's will for your life.

You don't want a life of always having to hear what God's will is for your life through others, even if they are great, godly people, because God is looking for a personal loving friendship with you. To have that kind of relationship, you must move your relationship with Him to a personal, day-to-day learning and walking-with-Him relationship.

One of the first steps in that journey is to learn His Word, understand His Word, and develop a love for learning from His Word. His Word is His personal message to you. To truly believe this, you have to experience it, and to experience it, you have to get into His Word. Let's start with some foundational understanding of the Bible.

The Bible: Prophecy and Fulfillment

The Bible is an extraordinary collection of sixty-six books, written by more than forty different authors across approximately 1,500 years. Despite the diverse backgrounds of its writers—ranging from kings, prophets, and shepherds to fishermen, physicians, and scholars—the Bible presents a unified story that centers on God's plan for humanity and the promise of redemption through Jesus Christ.

The Bible is divided into two main sections: the Old Testament and the New Testament. The Old Testament, made up of thirty-nine books, tells the story of God's covenant with His people and the history of life on earth before the birth of Jesus. It is filled with hundreds of prophecies that point toward the coming of the Messiah, the one who would bring salvation and fulfill God's promises. In contrast, the New Testament, consisting of twenty-seven books, focuses on the life, death, and resurrection of Jesus Christ. It reveals how Jesus came as the fulfillment of those ancient prophecies, offering salvation and establishing the early church.

Some of the most significant prophecies include His birth from a virgin (Isaiah 7:14), which was fulfilled when Jesus was born to Mary, a virgin (Matt. 1:22–23). The prophet Micah predicted that the Messiah would be born in

Bethlehem (Mic. 5:2), and indeed, Jesus was born in that town (Matthew 2:1). The Old Testament also prophesied that the Messiah would come from the line of King David (Jer. 23:5), which was confirmed in the genealogies recorded in the gospels (Luke 3:31).

Other prophecies foretold even more specific events in Jesus's life. Zechariah predicted that the Messiah would be betrayed for thirty pieces of silver (Zech. 11:12–13), which was fulfilled when Judas Iscariot accepted that exact amount to betray Jesus (Matt. 26:14–16). Isaiah spoke of the Messiah being "numbered with the transgressors" (Isa. 53:12), which was fulfilled when Jesus was crucified between two criminals (Luke 23:32–33). Psalm 22 even described the Messiah's hands and feet being pierced—centuries before crucifixion was a known form of execution (Ps. 22:16), a prophecy fulfilled in the crucifixion of Jesus (John 20:25–27). Isaiah also prophesied that the Messiah would be buried in a rich man's tomb (Isa. 53:9), which came to pass when Jesus was buried in the tomb of Joseph of Arimathea, a wealthy man (Matt. 27:57–60).

In total, Jesus fulfilled more than three hundred prophecies, a feat that is statistically beyond coincidence. The probability of one person fulfilling even ten of these specific prophecies is so small that it is often compared to covering the state of Texas in silver dollars, marking one, and then having someone pick out that marked coin while blindfolded.

Jesus didn't just claim to be the Messiah—His life and actions clearly demonstrated it. In Luke 4:17–21, He reads from the book of Isaiah in the synagogue and declares, "Today this scripture is fulfilled in your hearing." In John 10:30, He boldly states, "I and the Father are one," directly claiming both His divinity and His role as the promised Messiah.

The fulfillment of these prophecies affirms Jesus's identity as the long-awaited Messiah and the Son of God. His life, death, and resurrection stand as the ultimate testament to God's faithfulness and the fulfillment of His promises, offering salvation to all who believe.

The Truth about Jesus and His Resurrection

The truth about Jesus is foundational to Christianity: He lived, was crucified, and God raised Him from the dead. This was not just a symbolic event but a literal fulfillment of prophecies from the Old Testament, such as Isaiah 53, which foretold the suffering, death, and resurrection of the Messiah. These prophecies were written hundreds of years before Jesus's birth, pointing to a Savior who would take on the sins of the world, and they came to pass precisely as foretold.

The significance of this event goes beyond just religious belief—it's rooted in historical reality. While it may seem extraordinary, it's crucial to understand that this resurrection really did happen. In our book, we'll delve deeper into the spiritual and theological implications, but one of the most important questions people ask is: How do we know this is true, even 2,000 years later?

The Uniqueness of Jesus among World Religions

One day, one of our children asked my wife a profound question: "How do we know that Christianity is the true religion when there are so many others—like Buddhism, Islam, and others?" My wife's response was simple yet powerful: "Because Jesus is alive."

Most world religions center around founders who are no longer living. Buddha, Muhammad, and others died and remain dead. Their followers venerate their teachings but don't claim their leaders are alive today. Christianity, on the other hand, is built on the fact that Jesus was crucified, He died, and He rose again three days later. We don't worship a dead teacher—we worship a risen Savior.

The Resurrection: Eyewitness Testimony and Martyrdom

But how do we know for certain? This is where both faith and historical evidence come together. A wealth of historical documentation, including eyewitness testimonies, attests to Jesus's resurrection. One of the most compelling pieces of evidence is the behavior of His disciples. After Jesus was crucified, these men were initially fearful and in hiding. Yet, just days later, they boldly proclaimed that Jesus had risen from the dead. Why? They had seen Him alive with their own eyes.

The Apostle Paul speaks of this in 1 Corinthians 15:3–6, where he mentions that Jesus appeared to more than five hundred people after His resurrection. This letter is considered one of the earliest New Testament writings, penned only a few decades after Jesus's death, making it a close historical source. It would have been impossible for Paul to claim that five hundred people witnessed the risen Christ if it weren't true, as those witnesses were still alive and could have refuted the claim.

More importantly, almost all of the disciples went to their deaths proclaiming this truth. They faced torture, imprisonment, and execution, yet not one recanted their testimony. People don't willingly suffer and die for something they know is a lie. These men and women were fully convinced that Jesus had risen from the dead, and they were willing to die for that truth.

Historical Reliability of the Bible

In addition to the eyewitness accounts, there are many reasons to believe that the Bible itself is a historically reliable document. The Bible has been preserved through time with remarkable accuracy. For instance, the Dead Sea Scrolls, discovered in the mid-twentieth century, contained portions of the Old Testament dating back to the second century B.C. When compared to the modern versions of the Old Testament, the texts were nearly identical, proving the Bible has been transmitted faithfully over thousands of years.

Furthermore, no archaeological find has ever disproved a biblical claim. In fact, many discoveries have confirmed the Bible's historical accuracy. The ancient city of Jericho, the Pool of Bethesda (mentioned in John 5), and the existence of Pontius Pilate are just a few examples of archaeological evidence that supports the biblical narrative. In recent years, more discoveries continue to align with scripture rather than contradict it.

The Spread of Christianity: A Testimony to the Truth

Another historical fact to consider is the rapid spread of Christianity in the ancient world. How did a movement, born in a small, occupied territory like Judea, within a few decades spread across the Roman Empire? By all human logic, Christianity should have been a minor, obscure sect. Yet within three hundred years, it became the dominant religion of the Roman Empire, despite persecution from both Jewish and Roman authorities.

The early Christians didn't gain wealth, power, or fame for their beliefs—they faced constant danger. What could explain the explosive growth of this faith except that something miraculous had indeed happened? The resurrection of Jesus was not an event for a few people—it changed the course of history. The message of Jesus's victory over death gave people hope, and that hope was worth dying for.

The Gospels: Reliable Biographies of Jesus

The four gospels—Matthew, Mark, Luke, and John—are the primary sources for the life, death, and resurrection of Jesus. These books were written within the lifetime of eyewitnesses, which is crucial for historical accuracy. Scholars date the earliest gospel, Mark, to within thirty to forty years of Jesus's death, and the other Gospels shortly thereafter.

Compared to other ancient biographies, such as those about Alexander the Great, which were written hundreds of years after his death, the gospels stand out as remarkably close to the events they describe. Additionally, the gospels display remarkable consistency in their core message, despite being written by different authors for different audiences. While some skeptics claim that there are contradictions in the gospels, none of these alleged discrepancies affect the core message that Jesus died and rose again. Of course, there is a lot more evidence about the truth of who Jesus is and the reality and truth of the scriptures. I have just gotten your research started for you. If you are still not convinced that the Bible is a reliable source of truth, I encourage you to do more research if you are looking for the truth. I would also encourage you to talk to God and ask Him to help you find more truth.

Faith and Reason Work Together

Ultimately, belief in Jesus's resurrection is a matter of faith, but it is not blind faith. It is faith grounded in reason, history, and evidence. The Bible itself invites us to examine the truth. In Acts 17:11, the Bereans are praised because they "received the word with all readiness and searched the scriptures daily to find out whether these things were so." God doesn't ask us to believe without question—He invites us to seek the truth.

We'll explore in greater detail how the resurrection of Jesus changed the world and how this singular event continues to offer hope and life to all who believe. Rest assured, Jesus's resurrection is not just a religious claim—it's a historical reality backed by eyewitnesses, reliable documents, and the transformative power of lives changed forever. The question is not whether this event happened, but what you will do with the truth of it.

Learning and Following His Will through Scripture

My life over the several years since our great disaster has been about learning and following God's will. As we continue, I will keep sharing with you more about my spiritual journey, letting you know what God has shown me about how He wants us to live here on this earth pre-Heaven. I will continue to share with you a lot of scriptures. If you are like me, the temptation will be to blow through the scriptures as soon as you recognize them, saying to yourself that you have heard this one before. I'm sure you have heard several of these before, but please stop at every scripture. This is literally God speaking to us.

Think about that. *God.* The God of the universe, who made you, as well as all the universe, is noticing you and wants to speak to you. I challenge you to stop at every scripture and ponder it. The scriptures are far more valuable than what I have to say about them. When you read His words, ask Him to reveal Himself through His words. You might be surprised what He must share with you about it. Something interesting about reading scripture is that it is alive. We have heard this from pastors often, but it is true. When I say it is alive, I mean God uses these scriptures anew every time He brings us His Word. The last time you read the scripture, He might have been saying one thing to you, and the next time He might reveal something completely new from the same scripture. Don't miss that part of His interesting and fun personality.

The Necessity of Believing and Accepting All of God's Word

God also requires us to believe and adhere to the entirety of the Bible, not just select parts of it. Scripture emphasizes the importance of accepting all of God's Word. In 2 Timothy 3:16–17, it is stated, "All scripture is God-breathed and is useful for teaching, rebuking, correcting and training in righteousness, so that the servant of God may be thoroughly equipped for every good work." Jesus reinforces this in Matthew 4:4, saying, "Man shall not live on bread alone, but on every word that comes from the mouth of God," indicating the necessity of relying on the entirety of God's Word for our spiritual sustenance. Furthermore, James 1:22 urges believers, "Do not merely listen to the Word, and so deceive yourselves. Do what it says." Finally, Revelation 22:18–19 warns against altering the scriptures, underscoring the importance of accepting the Bible in its entirety: "I warn everyone who hears the words of the prophecy of this scroll: If anyone adds anything to them, God will add to that person the plagues described in this scroll. And if anyone takes words away from this scroll of prophecy, God will take away from that person any share in the tree of life and in the Holy City, which are described in this scroll." Thus, the Bible makes it clear that God expects us to believe and follow all His Word, and selectively believing or ignoring parts of it is not in alignment with His teachings.

Believing in God but not accepting all of what the Bible says can lead to significant spiritual and practical consequences or an incomplete or distorted understanding of His intentions. Spiritual growth and maturity come from a comprehensive understanding and application of scripture, and without embracing the entirety of the Bible, believers can be more susceptible to false teachings, as cautioned in Ephesians 4:14. Moreover, missing out on God's promises and blessings is often tied to disobedience to His Word, as indicated in Revelation 22:18–19. Proverbs 30:5–6 states, "Every word of God is flawless; he is a shield to those who take refuge in him. Do not add to his words, or he will rebuke you and prove you a liar."

The Power and Living Nature of God's Word

Hebrews 4:12 in the NIV says, "For the word of God is alive and active. Sharper than any double-edged sword, it penetrates even to dividing soul and spirit, joints and marrow; it judges the thoughts and attitudes of the heart." This verse paints a vivid picture of God's Word as not just text but a living, dynamic force that actively works in our lives. It cuts through to the core of who we are, reaching our soul, spirit, and even our innermost thoughts and intentions. The verse reminds us that God's Word isn't just for reading; it's meant to penetrate deeply, exposing what's really going on inside us. In the context of Hebrews 4, this powerful Word serves as both a warning and a guide, urging us to enter God's rest through true faith and obedience. It's not just about judgment but also about healing, convicting us of sin, aligning us with God's will, and offering us hope and transformation as we let it work deeply within us.

Therefore, while belief in God is foundational, accepting the entirety of the Bible is crucial. Without trusting and believing fully in the Bible, our faith may be reduced to mere stories rather than a living and active relationship with God. He is God, and there are no two ways around this. As God, He has every right to make decisions that are best for Him and for us.

Understanding this, it is crucial to recognize that God loves us more than we can ever imagine. When He makes decisions aligned with His great master plan, they are always in our best interest, even if we don't fully see or understand His reasons. We must trust this truth. As we continue to explore these concepts, we must lay the foundation that God loves us and desires the best for us all the time, guiding us through His complete and perfect Word.

In conclusion, the Bible is the foundation of an unshakable and abundant life, guiding us to align with God's true character and embrace His redemption. Scripture is key to understanding God's will and living a life that reflects His love and truth. By delving into the Bible, we clarify misconceptions, shed light on the myths, and learn from the past, all while growing closer to God. As we walk in His love and follow His Word, we open ourselves to the fullness of life He has promised—one rooted in His eternal truth and abundant grace.

Most importantly, will you only believe what's in the Bible when it makes you feel comfortable, or when you fully understand it? Do you turn away from what challenges you, or what doesn't fit with what you see around you? Do you demand physical proof for everything God says?

Why do you doubt anything in the Bible? This is a question that every believer needs to settle once and for all. Can you really pick and choose what's true in the Bible? Do you decide what you'll believe or obey? Or worse—do you make excuses, claiming that what God said doesn't apply to you or isn't relevant in today's world?

If you're truly seeking God and His will for your life, you can't play God yourself—deciding which parts of His Word are true and which aren't. That's not your job. Your job is to believe everything in the Bible and trust God to reveal understanding where you struggle. He promises to help you with your unbelief—if you give it to Him. Your job is simple: believe, even when it's hard. Trust Him to lead you to full understanding as you seek Him wholeheartedly.

Will you trust Him, or will you let doubt keep you from living in the fullness of His truth?

CHAPTER 11

The Love of God

O ne of the most fundamental parts of who God is—is Love. Does He love me, or am I somehow left out of His love? This was the first question I asked Him when I started abiding, although if I am totally honest the question was more like, "If you really loved me, why?" But the real question was, "Do you love me?" It is interesting because he does not always answer the questions that we ask. When I first asked this question, God took me on a journey of forgiveness as we have already discussed. Once He showed me how He had forgiven me and that I needed to forgive those who had harmed me, He then took me on a wonderful journey of understanding His love for me.

I know He has been described in the scripture as Love, God is Love. In 1 John 4:8 and 4:16, the Bible reveals that God is love, highlighting that love is not merely something God does, but it is who He is. This profound truth emphasizes that every action, command, and interaction from God is rooted in His perfect love. God's love is unconditional and sacrificial, as seen in the life and death of Jesus Christ. For believers, to know God is to experience and reflect this love in their own lives, as His love is the foundation of their relationship with Him and with others. How does this work?

God's Covenant Love in the Old Testament

God's love for humanity is a consistent and profound theme throughout the entire Bible, beginning in the Old Testament and flowing through to the New Testament. In the Old Testament, God's love is often displayed through His covenantal faithfulness. Even in the midst of rebellion, disobedience, and brokenness, God continually reaches out to restore and redeem His people. The covenants He established with figures like Noah, Abraham, and Moses reveal His desire to bring humanity back into relationship with Himself. Despite the fall of man and the sin that followed, God never abandoned His creation. In His love, He provided the Law—not as a means of oppression, but as a guide to lead His people to righteousness and holiness, showing them how to live in harmony with Him and others. The Old Testament prophets are filled with calls to return to God, a reflection of His grief over the brokenness of His people yet continues to pursue them with love.

The Ultimate Expression of God's Love in Jesus Christ

In the New Testament, God's love becomes incarnate in the person of Jesus Christ. Jesus is the ultimate expression of God's love—His willingness to step down from glory, live among us, and ultimately give His life for our redemption speaks to a love beyond comprehension. John 3:16 tells us that "God so loved the world that He gave His one and only Son," which reveals that God's love is not abstract but active and sacrificial. Jesus's ministry on earth was filled with acts of compassion, healing, and teaching, constantly reaching out to the marginalized, the broken, and the sinful. His love is unconditional, as seen when He forgives those who crucify Him, and when He invites even the most rejected and despised into His kingdom. The cross stands at the center of this love—the ultimate display of God's willingness to bear the weight of humanity's sin, to die in our place so that we might be reconciled to Him.

Does God Love Me Specifically?

The question of how much God loves an individual on a personal level is stated hundreds of times throughout the Bible. My real question was, "Do I believe what the Bible says, and does the Bible really apply to me? I needed to answer it once and for all. If you asked me if I believe the Bible, of course, my answer would be *yes*. So, do I believe every word of the Bible? My answer is *yes*.

Do I believe John 3:16? Yes, I believe I will have eternal life. So, if I believe that, why would I question *why* He would give me eternal life? Good question. God's love is not based on human merit or actions but is rooted in God's nature. It is truly who God is. He is Love. Think about that.

Many verses in the Bible express the idea of God's enduring and boundless love for individuals, and I am an individual, so that must apply to me. For instance, Romans 8:38–39 states, "For I am convinced that neither death nor life, neither angels nor demons, neither the present nor the future, nor any powers, neither height nor depth, nor anything else in all creation, will be able to separate us from the love of God that is in Christ Jesus our Lord." So, does that mean that there is no way He will ever stop loving me? There is nothing that I can do or not do, there is nothing that I can say or not say, there is nothing that I can believe or not believe that will ever cause Him not to love me.

Many times I have heard that in sermons or in Sunday school or just reading the Bible, so why do I question it? I believe we as believers need to settle this question. This is one fundamental place where our understanding of the truth of scripture that we asked in the last chapter comes in. Can I pick and choose what is true out of the Bible? What will I believe and obey? Or, will I come up with some lame excuse that what was said in the Bible is not relevant to me or not relevant in today's society? Will I believe what is said in the Bible only if I feel comfortable with it or if I fully understand it? Or if others also believe? Do I not believe it if it makes me feel uncomfortable or I don't see direct evidence of what is said in today's world? Do I need physical proof for everything that God says?

If I am going to seek God and know His will for my life, I'd better not play God and determine what is true and what is not of the Bible. Your job is not to evaluate truth in the Bible, as you cannot understand all the ways of God. As God told Job, "Where were you when I created the world?" Your role is simple: believe everything in the Bible and ask God for clarity and understanding when you find things that are confusing and don't make sense according to the world you are living in. God also says He will help us with our disbelief if we give it to Him. Our job is to simply, blindly, believe and allow God to lead us to a full understanding through seeking and trusting Him.

Ephesians 3:17–19 further emphasizes God's love: "So that Christ may dwell in your hearts through faith. And I pray that you, being rooted and established in love, may have power, together with all the Lord's holy people, to grasp how wide and long and high and deep is the love of Christ, and to know this love that surpasses knowledge—that you may be filled to the measure of all the fullness of God."

Jeremiah 31:3 says, "The Lord appeared to us in the past, saying: 'I have loved you with an everlasting love; I have drawn you with unfailing kindness.'"

First John 4:16 reminds us, "And so we know and rely on the love God has for us. God is love. Whoever lives in love lives in God, and God in them."

Reflecting on these scriptures, we see a consistent message: God's love is personal, unchanging, and all encompassing. The Bible repeatedly assures us of this truth. Therefore, the challenge is not in God's love being applicable to us but in our willingness to accept and trust in that love fully. Our faith journey involves moving past our doubts and embracing the completeness of God's Word, trusting that His promises are for each of us individually.

In conclusion, understanding the depth of God's love is foundational to living an unshakable and abundant life. As we align with His true character, shedding light on misconceptions and embracing unshakable redemption, we see that God's love is not an abstract concept—it's personal, unchanging, and limitless. Through the scriptures, we are reminded of His covenantal love, fulfilled in Christ, and His unwavering commitment to us. Trusting in this love helps us navigate our doubts, and as we embrace the fullness of His Word, we find peace, purpose, and the abundant life He has promised.

CHAPTER 12

Lord and Savior

U nderstanding God's boundless love is the foundation of our faith, but recognizing Jesus as our Lord and Savior takes that understanding to a transformative level. Accepting Jesus as Lord and Savior means acknowledging His authority in our lives and embracing the salvation He offers. This transition from knowing God's love to accepting His lordship is essential for a deeper, more personal relationship with Him. It is through this acceptance that we experience the fullness of His grace, guidance, and the eternal life promised to us.

We as believers hear these two aspects of Jesus so often together that I believe we think they are the same thing. We state that Jesus is our Lord and Savior as a declaration. Just stop for a minute and ask yourself if you believe this. If Jesus is your Savior, that means that you have chosen to accept His sacrifice, and you are now a Christian and will be with Him in Heaven.

Savior

In Luke 2:10–11, an angel tells us about Jesus as a Savior. He says, "But the angel said to [the shepherds], 'Do not be afraid. I bring you good news that will cause great joy for all the people. Today in the town of David, a Savior has been born to you; He is the Messiah, the Lord.'" In Titus 2:13, it states, "while we wait for the blessed hope—the appearing of the glory of our great God and Savior, Jesus Christ." Acts 4:12 emphasizes the exclusivity of salvation through Jesus: "Salvation is found in no one else, for there is no other name under Heaven given to mankind by which we must be saved." He is our Savior. We accept this and are so grateful for Him being our Savior.

When we call Jesus our Savior, we acknowledge that He saves us from sin, death, and eternal separation from God. The Bible teaches us that "all have sinned and fall short of the glory of God" (Rom. 3:23) and that "the wage of sin is death" (Rom. 6:23). However, through Jesus's sacrifice, we are forgiven and purified from all unrighteousness (1 John 1:9), granting us eternal life and victory over death (John 11:25–26).

Moreover, Jesus saves us from the wrath of God and eternal separation from His presence. Our sins create a barrier between us and God (Isa. 59:2). Still, Jesus reconciles us to Him, ensuring we are not shut out from His presence forever (2 Thes. 1:9). By accepting Jesus as our Savior, we are justified by His blood and rescued from the coming wrath (Rom. 5:9; 1 Thes. 1:10), securing a restored relationship with God and the promise of eternal life.

Lord

So, what does it mean that Jesus is our Lord? In Philippians 2:9–11, it says, "Therefore God exalted Him to the highest place and gave Him the name that is above every name, that at the name of Jesus every knee should bow, in Heaven and on earth and under the earth, and every tongue acknowledge that Jesus Christ is Lord, to the glory of God the Father." Jesus is acknowledged as the divine Son of God who came to save humanity from sin and is to be recognized as Lord and Master. "Lord" is a title used for God. Jesus Christ is often referred to as "Lord," signifying divine authority.

Calling Jesus our Lord means recognizing His supreme authority over our lives and submitting to His will. This acknowledgment goes beyond merely accepting Him as our Savior; it involves a commitment to follow His teachings, obey His commands, and allow Him to lead every aspect of our lives. In essence, it is a declaration that Jesus has the ultimate control, and we willingly surrender our own desires to align with His.

When we call Jesus our Lord, it means that we strive to live in accordance with His teachings. Jesus said in Luke 6:46, "Why do you call me, 'Lord, Lord,' and do not do what I say?" This implies that truly recognizing Him as Lord involves action and obedience. It means letting His words guide our decisions, our interactions, and our daily conduct. For example, in John 14:15, Jesus states, "If you love me, keep my commands." This reflects that loving Jesus and acknowledging Him as Lord are demonstrated through our obedience to His commandments.

Living with Jesus as our Lord transforms our lives. It influences our priorities, values, and behaviors. We exhibit the fruits of the Spirit as described in Galatians 5:22–23, which include love, joy, peace, patience, kindness, goodness, faithfulness, gentleness, and self-control. Additionally, acknowledging Jesus as Lord means that we trust Him with our future, casting all our anxieties on Him because He cares for us (1 Pet. 5:7). This trust is built on the understanding that His plans for us are for our good, as Jeremiah 29:11 reassures us: "For I know the plans I have for you," declares the Lord, "plans to prosper you and not to harm you, plans to give you hope and a future."

In practical terms, calling Jesus our Lord affects how we approach our relationships, our work, and our personal conduct. It compels us to love others as He has loved us (John 13:34), to work diligently as if working for the Lord (Col. 3:23), and to pursue holiness in our personal lives (1 Pet. 1:15–16). In doing so, we reflect His lordship in our actions and bear witness to His transformative power in our lives. This comprehensive surrender to Jesus as Lord is a journey of growing in faith, understanding, and obedience, continuously seeking to align our lives with His perfect will.

Declaration of Faith

So, when we declare that Jesus is our Lord and Savior, we are saying that we accept His sacrifice that allows us to be with God for eternity in Heaven. This acceptance is beautifully summarized in John 3:16, "For God so loved the world that he gave his one and only Son, that whoever believes in him shall not perish but have eternal life." However, recognizing Jesus as our Lord goes beyond this initial acceptance. It involves a lifelong commitment to follow Him, obey His teachings, and let His will guide every aspect of our lives. Romans 10:9 emphasizes this dual declaration: "If you declare with your mouth, 'Jesus is Lord,' and believe in your heart that God raised him from the dead, you will be saved."

Submitting oneself to Jesus as Lord, as described in the Bible, involves a personal and transformative relationship with Jesus Christ. This submission is not about losing our identity but about aligning our lives with His divine purpose. In Matthew 16:24, Jesus says, "Whoever wants to be my disciple must deny themselves and take up their cross and follow me." This means putting aside our selfish desires and embracing His path, even when it involves sacrifice. This transformative relationship is marked by a profound change in our hearts and minds, as described in Romans 12:2: "Do not conform to the pattern of this world but be transformed by the renewing of your mind. Then you will be able to test and approve what God's will is—his good, pleasing and perfect will."

When we fully submit to Jesus as our Lord, it affects every part of our lives. Our actions, decisions, and interactions reflect His lordship. We strive to live out His teachings, such as loving our neighbors as ourselves (Matt. 22:39) and forgiving others as we have been forgiven (Eph. 4:32). Additionally, we are called to serve others, following Jesus's example of humility and service. In John 13:14–15, Jesus washes His disciples' feet and says, "Now that I, your Lord and Teacher, have washed your feet, you also should wash one another's feet. I have set you an example that you should do as I have done for you." Living under His lordship also means trusting Him with our worries and burdens, as 1 Peter 5:7 encourages us: "Cast all your anxiety on him because he cares for you." This comprehensive submission leads to a life that not only acknowledges Jesus as Savior but also exemplifies Him as the guiding Lord of every aspect of our existence.

Story Time: Ethan Discovering His Lord

There was once a man named Ethan who grew up in a small town, surrounded by a community that cherished faith. From a young age, Ethan was taught about Jesus and the promise of eternal life. The message of John 3:16, "For God so loved the world that he gave his one and only Son, that whoever believes in him shall not perish but have eternal life," was a comforting assurance to him. Ethan held on to this promise tightly, finding solace in the thought of Heaven. He believed in Jesus as his Savior, attended church sporadically, and prayed when he needed something. However, his understanding of his faith stopped there. He never explored what it meant to live with Jesus as his Lord.

As Ethan entered adulthood, he faced numerous challenges and disappointments. His career was stagnant; despite his hard work, promotions and opportunities seemed to elude him. His relationships were strained, filled with misunderstandings and unresolved conflicts. He felt a constant sense of emptiness and unfulfillment, wondering why his life didn't reflect the peace and joy he had heard about in church. He prayed occasionally, asking God for success and happiness, but his prayers felt like they were hitting the ceiling and bouncing back. Ethan continued living for himself, making decisions based on his desires and limited understanding, without seeking God's guidance or wisdom.

One particularly difficult evening, after a harsh argument with his girlfriend and another rejection at work, Ethan sat alone in his apartment, feeling utterly lost. He stared at the ceiling, tears streaming down his face, and wondered why his life was so empty despite his belief in Jesus. In this moment of despair, he remembered an old friend, Michael, who always seemed to radiate a sense of peace and contentment, no matter the circumstances.

Desperate for answers, Ethan reached out to Michael. They met at a quiet café, and as they talked, Ethan poured out his heart, confessing his frustrations and confusion. Michael listened patiently, then shared his own journey of faith. He explained how he had learned not only to accept Jesus as his Savior but also to submit to Him as Lord. "It's about surrendering your own plans and desires," Michael said, "and seeking to live according to Jesus' teachings and guidance. Proverbs 3:5-6 says, 'Trust in the Lord with all your heart and lean not on your own understanding; in all your ways submit to him, and he will make your paths straight.'"

Michael's words struck a chord with Ethan. He realized he had been treating his faith like a safety net, something to fall back on, rather than a guiding force in his life. Determined to change, Ethan began to read the Bible with a new perspective. He prayed not just for blessings, but for guidance and understanding. He started attending a Bible study group, where he learned more about what it meant to follow Jesus wholeheartedly.

The journey was not easy. Ethan struggled with letting go of his own plans and trusting God's timing. There were moments of doubt and frustration, but he pressed on, remembering Michael's advice and the promise of Proverbs 3:5–6. Over time, Ethan noticed a transformation in his life. His decisions were now influenced by prayer and biblical principles, leading to a renewed sense of purpose and direction. His relationships improved as he practiced forgiveness and love, inspired by Ephesians 4:32: "Be kind and compassionate to one another, forgiving each other, just as in Christ God forgave you." He found joy in serving others, participating in community outreach programs, and helping those in need.

Ethan discovered that living with Jesus as Lord brought a depth of blessings and fulfillment that he had never experienced before. His career began to flourish, not because he chased success, but because he worked with integrity and dedication, as Colossians 3:23 advises: "Whatever you do, work at it with all your heart, as working for the Lord, not for human masters." His heart was filled with a peace that surpassed understanding, as promised in Philippians 4:7.

Through this journey, Ethan learned that true faith involves both accepting Jesus as Savior and submitting to Him as Lord, allowing God's guidance to shape every aspect of his life. The transformation wasn't just about outward success or happiness but a profound inner change that aligned his life with God's will. Ethan's story became a testament to the power of surrendering to Jesus as Lord, leading to a life marked by purpose, peace, and divine blessings.

Ethan realized that while he had been a good person, he hadn't fully embraced the idea of living a life that truly honored God. He recognized that his focus on earthly success had led him to miss out on the deeper spiritual rewards that awaited him.

Ethan's story teaches us that a life dedicated to doing God's will and storing up treasures in Heaven leads to a deeper, more profound experience in the afterlife. It reminds us that our actions on earth have eternal consequences.

Steps to Submission

Acknowledging Jesus as Lord and Savior

This involves confessing and believing that Jesus is the Son of God, the Savior of humanity, and the Lord of one's life. This acknowledgment is often expressed through prayer and a genuine commitment to follow Jesus. "If you confess with your mouth, 'Jesus is Lord,' and believe in your heart that God raised Him from the dead, you will be saved" (Rom. 10:9 NIV).

Repentance and Turning Away from Sin

Repentance is a central theme in submitting to Jesus and declaring Him as your Lord. It involves a genuine change of heart and a turning away from a life of sin. The Bible teaches that repentance is essential for forgiveness and reconciliation with God. "Repent, then, and turn to God, so that your sins may be wiped out, that times of refreshing may come from the Lord" (Acts 3:19 NIV).

Faith and Trust in Jesus

Submitting to Jesus requires placing trust and faith in Him. This means relying on Jesus for salvation, guidance, and the transformation of one's life. Faith is seen as the foundation of the Christian journey. "I have been crucified with Christ and I no longer live, but Christ lives in me. The life I now live in the body, I live by faith in the Son of God, who loved me and gave Himself for me" (Gal. 2:20 NIV).

Obeying God's Word

The Bible serves as a guide for Christian living. Submitting to Jesus involves a commitment to obeying His teachings and following the principles outlined in the Bible. This includes love for others, compassion, and a pursuit of righteousness. "Do not merely listen to the word, and so deceive yourselves. Do what it says" (James 1:22 NIV).

Living a Transformed Life

The transformation that comes from submitting to Jesus is reflected in a changed lifestyle. This may include a shift in priorities, attitudes, and behaviors. The Holy Spirit empowers believers to live according to God's will. "Therefore, if anyone is in Christ, the new creation has come: The old has gone, the new is here!" (2 Cor. 5:17 NIV).

Prayer and Relationship with God

Submitting to Jesus involves an ongoing relationship with God through prayer and communication. Christians are encouraged to pray, seek guidance, and develop a personal connection with Jesus. "Do not be anxious about anything, but in every situation, by prayer and petition, with thanksgiving, present your requests to God" (Phil. 4:6 NIV).

Participation in Christian Community

Being part of a Christian community, such as a church, is emphasized in the Bible. Believers are encouraged to fellowship with other Christians, share their faith, and support one another in their spiritual journey. "And let us consider how we may spur one another on toward love and good deeds, not giving up meeting together, as some are in the habit of doing, but encouraging one another." (Heb. 10:24–25 NIV).

As we come to the close of this unshakable part, the meaning of everything we've learned unfolds with profound clarity. We've explored the difference between merely seeing God as a Savior who rescues us and fully embracing Him as the Lord of our lives, to whom we submit all. This realization brings us to a crossroads—a moment where we must ask ourselves: What will we do differently? How will we let this truth transform us?

Who do you need to forgive? Is there someone who has wounded you deeply, and the bitterness has taken root in your heart? This is your moment to release that burden. Believe me this is not easy, but it is the best thing you can ever do for your own life. For your ability to live an Unshakable Life. You might need to set this book down, go before God, and extend the forgiveness you've been withholding. Maybe it's time to reach out to someone else, to seek forgiveness or to start the process of reconciliation.

There is such freedom waiting for you in this. Don't let this moment pass by without responding to what God is stirring in your heart. Whether it's the call to forgive, submit, or reconcile, make the right decision to change your life. This is your opportunity to walk into the fullness of the life God has prepared for you, a life marked by freedom, peace, and abundant love. Don't wait. Embrace the transformation that God is offering and watch as He does more than you could ever imagine.

Building Wealth on a Foundation of Faith and Stewardship

Building wealth on a foundation of faith and stewardship means aligning financial growth with the principles of trust in God and responsible management of resources. It's about recognizing that all we have is a gift from God, and our role is to steward those gifts wisely, making decisions that honor Him and serve others. By integrating faith into financial practices, wealth becomes more than just accumulation; it transforms into a tool for fulfilling God's purposes, blessing others, and leaving a lasting legacy that reflects His goodness and provision.

CHAPTER 13

God's Will and Our Wealth

We are about to make what might seem like a sharp turn from discussing profound spiritual and eternal matters to reflecting on wealth and money. At first glance, this shift may appear unusual, but money is one of the most significant aspects—both spoken and unspoken—by which we measure God's blessings and guidance. Without understanding God's perspective on money, it becomes challenging to grasp His nature and the ways He desires to richly bless us. If we only view finances and wealth as indicators of His blessings, we miss the broader and deeper ways God intends to enrich our lives. If we are not able to submit our wealth to the Lordship and leadership of Christ, our wealth will always be a struggle. Let us delve into His perspective on wealth and address this pressing issue through the lens of scripture.

The Bible provides a comprehensive view of wealth, highlighting its potential benefits and dangers. True wealth, as blessed by God, comes with peace, joy, and fulfillment, not just material abundance (Prov. 10:22). Jesus's teachings on stewardship (Matt. 25:14–30) and warnings about the love of money (1 Tim. 6:10, Matt. 6:24) emphasize the responsibility and risks associated with wealth. Generosity and contentment are key aspects of God's perspective on money, as reflected in 2 Corinthians 9:6–7 and Philippians 4:11–12. Ultimately, we are called to focus on eternal treasures over temporal riches (Matt. 6:19–21), understanding that God's blessings encompass far more than financial prosperity. By aligning our views with scripture, we can appreciate the myriad ways God desires to bless and guide us, beyond mere financial wealth.

As our Good Lord and the one who completely and fully loves us, do we believe that He wants to bless us? One of the most powerful parts of our life on earth is money. It is what makes the world go round. It seems that in the Bible, there is a lot of confusion about money. At least, a lot of believers are confused about it. How does money fit in understanding God's will for my life? How does my faith intertwine with money and how I manage it, as well as how much I can have? There are so many spoken and unspoken questions on this topic.

A Snapshot of Money and Wealth from God's Perspective

The Bible offers guidance on how to manage and spend money through various passages that emphasize principles of stewardship, contentment, generosity, and responsibility.

Stewardship and Ownership

The Bible teaches that everything belongs to God, and we are merely stewards or managers of the resources He has entrusted to us. This includes our money and possessions. The Parable of the Talents (Matt. 25:14–30) illustrates the concept of stewardship, where individuals are entrusted with different amounts and are expected to use them wisely. Most people never realize that one of the greatest stewardships of His gifts is our talents. We often get confused about what He has given us versus what we have accomplished on our own.

We must realize that we don't possess anything that He has not provided. This includes our talents, our skills, our hard work, and our education. Without His involvement in our lives, both now and in the past, we wouldn't have anything. In Philippians 2:13, we are reminded, "For it is God who works in you to will and to act in order to fulfill his good purpose." Therefore, our abilities and achievements are ultimately a reflection of His grace and provision. No matter your career—whether you're a doctor, an executive, a scientist, a plumber, or a homemaker—the temptation is to think you've achieved everything on your own. You studied for years, fought through challenges, and built something few others have accomplished. You might tell yourself, "I did this. I created my success." But the truth is, God did this. It's easy to believe that your greatest accomplishments are yours alone. You put in the work, you learned the skills, you faced the struggles. But scripture tells us a different story. "Every good and perfect gift is from above" (James 1:17), and that includes your intelligence, your skills, and your opportunities. God gave you the brain that thinks the way it does, the hands that work the way they do, and the resilience to persevere through hardship. Even the breath in your lungs is a gift from Him, as Psalm 139:13–14 reminds us: "For you created my inmost being you knit me together in my mother's womb. I praise you because I am fearfully and wonderfully made."

You are not the architect of your life—God is. This does not mean you are on his path, but he has designed an amazing path for you to be on if you step into it. He has already established the standards for what true accomplishment looks like, rooted in scripture and His divine plan. We often compare ourselves to others, adjusting our standards to make ourselves feel more significant. Whether you are at the top of your field or struggling, whether you are working in a so-called white-collar job or a blue-collar job, it's easy to be proud of your expertise, to think, "I've done this; I've earned this." But God's Word teaches us that it is He who equips us for every good work (2 Tim. 3:17). The path you've walked—the people you've met, the opportunities you've had—was all set in place by Him. In Ephesians 2:10, it says, "For we are God's handiwork, created in Christ Jesus to do good works, which God prepared in advance for us to do." Your success was never yours alone; it was always part of His design.

God blesses us so we may be a blessing to others (Gen. 12:2). Whether you're a scientist discovering life-changing cures, or a carpenter building homes, or even an athlete, your work is part of His greater plan. When we realize that, when we acknowledge His hand in all things, our lives change. The pressure to be better than others fades, and we see that we are great because of Him, not because of anything we've done on our own. As Proverbs 3:5–6 says, "Trust in the Lord with all your heart and lean not on your own understanding; in all your ways submit to Him, and He will make your paths straight." This is where true greatness comes from—walking in the path God has created, knowing He has done it all. When you live in this truth, your life becomes even greater, filled with purpose, blessing, and divine significance beyond what you could ever achieve on your own.

God's role in our lives is paramount, as He is the source of all our capabilities and resources. In 1 Corinthians 4:7, it is written, "For who makes you different from anyone else? What do you have that you didn't receive? And if you did receive it, why do you boast as though you did not?" This scripture emphasizes that everything we have is a gift from God. Recognizing this helps us remain humble and grateful, understanding that our successes are not solely our own doing but are enabled by God's generosity and guidance.

Prioritizing God

Matthew 6:24 states, "No one can serve two masters. Either you will hate the one and love the other, or you will be devoted to the one and despise the other. You cannot serve both God and money."

Contentment

First Timothy 6:6–10 teaches that the love of money can lead to harmful desires and discontentment. Instead, the focus should be on godliness and being content with what we have. True wealth is found in living a life pleasing to God and appreciating the blessings we already possess. The apostle Paul reminds us that we brought nothing into the world and can take nothing out of it, highlighting the temporary nature of material possessions. Therefore, we should cultivate a spirit of contentment, recognizing that having food and clothing is sufficient for our needs. By prioritizing spiritual growth and a close relationship with God over the pursuit of wealth, we can avoid the pitfalls of greed and find lasting satisfaction and peace.

Avoiding Debt

Proverbs 22:7 advises, "The borrower is a slave to the lender." The Bible cautions against excessive debt that can lead to financial bondage and encourages responsible borrowing. This proverb underscores the power dynamic that debt creates, where the borrower becomes subservient to the lender, often resulting in a loss of financial freedom. The Bible encourages us to live within our means and to practice wise stewardship of our resources. This includes planning and budgeting to avoid debt and to make thoughtful decisions when borrowing is necessary. Additionally, it promotes the principles of saving and generosity, suggesting that financial discipline and prudent management of resources lead to a more secure and liberated life. By avoiding the pitfalls of excessive debt, we can maintain our independence, reduce stress, and focus on more meaningful and spiritually enriching pursuits.

Planning and Wisdom

Proverbs are full of wisdom about managing money and making sound financial decisions. Proverbs 21:5 says, "The plans of the diligent lead to profit as surely as haste leads to poverty." Planning and wise decision-making are essential for financial success.

Generosity and Giving

The Bible places a strong emphasis on the importance of generosity and giving to those in need. This principle is clearly illustrated in 2 Corinthians 9:6–7, which states, "Whoever sows sparingly will also reap sparingly, and whoever sows generously will also reap generously. Each of you should give what you have decided in your heart to give, not reluctantly or under compulsion, for God loves a cheerful giver." Genuine generosity comes from a place of heartfelt joy and willingness, which is cherished by God.

Providing for Family

First Timothy 5:8 underscores the critical importance of taking care of one's family, emphasizing that it is a fundamental aspect of living out one's faith. The verse states, "Anyone who does not provide for their relatives, and especially for their own household, has denied the faith and is worse than an unbeliever." This verse highlights the integral role of family care in the practice of faith, suggesting that true faith is demonstrated through actions of love and provision for those closest to us.

Hard Work

Proverbs 13:11 offers a profound lesson on the value of honesty and diligence in financial matters. The verse states, "Dishonest money dwindles away, but whoever gathers money little by little makes it grow." This passage highlights the transient nature of wealth obtained through dishonest means, emphasizing that such gains are ultimately fleeting and unreliable. In contrast, it praises the virtues of hard work, persistence, and patience in accumulating wealth. By gathering money gradually and consistently, a person is more likely to see their wealth grow and sustain over time. The Bible thus promotes a strong work ethic and responsible financial management. It encourages individuals to earn their living through honest and diligent efforts, underscoring that the steady accumulation of resources, even if slow, leads to lasting prosperity. This approach not only ensures financial stability but also aligns with ethical and moral principles, fostering a sense of integrity and trustworthiness.

Honesty and Integrity

Proverbs 11:1 emphasizes the importance of honesty in financial transactions, stating, "The Lord detests dishonest scales, but accurate weights find favor with Him." This verse uses the metaphor of scales and weights to highlight the broader principle of integrity in all business dealings. Dishonest scales symbolize fraudulent practices and deceit, which are strongly condemned by God, while accurate weights represent fairness and honesty, earning divine favor. The Bible underscores that ethical behavior in managing money is essential for personal righteousness and contributes to building trust and just communities, making integrity in financial matters a fundamental principle.

Seeking God's Kingdom

Matthew 6:33 states, "But seek first His kingdom and His righteousness, and all these things will be given to you as well," teaching that prioritizing God's will and living according to His values should come before all else. By striving for spiritual growth and embodying virtues such as love, justice, and integrity, believers are assured that their material needs will be met. This verse encourages a shift from anxiety about daily provisions to trusting in God's provision, suggesting that aligning one's life with God's purposes leads to both spiritual fulfillment and the practical benefits of His care.

Living under God's blueprint for prosperity allows us to experience true abundance, where wealth serves His kingdom and reflects His love for others.

CHAPTER 14

Unlocking the Blessings of Tithing: Trusting God with Your Finances

Tithing is a topic that holds significant importance in discussions about finances from a biblical perspective. It has been a foundational practice for many religious communities. It has also been a subject of controversy and misuse, as people and organizations, including churches, have sometimes exploited this practice for financial gain.

In its biblical context, tithing refers to the practice of giving one-tenth of one's income or produce to support religious institutions and their activities. The word "tithe" literally means "one-tenth" or 10 percent. The concept is rooted in the Old Testament, with notable references in books such as Leviticus, Numbers, and Deuteronomy.

"A tithe of everything from the land, whether grain from the soil or fruit from the trees, belongs to the Lord; it is holy to the Lord" (Leviticus 27:30). This directive was intended to support the Levitical priesthood and the maintenance of the temple, ensuring that those dedicated to spiritual service were provided for.

Over time, the practice of tithing has been interpreted in various ways. Some modern interpretations emphasize that tithing is not just about supporting religious institutions but also about fostering a spirit of generosity and responsible stewardship. It is a way for believers to demonstrate their faith and commitment to God, trusting He will provide for their needs. Nevertheless, the potential for misuse arises when individuals or organizations manipulate the concept of tithing for personal or institutional gain rather than focusing on its intended purpose of worship and community support.

To properly understand tithing, it is crucial to refer to biblical texts and consider their historical and cultural context. By doing so, believers can discern the true meaning and purpose of tithing and separate it from any modern-day distortions. Ultimately, tithing should be viewed as an act of worship and a means of supporting believers' spiritual and communal lives rather than a mere financial obligation or a tool for exploitation.

Abraham's Tithe

The concept of tithing is first introduced in the Bible when Abraham gives a tithe to Melchizedek, a priest of the Most High God, in Genesis 14:18–20. This event marks the earliest biblical mention of tithing and sets a precedent for giving a portion of one's wealth as an act of worship and reverence.

Tithing under the Mosaic Law

Tithing became a formal practice under the Mosaic Law, integral to the religious system established for the Israelites. Leviticus 27:30–32 says and Numbers 18:21–24 reiterates that God commands the Israelites to bring a tenth of their crops, livestock, and other resources to support the Levites, who were tasked with the work of the tabernacle and had no inheritance in the land. In Malachi 3:8–10, the prophet rebukes the Israelites for neglecting their tithes and offerings. He challenges them to bring the full tithe into the storehouse, promising that God will open the floodgates of Heaven and pour out blessings in return.

A Deeper Dive into Old Testament Tithing

The Bible mentions several types of tithes, primarily in the Old Testament. These tithes served different purposes and were part of the Mosaic Law for the Israelites. The main types of tithes discussed in the Bible are the Levitical tithe, which we've discussed; The Festival Tithe (Tithe of Feasts), set aside for use during religious celebrations at the place of worship designated by God, encouraging communal worship and remembrance of God's blessings; The Poor Tithe (The Charity or Benevolence Tithe), given every third year to support the poor, widows, orphans, and foreigners residing in their land; and The King's Tithe (non-biblical but historical), a taxation by king similar in its percentage to support the king's rule. To tithe according to scriptural example, this is 23.3 percent plus the king's tax and additional offerings.

Additional Giving and Offerings

In addition to tithes, the Bible mentions several other forms of giving expected from the Israelites under the Mosaic Law. These offerings had specific purposes, ranging from worship and atonement to thanksgiving and voluntary giving. Here are the main types of offerings:

Burnt Offering

- Leviticus 1:1–17

- The burnt offering was a sacrifice of an animal, usually an entire bull, sheep, goat, or bird, completely consumed by fire. It symbolized atonement for sin, devotion, and surrender to God. It was one of the most common and frequent offerings, showing a person's complete dedication to God, symbolizing total commitment and seeking God's favor.

Grain Offering (Meal or Cereal Offering)

- Leviticus 2:1–16

- An offering of flour, oil, and incense, honoring God as the provider of food and sustenance, often accompanied by the burnt offering or other sacrifices. Part of the offering was burned, and the rest was given to the priests.

Peace Offering (Fellowship Offering)

- Leviticus 3:1–17

- A voluntary offering, symbolizing peace and fellowship with God, given as an act of thanksgiving, to fulfill a vow, or as a freewill offering. A portion of the meat was given back to the offeror to be eaten as a meal with family and friends, symbolizing communal fellowship.

Sin Offering

- Leviticus 4:1–35

- A mandatory offering, made to atone for unintentional sins and to seek forgiveness, for individuals and the entire community. The blood of the sacrifice was sprinkled before the altar, and specific portions of the animal were burned. The rest of the animal was often given to the priests.

Guilt Offering (Trespass Offering)

- Leviticus 5:14–6:7

- A required offering when someone sinned against God or their neighbor, particularly involving some form of restitution. The guilty party had to restore what was wrongfully taken or damaged and to add one-fifth of its value as compensation, followed by an animal sacrifice.

Freewill Offering

- Deuteronomy 16:10, Exodus 35:29

- A voluntary gift given out of gratitude or love for God, often in the form of animals, grain, or money, without any specific requirement or obligation. It could be given during times of celebration or when someone felt moved to offer something extra to the Lord.

Firstfruits Offering

- Exodus 23:19, Deuteronomy 26:1–11

- An offering of the first and best of the harvest to God, symbolizing trust in Him as the provider and gratitude for His blessings.

Votive Offerings (Vow Offerings)

- Leviticus 22:18–23, Numbers 6:21

- An offering in fulfillment of a vow or promise made to God, involving animals, grain, or other resources, depending on the type of vow and the circumstances.

The Half-Shekel Temple Tax

- Exodus 30:13–16

- A required tax levied on all adult male Israelites to help maintain the tabernacle and later the temple. Each man was required to give half a shekel as a temple tax, regardless of his wealth.

· **Offerings for the Poor (Charitable Giving)**

- Deuteronomy 15:7–11, Proverbs 19:17

- A moral and religious duty to care for those in need, though not labeled as a specific offering, including almsgiving, lending without interest, and generosity toward orphans, widows, and foreigners.

Thanksgiving Offering

- Leviticus 7:12–15

- A type of voluntary peace offering given in gratitude for God's blessings, offered to give thanks for specific blessings or deliverances. Part of the offering was eaten by the giver, while other portions were given to the priests and burned on the altar.

Additional Old Testament References on Tithing

The Old Testament contains several references that highlight the importance of tithing.

Malachi 3:8–12 challenges the Israelites to honor God with their tithes and offerings, promising abundant blessings in return.

Proverbs 3:9–10 encourages honoring the Lord with wealth and first fruits

Nehemiah 10:35–39 describes the commitment to bring tithes and offerings to the house of the Lord.

These passages collectively emphasize that tithing was a way to honor God, support religious institutions, and provide for the community's needs. Although these teachings were part of the Old Testament and the Mosaic Law, they offer principles that can be integrated with New Testament teachings on giving.

The New Testament shifts the focus from a strict percentage-based tithe to principles of generous and willing giving.

Corinthians 9:6–7: "The point is this: whoever sows sparingly will also reap sparingly, and whoever sows bountifully will also reap bountifully. Each one must give as he has decided in his heart, not reluctantly or under compulsion, for God loves a cheerful giver."

Luke 6:38: "Give, and it will be given to you. Good measure, pressed down, shaken together, running over, will be put into your lap. For with the measure you use, it will be measured back to you."

1 Corinthians 16:2: "On the first day of every week, each of you is to put something aside and store it up, as he may prosper, so that there will be no collecting when I come."

Acts 20:35: "In all things I have shown you that by working hard in this way we must help the weak and remember the words of the Lord Jesus, how he himself said, 'It is more blessed to give than to receive.'"

1 Timothy 6:17–19: "As for the rich in this present age, charge them not to be haughty, nor to set their hopes on the uncertainty of riches, but on God, who richly provides us with everything to enjoy. They are to do good, to be rich in good works, to be generous and ready to share, thus storing up treasure for themselves as a good foundation for the future, so that they may take hold of that which is truly life."

These passages emphasize giving with a cheerful heart, according to one's means, and in a spirit of generosity. The New Testament encourages believers to support the kingdom in the New Testament, believers are often described as a "royal priesthood," indicating a special role and responsibility in God's Kingdom. This concept, supported by several scriptures, emphasizes that all believers have a priestly duty to manage the resources God has entrusted to them, including tithes and offerings. 1 Peter 2:9 and Revelation 1:6 highlight that we are chosen to declare God's praises and serve Him as priests. While Jesus is our High Priest, believers share in the priestly responsibilities of stewardship, community care, and maintaining the church.

As priests, we are stewards of the resources God has given us. In the Old Testament, the tithe was used to support the Levitical priesthood and the work of the temple. The New Testament model of generosity extends beyond mere tithing; it includes all aspects of giving, such as offerings to support the church, missions, and the needy. This stewardship requires us to manage these resources wisely, ensuring they glorify God. Additionally, like the Old Testament priests, we are called to care for our community, including strangers, travelers, and the poor, as reflected in James 1:27. We are also responsible for supporting and maintaining the church, both physically and spiritually, contributing to church work, supporting staff, and participating in all kinds of ministry work.

The conversation of *how much* always comes up at this point. If we are to be generous, is there a measuring stick to help me know what generosity looks like? Of course, the Holy Spirit will lead and guide in all aspects of life including tithing but I would start with the 10% model and see where God takes you in your generosity.

In the New Testament, there are a few references that allude to the Old Testament practice of tithing, including the 10% tithe, although these references are not presented as commands for New Testament believers. Instead, they often acknowledge the practice as part of Jewish tradition and law. Here are some key passages:

Matthew 23:23 (NIV): "Woe to you, teachers of the law and Pharisees, you hypocrites! You give a tenth of your spices—mint, dill, and cumin. But you have neglected the more important matters of the law—justice, mercy, and faithfulness. You should have practiced the latter, without neglecting the former."

In this verse, Jesus acknowledges the practice of tithing even small garden herbs but emphasizes the importance of justice, mercy, and faithfulness over mere ritual observance.

Luke 11:42 (NIV): "Woe to you Pharisees, because you give God a tenth of your mint, rue and all other kinds of garden herbs, but you neglect justice and the love of God. You should have practiced the latter without leaving the former undone."

This passage is similar to Matthew 23:23, where Jesus critiques the Pharisees for their meticulous tithing while neglecting more significant moral responsibilities.

Hebrews 7:1–10: This passage discusses Melchizedek and Abraham's interaction, where Abraham gave Melchizedek a tenth of everything. The writer of Hebrews uses this Old Testament account to discuss the superiority of Melchizedek's priesthood and, by extension, the priesthood of Christ. While the focus is not on the practice of tithing itself, it acknowledges the historical practice of giving a tenth.

These references point back to the tradition of tithing, particularly in the context of Jewish law and practice, but they are not presented as direct instructions for the New Testament church. Instead, the New Testament teaching emphasizes the principles of generous, willing, and cheerful giving.

As we consider our role in giving, we should reflect on how we manage our tithes and offerings. Key questions include whether we are giving generously and cheerfully, supporting the church, and caring for those in need. Our goal should always be to glorify God and further His kingdom.

Where Should Tithes Be Given?

There is often much discussion about bringing the tithe into the storehouse, with some believing that the storehouse refers to the local church and that we are called to give our full tithe there. While that might be what God is leading you to do individually, scripture provides deeper insight as we study the tithe. The Bible calls believer's priests in the Kingdom of God, which brings both privileges and responsibilities. 1 Peter 2:9 declares, "But you are a chosen people, a royal priesthood, a holy nation, God's special possession, that you may declare the praises of him who called you out of darkness into his wonderful light." As priests under the High Priest, Jesus Christ, we are entrusted with managing the resources God provides, including the tithe.

In the Old Testament, the Jewish people brought their tithes to the temple, where the priests managed these offerings. Malachi 3:10 instructs, "Bring the whole tithe into the storehouse, that there may be food in my house." The tithe served multiple purposes: it supported the priests and Levites who ministered to the people (Numbers 18:21–24), provided for the needs of the community, and cared for the vulnerable, including widows, orphans, and foreigners (Deuteronomy 14:28–29). The priests sought God's guidance in distributing the tithe, ensuring that every portion was used according to His will.

Similarly, as priests today, we are responsible for the storehouse. This means that, like the Old Testament priests, we are accountable for where the tithe goes and how it is used. It is essential to seek God's direction and ask Him how He wants His tithe to be distributed, ensuring it fulfills His purposes in our lives and communities.

The New Testament provides several perspectives on where tithes and offerings can be directed. Here are some key areas to consider:

- Local Church Congregation—Galatians 6:6, 1 Timothy 5:17–18, and Exodus 25:1–2—allow the congregation to continue its ministries, teach the gospel, serve the community, and maintain the church.

- Support for Poor and Needy Christians—Romans 15:25–27, 1 Corinthians 16:1–4, and James 1:27—support individuals facing financial hardship, hunger, or other needs, a direct reflection of the early church's practice of providing for its members.

- Gospel Ministry and Preaching—Philippians 4:10–18, 1 Corinthians 9:13–14, and Acts 11:29—support local-church staff, missionary work, and global ministries, spreading the gospel beyond local congregations.

- Ministries Making Disciples—3 John 1:5–8—supports new church plants, ministries, and organizations dedicated to making disciples help ministries grow and multiply.

- The Holy Spirit's Leading—Acts 11:27–30—includes unexpected opportunities to give or support someone in need, disaster relief efforts, or other causes where God's prompting is evident.

- Healing and Compassion—Galatians 6:2—provides caring and support for those who are sick, grieving, or in need of emotional or physical healing, including healthcare ministries, counseling services, or supporting individuals facing medical needs.

- Community and Fellowship—Hebrews 10:24–25—supports ministries that build strong, loving communities and encourage fellowship, including local community groups, church gatherings, and Christian fellowships.

- Education and Wisdom—Proverbs 1:7—supports educational initiatives that align with biblical values, including Christian schools, Bible colleges, or programs that help people grow in their knowledge of God's Word.

- Reconciliation and Peace—Matthew 5:9—promotes peace, reconciliation, and forgiveness, including conflict-resolution ministries, counseling services, or programs aimed at fostering forgiveness and understanding.

- Hospitality and Welcome—Hebrews 13:2—supports ministries that welcome strangers and provide for those in need or in crisis. It is a beautiful expression of His love, including giving to homeless shelters, refugee assistance, or ministries that focus on hospitality.

You can see there are many ways to give to what is important to God. These scriptures provide a biblical foundation for many areas of giving, helping us align our actions with God's values and desires. In all giving, the key is to align with God's purposes and guidance, giving with a heart dedicated to His kingdom's work. Ask the Holy Spirit to guide you. Our objective is to be generous givers, finding joy in giving to what excites God. What excites Him should excite you! Start with a tithe—10%—but don't stop there. Give as God provides and ask Him for more income so you can be even more generous. Let this be a fun and fulfilling part of your relationship with Him. God is incredibly generous and a joyful giver to us, so reflect this part of His loving and joyful personality in your own giving!

Simple Steps to Begin Tithing as a Royal Priesthood

Tithing is more than just giving; it's about embracing your role as a priest in God's Kingdom. As a royal priest, you are entrusted with managing the resources He provides, including the tithe. This isn't about begrudgingly giving to the church out of guilt but about joyfully and generously stewarding the blessings God has entrusted to you.

Here's a practical way to start living out this responsibility:

1. **Open a Separate Tithing Account:** Go to your bank and open a separate checking account. This will serve as your "tithing account." Whenever you receive income, move 10% of it directly into this account. This simple act helps you release personal ownership of the money and recognize it as God's.

2. **Seek God's Guidance for Giving:** Treat the money in this account as God's provision for His purposes. Prayerfully ask where He wants you to direct these funds. You might feel led to set up regular payments to your local church, a ministry, or a person in need. Alternatively, you may sense God asking you to hold onto the funds until a larger need arises.

3. **Watch for Opportunities:** Be excited about the opportunities God will reveal. Sometimes, money accumulates in your account, waiting for a specific purpose He has planned. Trust that He will guide you to the right moment and the right place to use it.

4. **Give Cheerfully and Generously:** When God reveals where to give, do so with a cheerful and willing heart. Remember, this isn't just a transaction—it's an act of worship and partnership with God in His work on earth.

It's interesting that I haven't found any scripture that says our tithing should go through a non-profit or come with a tax write-off. Don't let the idea of non-profit status or tax deductions keep you from being obedient in your giving. God calls us to give generously from the heart (2 Cor. 9:7), trusting in His provision and reward, not in what the system offers in return. Now don't get me wrong. If God tells you to give somewhere that is giving a tax write-off, of course take the write-off. I'm only saying don't limit your giving to only what will give you a write-off. Ask God, and be obedient.

Story Time: John Learns What Tithing Is

John had grown up attending church with his family but had never really delved deep into the Bible. One Sunday, the pastor announced a new sermon series on the principles of giving and stewardship, which would include a study of tithing from both the Old and New Testaments. Intrigued, John decided to attend every sermon and embark on his own personal journey to understand tithing better.

Week 1—-Introduction to Tithing: During the first week of the sermon series, John learned about the concept of tithing in the Old Testament. The pastor explained how God had commanded the Israelites to give a tenth of their income and produce to support the Levites and maintain the temple. John had never considered this before. He started reading passages in the Old Testament, including Leviticus and Deuteronomy, which detailed the practice of tithing.

Week 2—The Heart of Giving: In the second week, the sermon shifted to the New Testament and focused on the teachings of Jesus. John discovered that while Jesus didn't explicitly command tithing, He emphasized the importance of giving from the heart. He remembered the story of the widow's offering in Mark 12:41-44, where Jesus praised the woman for giving all she had, even though it was a small amount. John began to understand that God valued the attitude and intention behind giving just as much as the amount.

Week 3—Giving in the Early Church: During the third week, John learned about the practices of the early Christian church. Acts 4:32–35 described how the believers shared everything they had, and no one was in need. John was moved by the idea of a community that cared for one another so deeply. He thought about the people in his own church who might be struggling and how his giving could make a difference.

Week 4—Personal Reflection and Decision: By the fourth week, John had spent hours studying the Old and New Testaments, reflecting on the sermons, and praying. He realized that tithing was not just about a fixed percentage but about a heart transformed by gratitude and compassion. John remembered a verse from 2 Corinthians 9:7: "Each of you should give what you have decided in your heart to give, not reluctantly or under compulsion, for God loves a cheerful giver."

John decided it was time to make a change in his life. He felt a sense of conviction and clarity. That Sunday, as the offering plate was passed around, John took a deep breath and placed his tithe envelope inside. It was the first time he had ever tithed, and it felt like a moment of profound significance.

The Impact of John's Decision

Over time, John continued to tithe faithfully, not out of obligation but out of gratitude for all that God had provided. He gave to his church, but he also got very excited about seeing opportunities to hear God's direction and give to other organizations that were doing God's work and he also decided to be more generous in his community, giving to those who needed help. He was having so much fun partnering with God with his giving and seeing the fruit of his giving expand. He even found some ministries that he loved and got involved with while supporting them. He found so much peace and joy, realizing that his giving expanded his life in ways that he never expected. He saw the positive impact of his giving within his church community, as more resources were available for ministry and helping those in need. He also found that as he gave more, he worried less about material possessions and trusted God's provision even more, realizing that God's promises were true. He tested God and found that God's blessings exceeded his imaginations. Not only in his personal income but also in every aspect of his life, he felt like he was being blessed.

John's journey through the Old and New Testaments about tithing had transformed his understanding of giving. It was no longer a mere ritual but a joyful act of worship and love for God and his fellow believers. John not only learned about tithing from the Bible but allowed God to shape his heart and actions, making him a cheerful and generous giver.

In conclusion, understanding tithing and aligning it with God's unshakable kingdom principles is crucial for living an abundant and purpose-driven life. Building wealth on a foundation of faith and stewardship means managing his resources with a heart of generosity and a focus on God's Kingdom. As we embrace God's blueprint for prosperity and purpose, we unlock the blessings that flow from living under His unshakable redemption and abundant grace.

CHAPTER 15

Breaking Free: What the Bible Teaches About Debt and Financial Freedom

A Flawed Foundation

The foundation of our world's financial system is built on dishonesty, something the Lord cannot bless. While He may use it for His purposes, He won't bless a system that enslaves those who participate in it. The system is designed so that the more one relies on debt, the more enslaved they become, echoing the biblical warning that the borrower becomes a servant to the lender (Prov. 22:7). This is not just a warning, but a timeless principle about the relationship between debt and bondage. Believers are called to live free and be servants to Christ, not to the systems of this world.

Debt and Financial Bondage

Debt is a significant theme throughout scripture. Romans 13:8 advises, "Let no debt remain outstanding, except the continuing debt to love one another, for whoever loves others has fulfilled the law." The only acceptable "debt" we should carry is love, a constant obligation that honors God's greatest commandment. Financial debt, on the other hand, burdens us and often distracts us from fulfilling God's purpose. Instead of being free to serve others and love generously, we become preoccupied with repaying our creditors.

In Deuteronomy 28:12, God's promise is that "You will lend to many nations but will borrow from none." This verse was part of the blessing God spoke over Israel if they obeyed Him, but the reverse, found in Deuteronomy 28:44, states that if they disobey, "The foreigner residing among you will rise higher and higher, but you will sink lower and lower. They will lend to you, but you will not lend to them." Debt is clearly tied to disobedience and the consequences that follow when we rely on borrowing rather than trusting in God's provision.

God, in His infinite wisdom, knows what is best for us. The dangers of debt are not just practical—they are spiritual. Debt enslaves us to a system that operates on human greed and exploitation, which is why God desires His people to be free from it. In Matthew 6:24, Jesus says, "No one can serve two masters. Either you will hate the one and love the other, or you will be devoted to the one and despise the other. You cannot serve both God and money." When in debt, instead of being fully available to God's work, our minds are consumed with how to manage our finances.

The Dangers of the Modern Financial System

In today's world, mortgages, credit cards, student loans, and national debts all serve to limit the freedom God desires for His people. The Bible teaches us to avoid placing ourselves in situations that would make us dependent on anyone but God. Galatians 5:1 reminds us, "It is for freedom that Christ has set us free. Stand firm, then, and do not let yourselves be burdened again by a yoke of slavery." Debt is a modern-day yoke of slavery.

Moreover, unsustainable growth fueled by debt has led to financial collapses throughout history. The Bible encourages us to build wisely and avoid quick fixes (Luke 14:28–30). God values foresight and planning, principles often ignored in today's debt-driven economy. Instead of counting the cost, many are enticed by the promise of instant gratification, which ultimately leads to financial ruin.

Integrity in Financial Dealings

The Bible also stresses the importance of integrity, fairness, and justice in financial dealings (Prov. 11:1). Financial systems that exploit the vulnerable or operate on deceit are detestable to the Lord (Lev. 19:35–36). In a world where financial gain often comes at the expense of others, God's people are called to higher standards.

God desires honesty and integrity even in the smallest financial dealings. The modern financial system, however, often rewards dishonesty, whether through hidden fees, predatory lending, or complex schemes that favor the wealthy over the poor. Believers must uphold the biblical standard of fairness, reflecting God's righteousness in all areas of life, including finances.

Godly Stewardship in a Broken System

Everything we have belongs to God, and He has entrusted us to manage it well. This includes living within our means, avoiding unnecessary debt, and practicing generosity (1 Cor. 4:2). By aligning our finances with God's Word, we can operate within this flawed system without becoming enslaved to it.

Contentment is a vital aspect of godly stewardship (Phil. 4:11–12) We are called to be content with what God has provided, resisting the constant pressure to accumulate more through debt. True contentment is found not in financial security but in trusting God's provision.

Focusing on Ownership and Freedom

One practical way to break free from financial enslavement is by focusing on ownership rather than borrowing. Proverbs 13:11 says, "Dishonest money dwindles away, but whoever gathers money little by little makes it grow." This principle encourages us to build wealth steadily and with integrity, avoiding the temptation to acquire through shortcuts or debt. By investing in tangible assets, owning property, and making wise financial decisions, we reflect God's principles and safeguard ourselves from the risks of debt.

Generosity as a Path to Freedom

At the heart of financial freedom is generosity (Prov. 11:24–25). When we give generously, we participate in God's economy, which operates on faith, trust, and provision. This counters the materialism and greed that drive the world's financial systems. The act of giving not only blesses others but also breaks the hold that wealth can have over our hearts. Second Corinthians 9:6–8 encourages us to trust that God will provide abundantly when we give freely, even when it seems counterintuitive.

Seeking God's Wisdom for Financial Decisions

Finally, we must seek God's wisdom in navigating the financial system (James 1:5). God knows the challenges we face in today's economic climate, and He is ready to guide us if we seek His direction. Through prayer and discernment, we can make financial decisions that honor Him and protect us from the pitfalls of debt and greed.

While we cannot fully escape the global financial system, we can operate within it with integrity, wisdom, and faith. Perhaps one day God will raise up a new system that reflects His principles of justice and stewardship. Until then, we are called to live with integrity, trusting in His provision and remembering that our true treasure is not found in earthly wealth, but in the eternal riches of His kingdom.

Walking in Freedom and Faith

This journey of financial freedom requires faith and courage. By leaning into God's Word and seeking His will, we can avoid the traps of the world's financial system and walk in the freedom Christ has provided (Heb. 13:5). We are reminded, "Keep your lives free from the love of money and be content with what you have, because God has said, 'Never will I leave you; never will I forsake you.'" Through stewardship, generosity, and wisdom, we can thrive in a broken system while keeping our eyes fixed on the eternal reward that awaits us.

Understanding the dangers of the modern financial system and its foundations of debt is crucial for living an unshakable and abundant life. Aligning with God's true character and embracing His principles of stewardship, freedom, and integrity are essential in breaking free from the bondage of debt. As we clarify misconceptions and shed light on the myths of wealth, we see that God's blueprint for prosperity is built on faith, contentment, and responsible management, not the flawed systems of this world. Living by God's standards of financial freedom allows us to walk in the unshakable redemption and abundance He has planned for us.

CHAPTER 16

True Riches: Unlocking God's Purpose for Wealth and Eternal Blessings

When God repeats something in the scriptures, it signifies a profound importance to Him. Among these repeated themes, money is mentioned more than seven hundred times, underscoring its significance in our spiritual journey, as God often links financial obedience to broader spiritual responsibilities. Jesus draws a direct connection between our management of worldly wealth and our capability to handle spiritual matters (Luke 16:10–11). "Whoever can be trusted with very little can also be trusted with much, and whoever is dishonest with very little will also be dishonest with much. So, if you have not been trustworthy in handling worldly wealth, who will trust you with true riches?"

This scripture challenges us to evaluate our stewardship over the resources and responsibilities we've been given. If we fall short, it prompts us to ponder the deeper implications: What spiritual blessings or "true riches" might we be missing out on due to our inadequacies in handling earthly wealth?

The Concept of True Riches in the Bible

The Bible contains several passages that discuss the concept of "true riches" or spiritual wealth as opposed to material wealth. Now, mind you, there is nothing wrong with material wealth as God is the provider of all good things. But we are exploring what will bring us wealth here on this earth as well as wealth for eternity. True riches transcend material possessions and lead to a deeper connection with God and His eternal kingdom.

Treasures in Heaven

One of the key passages on this topic is found in Matthew 6:19–21: "Do not store up for yourselves treasures on earth, where moths and vermin destroy, and where thieves break in and steal. But store up for yourselves treasures in Heaven, where moths and vermin do not destroy, and where thieves do not break in and steal. For where your treasure is, there your heart will be also" (NIV).

This passage emphasizes that true riches are not found in earthly possessions but in the treasures one accumulates in Heaven through righteous living and a focus on God. It challenges us to examine where our hearts lie—are we placing our trust in what we can accumulate on earth, or are we seeking eternal rewards that last forever?

Understand that God will provide us with abundant resources here on earth. However, the true riches we should be focused on are His eternal treasures. It all comes down to where we place our focus—on the temporary wealth of this world or the lasting, spiritual wealth found in God's Kingdom.

Spiritual Wealth Over Material Possessions

The book of Proverbs offers another profound insight in Proverbs 13:7: "One person pretends to be rich, yet has nothing; another pretends to be poor, yet has great wealth" (NIV).

This verse reminds us that true wealth isn't measured solely by material possessions. Qualities like integrity, contentment, and spiritual richness are what truly define a person's wealth (Prov. 13:7). Even those with little in the way of material goods may possess great spiritual wealth, which is far more valuable. Life's true meaning and riches don't come from an abundance of possessions but from other aspects such as faith, relationships, and inner peace. We must guard against the temptations of greed, which can distract us from the more meaningful pursuits of life (Luke 12:15).

Godliness with Contentment: True Gain

The pursuit of wealth in and of itself can lead to spiritual destruction (1 Tim. 6:6–10). It doesn't say money is evil, but rather the *love of money*—when wealth becomes an idol, it leads to all kinds of problems.

Spiritual Blessings: True Wealth

The Bible often contrasts worldly riches with spiritual blessings. In Ephesians 1:3, Paul writes: "Praise be to the God and Father of our Lord Jesus Christ, who has blessed us in the heavenly realms with every spiritual blessing in Christ." Spiritual blessings—wisdom, understanding, and righteousness—are far more valuable than any earthly treasure. Proverbs 3:13–15 echoes this sentiment:" "Blessed are those who find wisdom, those who gain understanding, for she is more profitable than silver and yields better returns than gold. She is more precious than rubies; nothing you desire can compare with her."

These verses point us toward the realization that God values the condition of our heart and mind more than our bank accounts. Wisdom, understanding, and righteousness are treasures that outlast anything this world has to offer (Mark 8:36). Jesus teaches us to prioritize our spiritual well-being over our material wealth, for true riches are those that will carry us into eternity.

Generosity and Contentment: Storing Up Heavenly Treasures

Being rich in good deeds and generosity not only blesses others but also stores up eternal rewards for those who give (1 Tim. 6:17–19). Contentment is a mark of true wealth because it reflects a trust in God's provision, no matter our earthly circumstances (Phil. 4:11–13).

Philippians 4:11-13 reminds us that contentment is part of true wealth:

> I have learned to be content whatever the circumstances. I know what it is to be in need, and I know what it is to have plenty. I have learned the secret of being content in any and every situation, whether well fed or hungry, whether living in plenty or in want. I can do all this through Him who gives me strength.

Eyes on God, Not on Wealth

In the end, God does not frown upon building wealth, but our purpose is to walk closely with Him, so He gives us the wealth He wants us to have for fulfilling His plans. The challenge is to keep our eyes fixed on God, using the resources He blesses us with to further His kingdom, rather than allowing wealth to distract us from our divine mission. By seeking first His kingdom, trusting in Him, and being generous in good works, we not only fulfill our purpose but also store up true treasures in Heaven—treasures that last for eternity.

Wealth as a Blessing and a Tool for God's Purposes

God's Word consistently teaches that wealth, when given by God, is intended to bless us and equip us to fulfill His purposes. God's desire is not for us to live in lack but to live in His abundant provision, using the resources He provides to further His kingdom and bless others. The Bible is filled with stories of individuals who were blessed financially as a result of their obedience and service to God, highlighting how God honors those who walk closely with Him.

Biblical examples of wealth as a blessing for obedience include:

- Abraham's Wealth and Covenant—Genesis 12:2–3, Genesis 13:2— According to God's promises, Abraham grew wealthy, but his wealth was always secondary to his relationship with God, and his heart remained focused on God's will.

- Joseph's Rise to Wealth and Power—Genesis 41:40–42—Enduring great trials, including being sold into slavery and unjustly imprisoned, Joseph's faithfulness to God never wavered. And God blessed him with power, influence, and material wealth, using him to save Egypt and the surrounding nations from famine.

- Solomon's Extraordinary Wealth—1 Kings 3:9–13— Solomon asked God for wisdom to lead His people, and in response, God gave him not only wisdom but also unparalleled riches.

Biblical Abundance

The Bible teaches that building an abundance of wealth is never accomplished by our own strength, intelligence, or willpower alone. Every example of wealth and abundance in scripture is rooted in obedience to God, seeking His will, and following His guidance. Proverbs 10:4 tells us, "Lazy hands make for poverty, but diligent hands bring wealth" (NIV), emphasizing the value of hard work and dedication, but this diligence must be done in partnership with God, not independent of Him.

True abundance comes from aligning our actions with God's principles and living a life of obedience. Deuteronomy 8:18 reminds us, "But remember the Lord your God, for it is He who gives you the ability to produce wealth" (NIV). "God is the ultimate provider, and it is through His blessing and favor that we are able to experience financial abundance" (Matt. 6:33). When we prioritize God's Kingdom and seek His will in all areas of our lives, including finances, He ensures that our needs are met and often blesses us with abundance.

Matthew 6:33 reinforces this truth, stating, "But seek first His kingdom and His righteousness, and all these things will be given to you as well" (NIV).

In addition to obedience, wise stewardship and generosity play key roles in building wealth according to biblical principles. Luke 16:10 teaches, "Whoever can be trusted with very little can also be trusted with much" (NIV), emphasizing that managing what we have well is essential to receiving more from God. Additionally, Proverbs 11:25 reminds us that "A generous person will prosper; whoever refreshes others will be refreshed." God's design for financial abundance involves not only receiving but also giving, as generosity reflects His heart and unlocks further blessings.

Ultimately, the path to building an abundance of wealth in a way that honors God is rooted in obedience, seeking His guidance, and faithfully managing what He has entrusted to us. Wealth is not a product of human effort alone but is the result of a life lived in close relationship with God, walking in His will and trusting in His provision.

The Purpose of Wealth

Wealth is a gift from God, intended to fulfill His purposes on earth (Deut. 8:18). Our ability to generate wealth comes from God, and it is meant to bless others, support ministries, and build up the community. As we accumulate wealth, we must seek God's guidance in how to use it (Prov. 3:5–6).

Wealth with a Purpose

God gives us wealth to equip us for the calling He has placed on our lives. Luke 12:48 says: "From everyone who has been given much, much will be demanded"" (NIV). As stewards of God's resources, we must use wealth to serve others and advance His kingdom. Proverbs 11:25 reminds us: "A generous person will prosper; whoever refreshes others will be refreshed" (NIV). Whether accumulating wealth for future use or giving it away, the key is to glorify God with what we have. As we seek His kingdom first and trust in His provision, we become faithful stewards, experiencing His blessings both now and for eternity.

Story Time: Frank and True Riches

Once upon a time in the bustling city of New York, a young man named Frank was consumed by a fervent desire to achieve great wealth. Raised in a modest home, he had witnessed his parents struggle to make ends meet, and he vowed that he would never live a life of financial hardship. Driven by ambition, he immersed himself in his studies, graduating at the top of his class from a prestigious business school. Frank quickly climbed the corporate ladder, landing a high-paying job on Wall Street.

In his twenties, Frank's life seemed to be the epitome of success. He wore tailored suits, drove a sleek sports car, and lived in a luxurious penthouse overlooking the city. His bank account swelled with each passing year, and he relished the envy and admiration of his peers. Yet, despite his outward success, Frank often felt a gnawing emptiness inside. He brushed it aside, attributing it to the pressures of his demanding career.

As Frank's wealth grew, so did his detachment from the people around him. He worked late into the night, rarely seeing his family or friends. Relationships became transactional, and his life was a constant whirlwind of meetings, deals, and lavish parties. The moments of silence, when they came, were filled with an unsettling loneliness that he drowned out with the noise of the city and the thrill of his next big financial conquest.

One crisp autumn evening, Frank attended a gala at a grand hotel. The room was filled with the city's elite, each person seemingly more successful and glamorous than the next. Amid the chatter and clinking glasses, Frank's gaze fell upon an elderly man who stood quietly in a corner, smiling warmly as he observed the crowd. Curious, Frank approached him and struck up a conversation.

The man introduced himself as Mr. Harrison, a retired businessman who had once been a titan of the finance world. As they talked, Frank learned that Mr. Harrison had amassed a fortune even greater than his own. Intrigued by the older man's serenity and genuine kindness, Frank asked him the secret to his happiness.

Mr. Harrison's eyes twinkled with wisdom as he spoke. "Frank, there was a time when I, too, believed that wealth was the pinnacle of life. I worked tirelessly, sacrificing everything to build my empire. But one day, I realized that despite all my riches, I was profoundly poor in the things that truly mattered— love, peace, joy, and meaningful relationships." He paused, then continued, "I found these truths in the Bible, and it transformed my life. All wisdom is from our heavenly Father."

Frank listened intently as Mr. Harrison continued. "The Bible teaches us that true wealth is not measured in material possessions. Proverbs 11:4 says, 'Wealth is worthless in the day of wrath, but righteousness delivers from death.' And in Matthew 6:33, Jesus tells us to Seek first His kingdom and His righteousness, and all these things will be given to you as well."

Mr. Harrison shared more scriptures, each one resonating deeply with Frank. "1 Timothy 6:17–19 advises the wealthy to do good, to be rich in good deeds, and to be generous. True riches come from a life aligned with God's will, filled with love, joy, and peace." He added, "Proverbs 3:13–15 speaks of the value of wisdom and understanding, saying they are more precious than rubies and nothing you desire can compare with them."

Mr. Harrison's words struck a chord deep within Frank. That night, as he stood on the balcony of his penthouse, the glittering city lights below him, he felt a profound sense of clarity. Tears welled up in his eyes as he realized that he had been chasing a mirage, a fleeting illusion of happiness that wealth could never truly provide.

Determined to change, Frank began to reevaluate his life. He cut back on his hours at work and started volunteering at a local shelter. He reached out to his estranged family, mending broken relationships and spending quality time with his parents. Frank also became involved in his community, using his financial acumen to help small businesses thrive.

As he shifted his focus from personal gain to the well-being of others, Frank began to experience a profound transformation. The emptiness that had once plagued him was replaced by a sense of fulfillment and peace. He found joy in the simple pleasures of life—in the laughter of children, the beauty of a sunset, and the warmth of genuine connections.

Frank's newfound purpose brought him closer to his faith as well. He began to understand the deeper meaning of spiritual wealth, embracing virtues such as love, kindness, and humility. He realized that true riches lay not in material possessions but in the richness of the soul and the impact one has on the lives of others.

Years later, Frank stood on the stage at a community event, sharing his journey with a captivated audience. He spoke of his rise to financial success and the emptiness that accompanied it, and how a chance encounter with a wise Christian man had led him to discover the true meaning of wealth. His story resonated with many, inspiring them to look beyond material gains and seek fulfillment in the things that truly matter.

Frank's life had come full circle. He had built a successful career and amassed wealth, but it was his transformation and commitment to living a life of purpose and integrity that brought him true happiness. In the end, Frank found that the greatest treasure of all was not in the riches he had once pursued so fervently, but in the love, joy, peace, and meaningful connections he had cultivated along the way, guided by the wisdom of the Bible and a meaningful relationship with God.

In conclusion, living an unshakable and abundant life starts with aligning our hearts and actions with God's true character and His blueprint for prosperity and purpose. When we build wealth on a foundation of faith and stewardship, we are not only blessed materially, but we unlock true riches—peace, wisdom, and eternal treasures. By clarifying misconceptions and shedding light on myths, we realize that wealth, while important, is a tool for advancing God's Kingdom, and our focus should always be on honoring Him. True abundance comes from embracing His purposes, walking in integrity, and using all that He entrusts to us for His glory.

Having spent more than twenty years in the investment world, I could easily fill an entire book with the good and bad sides of building wealth. Yet, nothing compares to God's perfect system. We've exposed the flaws of the enemy's financial system—a system that will keep you enslaved, always serving a master that promises much but delivers little. In contrast, God's system provides true freedom. It frees us in the world and, more importantly, it frees us in His kingdom. What is God leading you to do? This isn't about me telling you what you should do. It's about opening your eyes to what the Bible says on these topics and having the courage to ask God what He wants for your life.

Unshakable Riches: Understanding the Fullness of God's Covenant Wealth

The spiritual heritage passed down from Abraham, through Moses, and into our lives, shows how we are heirs to the promises of God through faith. It focuses on how the covenants with Abraham and Moses lay the groundwork for the New Covenant in Christ, revealing the full scope of God's blessings. Abraham's covenant teaches us that God's blessings are not just for him but for all his descendants—including us—who believe and follow God's will. These promises, fulfilled in the New Covenant through Christ, show the full scope of God's blessings, including protection, peace, spiritual well-being, and material abundance. By diving deep into this part of the story, you will see how your life is intricately connected to God's eternal promises, enabling you to live an unshakable life of abundance and blessing. This is not just history; it's a meaningful, impactful story that will transform how you see your purpose and God's provision for the rest of your life.

CHAPTER 17

Understanding Wealth in God's Plan for Us

Understanding how God promises to bless His people in the Old Testament is crucial for comprehending what true riches are. God's blessings, as described in scriptures like Genesis 12:2–3, Deuteronomy 28:1–14, and Jeremiah 29:11, encompass not only material prosperity but also spiritual well-being, protection, peace, and a hopeful future. These promises highlight that true riches go beyond mere financial wealth, involving a deep relationship with God, living righteously, and experiencing His favor in all aspects of life. Recognizing that God values obedience, faithfulness, and honoring Him as pathways to receiving His blessings helps us to prioritize spiritual growth and moral integrity. By aligning our lives with God's will, we position ourselves to receive the fullness of His blessings, which include peace, joy, and eternal hope, thus redefining our understanding of true wealth.

To further explore this, let's look at how God led Abraham and Moses as they guided the Israelites through the Old Testament. God promised to bless Abraham and make him a great nation, using him as a conduit for blessings to all peoples on earth. Similarly, under Moses's leadership, God provided the Israelites with rules and commandments designed to protect and bless them. These laws were not just restrictions but were meant to ensure their well-being, prosperity, and spiritual health. By following God's commandments, the Israelites were to experience His protection and blessings, illustrating that true riches come from a life lived in alignment with divine principles. Examining these stories, we see that God's intention has always been to lead His people into a comprehensive state of blessedness that encompasses every facet of life, reinforcing that true riches are found in faithful obedience and a close relationship with Him.

God's Promise to Abraham

God established a covenant between Himself and Abraham.: "I will bless you and make your name great so that you will be a blessing. I will bless those who bless you, and he who dishonors you I will curse, and in you, all the families of the earth shall be blessed" (Gen. 12:3). "And [Abraham] believed in the LORD, and He counted it to him as righteousness" (Gen. 15:6). Note: a covenant is a two-sided agreement or contract. God is saying that if you believe Him, He will follow through with His promise. Abraham's job was to believe what God was saying. Abraham did not have to do anything else other than watch God do His work after he believed.

Please understand before we go any further, that when God makes a promise, it is an immensely significant event with profound implications. God's promises are guaranteed by His divine nature, making them absolutely reliable (Num. 23:19). These promises form the bedrock of faith for believers, providing hope, guidance, and assurance of God's presence (Heb. 11:1). The Bible's narrative is woven with fulfilled promises, from Abraham becoming a great nation (Gen. 12:2–3) to the prophesied coming of the Messiah (Isa. 7:14, Matthew 1:22–23), showcasing God's impeccable track record. God's promises often carry eternal significance, such as the promise of eternal life through faith in Jesus Christ (John 3:16), offering hope that transcends earthly life. In times of uncertainty and difficulty, verses like Jeremiah 29:11 provide reassurance of God's benevolent plans. These promises also form the basis of God's covenants with humanity, shaping the course of salvation history. Reflecting His unconditional love and faithfulness, God's promises remain steadfast despite human shortcomings (Lam. 3:22–23). Understanding the magnitude of God's promises helps believers trust in His Word, finding hope and assurance in His divine plan.

The Key Elements and Significance of the Abrahamic Covenant

God promised Abraham that he would become the father of a great nation, even though he and his wife Sarah were initially childless and advanced in age

(Gen. 12:2, 15:4–5). This promise was fulfilled through the birth of Isaac and the subsequent growth of the Israelite nation.

God also promised Abraham a land for his descendants to inhabit (Gen. 12:7, 15:18), often referred to as the "Promised Land," which is associated with the region of modern-day Israel. A side note is that God promised Abraham the land of Israel—modern-day Israel. The enemy wants nothing more than to stop God's promises. He doesn't care when or how, but even 3,800+ years later, the enemy is still trying to eliminate God's promises made in the Bible. Why do you think that tiny country causes so much controversy around the world? Per square mile, there's no place on earth that attracts more media attention than Israel. Why? The enemy wants to make God a liar and therefore prevent the fulfillment of even one of His promises. Therefore, he will do his craft of lying to anyone who will listen about the realities of the origin of Israel. The enemy is crafty, but God will always be victorious.

God declared that through Abraham's descendants, all nations of the earth would be blessed (Gen. 12:3, 18:18). This is a reference to the coming of Jesus Christ, who has brought salvation to all humanity, as well as His blessing that can be seen in the contributions of believers in various fields. This also is a message that He will bless His people with an abundance that is clearly intended to bless His people, so that they can bless others.

As a sign of the covenant, God commanded Abraham and his male descendants to be circumcised (Gen. 17:10–14). This physical act symbolized their commitment to the covenant and set apart the descendants of Abraham as a distinct people. Abraham's faith was credited to him as righteousness before he was circumcised, and that circumcision served as a sign and seal of the righteousness that came from faith. Faith in God's promises is what leads to righteousness.

In Genesis 17:7, God directly tells Abraham that He will establish an "everlasting covenant" between Himself and Abraham's descendants. It is eternal and ongoing for a thousand generations (Ps. 105:8–10). The Abrahamic Covenant lays the groundwork for later covenants in the Bible, such as the Mosaic Covenant (given to Moses), the Davidic Covenant (given to King David), and the New Covenant (associated with Jesus).

Overall, the Abrahamic Covenant is a pivotal aspect of the biblical narrative, highlighting God's faithfulness, His plan for humanity's redemption, and the special relationship between God and the people of Israel.

Fulfillment of God's Promise

After God made the promise to Abraham, He fulfilled it. He did all that He promised to Abraham even when Abraham messed up. (That is a story for another time.) God fulfilled His promises to Abraham in several significant ways. First, the promise of land was realized when Abraham's descendants entered and settled in the land of Canaan, which became their historical and spiritual homeland. The promise of numerous descendants was fulfilled through Abraham's son Isaac, whose lineage became the Israelites. Lastly, the promise of blessings to all nations is understood as being fulfilled through Jesus Christ, a descendant of Abraham, who brings spiritual salvation to humanity. Through these fulfillments, God's promises regarding land, descendants, and blessings are realized, profoundly shaping the spiritual history and beliefs of millions worldwide.

God made Abraham the father of the great nation of the Jews and now the adopted nations of the world. In the process of fulfilling the covenant, Abraham's descendants, the Jews (who are also called Israelites), took quite a journey.

The Journey of the Israelites

Egyptian Slavery

During a time of severe famine, the descendants of Abraham settled in Egypt, seeking food. Initially, they were welcomed and allowed to thrive, but as their numbers grew, the Egyptians perceived them as a threat. The Israelites, as they came to be known, were enslaved by the Egyptian pharaohs, forced into hard labor, and subjected to harsh conditions. The Book of Exodus recounts their plight and introduces Moses, who was born during this period. Despite the Pharaoh's decree to kill all newborn Hebrew boys, Moses's mother placed him in a basket on the Nile, where the Pharaoh's daughter found him. Raised in the

Egyptian court, Moses was later chosen by God to lead his people out of slavery.

Exodus and the Ten Plagues

The Israelites leaving Egypt, known as the Exodus, marks a pivotal moment in the history of the Israelites. Under God's guidance, Moses confronted Pharaoh, demanding the release of his people. When Pharaoh refused, God unleashed a series of ten devastating plagues upon Egypt. One of the coolest things is that throughout the Bible God reveals little clues that show who He really is and how He works. If you ask, He'll show you. Each plague targeted a specific Egyptian god, showing that the God of Israel was more powerful. These plagues included the Nile turning to blood, swarms of frogs, gnats, and flies, the death of livestock, boils, hail, locusts, darkness, and finally, the death of the firstborn. Each plague demonstrated God's supremacy over Pharaoh's authority. Overwhelmed by the final plague, Pharaoh relented and allowed the Israelites to leave.

Wilderness Wanderings

The departure from Egypt was swift, and the Israelites began their journey through the wilderness. This period was fraught with challenges and miraculous events. They crossed the Red Sea on dry ground as God parted the waters, and they escaped the pursuing Egyptian army, which was then drowned. God led the Israelites toward the Promised Land—the land He had promised to their ancestor Abraham. However, the journey was not easy. Despite many trials, including a period of slavery brought on by the disobedience of earlier leaders, God remained faithful to His Word, guiding His people toward their destiny.

The Promised Land and Israelite Doubts

When the Israelites finally arrived at the edge of the Promised Land, Moses sent twelve men to scout it out to see how difficult it would be to take possession of the land God had promised them. When the spies returned, ten of them were filled with fear and doubt, while only two, Joshua and Caleb, believed that God would help them conquer the land. Because of the majority's unbelief, the Israelites faced hunger and thirst in the desert, but God provided manna from Heaven and water from a rock. Even though they witnessed countless miracles, the Israelites grumbled and complained, longing for the slavery they had left behind. As a result of their constant negativity, they were condemned to wander the desert for forty years until that doubting generation passed away.

One key takeaway in the Israelites' journey to the Promised Land is how their unbelief, doubt, and constant grumbling made their path more difficult. At every point where they doubted God's promises or complained about their circumstances, their progress was delayed. Instead of trusting in God's plan, they allowed fear and negativity to take over, which prolonged their journey and kept them from experiencing the blessings God had prepared for them.

The scriptures show a clear connection between their negative attitudes and the obstacles they faced. When the Israelites doubted they could conquer the Promised Land despite God's assurances, they were condemned to wander the desert for forty years. Their grumbling about food, water, and the hardships they encountered demonstrated a lack of faith in God's provision, resulting in harsher conditions and further delays. This story serves as a reminder that trust and faith in God's promises are crucial to experiencing His blessings, while doubt and negativity only hinder our progress.

So, pondering point, this gives you something to ponder the next time you want to grumble about your hardships or whatever else seems fun to grumble about.

The Ten Commandments and the New Covenant

At Mount Sinai, Moses received the Ten Commandments, a set of divine laws that would become the foundation of Israelite society. This moment marked the establishment of a new covenant between God and the Israelites, reinforcing their identity as God's chosen people. Despite their trials and grumbling, God remained steadfast in His commitment to the covenant He'd made with Abraham, promising to make his descendants a great nation.

The story of the Exodus and the wilderness wanderings underscores the themes of faith, perseverance, and divine faithfulness. God continued to guide and shape His people, despite the many obstacles they faced, proving that faith in His promises is essential, even when the journey is difficult.

Moses's Farewell Address

Moses's journey with the Israelites came to a close just before they entered the Promised Land. Due to an earlier act of disobedience, God did not permit Moses to enter Canaan. The incident occurred when the Israelites were encamped in the desert and faced a severe shortage of water. Complaining about their situation, they turned to Moses and Aaron, their leaders. God instructed Moses to speak to a rock to bring forth water for the people. However, in his frustration and anger, Moses struck the rock with his staff instead of speaking to it, as commanded. Although water gushed forth, demonstrating God's continued provision, Moses's action was seen as a failure to uphold God's holiness and commands. As a result, God decreed that neither Moses nor Aaron would lead the Israelites into the Promised Land. This incident served as a potent lesson about the importance of obedience, humility, and following God's instructions precisely.

As Moses neared the end of his life, he delivered his farewell address to the Israelites, which is recorded in Deuteronomy 28. Moses outlined the blessings and curses that would result from their obedience or disobedience to God's laws. He emphasized the covenant God had made with them, promising to bless them abundantly if they remained faithful and adhered to His commandments.

The blessings promised to the Israelites and to believers in Jesus, as detailed in Deuteronomy 28:1–14, include:

- Blessings in the City and in the Country: Prosperity in all aspects of life, whether in urban areas or rural settings

- Abundant Crops and Livestock: Fertility and productivity in agriculture and animal husbandry

- Fertility and Prosperity among the People: Growth and success within the community

- Provision of Food: Blessings in their daily sustenance and food provisions

- Success in Activities: General success and favor in all their endeavors

These blessings were seen as an extension of the Abrahamic Covenant, reaffirming the promise that God would be their God, protect them, and ensure their prosperity if they followed His will.

This is a covenant that God went into with the Israelites and now because of being adopted by God, this is a covenant for us. Remember that it is not a freebie. A covenant is a two-sided agreement. You do this and He will do that. Obedience was our side of the covenant, and all the rest is His side of the covenant.

In his farewell address, Moses also warned the Israelites of the dire consequences of disobedience. Deuteronomy 28:15–68 describes a series of curses that would befall the Israelites if they turned away from God, followed other gods, engaged in idolatry, or failed to keep His commandments. "Other gods" refer to anything in which people place their faith and trust instead of God, such as idols, wealth, power, or false deities:

- Suffering and Disease: The Israelites would face numerous illnesses and health issues, devastating their communities.

- Famine and Starvation: The land would fail to produce crops, leading to widespread hunger and starvation.

- Defeat and Exile: Enemies would conquer the Israelites, and they would be taken captive and exiled from their land.

- Economic Hardship: Poverty and economic ruin would plague the people, reversing any prosperity they'd once enjoyed.

- Social and Family Breakdown: Families would be torn apart, and social structures would disintegrate

Moses stressed that these calamities would effectively negate the blessings God desired to bestow upon them. It wasn't that God actively inflicted these curses, rather that turning away from God's commandments removed His hand of protection. When the Israelites chose their own strategies and ways instead of following God's guidance, they would become vulnerable to the world's dangers and challenges.

God's Faithfulness and Hope for Restoration

Despite the severe warnings, Moses assured the Israelites that there was always hope for restoration. If they repented and returned to God, they could experience reconciliation and the renewal of blessings. God's desire was always for His people to live in a covenant relationship with Him, enjoying His protection and blessings as long as the people remained faithful to His commandments.

Preparing for the Promised Land

Moses also prepared the Israelites for the next phase of their journey: the conquest of Canaan, the Promised Land. Knowing he wouldn't be allowed to enter the land himself, Moses appointed Joshua, his loyal assistant, as his successor. Joshua was tasked with leading the Israelites into Canaan and overseeing the conquest of the land that God had promised to their forefather Abraham.

Under Joshua's leadership, the Israelites approached the Jordan River, which they needed to cross to enter Canaan. God performed a miracle to facilitate their passage: He stopped the flow of the river, allowing the Israelites to cross on dry ground. This event marked the beginning of their military campaign to take possession of the Promised Land.

The first major challenge was the city of Jericho, which stood as a formidable fortress. Joshua, following God's specific instructions, led the Israelites in a unique strategy. For six days, they marched around the city once each day, with the Ark of the Covenant leading the procession. On the seventh day, they circled the city seven times. At the end of the seventh circuit, the priests blew their trumpets, and the Israelites shouted. By divine intervention, the walls of

Jericho collapsed, allowing the Israelites to capture the city. This victory demonstrated the power of obedience to God's plans and set the stage for further conquests.

Pondering Point: Do you require God's instructions to make perfect sense before you obey?

Conquest of the Promised Land

Over the following years, Joshua led the Israelites in a series of campaigns that gradually expanded their control over various regions of Canaan. Each victory was attributed to their obedience to God.

Interconnection of the Abrahamic Covenant and Mosaic Law

The Abrahamic Covenant and the Mosaic Law are interconnected in several significant ways. Circumcision, introduced in the Abrahamic Covenant, was reaffirmed in the Mosaic Law as a requirement for Abraham's descendants (Lev. 12:3). This practice indicated spiritual wealth, as it connected the Israelites to God's abundant provisions and protection. In the New Testament, or as we will talk about the New Covenant, the focus shifts to the circumcision of the heart, reflecting true spiritual richness in Christ. As Paul writes, "For in Christ Jesus neither circumcision nor uncircumcision has any value. The only thing that counts is faith expressing itself through love" (Gal. 5:6 NIV).

Extending the Blessing to All Nations

While the Abrahamic Covenant promised that all nations would be blessed through Abraham's seed, the Mosaic Law provided a practical framework for extending this blessing. It included specific instructions on how to treat foreigners and strangers who wished to join Israel and worship God. The Law emphasized that these outsiders were to be welcomed and treated fairly, with equal access to the religious life and covenant promises of Israel. Any foreigner who wanted to participate in the Passover had to be circumcised, symbolizing their full inclusion into the community (Ex. 12:48–49).

The Role of Obedience in Retaining the Blessings

The Mosaic Law detailed Israel's obligations to keep the covenant with God, tying obedience to these laws directly to receiving the blessings promised to Abraham and remaining in the land of Canaan (Deut. 4:1, 5:33). Failure to obey could result in losing these blessings.

Sacrificial System: Atonement and Purity

Additionally, the practice of offering sacrifices, which Abraham had followed, was codified in the Mosaic Law. This system of sacrifices was essential for ritual purity and the forgiveness of sins, ensuring that the Israelites could maintain the right relationship with God.

Living an Unshakable and Abundant Life

Understanding the Abrahamic Covenant and Mosaic Law is essential for grasping God's design for a life of unshakable faith and abundance. These covenants reveal the profound connection between obedience to God's commands and receiving His blessings—both material and spiritual. As believers, living in alignment with God's principles equips us to experience true wealth, which encompasses more than just financial prosperity. It includes peace, protection, spiritual growth, and the fulfillment of God's promises in every area of life.

Just as the Israelites were called to trust in God's plan, we too are called to live according to His will, ensuring that we remain in a place of blessing, protection, and divine favor.

CHAPTER 18

Application to Modern Believers

How This Applies to You

T he history of the Abrahamic Covenant and the Mosaic Law reveals what God has given us as believers today. It applies to all of us now, regardless of our background. These foundational covenants hold spiritual and practical significance, which shape our faith and our identities as heirs of God's promises.

The Foundation of all Believers

The Apostle Paul, in his letter to the Galatians, explains this connection beautifully. He writes in Ephesians 3:26–29:

> "For as many of you as were baptized into Christ have put on Christ. There is neither Jew nor Greek, there is neither slave nor free, there is neither male nor female; for you are all one in Christ Jesus. And if you are Christ's, then you are Abraham's seed, and heirs according to the promise."

Through faith in Jesus Christ, we become part of Abraham's family, regardless of our nationality, social status, or gender. This unity transcends all earthly divisions, making us part of something much greater—God's family.

Our side of the two-sided agreement with God, the New Covenant, is to believe God.

Through Christ, the fullness of God's promises—of protection, provision, an everlasting kingdom, and a direct, personal relationship with Him—is ours. By being baptized into Christ, we put on Christ and become part of His body, the Church. We inherit all the promises, blessings, and responsibilities of God's covenants, fully united in His plan for humanity. These covenants form the foundation of our identity and inheritance as God's people, making us joint heirs with Christ and partakers of all that God has promised to His people throughout history.

The New Covenant through Jesus

The New Covenant is the divine agreement established by God through the life, death, and resurrection of Jesus Christ. It fulfilled and completed the Mosaic Covenant made with Israel and is based on God's grace rather than human works or the ability to perfectly uphold the Law. The Covenant depends entirely on Christ's atoning sacrifice. Through faith in Christ, believers receive forgiveness of sins and are declared righteous before God.

The Holy Spirit indwells believers, writing God's Law on their hearts, which enables them to obey God from within, creating intimacy with Him. This direct relationship allows believers to access God through prayer and the Spirit, with Christ serving as the full revelation of God. In addition, the New Covenant establishes a new community of believers united by faith, removing barriers and ushering in the beginning of the messianic kingdom. This covenant transforms knowledge of God from an intellectual understanding to an experiential relationship. It deals with sin and fulfills God's promises to humanity, making intimacy with Him accessible to all by grace through faith in Jesus Christ.

The Superiority of the New Covenant

The New Covenant is often described as superior to the Mosaic Covenant, elaborating on its excellence, showing that the New Covenant is built on better promises and is mediated by Jesus Christ (Heb. 8:6–13). Unlike the old covenant, which was broken by Israel's unfaithfulness, this New Covenant is established by God Himself and written in the hearts and minds of believers. God promises forgiveness and intimacy, where all will know Him, from the least to the greatest. By making the first covenant obsolete, the New Covenant offers better hope and direct access to God.

Jesus: The High Priest of the New Covenant

Jesus's role as the ultimate High Priest is central to the New Covenant. His priesthood, established by a divine oath, differs from the Levitical priesthood, which was hereditary and temporary. Jesus's priesthood, in the order of Melchizedek, is eternal. Unlike the high priests of the Old Testament, who offered sacrifices for sins once a year, Jesus offered Himself as the final and perfect sacrifice. The tearing of the temple veil at His crucifixion signified the removal of the barrier between humanity and God, granting believers direct access to His presence. Jesus's priesthood is eternal, and His sacrifice was once for all (Heb. 9). As believers, we no longer need human mediators; instead, we can approach God confidently through Jesus.

Believers as Priests in the New Covenant

Because of Jesus's sacrifice, Christians are a chosen race and a royal priesthood (1 Pet. 2:9) with the responsibility to offer spiritual sacrifices, such as praise, worship, and a life surrendered to God. Believers now have direct access to God, the privilege of interceding for others, and the duty to proclaim the gospel. Jesus, as the mediator of the New Covenant, ensures that believers receive the promised eternal inheritance, liberating them from sin and granting them a permanent relationship with God.

Jesus Fulfills the Law

Jesus didn't come to abolish the Law but to fulfill it. He lived in perfect obedience to the Law and became the ultimate fulfillment of its demands. The core of the Law, as Jesus taught, is love—love for God and love for one's neighbor. The greatest commandments emphasize that love is the foundation of all God's instructions. By genuinely loving others, believers fulfill the moral requirements of the Law. Both Jesus and Paul confirmed that love encapsulates the entire Law, making it the guiding principle for the Christian life.

The Core Elements of the New Covenant

The New Covenant brings a shift in the relationship between God and humanity, focusing on forgiveness, grace, and intimacy. Central to this covenant is the forgiveness of sins through Jesus' sacrifice. It also promises a transformed heart and spirit, where believers receive a new heart from God and the indwelling of the Holy Spirit. The New Covenant ensures a direct relationship with God through Christ and offers eternal life to those who believe. Cleansing and atonement are provided through the blood of Jesus, and this covenant is universal, erasing distinctions between Jew and Gentile.

The Greatest Commandments: Love for God and Neighbor

Jesus emphasized that the entire Law and the prophets are fulfilled by two commandments: love for God and love for one's neighbor. Loving God with all one's heart, soul, and mind is the greatest commandment, calling for a complete devotion to God. The second greatest commandment, to love one's neighbor as oneself, flows naturally from the first. Jesus taught that genuine love for God must manifest in love for others.

By living according to these two commandments, believers fulfill the entire Law and reflect the heart of the New Covenant. Our obedience is not out of obligation but out of devotion, reflecting the essence of the Law in our lives. As believers, when we align with God's will and seek to honor Him through our actions, we fulfill the Law's intention.

Joint Heirs with Jesus

The New Covenant makes believers joint heirs with Jesus, inheriting eternal life, sharing in Christ's glory (Rom. 8:17) and the promises made to Abraham (Gal. 3:29). Through spiritual unity with Christ, believers share in His mission and blessings.

Grace in the New Covenant: God's Unmerited Favor

Grace in the New Covenant represents God's unmerited favor toward humanity, freely given through Jesus Christ. Unlike the Old Covenant, which was based on obedience to the Law, the New Covenant is grounded in grace, meaning that salvation and righteousness are not earned through human effort but are gifts from God.

The intent of grace is to reveal God's unconditional love and mercy, making forgiveness and reconciliation with Him available to all who believe in Jesus, empowering believers to live transformed lives, not by their own strength but through the indwelling of the Holy Spirit. Grace also removes the burden of striving to meet the Law's demands, allowing believers to rest in the completed work of Christ. It highlights that God's relationship with His people is built on love, not performance, and His grace continues to guide and sustain believers in their journey of faith.

The Importance of Obedience and the Covering of Grace

Obedience to God's commands and statutes remains vital in the New Covenant, as it reflects our love for Him and our desire to live according to His will. Jesus affirmed that love for God and neighbor fulfills the Law, and true obedience stems from a heart devoted to Him. While obedience is essential, it is impossible for humans to perfectly keep God's laws due to our sinful nature. This is where grace comes in—when we fail, God's grace through Christ covers our shortcomings, offering forgiveness and restoration. However, grace does not diminish the importance of obedience; instead, it empowers us to strive for holiness while trusting that God's grace will carry us when we stumble. Grace teaches us that while we should seek to obey, our salvation and relationship with God are not based on our flawless performance but on His love and mercy. Thus, grace complements obedience, ensuring that we can continue to pursue God's will without fear of condemnation when we fall short.

CHAPTER 19

Receiving God's Blessings

How do we truly receive God's blessings now as joint heirs with Jesus? Throughout the covenants, God repeatedly assures us that He will bless us. In the Abrahamic Covenant, an eternal covenant, God promises, "I will bless you and make your name great so that you will be a blessing. I will bless those who bless you, and he who dishonors you I will curse, and in you, all the families of the earth shall be blessed" (Gen. 12:3). This promise indicates that God will bless us abundantly so that we can, in turn, bless others. He assures us of making our name great, blessing those who bless us, and dishonoring those who dishonor us. Moreover, through us, all families of the earth will be blessed.

The Mosaic Covenant also includes promises of blessings:

> Blessings in the city and in the country; blessings of abundant crops and livestock; blessings of fertility and prosperity among the people; blessings in their basket and kneading bowl (i.e., in their food provisions); blessings in their coming in and going out (i.e., in all their activities). (Deut. 28:1–14)

As we've seen, to participate in the blessings of the New Covenant, we are called to love God and others. Do you believe you are participating in His blessings? Why or why not?

Several biblical principles lead to receiving God's blessings:

1. Believing in Jesus Christ as the Son of God and accepting Him as Lord and Savior is essential.

2. Genuine repentance for one's sins, recognizing, confessing, turning away from sinful behavior, and aligning our lives with God's will is vital.

3. Love and compassion, demonstrating compassion, forgiveness, and kindness, are central to the New Testament teachings.

4. Obedience to God's Word, living according to His commandments and teachings, aligning ourselves with His will and purpose pleases God.

5. Communication with God through prayer, expressing our dependence on Him and our desire to follow His guidance, strengthens our relationship with Him and aligns our hearts with His will.

6. Acts of charity, helping those in need and showing love through service, express our faith.

7. Thanking God for His blessings and provisions fosters a heart of contentment and appreciation, making us more aware of His continuous provision.

8. Trusting in God's plan and being patient, believing that God has a purpose for us and that His timing is perfect, we grow spiritually and ultimately receive His blessings.

9. Showing reverence and worshipping God as the ultimate authority and creator is essential, connecting us with God and reminding us of His greatness and our dependence on Him.

10. Obeying the moral and ethical guidelines of the Ten Commandments aligns us with God's will.

11. Engaging in the study and understanding of the Bible helps us grow in our knowledge of God and His plans for us.

Some of God's blessings manifest in spiritual growth and a closer relationship with Him, while other blessings are material prosperity. The New Testament encourages seeking God's Kingdom first, trusting that He will provide for our needs (Matt. 6:33). The focus should be on spiritual well-being and aligning our lives with God's will rather than seeking material gain as the primary goal. "We are God's handiwork, created in Christ Jesus to do good works, which

God prepared in advance for us to do" (Eph. 2:10). God will fulfill His work in us and provide what we need if we are willing to follow His plan.

As we walk closely with God, surrendering our will to His, He desires to give us a wonderful, abundant life. We should not seek this life for its own sake but accept His gifts as He lavishes blessings upon us. We must walk expecting the grand, abundant life from the Lord, living with gratitude and serving others. By lovingly following God's commandments, we understand that they are for our good, not to limit us. God's great abundance arrives in many ways, and we should watch for it with gratitude.

In times of recovery from disasters, we might overlook God's blessings if we focus only on our expectations. When we open our eyes to all the ways He blesses us, we become amazed at His grand abundance.

CHAPTER 20

God's Love and Our Participation

God's love for us is deep and profound, much like the love a parent has for their children. As a parent, you know the extent of your love for your kids, which is often beyond their comprehension. Similarly, God's love for us, His children, surpasses our understanding.

In His immense love, God has granted us a share in all the blessings He has received from the Father. These blessings are abundant and varied, so numerous that listing them all here would be impossible. However, they are available to us, ready for us to embrace.

Consider how, as a parent, you hope your adult children will appreciate and benefit from the inheritance and blessings of your family. They have the choice to either embrace and walk in these blessings or to distance themselves and miss out on the family's good inheritance.

In the same way, we have a choice to make. If we choose to align ourselves with Jesus and embrace His inheritance, we gain access to all the blessings He offers. This requires us to follow His will and live according to His teachings. By doing so, we can fully experience the richness of the inheritance God has prepared for us.

The Parable of the Lost Son

The Parable of the Lost Son illustrates this point beautifully:

> There was a man who had two sons. The younger one said to his father, "Father, give me my share of the estate." So, he divided his property between them. Not long after that, the younger son got together all he had, set off for a distant country, and there squandered his wealth in wild living. After he had spent everything, there was a severe famine in that whole country, and he began to be in need. So, he went and hired himself out to a citizen of that

country, who sent him to his fields to feed pigs. He longed to fill his stomach with the pods that the pigs were eating, but no one gave him anything. When he came to his senses, he said, "How many of my father's hired servants have food to spare, and here I am starving to death! I will set out and go back to my father and say to him: 'Father, I have sinned against Heaven and against you. I am no longer worthy to be called your son; make me like one of your hired servants.'" So, he got up and went to his father.

But while he was still a long way off, his father saw him and was filled with compassion for him; he ran to his son, threw his arms around him, and kissed him. The son said to him, "Father, I have sinned against Heaven and against you. I am no longer worthy to be called your son."

But the father said to his servants, "Quick! Bring the best robe and put it on him. Put a ring on his finger and sandals on his feet. Bring the fattened calf and kill it. Let's have a feast and celebrate. For this son of mine was dead and is alive again; he was lost and is found." So, they began to celebrate.

Meanwhile, the older son was in the field. When he came near the house, he heard music and dancing. So, he called one of the servants and asked him what was going on. "Your brother has come," he replied, "and your father has killed the fattened calf because he has him back safe and sound."

The older brother became angry and refused to go in. So, his father went out and pleaded with him. But he answered his father, "Look! All these years I've been slaving for you and never disobeyed your orders. Yet you never gave me even a young goat so I could celebrate with my friends. But when this son of yours who has squandered your property with prostitutes comes home, you kill the fattened calf for him!"

"My son," the father said, "you are always with me, and everything I have is yours. But we had to celebrate and be glad because this brother of yours was dead and is alive again; he was lost and is found" (Luke 15:11–32).

The Message: Walking in Faith

This powerfully illustrates how God, our loving Father, sees and treats us as His precious children. Some of us may run from His guidance, seeking our own path, while others stay close, choosing to obey and follow Him under His care. Yet, no matter our choices, God's heart remains unchanging. Like the father in the story of the prodigal son, He is always ready to welcome us back with open arms, showering us with love, acceptance, and restoration when we return. Even more incredible is the immense freedom and abundance available to those who remain under His protection. Too often, we miss the fullness of His blessings simply because we don't reach out in faith and accept them.

The Parable of the Prodigal Son highlights that no matter how far we stray or how much we squander, God delights when we come back to Him. He doesn't hold back; His love is unconditional. When the father said to the older son, "You are always with me, and all I have is yours," he revealed a deeper truth—everything had already been given, yet the son didn't walk in it. The older son didn't realize that the celebration, the inheritance, and the blessings were already his. Similarly, we often fail to walk in the fullness of what God has already provided, waiting for what's already ours. We don't have to wait for God to hand us the blessings—He already has. We need to step into the inheritance He's given us.

God has given us everything through His grace and mercy, just as He gave to the Jews through the Mosaic Covenant and even more through Jesus Christ. Like the older son, we have a choice. We can either walk in the gifts and blessings prepared for us, or we can miss out, wondering why life doesn't align with what we expected as children of the King. Many believers focus only on what they see directly before them, lacking faith in what God has already set in motion. It's time to open our eyes and recognize that there is so much more to this Christian life than we realize. The abundance and freedom of living in God's grace are available to us, but we must choose to embrace it with faith, gratitude, and a willingness to participate in the grand abundance of His promises.

Pondering Point: Are you either the younger son or the older son? Have you left your father, or have you lived without understanding the real blessings of living with your father? If so, what do you intend to do about it?

God's Best

As adopted heirs of the never-ending Abrahamic Covenant now under the New Covenant, we participate in God's favor and blessings. He wants to give us blessings in the city, abundant crops, fertility and prosperity, and blessings in our activities. He wants to bless us with abundance. This is the standard; He desperately wants to bless us. He also has a will and desire for greatness for each of us that is perfectly aligned with His great master plan. Sometimes, He uses giving and takes what we see as our blessings for His purposes, advancing His will. If we love Him, our desire should align with His. If He is our God and we know He loves us, our desire should be to follow His will, whatever the consequences. When we follow His will, whether it seems easy or hard, it will ALWAYS end in the greatest gifts for us and our families. This is only because He loves us more than we love ourselves. "God's best and none better." We must trust that no matter what it looks like today, the plan God has for us is great.

Blessed to Be a Blessing

The Bible repeatedly emphasizes that God desires to bless His people, not only for their benefit but so they can be a blessing to others. In Genesis 12:2–3, God speaks to Abraham, saying, "I will make you into a great nation, and I will bless you; I will make your name great, and you will be a blessing. I will bless those who bless you, and whoever curses you I will curse; and all peoples on earth will be blessed through you." This foundational promise reveals God's intention not just to prosper Abraham and his descendants but to use them as a channel through which His blessings flow to the entire world. God's blessings are not meant to stop with us—they are intended to reach others, expanding His goodness and love through acts of kindness, generosity, and service. When we receive God's blessings, whether spiritual, material, or relational, we are entrusted with a responsibility to extend those blessings to the world around us.

The New Testament continues this theme, particularly in 2 Corinthians 9:8–11, where Paul writes, "And God is able to bless you abundantly, so that in all things at all times, having all that you need, you will abound in every good work... You will be enriched in every way so that you can be generous on every occasion, and through us, your generosity will result in thanksgiving to God." This passage shows that God's provision is not only about fulfilling our personal needs but also enabling us to bless others. As we give, we reflect God's character and reveal His love to the world. Our generosity, made possible by God's blessings, leads others to thank and praise Him. When we understand that God's blessings are given to us for the purpose of blessing others, we align ourselves with His heart and His mission to spread His love and goodness throughout the earth.

This is truly the foundational message of understanding God's blessings: we are blessed to be a blessing to others. As we walk deeper in faith, we'll uncover more about how God blesses us and how we are called to participate in His promises. While some may mistakenly view this as a selfish approach—always seeking God's blessings and appearing to have a "give me" mindset—this perspective misses the heart of God entirely. Nowhere in scripture do we find a "give me" attitude encouraged. In fact, Acts 20:35 reminds us, "It is more blessed to give than to receive." The core of God's heart is to bless others, and we are a part of that "others" He longs to bless. We are both recipients and conduits of His blessings, meant to reflect His love and generosity to the world.

God desires to bless us immensely as we walk in His covenant, and a central part of the New Covenant is loving others. When we love, we are participating in God's mission to bless. This includes financial and/or material blessings but goes far beyond this. It includes sharing peace, joy, love, and, most importantly, the Kingdom of God. Romans 14:17 tells us, "For the Kingdom of God is not a matter of eating and drinking, but of righteousness, peace and joy in the Holy Spirit." When we extend these spiritual blessings to others—offering them God's love, kindness, and joy—we are sharing the essence of His kingdom. As we bless others in these ways, we become living expressions of God's love on earth, fulfilling His desire for us to be vessels of His abundant grace. The more we give of ourselves from the blessings that God has given us the more we align with God's heart and His purpose for our lives.

Obedience and Blessings

We know that God has given us an inheritance of great blessings; however, in his farewell address, Moses made it clear that the blessings came with a requirement of obedience. People often ask if God is a loving God. Why would He not just bless His children, obedience or not? Don't we live in the New Testament grace time frame anyway? Let's investigate this.

Would you give your disobedient children anything they wanted? If you are a good parent, the answer is *no*. You love that child too much to give them things that won't lead them to the ultimate reward you want them to have. The same is true with our heavenly Father. He wants all of us to participate in a loving relationship with Him for eternity in Heaven. He also wants us to be in Heaven with Him with all the rewards He intended to give us all along. He will give and take in such a way that leads us to His perfect will for our lives. This is why He gives us His laws to follow. For example, He says not to worship other gods. If we worship other gods and not the one true God, we will be left without the greatest blessing of all—spending eternity with Him in Heaven. God knows if you worship other gods, you won't enter Heaven. He wants to bless us abundantly in the earthly realm as well as the heavenly realm. The reality is that the obedience He requires is part of the blessings.

Let's look at an easy one: do not commit adultery. God knows that a long-term loving relationship with a spouse built on trust is one of the most fulfilling earthly relationships we can have. If we screw that up by having an affair, we could miss out on one of the greatest blessings He gives here on earth. If we follow His commandments, He will, in turn, give us more blessings. This is not restrictive but a part of our blessings.

Yes, we do live in a grace-filled world now in the New Testament due to Jesus's fulfillment of the Law. "Do not think that I have come to abolish the Law or the Prophets; I have not come to abolish them but to fulfill them" (Matt. 5:17).

This does not take away the need to follow the commandments but removes the death penalty for messing up.

Obedience and Participation

So, to participate in the blessings of God our Father, we must follow His commandments. When we follow His commandments, we will avoid the curses that come with disobedience and stay on track with His plan for our life, which is dripping with blessings He desperately wants us to have. Timing is everything. Because God is so loving, He knows exactly when the best timing would be for us to receive His blessings. He knows what we must learn and when, what His specific will is for our lives and what we need to fulfill His will. If our love for God is simply trusting that God's best is best for us and there is nothing better, we trust that as we follow His commandments, He is giving us everything we need when we need it, expecting His best. Sometimes, that is scarcity, and sometimes, it is great abundance. We must trust that God's will is perfect and that His love for us will provide exactly what we need when we need it.

In conclusion, understanding how to live an unshakable and abundant life is crucial for fully embracing the blessings God has prepared for us through His covenants. By aligning ourselves with God's true character, shedding light on misconceptions, and recognizing the inheritance we have as joint heirs with Christ, we unlock the promises and covenant blessings that God has graciously extended. Our journey is one of faith, obedience, and trust—knowing that God's will is perfect and that His blessings, both spiritual and material, flow from a relationship grounded in love and obedience. As we walk in faith and follow His commandments, we can live an abundant, unshakable life filled with His covenant blessings, trusting in His perfect plan for our lives.

The most incredible part of this journey is the realization that through Jesus, we have been adopted into His sonship and invited into the covenants of God's blessings. Wow. Think about that for a moment—God, in His love, is saying, "Let Me take care of you. Follow Me, and I will provide." What an indescribable blessing to be invited into His family to receive the honor and blessings He longs to pour on us! Are you willing to believe and accept that?

Have you asked God about this? Because yes—you, specifically you—are the one He is talking to. You are invited into the blessings of the covenants He made with His people. So, the question is: Are you going to walk in those blessings, trusting in His promises, or will you continue to trust in the world's system and the wisdom of the so-called greatest minds the world has to offer? The real question is, who will lead you—God, with His perfect plan for your finances and life, or the world? The choice is yours. The invitation is on the table—will you accept it?

CHAPTER 21

The Fall and Redemption of Humanity: A Story of Dominion

Creation and Dominion

When God created Adam, He granted him dominion over the earth (Gen. 1:28). As stated in Genesis 1:28: "God blessed them and said to them, 'Be fruitful and increase in number; fill the earth and subdue it. Rule over the fish in the sea and the birds in the sky and over every living creature that moves on the ground.'" This dominion was a gift from God, symbolizing His intention for humanity to govern and steward His creation. God didn't retain control over the earth for Himself or give just a portion of dominion to Adam; He gave complete control to Adam out of complete love and trust in His creation.

In the Garden of Eden stood two significant trees: the Tree of Life and the Tree of the Knowledge of Good and Evil. The Tree of Life provided ongoing life to Adam and Eve in their perfect state, symbolizing God's intention for humanity to live forever in His presence and blessing. The Tree of the Knowledge of Good and Evil represented moral autonomy—making choices independently from God's will. This setup ensured that God always had a real relationship with His creation, allowing them to choose either to remain dependent on Him or to walk away and live independently. This choice remains today, although now it comes from the other side of Adam and Eve's decision to give the dominion of the earth, which God gave them, to the enemy.

The Fall

God commanded Adam and Eve to eat freely from the Tree of Life, but He forbade them from eating from the Tree of the Knowledge of Good and Evil, warning them that doing so would lead to death (Gen. 2:16–17). Despite this command, the serpent (identified as the Devil) tempted Eve to eat the forbidden fruit by promising her that she would become like God, knowing good and evil (Gen. 3:1–5). Eve ate the fruit and gave some to Adam, who also ate it.

This act of disobedience against God's command brought sin and death into the world, severing humanity's close relationship with God. The immediate consequence was a loss of innocence, the realization of their nakedness, and the death of their connected spirit to God, prompting Adam and Eve to hide from God. When confronted, they confessed their sin, but the damage was done. God pronounced a curse on the serpent, the man, and the woman (Gen. 3:14–19) and expelled them from the Garden of Eden to prevent them from eating from the Tree of Life and condemning them to live forever in their fallen state (Gen. 3:22–24).

Consequences of the Fall

The curse affected all of creation. The ground was cursed, causing Adam to toil painfully for food. The harmonious relationship between humanity and creation was disrupted, and the world fell under the power of sin and death (Rom. 5:12–13 explains).

Through Adam's disobedience, the dominion over the earth, which was originally bestowed upon him as a gift from God and meant to be shared with all mankind, was handed over to the Devil. In that fateful moment, Adam relinquished the authority that had been fully given to him by God. While Adam may not have fully grasped the far-reaching consequences of his disobedience, the result was catastrophic. The world became a battleground between the will of God and the influence of the Devil. Yet, despite the Devil's newly gained dominion, God's unwavering love for humanity remained. In His mercy, God set in motion a plan of redemption, offering a way for mankind to be restored and for dominion to be reclaimed through His Son, Jesus Christ.

The Devil would do everything in his power to challenge and thwart the unfolding of this divine strategy, yet God would ultimately prevail. He would have to communicate His plan to people living under the Devil's dominion, guiding them to write it down, eventually forming the Bible—a direct line of communication between God and His beloved creation. The Bible would be His Word, one of the key ways He speaks to His people, reminding them that despite the Devil's schemes, His love for humanity never wavered.

God's love was so relentless that He would stop at nothing to save His children from the destruction the Devil had planned for them. Throughout history, He revealed pieces of His plan to various authors, ensuring that more than three hundred prophecies would foretell the coming of a Redeemer, and when Jesus fulfilled every single one, it would be undeniable proof of God's true plan for salvation.

Yet, there was a critical catch: God had to keep this plan hidden from the Devil. The Devil, consumed by hatred and believing he had defeated God, would unwittingly play into the plan by killing God's Son. The death of Jesus would fulfill the Law and provide the ultimate atonement for the sins that had entrapped humanity. If the Devil had known God's full plan, he would have tried to sabotage it, but God, in His infinite wisdom, relied on the Devil's own evil nature to bring the plan to fruition.

In the aftermath of Jesus's death and resurrection, God revealed the fullness of His plan to the world. Through more authors, He unfolded how each prophecy was fulfilled in Jesus, showing how His sacrifice was the cornerstone of redemption. The New Testament confirmed what was hidden in the Old Testament, revealing that Jesus was, indeed, the promised Savior.

Despite the mess the Devil caused, God's love for His creation was too powerful to be undone. He would do whatever it took to provide a way back for all His people, but because God is just, He would not force anyone to accept this master plan of salvation. Instead, He would offer it freely to all who see the truth, believe, and embrace His love. In this, God's character remains unshakable, and His redemption is available to all who choose it.

The Promise of Redemption

In Genesis 3:15, God said a descendant of the woman would crush the serpent's head, pointing to the ultimate defeat of the Devil Jesus Christ would come to redeem humanity from sin and restore God's rule. Throughout the

Old Testament, God revealed His plan through covenants and prophecies. This is where the covenant with Abraham comes in, promising that through his offspring, all the nations of the world would be blessed (Gen. 12:3). Isaiah 9:6–7 foretold the coming of a Messiah: "For to us a child is born, to us a son is given, and the government will be on his shoulders. And he will be called Wonderful Counselor, Mighty God, Everlasting Father, Prince of Peace. Of the greatness of his government and peace, there will be no end."

The Present and Future Dominion

According to the Bible, the dominion of the world is currently contested between God and the Devil. While Jesus has ultimate authority, the Devil still exerts influence over the fallen world. The Bible calls Satan the "god of this world" (2 Cor. 4:4) and "prince of the power of the air" (Eph. 2:2). Believers live in tension between these two powers, belonging to God's Kingdom but residing in a world influenced by the Devil. In John 18:36, Jesus stated, "My kingdom is not of this world," indicating that His kingdom operates in a spiritual sense rather than through earthly political authority. Believers are called to live by faith, trusting in God's promises and walking in His ways despite the challenges they face in this fallen world.

One day, Jesus will return and completely defeat Satan. Revelation 11:15 proclaims, "The kingdom of the world has become the kingdom of our Lord and of his Christ, and he will reign for ever and ever." The saints will then rule with Christ in a restored world under God's authority for eternity (Rev. 20–22).

The story of humanity's fall and redemption is a testament to God's unwavering love and faithfulness. Despite Adam and Eve's disobedience and the resulting dominion of the Devil, God had a plan to restore His creation. Through Jesus Christ, the rightful dominion is reclaimed, and believers are invited to participate in His kingdom. This story encourages us to trust in God's promises, walk in faith, and spread the message of His redeeming love to the world.

Real Story Time

In the beginning, the earth was filled with peace, beauty, and purpose. God had given dominion—authority, control, stewardship, and responsibility—over the whole world to Adam, His beloved creation, intending for humanity to steward it with care and love. But in a moment of disobedience, Adam gave away that authority to the Devil. The Devil got Adam to give him dominion by deceiving Eve and tempting both her and Adam to disobey God's command. When they ate the forbidden fruit, they rebelled against God, and through that act of disobedience, they unknowingly handed over their God-given authority to the Devil, allowing him to take control over the earth.

Adam didn't realize the weight of his decision, but with it, sin and death entered the world, and the earth became a battleground. The Devil, filled with hatred for God, knew that his move would separate God from His greatest love, His people. This was why the Devil did it, aiming to hurt God by separating Him from those He cherished most. Despite the chaos, God's love for humanity never wavered. God's greatest desire and love was to be with His people, and the Devil sought to exploit this, knowing it would cause pain to God. But God, in His unfailing love for His people, would not abandon His creation to destruction.

Instead, God, motivated by His deep love for humanity, put together a plan to win back His beloved people. He quietly set in motion the most intricate and brilliant plan ever conceived—a plan of redemption that would free mankind from the Devil's grip and restore the broken relationship between God and His cherished creation.

God knew that His plan would need to be hidden from the Devil, so He began revealing pieces of it to chosen men and women throughout history. These revelations were written down, and over time, they became the Bible. In it, God planted more than three hundred prophecies, each one a clue to the coming of the Savior, but the full picture was shrouded in mystery. If the Devil knew what was coming, he would surely try to destroy it. But God, in His wisdom, allowed the Devil to believe he was winning.

As the world groaned under the weight of sin, God's love persisted. After the fall of Adam, humanity began to experience the consequences of sin—separation from God, physical death, and a corrupted world. Yet, God, in His mercy, provided a way for people to temporarily atone for their sins through animal sacrifices while waiting for God's master plan to come together. This system began after the first sin in the Garden of Eden, when God made garments of animal skins to cover Adam and Eve's shame, signifying the first shedding of blood to cover sin. This set the precedent that life must be sacrificed to atone for the wrongdoing of humanity.

As the years passed, God formalized the system of sacrifices in the law He gave to Moses. The blood of animals, though imperfect, temporarily covered the sins of His people. These sacrifices pointed back to the first death in Eden, and year after year, animals were offered as a payment for sin. This was the only way to maintain a relationship with God, who is perfect and cannot fellowship with sin. The Israelites, often struggling to grasp the full extent of God's plan, relied on these offerings to restore their connection with Him. However, the sacrifices could never fully remove sin, and the burden of it continued to weigh on the world.

Then, at the perfect moment, God sent His Son, Jesus, into the world. Jesus lived a sinless life, but the Devil, blinded by his own hatred, didn't see the plan unfolding before his eyes. All he saw was a chance to kill the Son of God, to claim victory over his greatest enemy. The Devil whispered into the hearts of men, stirring them to betray, arrest, and crucify Jesus. And on that dark day, when Jesus breathed His last breath on the cross, the Devil rejoiced, believing he had finally defeated God.

But what the Devil didn't realize was that he had played right into God's hands. The death of Jesus wasn't a defeat—it was the fulfillment of every prophecy, the breaking of every chain. In that moment, Jesus bore the sin of the world, fulfilling the law and providing a way for mankind to be restored to God. His sacrifice was the final and perfect atonement, replacing the old system of animal sacrifices, and His resurrection three days later was the ultimate victory, a declaration that death and sin no longer had the final say.

In the years that followed, God revealed the fullness of His plan through more writers, and the New Testament unveiled the hidden prophecies that had pointed to Jesus all along. Piece by piece, the story came together, showing the world that Jesus was the Redeemer, the one sent to rescue them from the Devil's dominion.

The Devil, realizing too late what had happened, was furious. But there was nothing he could do to undo what God had accomplished. The door to salvation had been opened, and anyone who believed in Jesus could walk through it, escaping the Devil's hold forever.

Yet, in His perfect justice, God did not force anyone to accept this salvation. It was a gift offered freely to all who would believe. Those who recognized the truth and embraced God's love would find redemption, peace, and eternal life. The choice was theirs.

But now, knowing he had been defeated, the Devil shifted his strategy. He could no longer stop God's plan, but he could work to deceive as many of God's creations as possible, convincing them that the victory hadn't really been won. His new mission was to hide the blessings that came with God's Kingdom, to blind people to the truth, and to keep them from entering into the life and freedom God offered.

The Devil became a master of lies, manipulating people's perceptions of love, joy, peace, and purpose. He twisted God's gifts, creating false versions to distract and deceive. He whispered lies into hearts, telling people that they could find contentment in power, wealth, or pleasure rather than in God's presence. He now lures people into bitterness, unforgiveness, and anger, knowing that these things will block them from experiencing God's peace.

He now takes something as pure as love between a man and a woman and distorts it into lust and self-serving relationships, convincing people that fleeting passion could fill the void only God's love could truly satisfy. The Devil crafts imitations of joy—promising happiness through materialism or temporary thrills—while hiding the deep, unshakable joy that comes from a life in God's Kingdom.

He even attacks the peace God offers. Instead of trusting in God's plan, the Devil encourages people to seek peace through control, drugs, or false spirituality. He tempts them with shortcuts to achieve what only God could provide. The Devil has no original ideas, only perversions of what God has made good.

Through it all, the Devil's greatest lie is that there is a better way—his way—though it always leads to destruction. He manipulates hearts, offering the illusion of success while hiding the real blessings of walking in God's truth.

Yet, despite the Devil's efforts, God's love remains unwavering. He continues to reach out to His children, offering them the true gifts of His kingdom: love that is unconditional, peace that surpasses understanding, joy that overflows from His presence, and purpose that brings eternal meaning. God's plan is to rescue as many as possible, and the Devil's strategy is to stop them one by one—through deception, manipulation, and counterfeit promises.

The Devil knows his time is short, and his hatred for God fuels his relentless pursuit to lead people astray. But God's light continues to shine through, offering salvation, healing, and redemption to all who believe and walk into His kingdom. The battle rages on, but the victory is already won. God's people, armed with His truth and walking in His blessings, have everything they need to stand firm and live in the freedom He provides.

The rest of the story is that this will only play out for a little longer. We know that God has already won the battle with the Devil. Someday soon, Jesus will return. Now seated at the right hand of God in Heaven, He will come back to collect all who believe in Him and to send the Devil off to his eternal punishment. Sadly, all those whom the Devil has convinced to reject Jesus's gift of salvation will join him in eternal separation from God's love, joy, and peace.

But for those who have accepted Jesus, He will take them up to receive their eternal reward—life with Him forever in Heaven. The Devil knows this is set in stone, and there is nothing he can do to stop it. Jesus, in His great love and patience, is holding off His return, giving as many people as possible the chance to accept His gift of salvation. He is waiting for more to choose Him, to walk away from the Devil's fake gifts, and to embrace the real life He offers.

Jesus won't force anyone to accept this gift, but He will continue to offer it to everyone, hoping that all will come to salvation, though some may still refuse. His love even extends to those who reject Him, so He delays His return, holding off as long as possible in His eternal plan. In the meantime, our role as believers is to walk in God's peace, joy, and love, sharing His kingdom with others. We are called to offer His gift of salvation to everyone we can. Yet, as we live in a world where the Devil still holds dominion, we must keep the full armor of God on so we are not deceived or manipulated away from His kingdom. We must keep our eyes fixed on our eternal reward, knowing that one day soon, we will be with Him forever.

CHAPTER 22

Dealing with Spiritual Conflict as Believers

The spiritual conflict between God's Kingdom and the Devil's influence is an ongoing battle that believers face as we await the full establishment of God's rule on earth. Here are key ways the Bible teaches us to deal with spiritual conflict:

The Devil is a Defeated Foe

Although the Devil continues to exert influence in this world, the Bible teaches that his ultimate defeat was sealed through Jesus's death and resurrection. Colossians 2:15 says that Christ, "having disarmed the powers and authorities, made a public spectacle of them, triumphing over them by the cross." Jesus's victory broke the Devil's power over humanity. As believers, we stand on the truth that the enemy's influence has been rendered powerless in Christ (Col. 2:15). While the Devil continues to operate, his authority is ultimately shattered, and the future of his defeat is assured.

Believers Have Authority Over the Devil

Jesus gave His disciples authority over the Devil and demonic forces (Luke 10:19). He says, "I have given you authority to trample on snakes and scorpions and to overcome all the power of the enemy; nothing will harm you." This is symbolic of the authority believers have over spiritual forces of evil. As children of God, through their relationship with Jesus, believers share in this authority, enabling them to stand strong against the enemy's attacks. This authority is not from themselves but through the name of Jesus. Jesus's name is above every other name, and all—including demonic powers—will bow to Him (Phil. 2:9–11). When believers confront the enemy, they do so through the authority of Jesus's name, which holds supreme power over every force of darkness (Mark

16:17). Understanding that we as individuals do not have the authority or power to cast out demons but as believers with the Holy Spirit in us Jesus gives us His authority to cast out demons; we must be walking hand in hand with the Holy Spirit to do so.

Key Instructions

- "Submit yourselves, then, to God. Resist the Devil, and he will flee from you" (James 4:7). This is an active stance. By submitting to God's authority, standing firm in faith, and refusing to give in to fear or temptation, believers can cause the enemy to flee (1 Pet. 5:8–9).

- Be aware of the Devil's schemes. Paul writes that anything he has forgiven has been forgiven for the sake of the Corinthian believers in the presence of Christ "so that we would not be outwitted by Satan; for we are not ignorant of his designs" (2 Cor. 2:11). The Bible emphasizes that the Devil is a deceiver, the father of lies (John 8:44). His tactics include deception, accusations, temptation, and manipulation. By recognizing these schemes, believers are better equipped to stand firm and avoid being caught off guard.

- Take every thought captive. The Devil often tries to plant doubts, lies, and fears, but believers are called to capture these thoughts and filter them through the truth of God's Word (2 Cor. 10:4–5). By focusing on what is true, noble, and pure, believers can transform their thinking and resist the enemy's attempts to plant negative thoughts (Phil. 4:8). Thoughts shape behavior, so controlling them according to God's truth leads to victory. Thoughts create emotions, emotions create behavior, and behavior creates the results in your life. So, whatever a person thinks about will result in what their life becomes. Stand firm in faith, trusting in God's promises and continuing in prayer, worship, and obedience, no matter what the enemy brings (1 Pet. 5:8–9).

Speak the Word of God. Speaking and knowing God's Word enables believers to counter the Devil's deceptions and walk in truth. Of course, the easiest way to do this is to have the Word memorized.

- Walk in the Spirit and do not gratify the desires of the flesh. The Holy Spirit empowers believers to live according to God's will, making them less vulnerable to the Devil's attacks. The more believers walk in the Spirit, the more they experience God's protection and guidance.

- Put on the full armor of God (Eph. 6:10–18):
  - Belt of Truth: Grounding us in God's truth
  - Breastplate of Righteousness: Protecting our hearts through Christ's righteousness
  - Shoes of the Gospel of Peace: Helping us stand firm in peace
  - Shield of Faith: Deflecting the enemy's fiery darts
  - Helmet of Salvation: Guarding our minds with the assurance of salvation
  - Sword of the Spirit: The Word of God, our offensive weapon
  - Prayer: Maintaining continual communication with God for strength and guidance
  - Being alert and resisting the Devil's lies, temptations, and accusations helps us stand firm in obedience to God (1 Pet. 5:8–9).
  - Flee from temptation, avoiding compromising situations, noting that God provides a way out.

Cast Our Cares on God

1 Peter 5:7 and Philippians 4:6–7 encourage believers to trust God's care by casting all anxieties on Him through prayer. "And the peace of God, which transcends all understanding, will guard your hearts and minds in Christ Jesus" (Phil. 4:7). This act of trust brings peace and protects believers from the enemy's attacks.

Use Spiritual Weapons

Ephesians 6:10–18 and 2 Corinthians 10:3–5 describe spiritual weapons that demolish strongholds. These include prayer, faith, righteousness, truth, salvation, and the Word of God. Believers engage in spiritual warfare through the Holy Spirit's power, not by human strength.

Control Your Thinking According to the Word

Romans 12:2 and Philippians 4:8 stress renewing the mind through God's Word. By focusing on what is true, noble, and pure, believers can transform their thinking and resist the enemy's attempts to plant negative thoughts. Thoughts shape behavior, so controlling them according to God's truth leads to victory. Thoughts create emotions, emotions create behavior, and behavior creates the results in your life.

So, whatever a person thinks about will result in what their life becomes. This is why it's vital to recognize the power of your thoughts and understand that they are the starting point for everything you experience. If your mind is filled with negative or self-defeating thoughts, it will lead to discouraging emotions, which shape harmful behaviors and, ultimately, undesired results. Therefore, it's crucial to be intentional about your thoughts and choose ones that align with the truth of how God sees you. Don't fall into the trap of listening to the enemy's lies and letting those thoughts define you. Instead, take every thought captive (2 Cor. 10:5) and filter it through what you know God would want you to think about. By focusing on God's truth, you can create a life that reflects His purpose, peace, and abundance, living out the reality He has planned for you. Simply believe what God says in His Word (1 John 5:4). The authority of believers over the Devil is exercised through submitting to God, using Jesus's name, standing firm in faith, and relying on the Holy Spirit.

Ultimately, believers fight from a place of victory. Though the Devil continues to deceive, believers stand firm in the authority given by Jesus, walking in freedom and power through God's Kingdom.

The Rest of the Story

The Devil knows he is ultimately defeated but is determined to deceive as many as he can. His strategy now is to lie and manipulate, trying to keep people from accepting God's truth and living in His kingdom. He will counterfeit God's blessings, offering false versions of peace, love, and contentment. For example, he might tempt people with worldly success instead of God's true fulfillment or offer fleeting pleasures that mask true joy. Believers must recognize these lies, keep their eyes on Jesus, and live in the reality of God's promises.

One day, soon, Jesus will return. He is seated at the right hand of God and will come back to collect all who believe in Him. The Devil, along with those who reject God's offer of salvation, will face eternal punishment and separation from God's love, joy, and peace. Those who believe in Jesus will be taken up into eternal life with Him. The Devil cannot stop this future—it is set in stone. Until then, Jesus waits, offering the gift of salvation to as many as will believe, but He won't force anyone to accept it.

Believers are called to walk in peace, joy, and love while wearing the full armor of God to avoid being deceived by the enemy. As we live in a world where the Devil still operates, we keep our eyes on our eternal reward, standing firm in the victory Christ has already won. Is it possible that the Devil has convinced you of a false statement about something? What might you be believing that is not really from God?

Story Time: Thomas and His Armor

Once upon a time, in a small, quiet town, there lived a man named Thomas. Thomas was an ordinary man who worked hard at his job, loved his family, and tried to live a good life. Yet, lately, everything seemed to be falling apart. His job was in jeopardy due to company cutbacks, his marriage was strained, and he felt a pervasive sense of hopelessness that he couldn't shake.

Thomas began to notice that his problems seemed to multiply inexplicably. No matter how much effort he put into solving one issue, three more would spring up. He was constantly tired, emotionally drained, and found himself snapping at his loved ones. It was during a particularly rough night, as he lay awake in bed, that Thomas had a revelation: he was under attack. He recognized that these relentless difficulties were not just random misfortunes but orchestrated by an enemy who sought to break him.

Desperate for a solution, Thomas remembered a conversation he had with an old friend who mentioned the Armor of God from the Bible. His friend had explained how it was meant to protect believers from spiritual attacks. Skeptical but hopeful, Thomas decided to give it a try. He started with the belt of truth, trying to wrap himself in honesty and integrity. Initially, he felt a slight sense of clarity and conviction, but his problems persisted. Despite his best efforts to remain truthful in all things, the attacks continued unabated.

Next, he put on the breastplate of righteousness, striving to live a life of moral integrity and uprightness. He hoped that this would shield him from the relentless barrage of negativity. However, despite his commitment to righteousness, the waves of despair and frustration kept crashing over him. Nothing seemed to change, and he began to doubt the efficacy of this "armor."

It wasn't until a chance encounter with a wise, elderly man at his local church that Thomas's perspective began to shift. The elderly man, seeing Thomas's distress, invited him to sit and talk. He listened patiently as Thomas poured out his heart, sharing his struggles and his half-hearted attempt to use the Armor of God. The wise man gently explained, "Thomas, the Armor of God is not a set of trinkets or tokens. It is a full suit of spiritual protection that must be embraced completely. Each piece works together to shield and empower you against the enemy's attacks."

Feeling a spark of hope, Thomas decided to fully commit. He put on the full Armor of God: the belt of truth, the breastplate of righteousness, the gospel of peace as shoes for his feet, the shield of faith, the helmet of salvation, and finally, the sword of the Spirit, which is the word of God. He prayed fervently, asking for strength and guidance, and dedicated himself to living in accordance with God's will.

With all the armor in place, Thomas felt a change. The next time the enemy attacked, he stood firm. Temptations and doubts that once plagued him bounced off his shield of faith. His heart, protected by the breastplate of righteousness, remained steadfast. He found courage in the helmet of salvation, knowing that his future was secure in God's hands. And with a few decisive swipes of the sword of the Spirit, he used scripture to repel the enemy's lies and deceptions.

Thomas's life began to transform. His marriage improved as he communicated more lovingly and patiently. At work, he found new opportunities opening up, and his sense of hopelessness was replaced with a deep, abiding peace. He had tasted victory and knew that it was not his own strength but the power of God working through him.

From that day forward, Thomas committed to never taking off the Armor of God. He honored God by living each day fully clothed in the spiritual armor, ready to face whatever came his way. With the armor, he stood strong and confident, knowing that he was protected and empowered by the Creator of the universe. The enemy's attacks no longer held power over him, and he lived his life in victory, grateful for the divine protection and strength that had brought him through his darkest days. Thomas thanked God daily for this true gift, realizing that the Armor of God was a powerful testament to God's love and provision, enabling him to stand strong in the world.

In conclusion, living an unshakable and abundant life begins with understanding the spiritual battle we are in and aligning our lives with God's truth. We cannot afford to be passive or unaware, as the enemy constantly seeks to undermine our faith and joy. By putting on the full Armor of God and trusting in His unshakable redemption, we stand confidently in the face of trials, knowing that God has already provided everything we need to overcome. Aligning our thoughts and actions with God's true character allows us to shed the misconceptions and myths that lead to defeat, replacing them with His truth and victory. As we walk in this confidence, trusting in God's plan, we not only survive but thrive, reflecting the abundant life He desires for us in every situation.

CHAPTER 23

The 4th Dimension: Living in the Kingdom of God

What Is the Kingdom of God?

Being in the Kingdom of God is exactly this—living a life marked by righteousness, peace, and joy through the Holy Spirit (Rom.14:17). It's not about external rituals or following rules but about an inward transformation that aligns us with God's will. Righteousness comes from being in right standing with God; peace fills our hearts as we trust in His sovereignty, and joy overflows as we experience His presence and grace. When we live in the Kingdom of God, we walk in His truth, are grounded in His peace, and are uplifted by His joy, reflecting His love in everything we do. There's a song that joyfully proclaims, "Righteousness, peace, and joy—that's the Kingdom of God! Don't you want to be a part of the kingdom? Come on, everybody!" This joyful invitation mirrors God's call for us to step into His kingdom life, where righteousness, peace, and joy are our daily experiences through His Spirit.

The idea of the "4th Dimension" isn't directly mentioned in the Bible, but it symbolizes living by faith in God's Kingdom. When Jesus teaches us to pray in the Lord's Prayer (Matt. 6:9–13), He says, "Your kingdom come, your will be done on earth as it is in Heaven." This means God wants His Kingdom to be present here on earth and for us to follow His will in our lives.

We can do this supernaturally by accepting His gifts of righteousness, peace, and joy and walking in these gifts daily. When we fully embrace what God offers, we experience the Kingdom of God in a way that is truly supernatural. His righteousness transforms our hearts, His peace guards our minds, and His joy strengthens our spirits, allowing us to live above the challenges of this world. This is the abundant life Jesus spoke of—one where we are not bound by circumstances but empowered by the Holy Spirit to walk in God's

Kingdom reality every day. Through this supernatural life, we become living testimonies of God's grace, demonstrating His kingdom here on earth.

Kingdom Living Now: Walking in God's Victory Today

With this understanding, we can see how we are invited to experience God's Kingdom right here on earth, living abundantly with His gifts of righteousness, joy, and peace. As Romans 14:17 reminds us, the Kingdom of God is about these very things, and they are available to us now through the Holy Spirit. If we choose to accept God's gifts, we can live a life marked by His righteousness, where our hearts are in alignment with His will, His peace that transcends all understanding, and His joy that sustains us in every circumstance. This is not just a future promise but a reality we can step into today, fully embracing the abundant life God offers us in His kingdom.

Kingdom living isn't something reserved for the distant future—it starts now. As believers, we are called to live in the reality of God's Kingdom, even as we reside in a world that is still influenced by the enemy. Jesus declared that His kingdom is not of this world, yet we are already citizens of that heavenly kingdom (John 18:36). Living in this kingdom reality means actively applying God's truth to every part of our lives. It means putting on the Armor of God, standing firm against the enemy's schemes, and walking in the abundant life that Christ promised us.

In the present, we are equipped to live out God's peace, joy, and purpose through the Holy Spirit who dwells within us. We experience His kingdom by submitting to His rule over our lives, resisting the enemy's lies, and using the spiritual tools God has given us—faith, righteousness, His Word, and prayer. Kingdom living now is about reflecting God's light in this world, spreading His love, and walking in the authority we have as His children, even as we face the trials of a fallen world.

Kingdom Living in the Future: The Fullness of God's Rule

We also look forward to the day when His rule will be fully established on earth. This future reality, when Christ will return and defeat the enemy once and for all, is our ultimate hope. In this future kingdom, all pain, suffering, and spiritual conflict will cease. "He will wipe every tear from their eyes. There will be no more death or mourning or crying or pain, for the old order of things has passed away" (Rev. 21:4).

While we engage in spiritual battles today, knowing that the enemy's power is temporary gives us unshakable confidence. One day, when Jesus returns, the Devil will be defeated, and God's Kingdom will be fully established on earth. We will reign with Him in a restored creation, where peace, joy, and righteousness are not just hopes but the eternal reality. Understanding both the now and future aspects of kingdom living empowers us to live victoriously in the present, knowing that the future promises far more than we could ever imagine.

Living in Victory: The Present and the Promise

Living an unshakable life means embracing the reality of God's Kingdom now while eagerly awaiting its future fulfillment. We are called to live in God's victory today, applying His truth to our thoughts, emotions, and behaviors. Yet, we also live with the expectation that one day, His kingdom will fully come, and we will see His reign established over all things. Trusting in God's promises, walking in His Spirit, and renewing our minds daily to align with His will allow us to live a life of purpose, confidence, and abundance in both the present and the future.

Living by Faith

Living in God's Kingdom means living by faith, as defined in Hebrews 11:1: "Faith is confidence in what we hope for and assurance about what we do not see." This faith allows us to trust in God's promises even when they are not visible, guiding our actions and shaping our outlook on life. 2 Corinthians 5:7

reinforces this idea: "For we live by faith, not by sight." Biblical examples, such as Abraham obeying God's call to leave his homeland (Heb. 11:8–10) and Moses leading the Israelites out of Egypt (Heb. 11:24–29), illustrate the power of living by faith. Jesus also teaches us to trust in God's provision for our daily needs in Matthew 6:31–33, encouraging us to seek first His kingdom and righteousness, trusting that all our needs will be met.

Living by faith empowers us to act courageously and persevere through trials (James 1:2–4). This perspective helps us to consider trials as opportunities for growth, knowing that the testing of our faith produces perseverance and leads to spiritual maturity. By stepping out in obedience, relying on God's guidance and provision, and enduring challenges with the assurance that God is at work in our lives, we embody the principles of God's Kingdom.

Experiencing God's Presence

Living in God's Kingdom means experiencing God's presence in our lives. Psalm 16:11 says, "You make known to me the path of life; you will fill me with joy in your presence." This highlights the joy and fulfillment that come from being close to God.

Living in the Kingdom of God, or the 4th Dimension (this is my way of explaining it and is not found in the Bible), is a journey of faith, submission, vigilance, and a renewed mind. As we align our lives with God's will, we experience His righteousness, justice, and peace. This way of living is open to everyone who repents and believes, offering a present reality and a hopeful future based on God's promises.

Practical Steps of Living in the Kingdom of God Now

Living in the Kingdom of God on earth involves practical actions and a transformed way of being. Firstly, embracing the teachings of Jesus and striving to live according to God's commandments is essential. This means showing love, compassion, forgiveness, and humility in our daily interactions, thereby reflecting God's character. Regular prayer and worship are also crucial, as they help align our hearts and minds with God's will, inviting His presence into our lives and communities.

Acts of service, kindness, and charity are tangible ways to manifest the values of the Kingdom of God, demonstrating God's love and justice on earth. Building community is another key aspect, where engaging in fellowship with other believers, supporting one another, and working together to promote joy, love and peace becomes central. This requires putting aside grumbling and gossip as community activities. Additionally, spreading the Gospel and sharing the message of Jesus and the hope of the Kingdom of Heaven with others is vital in extending God's love and truth to those who have not yet encountered it.

Knowing we are in the Kingdom of God can be discerned through several indicators. One such sign is the inner peace and joy that comes from the presence of the Holy Spirit, which surpasses all understanding as described in Philippians 4:7. Growth in the fruit of the Spirit, such as love, joy, peace, patience, kindness, goodness, faithfulness, gentleness, and self-control (Galatians 5:22–23), also evidences our life in the Kingdom. A sincere desire to obey God's commands and live according to His principles shows our alignment with His will. Furthermore, the transformative work of the Holy Spirit in changing our hearts and minds to be more Christlike is a hallmark of living in God's Kingdom. This transformation leads to a sense of purpose and mission, as we recognize that our lives have a divine purpose and are called to fulfill God's mission on earth, bringing His love and truth to the world.

Story Time: The 4th Dimension—Walking in the Kingdom

Dan lived in a quaint little town nestled between rolling hills and a serene river. On the surface, his life appeared content and ordinary. He had a small house, a steady job at the local mill, and a close-knit circle of friends. The townsfolk knew him as a quiet, dependable man who always did what was expected of him. But beneath this calm exterior, Dan felt a nagging sense of emptiness—a void that he couldn't quite understand or fill.

His days were a routine of work, meals, and sleep, punctuated by the occasional social gathering or church service. Dan was a man of habit, but these habits had begun to feel like shackles. The predictability of his life, once comforting, now felt suffocating. He attended church every Sunday, said his prayers, and read his Bible, but the words felt hollow. He knew there was supposed to be more to faith but didn't know how to access it.

One morning, during his usual bible and prayer time, Dan cried out in frustration, "Lord, I don't understand what You have planned for me. I want to see what You see, to know Your will. I want to know more about you. I know there is more. When I read your words, I see that I am not experiencing everything that is in your Word. How can I experience more of you? Please show me the way."

The next day, Dan noticed something unusual as he walked through the town's marketplace. Above the noise and clamor, a thick, ethereal cloud hung in the air, casting a heavenly glow over everything it touched. People walked with their heads down, avoiding the cloud or ignoring it completely. But Dan, feeling something stirring inside him, decided to lift his head into the cloud.

At first, everything was foggy. The world seemed distant, but then, a small light appeared. As Dan focused on it, the fog lifted, and he was filled with an overwhelming sense of peace, joy, love and clarity. He saw the townspeople as souls connected by a web of love, fear, joy, and pain. Dan started to realize that his entire perception of life on Earth had transformed. The world continued to become clearer and different than he had ever seen it. He began to see the world and its people through God's eyes, and what he saw filled him with a love and understanding that he had never known before.

The townspeople, once just familiar faces in the crowd, became intricate souls, each bearing the weight of their own struggles, hopes, and fears. Those who had hurt him in the past no longer stirred feelings of anger or resentment; instead, Dan felt deep compassion for them as he saw the pain and wounds that had driven their actions. He realized that what he had once dismissed as laziness in others was often the result of a life crushed by defeat, a defense mechanism born out of hopelessness rather than true indifference.

As Dan walked through the town, he saw potential in people and things he had never noticed before, recognizing the seeds of greatness and beauty that lay hidden beneath the surface. It was as if a veil had been lifted from his eyes, revealing the divine purpose woven into every life around him. More than that, he saw angels ministering to the townspeople, unseen by those who hurried by, their presence a quiet testament to God's care and protection.

These celestial beings moved among the people, guiding, comforting, and shielding them in ways that went unnoticed by most, but Dan saw it all clearly. He felt the deep, abiding love that God had for each person, a love so vast and pure that it overwhelmed him. Dan's heart was transformed in that moment, filled with a peace and clarity that he had never experienced. He had seen through God's eyes, and the world would never look the same to him again.

For a while, Dan lived in this divine perspective. He became a beacon of hope and wisdom in the town, guiding people with compassion and love. But then, as the days passed, Dan began to grow weary. The distractions and temptations of daily life tugged at him. He found himself lowering his head out of the cloud, choosing the ease of his old life over the divine clarity he had come to cherish.

With his head out of the cloud, Dan's life began to unravel. The peace he once knew slipped away, replaced by confusion and frustration. His relationships grew strained, and his heart felt heavy with the weight of regret. One day, standing among the wreckage of his choices, Dan fell to his knees in despair. He cried out to God for forgiveness. "Lord, I have lost my way. I need You. Please let me see again as You see."

In that moment of repentance, the cloud returned, and Dan lifted his head once more into its light. This time, however, God spoke to him. "Dan," came a voice filled with love, "I forgive you, but to keep your head in this cloud, to remain in My presence, you need more than just the desire. You need My protection. Put on the armor of God."

Dan listened closely as God continued, "Put on the belt of truth to keep your thoughts grounded in My Word. Wear the breastplate of righteousness so your heart stays aligned with Me. Walk in peace, so your feet will not stumble. Take up the shield of faith to guard against doubt and distraction. Let the helmet of salvation protect your mind, and wield the sword of My Spirit, which is My Word."

With the armor of God securely in place, Dan felt stronger and more secure than ever. He could now walk with his head in the cloud and the rest of him protected from the temptations and struggles that once pulled him away. He could feel God's wisdom and love guiding him in every step.

It was after Dan's transformation that the townspeople began to take notice. His life, now marked by unwavering peace and divine clarity, stood out to those around him. People like Anna, the shopkeeper, and Thomas, the town's blacksmith, were intrigued by the change in Dan. They had seen him fall and rise again, stronger than before, and it piqued their curiosity.

Anna had always been a practical woman. She had watched Dan go through his struggles and was wary of what she saw as his "head in the clouds" approach to life. But now, seeing the change in him, she wondered if there was more to it. Thomas, who had always been skeptical of anything spiritual, had begun to notice a difference in how Dan carried himself—steadier, more confident, yet filled with compassion and understanding.

One evening, as Dan walked through the marketplace, Anna approached him. "Dan," she asked hesitantly, "how is it that you have such peace? I've seen you go through hard times, but now, there's something different about you."

Dan smiled and invited her to join him for a walk. As they strolled through the town, Dan shared his story. He spoke of the cloud, of how he had once lowered his head and lost his way, and of how God had restored him with the armor that kept him protected. Anna listened intently, her heart stirring with a desire to experience the same peace and clarity that Dan described. She said that she had seen the cloud but just ignored it. Dan said trust it. Stick your head in the cloud with me and see what I see. See what God sees. Hear what God is speaking to you, daily and even sometimes, minute by minute or even sometimes step by step as I walk. He is speaking to me in the cloud all the time. I want you to experience this with me.

The next day, Anna made the decision. With some trepidation, she lifted her head into the cloud. At first, she felt the same fog and confusion that Dan had experienced, but then, the light appeared. As she focused on it, her heart filled with peace, and she saw the people around her not as they appeared but as God saw them. She actually could hear God speak to her some of the most amazing and loving things she had ever heard. Anna's life was transformed, and she, too, put on the armor of God so that she would not be distracted from the most amazing thing that she had ever experienced. It was like Heaven on earth, walking through the town with her head lifted high.

Word spread quickly through the town. Thomas, who had always scoffed at spiritual things, found himself drawn to the change in Anna. After hearing her story, he, too, decided to lift his head into the cloud. Soon after, others followed—Martha, the baker's wife, and James, the schoolteacher. One by one, they stepped into the cloud and experienced the same divine clarity and love that had transformed Dan's life.

Of course, not everyone joined. Peter, the town tailor, laughed at the idea, calling it foolishness. He and a few others refused to believe that anything so intangible could make such a difference. But even as they scoffed, they couldn't deny the change they saw in their neighbors.

Those who had entered the cloud became a force of love and light in the town. They treated each other with kindness and compassion, guided by the wisdom they received from God's perspective. Together, they brought about changes that reflected the love and peace of the Kingdom of God. The town, once divided by petty disagreements and fears, began to transform into a community marked by unity, love, and purpose.

Dan's story and the stories of Anna, Thomas, Martha, and James continued to spread throughout the town and beyond, becoming a testament to the power of seeing life through God's eyes and living protected by the armor of God. People spoke of the man who had first lifted his head into the cloud and how his example had led others to do the same. The town was forever changed by the choice of one man to walk with his head in the cloud and the willingness of others to follow.

And so, Dan, along with the others who joined him, lived with their heads lifted high into the heavenly cloud—not because they feared losing the divine perspective again, but because they had come to understand that this was where true life was found. With the armor of God protecting them, they walked with confidence, bringing light, love, and wisdom to their town, forever changed by the presence of God.

Conclusion: Living an Unshakable and Abundant Life

Understanding what it means to live an unshakable and abundant life is essential to experiencing the full reality of God's Kingdom both now and in the future. This chapter has sought to clarify misconceptions and shed light on the truths of God's character and His redemptive plan. We've seen that God's Kingdom is marked by righteousness, peace, and joy through the Holy Spirit (Rom. 14:17) and that this kingdom is available to us now if we choose to walk in His gifts daily. Living with unshakable confidence in God's plan, trusting His faithfulness through trials and redemption, empowers us to rise above the difficulties of this world. As we align our lives with His kingdom today, we experience a supernatural life filled with His presence and abundant provision. And as we look forward to the fullness of His kingdom in the future, we live with the hope and assurance that one day, all things will be made new, and we will reign with Christ in perfect peace. Understanding and embracing this dual reality of the present and future kingdom equips us to live in victory, both now and for eternity.

CHAPTER 24

How to Walk in the World
But Not of the World

The phrase "walk in the world but not of the world" signifies that as Christians, believers are called to engage with society and live in the world, yet they should not adopt the secular world's values, behaviors, or priorities. Instead, they should maintain a distinct, Christlike way of life, reflecting their faith in all they do.

In John 17:14—16, Jesus prays for His disciples, saying, "I have given them your word, and the world has hated them, for they are not of the world any more than I am of the world. My prayer is not that you take them out of the world but that you protect them from the evil one." Here, Jesus acknowledges the tension believers face: living in a world that often opposes their faith. His prayer is for their protection, not removal, emphasizing the need for believers to remain in the world to be His witnesses while relying on God's protection against evil influences.

Romans 12:2 instructs believers, "Do not conform to the pattern of this world but be transformed by the renewing of your mind. Then you will be able to test and approve what God's will is—his good, pleasing, and perfect will." This verse highlights the importance of a renewed mind, one that discerns and follows God's will rather than succumbing to worldly patterns. Transformation through a renewed mind enables believers to live out God's will, showcasing a life that contrasts with secular norms.

James 1:27 emphasizes practical holiness: "Religion that God our Father accepts as pure and faultless is this: to look after orphans and widows in their distress and to keep oneself from being polluted by the world." True religion involves compassionate actions toward the needy and maintaining purity by avoiding worldly corruption. This verse underscores the dual responsibility of social engagement and personal holiness.

First John 2:15–17 warns against loving the world: "Do not love the world or anything in the world. If anyone loves the world, love for the Father is not in them. For everything in the world—the lust of the flesh, the lust of the eyes, and the pride of life—comes not from the Father but from the world. The world and its desires pass away, but whoever does the will of God lives forever."

This passage contrasts worldly desires with the eternal nature of God's will. It calls believers to prioritize their love for God over worldly attractions, emphasizing that true fulfillment and eternal life come from doing God's will.

Living a Christian Life in This World

Walking in the World but Not Being of It

To walk in the world but not be of the world, believers must engage with society without adopting its secular values. By following Christ's teachings, renewing their minds, practicing compassionate and holy living, and prioritizing their love for God, Christians can navigate the world while reflecting the distinct, transformative power of their faith. This balance allows believers to be a light in the darkness, demonstrating Christ's love and truth to those around them without conforming to the patterns of this world.

The Spiritual Battle We Face

We are in the midst of a spiritual battle that God will ultimately win. Currently, God's enemy holds dominion over the world, but Jesus's sacrifice for our sins has established His kingdom. By accepting His sacrifice, we become part of His kingdom now. Jesus's victory allows individuals to choose to be part of His kingdom or remain under the enemy's rule. At His second coming, Jesus will reclaim the world He has already won. Those who have not accepted His gift will remain under the enemy's dominion and suffer the penalties given by God to the enemy for eternity. God's plan includes waiting as long as needed to give more individuals the chance to accept His gift.

The Daily Choice: God's Kingdom or the Enemy's Dominion

While we are here on this earth, we have a choice every day to walk in His kingdom or in the enemy's dominion. We can choose to walk step by step, hearing God's words of wisdom if we believe, or we can keep ourselves out of the kingdom by walking without faith and only hearing the enemy's words of destruction, trying to navigate this world without God's loving wisdom. James 1:5 assures us, "If any of you lacks wisdom, you should ask God, who gives generously to all without finding fault, and it will be given to you." This wisdom is available to those who choose to walk in God's Kingdom and seek His guidance.

Equipped for Victory: The Tools of Spiritual Warfare

In the meantime, God has provided us with tools to live a successful Christian life. These include the full armor of God, submission to God, alertness to the enemy's tactics, fleeing temptation, casting our cares on God, walking in the Spirit, controlling our thoughts, and believing everything in the Bible. Ephesians 6:11–13 encourages us to "put on the full armor of God, so that you can take your stand against the Devil's schemes. For our struggle is not against flesh and blood, but against the rulers, against the authorities, against the powers of this dark world and against the spiritual forces of evil in the heavenly realms." This means that believers are not defenseless in this world but rather equipped by God to stand firm in their faith.

Choosing to Walk in God's Kingdom

By using these tools and choosing to walk in God's Kingdom daily, believers can live victoriously in the world while staying true to their faith and advancing God's Kingdom. As 2 Corinthians 5:7 reminds us, "For we live by faith, not by sight." This daily choice determines whether we experience the blessings and guidance of God's Kingdom or struggle under the enemy's dominion. We cannot live simply by what we see and understand of this world, as the enemy has dominion here. We must believe and trust that God's Kingdom is here and available for us to walk in, whether we see it or not, as His Word says.

Living in the Kingdom of God While on Earth

Living in the Kingdom of God while on earth requires aligning our perspective with what the Bible declares, even when our earthly reality may seem contradictory. The Bible teaches that the Kingdom of God is present here and now, accessible through faith in Christ. In Luke 17:20–21, Jesus said, "The Kingdom of God is within you." This indicates that God's reign is not merely a future hope but a present reality for believers who live under His rule. To live in the kingdom while on earth means to walk by faith, not by sight (2 Cor. 5:7), trusting in God's promises over what we see in the natural world.

Renewing Our Minds and Living as Citizens of Heaven

It involves renewing our minds to align with kingdom principles (Rom. 12:2) and recognizing that we are citizens of Heaven (Philippians 3:20). Though we live in a fallen world, the kingdom exists within us, transforming our lives and actions as we believe and act on God's Word. By embracing this reality, we demonstrate our faith that God's Kingdom is advancing on earth, even when circumstances seem to suggest otherwise.

Walking in Holiness and Compassion

An essential part of living in God's Kingdom is walking in holiness and compassion. As believers, we are called to love others as Christ loved us, forgiving offenses and showing mercy. The more we understand God's love and His desire for reconciliation, the more we reflect His heart in our relationships. The act of walking in the Kingdom is not just about personal faith but also about loving others and leading them toward God's light through our actions, words, and attitudes.

Eternal Perspective: Living for God's Glory

Finally, living with an eternal perspective transforms how we view our time on earth. Knowing that we are part of God's eternal kingdom should motivate us to live for His glory in everything we do. This includes making decisions with eternal consequences in mind, storing up treasures in Heaven (Matt. 6:20), and realizing that our actions here have a lasting impact in God's eternal kingdom.

We must live each day knowing that we are preparing for a seamless transition into eternity, where we will continue to walk with God.

Story Time: John Living by Biblical Principles

John grew up in a typical middle-class family, living a normal life according to worldly standards. He worked an office job, was focused on success and pleasure, and didn't give much thought to spiritual things. Though he went to church sometimes, he didn't apply the Bible to his day-to-day life. One day, a coworker named James told John about his faith in Christ. James explained the gospel and the life transformation he experienced when he surrendered his life to following Jesus. Convicted of his sin and need for salvation, John repented and believed in Jesus.

John's life began to change as he took steps to live out his new faith. He started reading the Bible, studying verses that caught his attention. He discovered the passage in Ephesians 6:11–18 about the full armor of God and decided to take it to heart. Rather than reacting with anger when coworkers treated him badly, John submitted those situations to God, asking the Holy Spirit to help him respond with patience and kindness.

John also took to heart the warning to be alert and resist the Devil. He recognized temptations and negative influences in his life and actively resisted them. He distanced himself from toxic relationships and sought the company of those who shared his newfound faith. He avoided situations that could lead him astray and sought refuge in prayer when faced with challenges. Casting his cares on God became a natural response as he learned to trust in the Lord's guidance and provision.

John began to walk in the Spirit, allowing God to lead him in all aspects of his life. He cultivated a life of prayer and worship, deepening his relationship with the Creator. As he grew spiritually, he found it easier to control his thinking according to the Word of God. His thoughts became more aligned with love, joy, peace, patience, kindness, goodness, faithfulness, gentleness, and self-control. Over time, John's transformation was evident to those around him. His family noticed a newfound sense of peace and joy in him. His coworkers admired his integrity and compassion. He became an active member of his local church, volunteering his time and talents to help others in need.

As the years went by, John's life looked drastically different from the one he had led before. He had indeed put on the full armor of God, submitted to God, been alert and resisted the Devil, fled from temptation, cast his cares on God, walked in the Spirit, and controlled his thinking according to the Word. When the time came for John to leave this earthly life, he did so with the assurance of great rewards in Heaven. He had glorified God through his transformed life, and as he entered the gates of Heaven, he heard the words, "Well done, good and faithful servant."

Living by the Spirit: Navigating the World as a Follower of Christ

Living as a Christian in today's world presents unique challenges. We are called to live in a world that often pulls us in the opposite direction of our faith, but we are also called not to be of this world. Jesus Himself prayed for His followers, saying, "They are not of the world, even as I am not of it" (John 17:16). This means that while we live among the culture, values, and pressures of society, we are called to live according to a different standard—God's standard. But how do we do this? How can we navigate the daily struggles, temptations, and conflicts of this world without being consumed by them?

The answer lies in walking by the Spirit and allowing God to shape our character through the fruit of the Spirit. These are not simply behaviors to adopt; they are the evidence of a life transformed by Christ. As we grow in our relationship with God, the Holy Spirit produces these fruits in our lives, enabling us to reflect God's character to the world around us. The fruit of the Spirit—love, joy, peace, patience, kindness, goodness, faithfulness, gentleness, and self-control—serve as both the foundation and the guide for living as a Christian in this world.

Walking in the Spirit means choosing to respond to the world not out of our flesh or selfish desires but out of the character that God is shaping within us. It's about living with love when hatred is easier, choosing joy in the midst of despair, embracing peace in a world of chaos, and practicing patience when everything urges us to rush ahead. By living out the fruit of the Spirit, we reflect Christ's presence in our lives, becoming beacons of His love and truth in a world that desperately needs both.

As Christians, we are not called to withdraw from the world but to engage with it in a way that glorifies God. Living by the fruit of the Spirit allows us to live in this world while staying rooted in God's truth, showing the world what it means to walk with Him. Through this lifestyle, we become the salt and light that Jesus speaks of in Matthew 5:13–16, bringing hope, peace, and love to those around us while remaining steadfast in our faith.

Understanding the Nature of Biblical Love

Love is much deeper than mere affection or emotion—it is a selfless, sacrificial commitment to the well-being of others. In 1 Corinthians 13, often called the "love chapter," love is described as patient, kind, not envious or boastful, and always protecting, trusting, hoping, and persevering. Love has many meanings in the English language, and the love God talks about here is all-encompassing. Agape love, the highest form of love in the Bible, is selfless, unconditional, and sacrificial. It reflects God's nature, demonstrated through Jesus's sacrifice, and calls us to love others without expecting anything in return. This kind of love seeks the well-being of others regardless of circumstances.

Eros love refers to romantic or passionate love, while phileo love is the deep friendship and brotherly love that binds people in loyalty and affection. Storge love is the natural, familial love that exists within families. Together, these types of love, with agape at the foundation, guide us in how we relate to others, helping us to reflect God's love in every aspect of life—from friendships and families to romantic relationships. Love, according to the Bible, is central to the Christian faith; it reflects God's nature.

First, John 4:8 tells us that "God is love," and Jesus commands us to love God with all our heart and to love our neighbors as ourselves (Matt. 22:37–39). This kind of love, or "agape" love, is unconditional and rooted in a desire to serve and give, just as Christ gave Himself for us. Love is transformative and life-giving. Love is the greatest because it is the foundation of every aspect of the

Christian life (1 Cor. 13:13). Love has the power to heal, reconcile, and unite people, breaking down barriers and fostering peace. The sacrificial love of Jesus on the cross is the ultimate example of love's power to change lives and restore broken relationships (John 15:13). This kind of love enables us to forgive, show compassion, and extend grace, even when it is difficult. Love covers over sins (1 Pet. 4:8) and brings light into the darkest situations, reflecting God's heart for humanity.

How to Get Love According to the Bible

Love originates from God, and we receive it from Him and reflect it on others. First, we experience God's love through Christ. God's love for us is not based on our worthiness but on His grace and mercy. Understanding and accepting this love is the starting point for truly loving others. As we stay connected to God through prayer, worship, and studying His Word, His love flows through us, enabling us to love others. Second, we grow in love by abiding in God (John 15:4). Abiding in His love means obeying His commandments and living in close relationship with Him (John 15:9–10). Third, the Holy Spirit plays a vital role in producing love in our hearts. The Holy Spirit fills us with God's love (Rom. 5:5) and empowers us to love others in ways that we couldn't do on our own (Gal. 5:22). Fourth, love grows through acts of service and obedience to God's Word (1 John 3:18). Lastly, faith and love are intertwined (Gal. 5:6). It motivates us to live a life that glorifies God and blesses others.

The Nature of Biblical Joy

Biblically, joy is much more than a fleeting feeling of happiness—it is a deep, enduring sense of peace and gladness that flows from a relationship with God. There is a true godly power that comes from joy. God produces it within us as we walk closely with Him (Gal. 5:22–23). Unlike happiness, which can change with circumstances, biblical joy is rooted in the certainty of God's love, promises, and presence in our lives and remains constant, even in hard times (Rom. 8:28).

Joy is life-changing and transformative (Neh. 8:10). More than an emotional boost, it is a source of divine strength. It gives us the resilience to endure hardships, face trials, and keep pressing forward in faith. Joy renews our spirits, provides hope, and helps us overcome fear and despair because it directs our focus away from our challenges and onto the goodness and faithfulness of God. James 1:2–3 encourages believers to "consider it pure joy" when facing trials because those trials produce perseverance and spiritual growth. Joy allows us to view life through God's perspective, trusting that He is always shaping us and that His plans for us are good.

How to Get Joy According to the Bible

First, joy comes from a relationship with God (Ps. 16:11), meaning that when we spend time in prayer, worship, and the study of God's Word, we draw closer to Him and experience the fullness of joy. Second, joy is found in obeying God's Word. (Ps. 19:8). Third, trusting God brings joy, especially during difficult times (Rom. 15:13). When we place our trust in God, we experience joy because we know He is in control and He is faithful. Fourth, joy comes from the Holy Spirit, who produces joy in our hearts as we walk closely with Him (Gal. 5:22). Lastly, hope in salvation is the greatest source of joy. Knowing that we are saved through Jesus Christ fills us with unshakable joy because it is anchored in the certainty of eternal life with God (1 Pet. 1:8–9). This joy is transformative, giving us the strength to persevere and live with confidence, knowing that nothing can separate us from the love and goodness of God.

The Nature of Biblical Peace

Biblical peace, often referred to as "shalom," is not just the absence of conflict or worry—it is a deep sense of tranquility and wholeness that comes from being in right relationship with God. This peace, in the Bible, encompasses harmony, completeness, and well-being. Peace is also a fruit of the Holy Spirit (Gal. 5:22–23), which means that it is a gift God cultivates in our hearts as we walk with Him. Biblical peace transcends circumstances, remaining steadfast even in the midst of difficulties because it is grounded in the assurance of God's sovereignty and care (Isa. 26:3).

The power of peace is transformative and protective, a supernatural peace that shields us from fear, anxiety, and despair, enabling us to remain calm and steadfast in the face of trials. Peace helps us focus on God rather than being overwhelmed by the chaos around us, allowing us to live with confidence and trust in His plan. This peace also empowers us to extend grace and love to others, even in conflict, reflecting God's peace in our relationships and communities (Matt. 5:9).

How to Get Peace According to the Bible

First, peace comes from a relationship with God (Rom. 5:1). When we are in right standing with Him, we experience the peace that comes from knowing we are forgiven and loved. Second, peace is found in trusting God (Isa. 26:3), laying down our anxieties, and believing that He is in control, even when we can't see the outcome. Third, peace is cultivated through prayer (Phil. 4:6–7), trusting God to handle our concerns, and His peace fills our hearts and minds, replacing anxiety with calm assurance. Fourth, peace comes from obedience to God's Word (Ps. 119:165). Lastly, as we walk in step with the Holy Spirit, He cultivates peace in our hearts (Gal. 5:22), enabling us to experience true inner calm and extend peace to those around us.

The Nature of Biblical Patience

Patience is much more than merely waiting without complaint—it is the ability to endure difficult circumstances, delays, or suffering without giving in to anger, frustration, or despair. Patience is often described in the Bible as "long-suffering" (Gal. 5:22–23). It reflects a calm, steadfast trust in God's timing and purposes. Patience requires humility, knowing that God's plan is far better than our own, and it strengthens our faith as we learn to depend on His perfect timing (Ps. 37:7).

The Power of Patience lies in its ability to shape our character and deepen our relationship with God. James 1:3–4 tells us that the testing of our faith produces perseverance and that perseverance leads to maturity and completeness. Patience enables us to endure trials and grow spiritually as we trust in God's plan, even when it feels delayed or unclear. It helps us stay faithful through challenging seasons, knowing that God is working behind the scenes, often in ways we cannot see (Rom. 8:25). Patience also transforms our relationships with others, allowing us to extend grace, love, and understanding, even when people or situations are difficult (Eph. 4:2).

How to Become Patient According to the Bible

Trusting in God's timing is essential for cultivating patience. "Wait for the Lord; be strong, and let your heart take courage; wait for the Lord!" "We also glory in our sufferings, because we know that suffering produces perseverance; perseverance, character; and character, hope" (Ps. 27:14). Patience is often developed through life's hardships as we learn to rely on God, allowing Him to use those experiences to build our faith and shape our character (Rom. 5:3–4). When we feel our patience waning, we can ask God to empower us through His Spirit, giving us the endurance we need to remain steadfast (Col. 1:11). Meditating on God's Word helps us grow in patience (Rom. 15:4) By focusing on God's promises and the examples of patient faith in the Bible, we are encouraged and equipped to be patient ourselves. Lastly, walking in the Spirit allows us to bear the fruit of patience in our lives.

The Nature of Biblical Kindness

Kindness is more than being polite or nice; it is a deep-rooted quality God cultivates in us, involving a heart of empathy, care, and a desire to uplift others (Eph. 4:32). Kindness has the power to soften hardened hearts and bring healing to strained relationships. It also has a ripple effect—when we show kindness, it often inspires others to do the same, leading to a community that reflects God's love. Kindness breaks down barriers, opens doors for reconciliation, and allows others to experience God's compassion through our actions.

How to Get Kindness According to the Bible

Kindness flows from our relationship with Christ. First, abiding in Him allows us to bear the fruit of kindness naturally (John 15:5). Second, we are called to imitate Christ's example of kindness, who showed compassion to the outcasts and sinners (Matt. 9:36) Third, prayerfully asking the Holy Spirit to develop kindness in our hearts, even in challenging situations, is essential. Fourth, meditating on God's Word equips us to act kindly. Finally, practicing kindness in small, everyday moments helps us build this trait into our character.

The Nature of Biblical Goodness

Goodness in the Bible refers to uprightness in heart and life, and it flows from the character of God (Ps. 34:8). It is not simply avoiding wrong but actively pursuing righteousness and doing what is beneficial for others. As a fruit of the Spirit, goodness is rooted in moral integrity and the desire to see God's will done in our lives and in the world around us. Acts of goodness—whether in standing for justice, helping those in need, or living with integrity—open doors for others to see God's love in action. Goodness attracts people to the gospel because it reveals the depth of God's care and His desire for their well-being.

How to Get Goodness According to the Bible

Abiding in Christ is necessary to grow in goodness (John 15:5). And looking to scripture as our moral compass helps us discern what is right and just. Practicing goodness in our daily lives, even in small ways, helps it become a natural part of who we are, and asking the Holy Spirit to guide us in doing what is right and good, even when it is difficult, strengthens this virtue.

The Nature of Biblical Faithfulness

Faithfulness—characterized by loyalty, steadfastness, and reliability— reflects God's unchanging character. His promises are sure, and His love never fails (Lam. 3:22–23). Faithfulness as a fruit of the Spirit involves staying true to God, His Word, and the people we are committed to, even when it is challenging. It builds trust and stability in relationships; it provides security and deepens connections.

How to Get Faithfulness According to the Bible

Faithfulness is nurtured by trusting in God's faithfulness first. As we experience His reliability and love, we are empowered to be faithful to Him and others. First, abiding in Christ strengthens our ability to remain steadfast. Second, reading God's Word and remembering His promises gives us the endurance to remain faithful. Third, prayer is vital in times of struggle, helping us stay committed even when it's difficult.

The Nature of Biblical Gentleness

Gentleness in the Bible refers to humility, meekness, and a calm spirit. It is strength under control, often described as the opposite of harshness or aggression. Jesus embodies gentleness (Matt. 11:29). Gentleness reflects a heart that trusts God and responds to others with love and care. It has the power to heal relationships and diffuse tension (Prov. 15:1) and allows for deeper communication, creating safe spaces for honesty and vulnerability. Gentleness is also transformative in our relationship with God, as it opens our hearts to His correction and guidance with humility.

How to Get Gentleness According to the Bible

Gentleness is cultivated by walking with God. First, abiding in Christ produces gentleness in our lives (John 15:5). Second, following Christ's example of humility and service helps us grow in gentleness. Third, relying on the Holy Spirit empowers us to respond gently in situations where we might otherwise be harsh. Finally, reflecting on the kindness of God, who deals with us gently, teaches us to extend that same grace to others.

The Nature of Biblical Self-Control

Self-control is the ability to restrain one's impulses, desires, and emotions in order to align with God's will. More than willpower, it is the Spirit-led discipline that helps us make choices that honor God. Self-control protects us from falling into sin and enables us to live in obedience to God's commands (Tit. 2:11–12). It empowers us to live a disciplined life not ruled by our emotions or desires but by God's wisdom.

How to Get Self-Control According to the Bible

Self control is developed through the power of the Holy Spirit. First, abiding in Christ helps us grow in self-control (John 15:5). Second, studying scripture equips us with wisdom to know what God's will is, helping us resist temptation. Third, prayer is vital for strength in moments of weakness. Finally, practicing self-discipline in small areas of life helps us develop the capacity to exhibit self-control in more significant matters.

Living in the Fruit of the Spirit: A Powerful Witness and Shield

I go into such detail about the fruit of the Spirit because these characteristics are among the most compelling traits that draw others to a person. When people truly abiding in the Lord and display love, joy, peace, patience, kindness, goodness, faithfulness, gentleness, and self-control, they are naturally attracted to others.

These traits are a reflection of who God is, and when we walk closely with Him, the fruit of the Spirit becomes evident in our lives. It demonstrates the transformative power of a life surrendered to Christ. We experience these blessings in our own lives, and we are able to share the fruit of the Spirit with everyone around us, offering the love, peace, and joy that only God can provide. It is also a strong defense against the enemy, acting as a spiritual shield, repelling the enemy's attempts and strengthening our walk with the Lord, making us even more effective in His kingdom.

Story Time: A Fruit-filled Approach to Life

The Ripple of Grace

In the small town of Willow Creek, nestled between rolling hills and streams, lived a man named Thomas. He was a quiet man, often unnoticed by those around him, but he lived with an unwavering commitment to God. Thomas wasn't wealthy, nor was he particularly influential, but he had something that set him apart—he lived by the fruit of the Spirit. His life was marked by love, joy, peace, patience, kindness, goodness, faithfulness, gentleness, and self-control.

Thomas had lived in Willow Creek for as long as anyone could remember. He ran a small hardware store, where every customer was greeted with a smile and a kind word. Most didn't know the depth of Thomas's faith, but those who spent time around him couldn't help but feel the presence of something different, something peaceful and good.

One day, a young man named Alex came into the store. Alex was new to Willow Creek and had moved there to escape the chaos of his past. He carried the weight of bitterness, disappointment, and a broken heart. His eyes were cold, and his manner was curt. He wasn't looking for friendship; he wasn't looking for help—he was just looking to be left alone. But Thomas saw more than the hardened exterior. He saw a man in need of love.

"Can I help you with anything?" Thomas asked with his usual warm smile as Alex shuffled through the aisles.

Alex grunted, not looking up. "Just looking."

Thomas didn't press him, but there was something in the way he responded that caught Alex off guard. "Take your time," he said, his tone patient, almost peaceful.

Over the next few weeks, Alex became a regular at the store. At first, it was just for supplies, but eventually, he began to linger, drawn to the quiet, gentle presence of Thomas. One day, after a particularly hard morning where Alex's frustration had boiled over into an argument with a neighbor, he came into the store, his hands trembling with anger.

"Rough day?" Thomas asked with that same calm voice.

Alex slammed a hammer on the counter. "You could say that."

Thomas didn't react to the aggression. Instead, he looked Alex in the eyes, his expression full of compassion. "I've had those days too."

For a moment, Alex stood there, expecting a lecture or an argument. But there was none. Only kindness.

"What's your deal?" Alex asked, more puzzled than angry now.

"What do you mean?"

"You're always like this. Calm. Happy. Why?"

Thomas smiled. "I'm not always happy. But I do have joy. There's a difference."

Alex scoffed. "What's the difference? Sounds like the same thing to me."

Thomas leaned on the counter. "Happiness depends on what's happening around you. Joy comes from something deeper. For me, it's my faith in God. Even when things don't go right, I know He's with me. That's what keeps me going."

Alex was silent, staring at the man in front of him. He wasn't used to this kind of answer. Most people would have shrugged him off or lectured him about his attitude. But Thomas didn't seem to need anything from him. He just...cared.

Over the next few months, Alex began to visit Thomas regularly, not just for supplies but for conversation. Slowly, his guard began to come down. He learned that Thomas's wife had passed away years ago and that Thomas had faced his own share of heartache. Yet, through it all, Thomas spoke of how God had been his anchor, how the fruit of the Spirit—especially love, patience, and self-control—had kept him steady when everything else seemed to crumble.

One day, Alex broke down. In the middle of the store, he confessed his own heartache—how his wife had left him after years of fighting, how his job had fallen apart, how he had come to Willow Creek to escape his failures. He expected Thomas to offer some pity or empty words of encouragement, but instead, Thomas placed a hand on his shoulder.

"God hasn't left you, Alex. He's been with you the whole time. He brought you here for a reason."

Tears welled up in Alex's eyes. "How can you believe that? After everything that's happened to you?"

Thomas smiled, his eyes kind but full of strength. "Because I've seen Him work through it all. Every trial, every loss, He's been there, shaping me. It's not always easy, but He's faithful."

Alex didn't say anything for a long time. But something shifted in him that day.

Over time, Alex began attending church with Thomas, slowly opening up to the idea of faith. The more he listened, the more he felt the weight of his past lifting. He started to see the world through a new lens—one of hope, not despair. As he experienced God's love and forgiveness, the fruit of the Spirit began to take root in his own life.

People in the town began to notice the change in Alex. His once-hard demeanor softened. He started to repair relationships he had damaged, even reaching out to his estranged wife. Though their marriage wasn't fully restored, there was forgiveness and healing. He became known for his kindness, his patience, and his willingness to help others, much like Thomas.

One cold winter day, the town faced a crisis. A major storm had hit, cutting off power and supplies. People were stranded, and tensions were rising. But Thomas and Alex, now partners in the hardware store, stepped up. Together, they worked to organize a relief effort, using their store as a hub to distribute food, blankets, and supplies. Alex, who had once been consumed by his own pain, was now at the forefront of helping others.

During that storm, something beautiful happened. The whole town came together, inspired by the kindness and leadership of these two men. Neighbors who had once been at odds found themselves working side by side. Strangers became friends. And through it all, there was a sense of peace that settled over Willow Creek despite the chaos of the storm.

Years later, after Thomas had passed away, people would still talk about him. They didn't speak of his wealth or accomplishments but of his kindness, his love, his gentleness, and his faithfulness. He had left a legacy—not in material things, but in the lives he had touched. Alex, who had once been broken and lost, had become a pillar in the community, carrying on the legacy of living by the fruit of the Spirit.

In the end, the impact of Thomas's life wasn't measured by the store he had run or the words he had spoken, but by the countless lives that were changed because he had chosen to live out the love, joy, peace, patience, kindness, goodness, faithfulness, gentleness, and self-control that God had placed in his heart.

Thomas's life was a testament to the power of living by the Spirit—a ripple of grace that started in a small town and spread far beyond. And Alex, once hardened by life's pain, had become a living example of how God can transform even the most broken heart, using it to bring light and hope to the world.

Conclusion: Living an Unshakable and Abundant Life

Understanding how to live an unshakable life rooted in God's Kingdom is essential to navigating the challenges and trials we face on earth. It empowers us to embrace an abundant life, one that aligns with God's true character and His redemptive plan. The importance of clarifying misconceptions about God's nature and shedding light on the myths that often cloud our understanding cannot be overstated. As we align our lives with God's truth, trusting His plan through trials and redemption, we develop unshakable confidence in His ability to bring us through. Living by the Spirit and walking in the world, but not of it, is how we experience the fullness of life God intends for us and how we advance His kingdom on earth.

Unshakable confidence—that's what God gives us. And make no mistake, the enemy is real. He is after you, relentlessly seeking to destroy what God has lovingly built in you. Why? Because God loves you so much, and in his hatred for God, the enemy will stop at nothing to ruin you. Are you going to let him? Now, it is your choice: are you going to let the enemy and his schemes tear you down, or are you going to stand firm behind enemy lines, faithful to your true King?

Believe me, I wasn't always standing firm during our hardest times. The enemy nearly had me. He tried relentlessly, whispering lies that almost pulled me into complete destruction. He already had me into anger and bitterness. I was on the edge, ready to give up on the promises of God and turn to the world for peace—a peace that never really satisfies. The enemy's snare was set, and I was close to being trapped. But then, God did what He always does—He sent His saints. They reached out a hand when I couldn't find my own way out. If it wasn't for them, I might have been lost. I might have given up on the God who never gave up on me.

Maybe that's what this book can be for some of you—a hand reaching out, offering hope in your darkest moments. And maybe, just maybe, you are being called to be that hand for someone else. We cannot walk this journey alone. We need each other, and we need to pull as many as we can into the peace of God's presence, into the shelter of the cloud where His protection and guidance flow.

So, I urge you—whether you're the one needing a hand or the one offering it—don't hesitate. Don't wait. There is peace and freedom waiting, but sometimes it takes the courage to reach out or accept the help that's offered. Together, we can stand firm in the face of the enemy's attacks, walking with God and offering help to others to walk into His love and peace.

We are living in a world where the enemy has dominion, but we don't belong to him. No, we belong to God's Kingdom, and we have access to a whole different realm—the 4th dimension. Imagine walking through this life, right in the middle of the enemy's territory, with God's complete protection surrounding you. The Holy Spirit speaks to you, guiding your every step. You are armored up, wearing the full armor of God, and you are undeterred in doing Kingdom work. That's the life God offers—He speaks to us in the cloud, showing us where to move, how to avoid the enemy's traps, and how to walk in victory, even when the enemy's attacks are fierce.

Now, can you picture the strength that comes when we walk in this confidence, not just alone but with our family and friends beside us, all of us tuned into God's voice, our heads in the cloud, our armor on 24/7? This is my journey—to share this truth, to spread the incredible news of God's loving protection and unshakable confidence to everyone I can. Life becomes a joy-filled adventure when we follow His lead, standing firm in His love and protection, and it's even more exhilarating when we do it together with those we love the most.

So, what has God challenged you to do with this? Will you commit to keeping your head in the cloud and your armor on, not just for yourself but for your family and friends? This is when life becomes truly amazing. When we walk in the fruit of the Spirit—love, joy, peace, patience, kindness, goodness, faithfulness, gentleness, and self-control—it's like it's magnetic. People will want to be around you, drawn to the life you carry in Christ. And that's your moment to invite them in, to bring them into the cloud with you, into God's protection and His unshakable confidence. Who do you need to invite into God's cloud today? Because this—this life of walking with Him, fully armored, fully confident—is what life is all about.

As believers, our actions and decisions on earth have eternal consequences. By focusing on God's will, rather than seeking immediate gratification or worldly success, we store up treasures in Heaven, as Jesus taught. Our lives become a reflection of obedience and faithfulness, not just for rewards in this life, but for an eternal inheritance that will glorify God forever.

This section also clarifies common misconceptions about rewards, reminding us that while we are already part of God's eternal Kingdom, we must continue to live in alignment with His purposes. The rewards promised in scripture are not merely for personal gain but are meant to be offerings back to God, reflecting His grace and character in our lives. With an eternal mindset, we can face trials and challenges, trusting in God's plan, knowing that our faithfulness will be richly rewarded in ways that magnify His glory.

An Eternal View on Life emphasizes that living for eternity impacts our daily choices. As we walk in the world but remain rooted in God's Kingdom, our perspective shifts toward long-term, spiritually significant decisions.

CHAPTER 25

An Eternal View of Life

Cultivating an Eternal Perspective

To live a successful Christian life, we must cultivate an eternal perspective, recognizing that our actions and decisions on earth have lasting implications beyond our immediate circumstances. While it is natural for us to focus on the short-term—today and tomorrow—we often miss the broader, divine narrative that God is weaving through our lives. When we don't see immediate results or solutions, this short-term thinking can lead us to question God's love and plan. However, faith invites us to trust in God's ultimate purpose and timing, even when we cannot see the immediate benefits.

A Spiritual Reality: You Will Never Die

As we saw in the section on the fall of Adam and Eve, when you become a believer in Christ, you move from death to life. Your spirit, which was once dead, becomes alive in Him. This is exactly what God was telling Adam and Eve when He said, "But of the tree of the knowledge of good and evil, you shall not eat, for in the day that you eat of it you shall surely die" (Gen. 2:17). Although Adam and Eve didn't physically die immediately, they experienced spiritual death—a separation from God.

You were born into this same spiritual death, but when you accepted Jesus's sacrifice, God brought you from spiritual death to spiritual life. As Ephesians 2:1–5 tells us, "And you He made alive, who were dead in trespasses and sins...But God, who is rich in mercy, because of His great love with which He loved us...made us alive together with Christ." This is the transformative power of salvation: your spirit is no longer dead but alive in Christ.

You, as a person, will continue on forever. Your physical body will need to be renewed because it is part of the temporary physical world, but your spirit—your true self—will never die. Instead, it will continue to grow, deepen, and flourish in the presence of God, experiencing His love, wisdom, and guidance for all eternity. This is the promise we hold as believers: life everlasting, never-ending growth in the things of God, and eternal fellowship with Him. The gift of God is eternal life (Rom. 6:23). Embrace this truth, and live with the assurance that you will never die. This is the core of Jesus's promise in John 11:25–26: "I am the resurrection and the life. He who believes in Me, though he may die, he shall live. And whoever lives and believes in Me shall never die."

The Dual Nature of Life: Physical and Spiritual

Your life now has two dimensions: a physical life and a spiritual life. Yes, your body is part of the physical world and will eventually die—this is a reality we all face as part of the fallen creation. As Ecclesiastes 3:20 says, "All go to the same place; all come from dust, and to dust all return." Our physical bodies age, grow tired, and will eventually return to the earth.

Focus on the Eternal: Your Spiritual Life

This spiritual life is what truly matters. If we have a heavenly focus, we will prioritize our spiritual life over our temporary physical existence. Your spirit will continue to grow, mature, and learn about spiritual things even after your physical body is gone. "Set your mind on things above, not on earthly things. For you died, and your life is now hidden with Christ in God. When Christ, who is your life, appears, then you also will appear with Him in glory" (Col. 3:2–4). As you focus on your spiritual life, you realize that eternal life has already begun. You are already living in eternity, and as Jesus declared, "Very truly I tell you, whoever hears my word and believes him who sent me has eternal life and will not be judged but has crossed over from death to life" (John 5:24).

Your spirit will continue to grow, mature, and learn about spiritual things even after your physical body is gone. The Apostle Paul reinforces this truth in 2 Corinthians 4:16-18:

> "Therefore, we do not lose heart. Though outwardly we are wasting away, yet inwardly we are being renewed day-by-day. For our light and momentary troubles are achieving for us an eternal glory that far

outweighs them all. So we fix our eyes not on what is seen, but on what is unseen, since what is seen is temporary, but what is unseen is eternal."

Eternal Life: A Journey of Growth

As a believer, you are on an eternal journey, and your spiritual life will never cease. Even though your body will grow old and tired, your spirit will continue to be renewed, transformed, and shaped by God's presence. You will continue to live, grow, and experience the fullness of life in God's Kingdom forever. In 1 Corinthians 15:42–44, Paul explains this beautifully: "The body that is sown is perishable, it is raised imperishable; it is sown in dishonor, it is raised in glory; it is sown in weakness, it is raised in power; it is sown a natural body, it is raised a spiritual body."

Though your physical body may wear out, your spirit will live forever in God's presence. As you focus on your spiritual life, you realize that eternal life has already begun. You are already living in eternity, and as Jesus declared in John 5:24, "Very truly I tell you, whoever hears my word and believes him who sent me has eternal life and will not be judged but has crossed over from death to life."

You Will Never Die

Our Time on Earth: A Ninety-Year-Long Job Interview

Our time on earth can be viewed as a metaphorical ninety-year-long job interview, an opportunity to demonstrate our obedience and faithfulness to God's will. During this period, our objective is to do His will, storing up treasures in Heaven (Matt. 6:19–20). These treasures are not merely for our future blessings but are gifts we can offer to God throughout eternity. This perspective shifts our focus from seeking immediate gratification to living with an awareness of our eternal destiny.

Preparing for Eternal Life: A Journey of Obedience

Our ultimate purpose as believers is to live forever with God, and our time on earth is an opportunity to prepare for that eternal life. In Heaven, we will experience the fullness of God's presence, serving and loving Him with all our hearts, souls, and minds. This eternal life is a continuation of our earthly relationship with God, where we will follow all His commands with joy and a heart fully aligned with His will. "No longer will there be any curse. The throne of God and of the Lamb will be in the city, and His servants will serve Him. They will see His face, and His name will be on their foreheads" (Rev. 22:3–4).

In Heaven, obedience to God will be natural, as we will be fully perfected in Him. But while we are here on earth, we are learning how to follow God's will and demonstrating to Him our deep desire to be obedient to His commands. This life is a preparation for the responsibilities or work God will give us in Heaven, as He will entrust us with greater things based on our faithfulness on earth. Jesus teaches us this principle in Luke 16:10, "Whoever can be trusted with very little can also be trusted with much, and whoever is dishonest with very little will also be dishonest with much."

Obedience is Key, Not Perfection

It's important to understand that our time on earth is not a measure of our worth but of our obedience. God is not grading us on our failures or successes in terms of earthly achievement; He is looking at the heart that says *"yes"* to Him. The story of the thief on the cross is a powerful example of this. In Luke 23:42–43, the thief acknowledges Jesus as Lord in his final moments, and Jesus assures him, "Truly I tell you, today you will be with me in paradise." The man's past failures didn't disqualify him from eternal life. It was his decision to turn to Jesus in obedience at that moment that mattered.

God's character is such that He is always focused on *now* forward. God is not concerned with the mistakes of the past; He is calling us to start anew, focusing on our present obedience and our future commitment to following His will. The Apostle Paul, who once persecuted Christians, became one of the greatest servants of Christ. "But one thing I do: Forgetting what is behind and straining toward what is ahead, I press on toward the goal to win the prize for which God has called me Heavenward in Christ Jesus" (Phil. 3:13–14).

This concept applies to our everyday lives as well. From now forward, we live each day knowing we won't always get everything right. The key is not to get stuck in those moments. When we stray from His path, we have a choice: we can dwell on our mistakes, which is one of the enemy's strategies to keep us from pursuing God's will, or we can simply acknowledge it, say we're sorry, and move forward. Life with God is always about *Now Forward*, pressing on without looking back in regret. God's character is not one of condemnation but of grace and mercy. The moment we turn to Him and commit to walking in His will, He welcomes us into the next chapter of our journey with Him.

Earthly Life as a Training Ground for Heaven

Our lives on earth are like a training ground for eternity. The responsibilities we are given in Heaven will be directly linked to how we follow God's will here on earth. Jesus highlights this in the Parable of the Talents in Matthew 25:14–30. The master praises the faithful servants who invested and multiplied the talents they were given, saying, "Well done, good and faithful servant! You have been faithful with a few things; I will put you in charge of many things. Come and share your master's happiness!" (Matt. 25:21). How we steward the resources, gifts, and opportunities God gives us on earth will determine the level of responsibility we are given in Heaven.

It's not about doing great things in the eyes of the world but about being faithful to the tasks and opportunities God sets before us. Whether it's loving our neighbors, serving our families, or using our talents for His glory, God is watching our faithfulness. In Heaven, those who have been faithful in small things will be entrusted with greater responsibilities, as Jesus says in Luke 19:17: "Well done, my good servant! Because you have been trustworthy in a very small matter, take charge of ten cities."

Moving Forward: It's About the Now

If you've failed in the past, know that it doesn't disqualify you from receiving God's best. His grace is sufficient, and He is always focused on your future. Lamentations 3:22–23 reminds us that "His compassions never fail. They are new every morning; great is your faithfulness." God's character is not one of condemnation but of grace and mercy. The moment we turn to Him and commit to walking in His will, He welcomes us into the next chapter of our journey with Him.

Your past disobedience does not define you. What matters to God is your decision today. His focus is always on the present and the future—how you will live now and in the days ahead. As Paul encourages us in Romans 12:1–2, "Do not conform to the pattern of this world, but be transformed by the renewing of your mind. Then you will be able to test and approve what God's will is—His good, pleasing and perfect will."

Heaven: A Place of Joyful Obedience

In Heaven, obedience to God will not be burdensome but a joy. We will love and serve God and all those who are in Heaven with us. Revelation 21:4 promises, "He will wipe every tear from their eyes. There will be no more death or mourning or crying or pain, for the old order of things has passed away." In the presence of God, our desires will be perfectly aligned with His, and we will experience the fulfillment of living out His will without the struggles and distractions of this earthly life. We will always say "yes" to God's commands, not out of obligation, but because our hearts will be fully in sync with His.

The time we have on earth is a precious opportunity to prepare for this eternity. With each act of obedience, we are demonstrating to God that we have a deep desire to follow His will and live according to His commands. As we align ourselves with His purposes now, we are preparing ourselves for the responsibilities He will entrust to us in Heaven.

Start Now, Press On

Your ninety years (or however long God gives you on earth) is not just a temporary existence but a period of preparation for eternity. The choices you make today—the way you serve God, the obedience you demonstrate, and the love you show to others—are preparing you for an eternal life of joy, service, and worship in God's presence. The good news is that it's never too late to begin living with an eternal perspective. God is always inviting you to step forward from now and follow Him faithfully, preparing for the eternal responsibilities and joy that await you in Heaven.

True Rewards are Eternal

Many people focus on the rewards they hope to receive from God in this life, expecting blessings such as wealth, success, or comfort. However, scripture reminds us that the true rewards God promises are not limited to our earthly existence but are ultimately reserved for eternity. Colossians 3:2–4 urges us, "Set your minds on things above, not on earthly things...When Christ, who is your life, appears, then you also will appear with him in glory." Similarly, Philippians 3:20–21 reminds us, "But our citizenship is in Heaven. And we eagerly await a Savior from there...who...will transform our lowly bodies so that they will be like his glorious body." Our earthly life is temporary, but the rewards of faithfulness, obedience, and perseverance are eternal. By keeping our eyes fixed on the promise of Heaven, we gain a perspective that helps us endure hardships, knowing that our true inheritance is not of this world but awaits us in eternity (Heb. 10:34). Instead of focusing solely on immediate blessings, we should live in anticipation of the eternal joy and glory that await us in the presence of our Lord.

Aligning with God's Eternal Purposes

By keeping an eternal view, we align our lives with God's eternal purposes, ensuring that our short-term thoughts and actions contribute to a lasting legacy in God's Kingdom. Our time on earth is not just about securing immediate benefits but about proving our faithfulness and preparing to live forever in God's presence. This eternal focus transforms how we live daily, driving us to pursue His will wholeheartedly and trust in His perfect plan for our lives.

Treasures and Rewards in Heaven

Living with an eternal perspective transforms how we approach life, aligning our goals and actions with God's greater plan and emphasizing the significance of storing treasures in Heaven. God instructs us to store up these treasures, highlighting their importance and the rewards that come from living a life pleasing to Him. These rewards are tangible evidence of our obedience and faithfulness, serving as a testament to a life well lived in accordance with God's will. Therefore, they should be a significant focus for us now, guiding our decisions and actions.

The Bible's Emphasis on Treasures

The Bible frequently discusses treasures and rewards, underscoring their importance. In Matthew 6:19–21, Jesus advises, "Do not store up for yourselves treasures on earth, where moths and vermin destroy, and where thieves break in and steal. But store up for yourselves treasures in Heaven, where moths and vermin do not destroy, and where thieves do not break in and steal. For where your treasure is, there your heart will be also." This passage clearly indicates that earthly treasures are temporary and vulnerable, while heavenly treasures are eternal and secure. By focusing on accumulating spiritual treasures, we shift our priorities from the fleeting to the everlasting.

Making Decisions with Eternal Significance

Living with an eternal perspective means making decisions with a long-term view, considering how our actions today will impact our eternal future. When we focus on eternity, we are more likely to prioritize activities that have lasting spiritual significance over those that offer immediate but temporary gratification. For instance, investing time in building relationships, sharing the gospel, serving others, and growing in our faith takes precedence over pursuing wealth, status, or other worldly achievements.

Jesus's Promise of Rewards

Revelation 22:12 emphasizes the significance of rewards: "Look, I am coming soon! My reward is with me, and I will give to each person according to what they have done." Jesus's promise to bring rewards for our deeds highlights that rewards are not only significant to God but will also be significant to us in eternity.

Navigating Life with an Eternal Focus

By focusing on eternity, we make decisions differently. We become more mindful of our spiritual growth, more intentional in our actions, and more diligent in seeking God's will. This eternal focus helps us to navigate life's challenges with a perspective that sees beyond the present moment, recognizing the lasting impact of our faithfulness. It encourages us to persevere, knowing that our efforts are not in vain and that God rewards those who earnestly seek Him.

Living with an eternal perspective means valuing the rewards and treasures that come from a life of obedience and faithfulness to God. These rewards are a testament to a life well lived in accordance with His will and serve as a motivating factor for us to prioritize what truly matters. By making decisions with eternity in mind, we align our lives with God's purposes, ensuring that our actions today contribute to our eternal joy and the fulfillment of God's Kingdom.

God's Intention for Us to Rule and Reign with Him

From the moment of creation, God designed humanity to have dominion over the earth (Gen. 1:28), and though sin disrupted this plan, it has been restored through Christ. God's magnificent plan for us extends far beyond salvation—it includes reigning with Him in His eternal kingdom. Revelation 5:9-10 declares that believers are made "a kingdom and priests to serve our God, and they will reign on the earth." This is not merely a role of power but of glorifying God through humble and righteous leadership, showing His love and wisdom to all of creation. The beauty of this promise is that we won't only experience

His eternal kingdom, but we'll be entrusted with the joy of co-reigning with Him for eternity.

The Joy of Serving in Heaven

In Heaven, service won't feel like work as we know it on Earth—it will be a joyful, fulfilling extension of our worship. Revelation 22:3 assures us that "His servants will serve Him," but this service will be entirely satisfying because it will be in perfect harmony with our God-given gifts and desires. The work we will do in Heaven will be a continuation of the good works we began on earth, amplified and perfected in the glorious presence of God. Revelation 20:6 expands on this, stating, "Blessed and holy are those who share in the first resurrection...they will be priests of God and of Christ and will reign with him for a thousand years." This promise underscores the honor and authority bestowed on those who faithfully serve God, granting them significant roles in His eternal kingdom—a kingdom that reflects joy, purpose, and divine leadership.

In Heaven, our role will be to serve, lead, and reign under Christ's authority, reflecting the humble service we lived on earth. True leadership in God's Kingdom comes not from seeking power but from a heart of love, humility, and obedience to God's will.

Who Will Rule and Reign with Christ?

Not everyone will automatically rule with Christ; this privilege is given to those who have faithfully followed Him and endured in their faith. "If we endure, we will also reign with Him" (2 Tim. 2:12). Faithfulness, perseverance, and obedience are the keys to ruling with Christ. The meek and humble, those who serve others with a pure heart, are those God will trust with authority in His kingdom (Matt. 5:5). "Blessed are the meek, for they will inherit the earth." The faithful and humble will reign, not for personal gain, but for the glory of God. And those who are faithful with small things will be entrusted with greater responsibility (Matt. 25:21).

What Do We Need to Do on Earth to Rule with Him?

This demonstrates that our actions, faithfulness, and service on earth prepare us for our future role in Heaven. Luke 16:10 reinforces this, stating: "Whoever can be trusted with very little can also be trusted with much."

While this opportunity to rule and reign with Christ is available to all believers, it is not something everyone will achieve in the same measure. Only those who remain faithful and obedient will be given greater responsibility in the kingdom of Heaven. Revelation 22:5 states, "And they will reign forever and ever," but this reign is reserved for those who have served faithfully. In Luke 19:17, Jesus illustrates this by rewarding the faithful servant with authority over ten cities. This shows that our roles in eternity are directly tied to how we serve God now. Furthermore, 1 Corinthians 6:2-3 highlights the astonishing authority believers will have in judging the world and even angels, pointing to the significant responsibility we will carry in God's Kingdom (1 Cor. 6:2–3). Yet, this authority is not based on human pride but on God's grace and how we live out our calling on earth.

The Criteria for Reigning with Christ

The Bible sets forth clear criteria for who will reign with Christ: faithfulness, stewardship, obedience, and humility. Jesus consistently taught that those who are faithful with small responsibilities on earth will be entrusted with greater authority in His kingdom. In Matthew 20:25-28, He explains that true greatness comes through serving others, not through seeking power or influence. Those who humbly serve others will be exalted by God, as Luke 14:11 says, "For everyone who exalts himself will be humbled, and he who humbles himself will be exalted."

Believers will be judged and rewarded based on the quality of their work for God's Kingdom (1 Cor. 3:12–15, 2 Cor. 5:10). Those whose work endures through testing will receive eternal rewards and responsibilities. As we explore this further in the coming chapters, we will see that our faithfulness, stewardship, and humble service on earth prepare us for the privilege of reigning with Christ in His eternal kingdom.

The Eternal Joy of Humble Leadership

Ruling and reigning with Christ is a joyful, eternal reward that reflects God's original plan for humanity. The work we do now in obedience and service to Him will not only bring glory to God but will prepare us for greater responsibilities in His kingdom. This reign is not born of pride or ambition—it is God's plan, and it will be carried out in humility and love. Those who serve faithfully on earth will experience the joy of serving and ruling in Heaven, co-reigning with Christ in perfect harmony with His will. We are invited into this glorious future, where our humble service now leads to eternal joy and fulfillment in the presence of our Creator.

The Judgment Seat of Christ

Living with an eternal perspective means recognizing that one day, every believer will stand before the judgment seat of Christ to be evaluated for how we've lived as believers. As 2 Corinthians 5:10 states, "For we must all appear before the judgment seat of Christ; that everyone may receive the things done in his body, according to that he hath done, whether it be good or bad." This judgment is not about determining our entrance into Heaven, which is secured through faith in Jesus Christ, but about assessing the degree of rewards and responsibilities we will carry into eternity (Luke 19:15–17).

The judgment seat of Christ, also known as the Bema Seat, is a place of reward for believers. As Paul writes that our works will be tested for their eternal value, and only those that endure will result in reward (1 Cor. 3:12–15), "If anyone builds on this foundation using gold, silver, costly stones, wood, hay or straw, their work will be shown for what it is, because the Day will bring it to light. It will be revealed with fire, and the fire will test the quality of each person's work. If what has been built survives, the builder will receive a reward. If it is burned up, the builder will suffer loss but yet will be saved—even though only as one escaping through the flames." This passage highlights that our works will be tested for their eternal value, and only those that endure will receive in reward.

Every believer will hear "Welcome home," but not every believer will hear "Well done, my good and faithful servant." While all believers are equally loved by God, they will not be equally rewarded.

Jesus's teachings consistently emphasize that our works, attitudes, motivations, how we manage what He gives us, our evangelism efforts, and how we love others—it all matters. As we have identified before but is so critical to this discussion, in Matthew 6:19–21, Jesus tells us, "Do not store up for yourselves treasures on earth, where moths and vermin destroy, and where thieves break in and steal. But store up for yourselves treasures in Heaven, where moths and vermin do not destroy, and where thieves do not break in and steal. For where your treasure is, there your heart will be also." Our lives need to be focused on something more than what we get in this world and will be meaningful throughout eternity (Matt. 6:19–21).

Furthermore, Jesus longs to give us the maximum reward possible on that day. It will bring Him great joy to reward those who have faithfully served Him. Hebrews 11:6 reminds us, "And without faith it is impossible to please God, because anyone who comes to him must believe that he exists and that he rewards those who earnestly seek him." This assurance motivates us to live lives of faithfulness and devotion, knowing that God is a rewarder of those who diligently seek Him (Heb. 11:6).

The Bible makes it clear that on Judgment Day, God won't only assess what we did but why we did it. Our actions are weighed in light of the intent behind them, and it is the purity of our motives that truly matters. The Lord "searches the heart and examines the mind," rewarding each person according to their conduct and the condition of their heart (Jer. 17:10). God reminds Samuel that, unlike humans, He looks beyond outward appearances and sees the heart (1 Sam. 16:7). Our religious duties—whether prayer, giving, or service—only hold eternal value if our hearts are aligned with God's will and we are motivated by love for Him rather than seeking approval from others (Matt. 6:1–4). Those who seek human recognition for their good deeds have already received their reward in full. True righteousness, however, is practiced in secret with pure intentions and will be openly rewarded by the Father (Luke 18:9–14). Scripture reveals more instances about intentions of the heart in the story of Ananias and Sapphira (Acts 5:1–11) and in the poor widow's small offering was praised by Jesus because it came from a place of true sacrifice and sincerity (Mark 12:41–44).

Living with an eternal perspective means understanding that our earthly lives are a preparation for eternity. Every action, decision, and moment is significant as we await the day we will stand before the judgment seat of Christ. By focusing on eternity, we make decisions differently, prioritizing spiritual growth, obedience, and service to God. Our works, attitude, motivation, management of God's gifts, evangelism efforts, and love for others all contribute to the rewards we will receive. Jesus desires to reward us richly, and by living with this eternal focus, we align our lives with His purposes, ensuring that our efforts today contribute to our eternal joy and fulfillment in His kingdom.

At the Second Coming, Final Judgment, New Heaven, and New Earth

Another key time when God distributes rewards is at the Second Coming of Christ and the *Final Judgment*. This happens after Jesus returns to establish His millennial kingdom, and all people—both believers and unbelievers—are judged at the Great White Throne Judgment. However, believers' rewards are already given at the Bema Seat, so this final judgment focuses more on assigning eternal roles and responsibilities. In Revelation 22:12, Jesus says, "I am coming soon! My reward is with me, and I will give to each person according to what they have done." Similarly, Matthew 16:27 echoes this idea, saying the Son of Man will come in glory and reward each person for their deeds (Rev. 22:12; Matt. 16:27). This time of judgment affirms God's justice, as everyone is given what they deserve, but for believers, it is a joyful moment of receiving their eternal inheritance.

Rewards in the New Heaven and New Earth

Following the final judgment, believers will receive their eternal rewards in the New Heaven and New Earth. After the final resurrection, God establishes His eternal kingdom, and believers enter into their everlasting roles. At this point, believers' eternal responsibilities, authority, and privileges are distributed, often based on how faithfully they lived their lives on Earth.

Luke 19:17 illustrates this idea in the parable of the talents, where a faithful servant is told, "Well done, my good servant! Because you have been trustworthy in a very small matter, take charge of ten cities." Similarly, Matthew 25:21 emphasizes that those who were faithful with what they were given on earth will be trusted with more in Heaven. These eternal rewards include increased responsibilities, levels of authority, and perhaps even different degrees of joy and glory. This moment celebrates the fulfillment of God's promises to His people, showing that their faithfulness on earth has eternal significance.

The Eternal Significance of Rewards

In Heaven, rewards are not just about individual recognition but about fulfilling the larger purposes of God's Kingdom. Believers' rewards reflect how they partnered with God during their earthly lives and will directly impact their eternal responsibilities in the new creation. Whether it's receiving crowns, being entrusted with leadership, or experiencing deeper joy, these rewards are a testament to God's justice and grace. As Revelation 22:12 reminds us, these rewards come from the hand of Jesus Himself, ensuring that believers live forever in the abundance and joy of God's Kingdom.

God's View on Rewards

Rewards are a big deal to God. Throughout the Bible, God discusses treasures and rewards. If we take rewards seriously, our heavenly experience can be significantly different. God encourages us to focus on storing up treasures and building rewards in Heaven rather than earthly treasures. Understanding the importance of these heavenly rewards can profoundly shape our lives, directing our focus away from temporary, earthly gains and toward eternal, spiritual investments.

In Matthew 5:12, Jesus encourages us to rejoice and be glad when we face persecution for His sake because "great is your reward in Heaven." This promise of a great reward underscores the value God places on enduring faithfulness and righteousness, even in the face of adversity. It reassures believers that their sacrifices and suffering for Christ's sake are not in vain but are recognized and will be richly rewarded by God.

The book of Revelation also provides vivid imagery of rewards in Heaven. Revelation 2:10, for example, speaks of the "crown of life," given to those who remain faithful unto death: "Be faithful, even to the point of death, and I will give you life as your victor's crown." This crown symbolizes eternal life and honor granted to those who persevere in their faith, demonstrating that God rewards not only our faithfulness but also our endurance and loyalty.

Paul, in his letters, often discusses the theme of running a race to win an imperishable crown. In 1 Corinthians 9:24–25 writes, "Do you not know that in a race all the runners run, but only one gets the prize? Run in such a way as to get the prize. Everyone who competes in the games goes into strict training. They do it to get a crown that will not last, but we do it to get a crown that will last forever." This metaphor of an athletic race highlights the discipline, effort, and dedication required to attain heavenly rewards. It encourages believers to strive for spiritual excellence, knowing that their rewards are eternal and imperishable.

I want to take you on a journey through the scriptures because when God repeats something, He wants us to understand it deeply. By delving into numerous passages, you'll see a clear pattern: God is profoundly committed to rewarding His followers. This isn't a minor theme; it's central to His nature. The idea of rewards from God is consistently reinforced throughout the Old and New Testaments, showcasing His promise to bless us for our faithfulness and obedience. Let's dive deep into God's Word together and uncover the undeniable truth of His generous nature—God delights in rewarding His people.

God Promises Rewards All Over the Scriptures for Obedience to Him

God's Word reveals a wide range of rewards that He desires to give His people. These rewards are given based on our faithfulness, obedience, love, and devotion to Him. They include both blessings we experience in this life and eternal rewards that will be fully realized in Heaven. Understanding the different types of rewards that God promises, when we can expect them, and the assurance we have in scripture that we can count on them, I believe, is critical to understanding God's nature and how much He loves us. The Bible consistently emphasizes that God rewards those who faithfully follow His ways, perform acts of kindness, and endure trials for His sake. These rewards, both temporal and eternal, reflect God's justice, generosity, and deep love for His people. It is through our obedience, humility, and perseverance that we store up treasures in Heaven, ensuring an eternal inheritance that far surpasses any earthly gain.

Types of Rewards in Scripture

God Himself Is Our Reward

The Bible is rich with promises of rewards, both in this life and in eternity. These rewards are not merely material but often spiritual and eternal, designed to reflect God's justice, grace, and desire to bless His faithful servants. Throughout scripture, God assures believers that their faithfulness, generosity, obedience, and perseverance will be rewarded.

In Genesis 15:1, we see God speaking directly to Abram, saying, "Do not be afraid, Abram. I am your shield, your very great reward." Here, God reassures Abram that His presence is the ultimate reward, far surpassing any material blessing. God Himself is the prize for those who seek Him—a relationship that offers protection, love, and eternal blessings. This same promise echoes through Psalm 73:25-26, where the psalmist declares, "Whom have I in Heaven but you? And earth has nothing I desire besides you...God is the strength of my heart and my portion forever."

God Promises Us Justice

Proverbs 11:18 "The wicked earns deceptive wages, but one who sows righteousness gets a sure reward."

Romans 2:6 "He will render to each one according to his works."

Psalm 58:11 "Mankind will say, 'Surely there is a reward for the righteous; surely there is a God who judges on earth.'"

Hebrews 6:10 "For God is not unjust so as to overlook your work and the love that you have shown for his name in serving the saints, as you still do."

Rewards for Faithfulness and Obedience

In addition to all the passages in this chapter about what God rewards us for, The Bible consistently shows that God rewards faithfulness and obedience. Consider:

Exodus 23:25 God promises the Israelites, "Worship the Lord your God, and His blessing will be on your food and water. I will take away sickness from among you." Obedience to God brings physical and spiritual rewards.

Ruth 2:12 shows a profound blessing pronounced by Boaz: "May the LORD repay you for what you have done. May you be richly rewarded by the LORD, the God of Israel, under whose wings you have come to take refuge." Boaz acknowledges that Ruth's faithfulness to her mother-in-law and her decision to seek refuge under God's wings are actions that will be richly rewarded by God. This verse shows how acts of kindness and obedience, even when unnoticed by the world, are seen and rewarded by the Lord.

Proverbs 11:18 lays out the principle of divine justice: "A wicked person earns deceptive wages, but the one who sows righteousness reaps a sure reward." Proverbs consistently teach that while wickedness may lead to temporary gain, true and lasting rewards come only to those who live righteously before God. The idea of reaping a "sure reward" emphasizes the permanence and reliability of God's promises to the faithful.

Romans 2:6 Paul writes that God "will repay each person according to what they have done." This New Testament passage, which echoes the sentiments of the Old Testament, reminds believers that God's justice is both fair and certain. Whether in this life or in the life to come, God rewards individuals based on their obedience to Him.

Galatians 6:9 encourages believers not to grow weary in doing good: "Let us not become weary in doing good, for at the proper time we will reap a harvest if we do not give up." This verse is a reminder that persistence in righteousness brings about a harvest, even when immediate results are not visible. God's timing is perfect, and His rewards for those who persevere in faith are assured.

Deuteronomy 28:1–2 underscores the rewards of obedience: "If you fully obey the Lord your God...all these blessings will come on you and accompany you if you obey the Lord your God." This chapter lists the blessings God promises to those who are faithful, including prosperity, protection, and peace.

1 Samuel 24:19 "May the LORD reward you well for the way you treated me today." God rewards those who act with kindness and mercy, even in difficult circumstances.

Psalm 19:9–11 "The decrees of the LORD are firm, and all of them are righteous...By them your servant is warned; in keeping them there is great reward. Obeying God's Word brings great reward, both in protection and blessings."

Psalm 58:11 "Then people will say, 'Surely the righteous still are rewarded; surely there is a God who judges the earth.'" God rewards the righteous, affirming His justice and sovereignty over the earth.

Isaiah 40:10 "See, the Sovereign LORD comes with power, and He rules with a mighty arm. See, His reward is with Him, and His recompense accompanies Him." God brings rewards for those who are faithful and serve Him, coming in power to give just compensation.

Isaiah 61:11 "For as the soil makes the sprout come up and a garden causes seeds to grow, so the Sovereign LORD will make righteousness and praise spring up before all nations." Faithfulness and righteousness are rewarded as they lead to God's promises being fulfilled and honored before all nations.

Hebrews 6:10 "God is not unjust; He will not forget your work and the love you have shown Him as you have helped His people and continue to help them." God remembers acts of love and service, rewarding those who show faithfulness.

Hebrews 11:6 "And without faith it is impossible to please God...He rewards those who earnestly seek Him." God rewards those who seek Him in faith, making faithfulness a vital part of receiving His blessings.

Rewards for Generosity and Kindness

Jesus, too, places great emphasis on the rewards for generosity and kindness.

Matthew 6:3–4 Jesus teaches, "But when you give to the needy, do not let your left hand know what your right hand is doing...Then your Father, who sees what is done in secret, will reward you." This passage highlights the importance of humility in giving. God sees the heart behind every act of generosity, even when others do not, and He promises to reward those who give quietly and selflessly.

Mark 9:41 Jesus assures His followers that no act of kindness, no matter how small, goes unnoticed: "Truly I tell you, anyone who gives you a cup of water in my name because you belong to the Messiah will certainly not lose their reward." This verse emphasizes that even the simplest acts of service, when done in Jesus's name, carry eternal significance and will be rewarded by God.

Luke 6:35 Jesus expands this principle by teaching about loving enemies: "But love your enemies, do good to them, and lend to them without expecting to get anything back. Then your reward will be great." Loving those who cannot repay us is a powerful demonstration of God's love, and Jesus promises that such actions will result in "great" rewards from the Father.

Luke 14:12–14 Jesus instructs, "When you give a banquet, invite the poor, the crippled, the lame, the blind...you will be repaid at the resurrection of the righteous." Here, Jesus emphasizes that true generosity is giving to those who cannot repay us. He assures that such acts will be repaid in eternity, pointing to the resurrection as the time when God's rewards will be fully realized.

Proverbs 19:17 further underscores this truth: "Whoever is kind to the poor lends to the Lord, and He will reward them for what they have done." This verse reveals that generosity toward the needy is seen by God as an investment in His kingdom, and He promises to personally repay those who give out of love and compassion.

Proverbs 28:27 teaches that generosity is rewarded by God: "Whoever gives to the poor will not want, but he who hides his eyes will get many a curse." This verse underscores the importance of helping those in need. Those who are generous will be taken care of by God, while those who ignore the poor will face consequences. God sees the act of giving and responds by ensuring the giver will not be in need.

Ecclesiastes 11:1 highlights the concept of trust and future reward: "Cast your bread upon the waters, for you will find it after many days." This verse encourages believers to give generously without immediate expectation of return, trusting that in time, their generosity will come back to them. God honors those who give freely, and although the reward may not be instant, it is guaranteed in the future.

Matthew 10:42 Jesus assures that even the smallest acts of kindness are noticed and rewarded: "And whoever gives one of these little ones even a cup of cold water because he is a disciple, truly, I say to you, he will by no means lose his reward." This passage emphasizes that no act of service is too small when done with the right heart. God promises to reward even the smallest gesture of kindness done in His name.

Matthew 25:40 Jesus reveals that acts of kindness toward others are seen as acts of service to Him: "And the King will answer them, 'Truly, I say to you, as you did it to one of the least of these my brothers, you did it to me.'" This verse demonstrates that when we care for the needy and show compassion to others, we are serving Christ Himself. Every act of love and kindness toward others is eternally significant and will be rewarded by God.

2 Corinthians 9:6–8 Paul emphasizes the principle of sowing and reaping in generosity: "The point is this: whoever sows sparingly will also reap sparingly, and whoever sows bountifully will also reap bountifully. Each one must give as he has decided in his heart, not reluctantly or under compulsion, for God loves a cheerful giver." This passage teaches that generosity brings abundant blessings. God loves when we give joyfully, and He promises to provide for us abundantly so that we can continue to do good works.

Hebrews 6:10 reassures believers that God does not forget their acts of service and love: "For God is not unjust so as to overlook your work and the love that you have shown for his name in serving the saints, as you still do." This verse reminds us that God remembers every act of love and service done in His name. He is just, and He will reward those who faithfully serve others and demonstrate His love.

Rewards for Faithful Stewardship

Matthew 25:19–23 Jesus tells the Parable of the Talents, where a faithful servant is commended: "Well done, good and faithful servant! You have been faithful with a few things; I will put you in charge of many things. Come and share your master's happiness!" This parable illustrates that faithfulness in managing what God entrusts to us, no matter how small, will result in greater responsibilities and joy in God's Kingdom.

Luke 19:15–19 The parable of the ten minas shows a similar reward: "Well done, my good servant! Because you have been trustworthy in a very small matter, take charge of ten cities." Jesus teaches that faithfulness in small tasks will be rewarded with greater responsibility and honor in eternity.

Colossians 3:23–24 provides further encouragement: "Whatever you do, work at it with all your heart, as working for the Lord, not for human masters, since you know that you will receive an inheritance from the Lord as a reward." This passage reminds believers that their efforts, when done for the Lord, are not in vain. God promises an eternal inheritance for those who serve Him wholeheartedly.

1 Corinthians 3:8 reinforces the rewards for faithful labor: "The one who plants and the one who waters have one purpose, and they will each be rewarded according to their own labor." Every faithful act in God's service is seen and rewarded.

Rewards for Spiritual Sacrifice and Perseverance

Matthew 19:27–29 Jesus reassures His disciples, saying, "Everyone who has left houses or brothers or sisters...for my sake will receive a hundred times as much and will inherit eternal life." This profound promise affirms that sacrifices made in this life for the sake of the gospel will be richly rewarded both now and in eternity.

Hebrews 11:25–26 We see the example of Moses, who "regarded disgrace for the sake of Christ as of greater value than the treasures of Egypt because he was looking ahead to his reward." Moses's willingness to endure hardship and forsake worldly treasures demonstrates the eternal perspective that is necessary to receive God's lasting rewards.

Hebrews 6:10 reminds us that "God is not unjust; He will not forget your work and the love you have shown Him as you have helped His people." This assures believers that no act of love or service goes unnoticed by God, and He is faithful to reward those who labor in His name.

2 Timothy 2:12 Paul also emphasizes: "If we endure, we will also reign with Him." This promise reveals that enduring trials and remaining faithful leads to the reward of reigning with Christ in His eternal kingdom.

James 1:12 We find encouragement for those who persevere under trial: "Blessed is the one who perseveres under trial because, having stood the test, that person will receive the crown of life." Enduring trials leads to the reward of eternal life.

Revelation 2:10 speaks to those facing persecution: "Be faithful, even to the point of death, and I will give you life as your victor's crown." Jesus promises eternal life to those who remain faithful despite suffering.

Rewards for Private Devotion and Sincere Worship

God values private devotion and rewards sincere acts of worship, prayer, and fasting.

Matthew 6:5–6 Jesus teaches, "But when you pray, go into your room, close the door and pray to your Father, who is unseen. Then your Father, who sees what is done in secret, will reward you." This teaches us that God rewards genuine prayer and devotion done in humility.

Matthew 6:16–18 reinforces this idea. "But when you fast, put oil on your head and wash your face...your Father, who sees what is done in secret, will reward you." This verse highlights the spiritual rewards of fasting, done not for human recognition but for God.

Psalm 37:4 "Take delight in the LORD, and He will give you the desires of your heart." This reminds us that when our hearts are focused on worshipping God, He rewards us by fulfilling our desires in accordance with His will.

Isaiah 40:31 promises rewards for those who wait on God: "But those who hope in the Lord will renew their strength. They will soar on wings like eagles." God rewards those who patiently seek Him with spiritual renewal and strength.

Eternal Crowns and Glory

1 Corinthians 9:24–25 compares the Christian life to a race: "Run in such a way as to get the prize... They do it to get a crown that will not last, but we do it to get a crown that will last forever." Paul's metaphor highlights the importance of perseverance, with the promise of receiving an eternal crown that far surpasses any earthly reward.

1 Peter 5:4 speaks of a specific reward for faithful shepherds: "And when the Chief Shepherd appears, you will receive the crown of glory that will never fade away." This crown is a special reward for those who faithfully care for God's people.

James 1:12 "Blessed is the one who perseveres under trial because, having stood the test, that person will receive the crown of life that the Lord has promised to those who love him." This shows that enduring trials in faith leads to the reward of eternal life.

Revelation 22:12 Jesus promises, "Look, I am coming soon! My reward is with me, and I will give to each person according to what they have done."

Fullness of Reward in the Judgment

Revelation 11:18 speaks of God's final judgment: "For rewarding your servants the prophets and your people who revere your name, both great and small." In the final judgment, God will reward all those who have served Him faithfully.

2 John 8 warns believers: "Watch out that you do not lose what we have worked for, but that you may be rewarded fully." This is a call to stay vigilant in our faith to receive the full reward that God has prepared for us.

These verses, taken together, paint a rich and detailed picture of the rewards God promises to those who love, serve, and obey Him. Whether through acts of kindness, faithful stewardship, endurance through trials, or private devotion, God's rewards are both spiritual and eternal, far surpassing any earthly gain. This theme of reward underscores God's justice, grace, and desire to bless His children as they walk in His ways.

Are These Rewards Promised, and Can We Count on Them?

Yes, the rewards described in scripture are fully promised, and we can absolutely count on them. God is faithful to fulfill His promises, and His Word assures us that our labor in the Lord is never in vain (1 Corinthians 15:58). While some rewards may be experienced in this life—such as spiritual growth, peace, and blessings—many of the rewards God promises are eternal and will be fully realized in Heaven.

God's promises are unwavering, and scripture consistently teaches that He rewards those who diligently seek Him, faithfully serve Him, and live according to His will (Hebrews 11:6). As believers, we can trust that these rewards are guaranteed, and they are distributed according to our faith, obedience, love, and devotion to Him.

God's rewards encompass both present blessings and eternal treasures. They are certain and will be given based on our faithfulness to Him, with the ultimate fulfillment of these rewards being realized in eternity.

Why Focus on Building Rewards and Treasures in Heaven?

As we have seen, the concept of storing treasures in Heaven is rooted in scripture and provides us with a framework for understanding how our actions, faithfulness, and spiritual growth during our earthly lives have eternal significance. While the Bible does not offer extensive details about the exact nature of these treasures or rewards, it provides key principles and insights that encourage believers to prioritize heavenly rewards over earthly gain.

Fully Known and Fully Loved in Heaven

In Heaven, we are fully known and fully loved, surrounded by endless light and the presence of Jesus, where every desire is fulfilled, and every hope is realized. It is a place of eternal worship and deep, unbroken communion, a home where love reigns and where every moment is filled with overwhelming joy and peace.

Glorifying God through Rewards

The ultimate purpose of these heavenly rewards is to glorify God. In Heaven, whatever treasures we have stored up will be used to magnify God's goodness, wisdom, and grace. Jesus taught in Matthew 5:16 that our good works should shine before others, leading them to glorify our Father in Heaven. This principle extends into eternity, where the rewards we receive will continually reflect God's character and bring honor to His name.

Building Communion with Other Believers

Scripture indicates that Heaven will be a community of believers united in Christ (Heb. 12:22–23). The treasures we store in Heaven could contribute to this sense of unity and shared purpose among believers. These rewards might enrich our relationships and foster deeper bonds within the community of the redeemed, helping us experience the fullness of life together in God's eternal kingdom.

The Mystery of Unknown Blessings

1 Corinthians 2:9 says, "No eye has seen, no ear has heard, and no human mind has conceived the things God has prepared for those who love him." There are dimensions of heavenly rewards that are beyond our comprehension. The treasures we store in Heaven might be part of these unimaginable blessings that

God has in store for us—things far greater than anything we can currently grasp.

While the specifics of how we will use the treasures we store in Heaven remain a mystery, the Bible provides ample encouragement to live a life focused on eternal rewards. These rewards won't only bring us joy and fulfillment, but, more importantly, they will glorify God and contribute to His eternal kingdom plan.

The Ultimate Gift to God

Perhaps the most profound potential benefit of storing treasures in Heaven is that these rewards and treasures might be what we have for eternity to offer to our heavenly Father. God provides us with everything we need to live and will be with us in Heaven for eternity. What a blessing it could be to have our rewards and treasures stored up in Heaven, ready as a gift to Him. Consider it: what else would we have to offer as a sacrifice in Heaven?

Imagine the incredible moment of standing before Jesus, holding all the treasures and rewards He lovingly stored up for us. Now, picture the joy of giving them back to Him in pure worship as our eternal offering to the One who gave us everything. These treasures aren't just rewards—they're precious gifts we potentially get to lay at His feet, showing our love and gratitude for all He's done.

But now, imagine the emptiness if we had nothing to give back, nothing to offer in return. How profound it would be to have these heavenly rewards ready, stored up as a sacrifice of praise to our heavenly Father! What a blessing it would be to have something of eternal value to present to Him, not because He needs it, but because it's our way of saying, "This is for You, Lord."

God's instruction to store treasures in Heaven reflects His desire for us to prioritize eternal values over temporary gains. It aligns with His love for us and His desire to see us grow in spiritual maturity, experience the joy of selfless living, and invest in His kingdom's work on earth. Ultimately, the specifics of how we'll use our treasures in Heaven are beyond our current understanding. The focus should not solely be on what we will receive or do in Heaven but on cultivating a genuine relationship with God, living in obedience to His teachings, and pursuing a life of love and service.

The concept of storing up treasures in Heaven serves as a motivation for living a life that pleases God and reflects His values. Our understanding of Heaven and the specifics of how we will use our stored treasures is limited. The Bible provides us with a glimpse, but it's not meant to be an exhaustive description. The main emphasis is on living a life that honors God and follows His teachings, resulting in the accumulation of treasures that have eternal significance and rewards in His presence. Obedience tells us that it is important to Him, so it should be important to us (Matt. 6:19–21).

Story Time: An Eternal View on Life—The Story of Evelyn and Michael

Evelyn stood in her garden, the soft hum of bees flitting between the flowers she had so carefully nurtured over the years. Her hands, calloused from years of tending to her plants, were a testament to the beauty she had cultivated, but today, her heart felt heavy. The weight of her 90 years on earth was catching up to her, and as the sun cast its golden glow across the land, she reflected on her life's purpose.

"I thought by now I'd see more results," Evelyn whispered to the wind. "I've been faithful, Lord. I've given, served, loved ... but was it enough?"

In Heaven, Michael, a member of the great cloud of witnesses, watched over Evelyn. Michael had lived in the same small town as Evelyn many decades before. They never knew each other on Earth, but in Heaven, Michael had seen her life unfold. He had watched as she selflessly cared for others, worked humbly in the church, and poured her heart into people who could never repay her.

"Is she asking that question again?" Michael smiled softly. He understood the struggle between Heaven and Earth—between what we see now and what God is preparing for eternity. And now, he watched, knowing that Evelyn, like so many believers, had focused on the immediate, the visible, and the tangible, often unaware of how her faithfulness echoed into eternity.

Evelyn turned away from the garden, sitting on a worn bench nearby. Her mind wandered to moments she had considered insignificant conversations she had with lonely strangers, donations given to those who would never know her name, and prayers offered in the stillness of the night. "What do these little things matter?" she had often thought.

The Struggle of Earthly Perspective

In Heaven, Michael understood that tension well. He, too, had once lived on earth, focusing on the short-term rewards and the visible successes. Before he passed away, Michael often questioned the value of the sacrifices he made for others. "I'm just one person. How can anything I do make a lasting difference?" he had often asked.

But that was before he entered eternity.

Now, standing in the presence of God, Michael saw everything clearly. The seemingly small acts of kindness, the unnoticed moments of faithfulness, the prayers no one else knew about—those were the moments that mattered most. Each one, Michael realized, was a treasure stored in Heaven, a crown laid at Jesus's feet in worship.

Heaven's Perspective Unveiled

As Evelyn sat in her garden, her heart ached with the question of whether her life had truly made an impact. Then, a breeze stirred the leaves, and in that quiet moment, she heard a still, small voice deep in her spirit.

"Your treasures are not lost, Evelyn. They're waiting for you."

Tears welled up in Evelyn's eyes as she recognized the voice of her Savior. In that instant, she saw a glimpse of Heaven—a place of unimaginable beauty, where every act of love, every sacrifice, and every moment of obedience was carefully gathered by God. These weren't just rewards for her enjoyment; they were offerings she would one day lay at the feet of Jesus.

In the vision, Evelyn saw Michael standing there, a man she had never met but one who had also lived for eternity. His face radiated joy as he placed a crown at Jesus's feet. Evelyn understood then that it wasn't about how much the world noticed her or how successful she seemed. It was about how her faithfulness had contributed to the eternal tapestry of God's Kingdom.

Michael looked at Evelyn and smiled. "We were never meant to see it all while still on earth, but now you'll understand the eternal view of life. Every moment of faithfulness echoes here."

The Joy of Eternal Reward

Evelyn returned from her vision, tears streaming down her face, but this time, they were tears of joy. She could now see that her life, full of quiet acts of devotion, was not wasted. The treasures she had stored up in Heaven were not only rewards for her but also reflections of the glory and love she had for Jesus.

On that worn bench, she prayed, "Thank you, Lord, for showing me that everything I've done matters. It's all for you. I will gladly give it all back to you one day."

In Heaven, Michael's heart swelled with joy as he watched Evelyn's transformation. He remembered the day he, too, had received his crown from Christ and how he had knelt in awe, laying it at the feet of his Savior. Now, Evelyn was preparing for her own moment—her chance to worship the Lord with the treasures she had stored in Heaven.

The unseen kindness, the prayers in secret, the service without recognition—each act was a gift for her to return to God. And in Heaven, Michael knew that when Evelyn arrived, she would be greeted with those simple but powerful words: "Well done, good and faithful servant. Enter into the joy of your Lord."

The Eternal Perspective

The years passed quickly after that day, and Evelyn lived with a new sense of peace. She understood that her time on earth was merely the beginning, a "ninety-year-long job interview," as she sometimes called it. Every decision, every moment, was preparing her for eternity.

When Evelyn finally took her last breath, she entered Heaven with joy in her heart, and Michael was there to greet her. "You made it," he said warmly.

Evelyn looked around and saw the beauty of Heaven, the treasures that awaited her, and the presence of the Lord shining brighter than anything she had ever imagined.

And as she knelt before Jesus, the crown of her faithfulness in her hands, she laid it at His feet, saying, "This is for You, Lord. Everything I did was for You."

In that eternal moment, Evelyn knew with complete certainty that her life had mattered—not just for the short span of years she had lived on earth, but for all eternity. Her treasures were not just rewards; they were her eternal love offering to the Savior who had given her life everlasting.

And as Michael watched, he knew that Evelyn's story was only beginning. The joy of eternity, the worship of the King, the fulfillment of purpose—this was what living with an eternal perspective was all about. Every act of faithfulness on earth was a building block in the eternal kingdom, a legacy that would last forever.

In Conclusion

Understanding the importance of living an unshakable and abundant life with an eternal perspective is crucial for our Christian journey. By aligning ourselves with God's true character and plan, we embrace His vision for eternity rather than becoming entangled in the fleeting concerns of the world. An unshakable life means building our foundation on God's promises, remaining steadfast through trials, and storing up treasures in Heaven, not for our gain but as offerings of love and gratitude to God. As we live in alignment with His will, we shed light on the common misconceptions that material success or immediate gratification defines a blessed life. Instead, true abundance is found in our spiritual growth, eternal rewards, and the impact of living out God's love and grace in our everyday choices.

This eternal perspective, as reflected in *Clarifying Misconceptions: Shedding Light on the Myths* and *Unshakable Redemption: Embracing God's Eternal Perspective*, guides us to see life as part of a greater divine plan. By viewing our earthly existence as a preparation for eternity, we cultivate a life that honors God, builds His kingdom, and prepares us for the eternal joy awaiting us. When we understand that our actions have eternal significance, we are empowered to make decisions with a purpose, knowing that our ultimate reward is glorifying God and sharing in His everlasting glory. Living an abundant life, in this sense, is not about earthly prosperity but about thriving spiritually, trusting God's timing, and walking in the fullness of His eternal plan for our lives.

CHAPTER 26

How to Store Up Treasures in Heaven

Storing Treasures in Heaven: Aligning Our Lives with Eternal Values for God's Kingdom

In the teachings of Jesus, the concept of storing treasures in Heaven emerges as a profound principle that touches every facet of Christian life. Far from being a call to renounce worldly wealth, it is an invitation to align our lives with eternal values, to engage in acts of righteousness that reflect God's Kingdom, and to grow in a relationship with Christ that culminates in eternal joy and reward. This principle weaves together themes of faith, character development, sacrificial love, and the pursuit of God's Kingdom. Let us explore these themes in depth, guided by scripture and enriched by the Bible's wisdom.

Faith in Jesus Christ: The Cornerstone of Eternal Investment

Storing up treasures in Heaven begins with faith in Jesus Christ, the bedrock of our spiritual lives. This faith is not a mere intellectual assent but a transformative trust in the redemptive work of Christ and a wholehearted commitment to follow Him. As Jesus asserts in John 14:6, "I am the way and the truth and the life. No one comes to the Father except through me." This foundational truth highlights that without faith in Christ, every attempt to store treasures in Heaven is futile. The Apostle Paul reinforces this in Ephesians 2:8-9, emphasizing that it is by grace through faith that we are saved. Faith in Christ is the beginning of our eternal relationship with God and the framework within which all other spiritual activities gain meaning. The call to store up treasures in Heaven is, at its core, a call to deepen our faith in Christ, allowing His teachings to shape our values and actions.

Acts of Righteousness: The Currency of the Kingdom

In the Sermon on the Mount, Jesus warns against performing acts of righteousness for public acclaim, instead encouraging believers to seek God's approval in secret (Matthew 6:1-4). This passage reveals the essence of what it means to store treasures in Heaven. True righteousness is rooted in love for God and neighbor, expressed through humility, justice, and mercy. Isaiah 58:6-7 reminds us that God desires acts of justice that set the oppressed free, share bread with the hungry, and shelter the homeless. The biblical vision of righteousness is not limited to religious rituals but extends to acts of justice and compassion. In Micah 6:8, we are reminded, "He has shown you, O mortal, what is good. And what does the Lord require of you? To act justly and to love mercy and to walk humbly with your God." Such deeds, done with a heart aligned with God's purposes, are treasures that neither moth nor rust can destroy (Matthew 6:19-20). They are investments in the eternal kingdom, reflecting God's own character and advancing His redemptive plan.

Honoring Parents: A Promise of Long Life

Ephesians 6:2-3 God's command to **honor your father and mother** comes with a promise: a long and fulfilling life. This blessing is rooted in the importance of respecting and caring for parents, and it reflects God's desire for healthy and loving family relationships that mirror His care for His children.

Generosity: Reflecting God's Abundant Grace

Generosity in scripture is more than an act of giving; it reflects the character of God, who "did not spare his own Son, but gave him up for us all" (Romans 8:32). The call to generosity is both a command and an opportunity to participate in God's mission. Acts 20:35 underscores the principle that "it is more blessed to give than to receive," pointing us toward a life of joyful, sacrificial giving that mirrors God's grace. Proverbs 11:25 states, "A generous person will prosper; whoever refreshes others will be refreshed." This biblical truth emphasizes that generosity is not about losing but about gaining what are truly valuable treasures in Heaven. The Apostle Paul, in 2 Corinthians 9:6-7, highlights that God loves a cheerful giver and that such giving results in spiritual enrichment both for the giver and the recipient. Thus, generosity is a tangible expression of our faith and a key means of investing in the eternal work of God's Kingdom. Luke 6:38 states that the act of giving is closely tied to receiving blessings from God. Jesus teaches that **generosity** will result in a return that is "pressed down, shaken together, and running over." God honors those who give freely, and their generosity results in abundant spiritual and material blessings.

Overcoming Sin: The Crown of Life

Revelation 3:21: The **crown of life** is promised to those who overcome sin and remain faithful to Christ. Victory over temptation and steadfastness in faith are rewarded with eternal life, symbolized by this special crown. It is a mark of triumph for those who have persevered and stayed true to their faith in Jesus.

Sacrifices and Service: The Path to Eternal Reward

The call to present our bodies as "living sacrifices, holy and pleasing to God" (Romans 12:1) is central to the Christian life. Biblical sacrifice is not simply about giving up something of value; it is about offering ourselves fully to God's purposes. Jesus Himself is the ultimate model of sacrificial service, declaring that "the Son of Man did not come to be served, but to serve, and to give his life as a ransom for many" (Matthew 20:28). Following Christ's example, we are invited to lay down our lives in service to others, knowing that such sacrifices are not in vain but are richly rewarded in eternity. Hebrews 13:16 adds, "And do not forget to do good and to share with others, for with such sacrifices God is pleased." Every act of self-giving love is a seed sown into the eternal harvest, a treasure stored in the kingdom where Christ reigns.

Crown of Glory for Faithful Shepherds

1 Peter 5:4 God promises a **crown of glory** for those who faithfully shepherd His people. Spiritual leaders and pastors who lead with humility and care are rewarded in Heaven with honor and recognition. This crown signifies the eternal value of guiding God's flock and faithfully nurturing His people.

Welcoming Others: A Prophet's Reward

Matthew 10:41-42: Welcoming others in the name of Christ is an act that holds eternal significance. Jesus assures that even small acts of kindness, like offering a cup of cold water, are seen and rewarded by God. Those who honor prophets and righteous people share in their spiritual rewards, demonstrating that hospitality is valued in God's Kingdom.

Faithfulness in Little Things

In Matthew 25:21, Jesus emphasizes the importance of faithfulness in small tasks. Those who are trustworthy with what they are given will be entrusted with greater responsibilities in God's Kingdom. This principle reminds us that God values even seemingly insignificant acts of faithfulness.

Forgiveness and Love: The Heartbeat of the Kingdom

In the Lord's Prayer, Jesus teaches us to ask for forgiveness "as we also have forgiven our debtors" (Matthew 6:12), linking our forgiveness from God with our willingness to forgive others. Forgiveness is not optional in the Christian life; it is essential for storing treasures in Heaven. Matthew 6:14-15 makes it clear: "For if you forgive other people when they sin against you, your heavenly Father will also forgive you." Forgiveness is an act of grace that reflects God's own nature and releases us from bitterness, freeing us to live in the fullness of God's love. 1 John 4:7-8 commands us to "love one another, for love is from God, and whoever loves has been born of God and knows God." Love is the highest virtue in the Christian life (1 Corinthians 13:13), and it is through love that we fulfill the law (Romans 13:10). When we love and forgive others, we align ourselves with the very heart of God, storing up treasures that resonate with the eternal nature of His kingdom.

Enduring Trials and Persecution: The Path to the Crown of Life

The Christian life is marked by trials, yet Scripture encourages us to view these as opportunities to store up treasures in Heaven. James 1:12 declares, "Blessed is the one who perseveres under trial because, having stood the test, that person will receive the crown of life that the Lord has promised to those who love him." Endurance in the face of suffering is not just a passive waiting but an active trust in God's sovereign plan. Romans 5:3-4 reveals that suffering produces perseverance, perseverance produces character, and character produces hope—a hope that does not disappoint because it is rooted in God's love (Romans 5:5). In 2 Corinthians 4:17, Paul reminds us that "our light and momentary troubles are achieving for us an eternal glory that far outweighs them all." Every hardship, when endured with faith, adds weight to the treasures we are storing up in Heaven, pointing us toward the eternal reward that awaits those who remain steadfast in Christ.

Seeking God's Kingdom First: The Divine Priority

In Matthew 6:33, Jesus offers a powerful promise: "But seek first his kingdom and his righteousness, and all these things will be given to you as well." This is not merely a command to prioritize spiritual matters but an invitation to align every aspect of our lives with God's redemptive purposes. Seeking God's Kingdom involves making His will our highest aim, ensuring that our decisions, goals, and pursuits are centered on advancing His rule in our lives and in the world. Colossians 3:1-2 command us to "set your hearts on things above, where Christ is, seated at the right hand of God." This eternal perspective shifts our focus from temporal concerns to the eternal realities of God's Kingdom. As we invest our time, energy, and resources in kingdom values, we lay up treasures that cannot be shaken, securing a reward that endures forever.

Living in Light of Eternity: The Christian Worldview

The call to store treasures in Heaven is rooted in the biblical worldview that sees this life as preparation for eternity. Colossians 3:2 instructs us to "set your mind on things above, not on earthly things." This mindset is essential for making choices that reflect eternal values rather than temporary gain. In 2 Peter 3:11-12, believers are challenged to live holy and godly lives in light of the coming day of the Lord, recognizing that "the earth and everything done in it will be laid bare." This eternal perspective not only motivates righteous living but also provides comfort in the face of life's uncertainties. In Hebrews 11:13-16, the patriarchs are commended for living as "strangers and exiles on the earth," looking forward to the city whose architect and builder is God. To live with eternity in mind is to recognize that our true home is with God and that our treasures should be stored there, where they will never perish.

Eternal Perspective and True Riches: Valuing What Lasts

In a world that prizes wealth and status, Jesus' command in Matthew 6:19-20 to "store up for yourselves treasures in Heaven" stands as a radical countercultural call. True wealth, according to scripture, is not found in material possessions but in spiritual growth, godly character, and an intimate relationship with God. Luke 12:15 warns, "Watch out! Be on your guard against all kinds of greed; life does not consist in an abundance of possessions." The parable of the rich fool (Luke 12:16-21) illustrates the futility of hoarding wealth without being "rich toward God." True riches are measured by the depth of our faith, the strength of our character, and the extent to which our lives are aligned with God's eternal purposes. In Revelation 3:18, Jesus advises the church to "buy from me gold refined in the fire," symbolizing the spiritual riches that come from a life purified through obedience and faith. These are the treasures that truly endure and will be rewarded in eternity.

Detachment from Materialism: The Call to Spiritual Freedom

The pursuit of material wealth is a significant obstacle to storing treasures in Heaven. 1 Timothy 6:10 warns, "For the love of money is a root of all kinds of evil." This love of money can lead to greed, corruption, and a life centered on self rather than God. Jesus emphasized the impossibility of serving both God and money in Matthew 6:24, stating that "no one can serve two masters." The call to store treasures in Heaven is a call to freedom from the tyranny of materialism, inviting us to live generously and simply, with hearts fully devoted to God. Hebrews 13:5 advises, "Keep your lives free from the love of money and be content with what you have because God has said, 'Never will I leave you; never will I forsake you.'" Contentment rooted in God's presence is the key to spiritual freedom and the foundation for storing treasures that last.

Investment in Kingdom Values: Building on the Eternal Foundation

Storing up treasures in Heaven involves a conscious investment in values that align with God's Kingdom. This includes spreading the gospel, practicing righteousness, and serving others in ways that reflect God's love and justice. In Matthew 25:21, the faithful servant hears the words, "Well done, good and faithful servant!" This affirmation is not based on earthly success but on a life lived in faithful obedience to God's will. In 1 Corinthians 3:11-15, Paul explains that "no one can lay any foundation other than the one already laid, which is Jesus Christ." The quality of our works, whether built with gold, silver, or costly stones, will be tested by fire. Only that which is built on the foundation of Christ will endure, resulting in a reward that reflects our alignment with God's Kingdom purposes.

Eternal Rewards: The Crown Awaiting the Faithful

While salvation is a gift of grace, the Bible speaks of rewards based on our deeds. Revelation 22:12 emphasizes, "Look, I am coming soon! My reward is with me, and I will give each person according to what they have done." The word "done" highlights the significance of one's actions in determining their eternal reward. The Greek terms suggest ongoing, habitual actions, while the Hebrew context emphasizes deeds as expressions of moral character. Together, they point to the cumulative impact of a person's life, reflecting their alignment with or against God's will. This verse emphasizes that Jesus will reward each person based on the entirety of their deeds, underscoring the importance of living faithfully and intentionally. Timothy 4:7-8 speaks of the "crown of righteousness" awaiting those who have fought the good fight, finished the race, and kept the faith. The promise of eternal reward motivates us to live with purpose, knowing that our labor in the Lord is never in vain (1 Corinthians 15:58). These eternal rewards and honors from God motivate us to live faithfully and obediently.

Loving God Above All: The Highest Treasure

Jesus taught in Matthew 6:21, "For where your treasure is, there your heart will be also." The call to store treasures in Heaven ultimately points to the priority of loving God above all else. Deuteronomy 6:5 commands us to "Love the Lord your God with all your heart and with all your soul and with all your strength." This love for God is the essence of what it means to store treasures in Heaven, for it directs our affections, decisions, and desires toward what is most valuable—God Himself. The greatest commandment, to love God and love our neighbor (Matthew 22:37-39), encapsulates the essence of storing treasures that last. When our hearts are fully devoted to God, our lives naturally reflect His priorities, and we lay up treasures that are imperishable and incorruptible.

This list highlights that God's rewards, treasures, and blessings are for a wide range of righteous actions, faithfulness, and heart attitudes. Each of these rewards is grounded in our relationship with God and reflects His justice, grace, and abundant generosity.

Building Character: The Refining Process of Eternal Worth

The journey of storing treasures in Heaven is closely tied to character formation. Romans 5:3–4 outlines a progression from suffering to perseverance, perseverance to character, and character to hope. This process of refinement is essential for living a life that is pleasing to God and aligned with His purposes. Our character is shaped in the context of trials and challenges, leading to treasures that bear eternal value. In 1 Peter 1:6–7, Peter describes faith as more precious than gold, refined by fire, resulting in "praise, glory, and honor when Jesus Christ is revealed." The cultivation of Christlike character is itself a treasure, for it prepares us to fully enjoy the eternal inheritance that God has prepared for those who love Him.

Avoiding Earthly Worries: Trusting in God's Provision

Anxiety about material concerns often hinders our ability to focus on heavenly treasures. Philippians 4:6–7 counsels believers, "Do not be anxious about anything, but in every situation, by prayer and petition, with thanksgiving, present your requests to God." This posture of trust frees us from the distractions of earthly worries, enabling us to invest in what truly matters. Jesus's teaching in Matthew 6:25–34 reinforces this: by seeking first the Kingdom of God, we are released from the burdens of worldly anxiety and are free to store treasures in Heaven with joyful confidence.

Treasures in Heaven Versus Rewards

The Bible makes a clear distinction between treasures in Heaven and rewards in Heaven, though they are related concepts, both integral to understanding the eternal nature of our faith and actions.

Treasures in Heaven

Treasures in Heaven refer to the spiritual blessings and acts of righteousness that believers store up for their eternal life with God. The Greek word for treasures, "θησαυρός" (thēsauros), signifies a storehouse of valuable things. These treasures represent the accumulated goodness, faithfulness, and love demonstrated during one's earthly life.

Treasures in Heaven are built through actions that reflect God's character, such as acts of kindness, generosity, and faithfulness. They signify a believer's relationship with God and commitment to His will. For example, in Luke 12:33–34, Jesus explains, "Sell your possessions and give to the poor. Provide purses for yourselves that will not wear out, a treasure in Heaven that will never fail, where no thief comes near, and no moth destroys. For where your treasure is, there your heart will be also."

Rewards in Heaven

Rewards in Heaven, described by the Greek word "μισθός" (misthos), pertain to the compensation or recognition believers receive from God for their faithful service and obedience. These rewards are not about earning salvation, which is a gift of God's grace, but rather about receiving acknowledgment for living a life of faith and service.

In 1 Corinthians 3:8, Paul writes, "The one who plants and the one who waters have one purpose, and they will each be rewarded according to their own labor." This passage highlights that rewards are based on the quality and faithfulness of one's work in God's Kingdom. Jesus also speaks about rewards in the Sermon on the Mount.

The Relationship and Distinction

While both treasures in Heaven and rewards in Heaven emphasize the importance of living in accordance with God's will and the eternal nature of the Christian faith, they differ in focus. Treasures in Heaven are the spiritual wealth accumulated through one's relationship with God. This includes intangible spiritual gains like peace, joy, and a closer relationship with God. On the other hand, rewards are specific acknowledgments from God for one's faithful actions, often described in the context of judgment and recompense for deeds done in faith. This dual emphasis encourages us to prioritize our spiritual lives, ensuring our hearts are set on the eternal rather than the temporary.

Story Time: Building Treasures in Heaven

Grace and Ethan were two remarkable individuals admired by their community. Grace was a devout woman who centered her life around her faith, dedicating herself to serving God and others. Her days were filled with acts of kindness, volunteer work, and moments of deep prayer. She was known for her unwavering commitment to blessing those around her, always putting others' needs before her own. Her focus on God and blessing her community resulted in a life that was not only blessed but also deeply fulfilled and prosperous. Grace's prosperity was evident in the joy and contentment she exuded, a reflection of her selfless devotion and the blessings she received in return.

On the other hand, Ethan was a respected member of the community, admired for his hard work and dedication to his family and business. He lived a very prosperous life, having built a successful career that provided well for his loved ones. Ethan was friendly and well-liked, often seen engaging with neighbors and colleagues. However, unlike Grace, Ethan's free time was primarily focused on how he could make his own life better. He invested his energy and resources into enhancing his personal comfort and security, seeking ways to increase his wealth and enjoy the fruits of his labor.

While both Grace and Ethan lived prosperous lives, the focus of their efforts differed significantly. Grace's life was marked by a relentless pursuit of blessing others and finding joy in giving and serving. Her prosperity was a byproduct of her selflessness and her deep connection to God. Ethan's prosperity, though equally evident, was more self-centered, driven by his desire to improve his own circumstances and ensure his family's well-being.

The contrast between Grace's and Ethan's lives highlights the different ways people can achieve prosperity and fulfillment. Grace's eternal perspective and dedication to serving others brought her a deep sense of purpose and spiritual richness. Ethan's focus on personal gain and comfort provided him with material success but lacked the profound sense of fulfillment that comes from living a life devoted to the well-being of others.

Upon their arrival in Heaven, Grace found herself in a place of extraordinary beauty and splendor. She was surrounded by vibrant colors, breathtaking landscapes, and a profound sense of peace. She was welcomed by a chorus of angels and felt an overwhelming sense of joy. Grace's acts of service and selflessness on earth had blossomed into an eternal reward of unimaginable proportions.

Ethan found himself in Heaven, but his surroundings were simpler. While still beautiful and serene, they paled in comparison to the paradise Grace was experiencing. He was content and at peace but couldn't help but wonder about the stark difference between his heavenly abode and responsibilities and what he observed Grace's abode and responsibilities seemed to be.

Grace explained to Ethan that the rewards in Heaven were not about comparison but about the overflow of a life lived in alignment with God's will. She shared how her acts of service and selflessness on Earth had paved the way for the heavenly treasures she was now experiencing.

Ethan realized that while he had been a good person, he hadn't fully embraced the idea of living a life that truly honored God. He recognized that his focus on earthly success had led him to miss out on the deeper spiritual rewards that awaited him.

Grace and Ethan's story teaches us that a life dedicated to doing God's will and storing up treasures in Heaven leads to a deeper, more profound experience in the afterlife. It reminds us that our actions on earth have eternal consequences.

Pure Motives in Acts of Righteousness

Jesus reinforces this in *Matthew 6:1–4*, where He warns against performing righteous acts to be seen by people. Those who seek human recognition for their good deeds have already received their reward in full. True righteousness, however, is practiced in secret with pure intentions and will be openly rewarded by the Father. The parable of the Pharisee and the tax collector (*Luke 18:9–14*) further illustrates this truth. The Pharisee's self-righteous prayer was rejected, while the humble tax collector, seeking only God's mercy, was justified.

Examples of Intent in Scripture

In the story of Ananias and Sapphira (*Acts 5:1–11*), the couple's deceitful intent in their giving led to severe judgment. This shows that God sees beyond the external appearance of generosity and discerns the heart's true motives. Conversely, in *Mark 12:41–44*, Jesus praises the poor widow's small offering because it comes from a place of true sacrifice and sincerity. This demonstrates that it is the intent and sacrifice behind an act that matters most to God.

Living with Integrity Before God

These examples remind us that God not only observes our actions but also judges the motives behind them. Whether we are serving, giving, or praying, the true value lies in our heart's alignment with God's will. Living with sincerity and purity of heart, seeking to honor God rather than gain human approval, is what ultimately pleases the Lord and leads to eternal rewards

The Importance of Intent in God's Judgment

Jesus's words in Matthew 7:21–23 are some of the most sobering in scripture: "Not everyone who says to me, 'Lord, Lord,' will enter the kingdom of Heaven, but only the one who does the will of my Father who is in Heaven. Many will say to me on that day, 'Lord, Lord, did we not prophesy in your name and in your name drive out demons and, in your name, perform many miracles?' Then I will tell them plainly, 'I never knew you. Away from me, you evildoers!'" Here, Jesus reveals that even those who did seemingly great works in His name could be rejected if their motives were wrong. Why? Because their hearts were far from Him. Their actions were not driven by love, humility, or a desire to truly honor God. Instead, they were likely motivated by self-interest, pride, or the pursuit of recognition. God is not fooled by outward displays of religiosity—He sees the heart (1 Samuel 16:7).

This is a critical reminder that God won't reward actions done with impure motives, even if they appear righteous on the outside. It is not enough to simply go through the motions of religious life. Hebrews 4:12 tells us, "For the word of God is alive and active. Sharper than any double-edged sword... it judges the thoughts and attitudes of the heart." God's Word reveals and exposes our true intentions. Are we seeking to please God, or are we trying to manipulate the system for our own gain?

No Shortcuts in the Kingdom: Walking in Genuine Faith

In our pursuit of heavenly rewards, we must recognize that there are no shortcuts or quick fixes. God's Kingdom operates on principles of truth, love, and integrity. Galatians 6:7–8 warns, "Do not be deceived: God cannot be mocked. A man reaps what he sows. Whoever sows to please their flesh, from the flesh will reap destruction; whoever sows to please the Spirit, from the Spirit will reap eternal life." The rewards that truly matter in Heaven come from a life lived in sincere obedience to God's will, walking in step with the Holy Spirit, and allowing His love to flow through us.

Our faith journey is about far more than just securing rewards in Heaven. It is about cultivating a deep, authentic relationship with the Lord, where we are shaped into His likeness. Jesus invites us to abide in Him (John 15:5), promising that as we remain connected to Him, our lives will naturally bear fruit that brings glory to God. This fruit is not born out of striving for rewards but out of a genuine love for Jesus and a desire to live in accordance with His will.

The real treasure is being able to offer our lives back to Jesus as a sacrifice of worship, knowing that we have walked in genuine faithfulness. The crowns and rewards we receive are not for our own glory; they are meant to be laid at the feet of Jesus in reverence and adoration (Rev. 4:10–11).

Guarding Our Hearts and Examining Our Motives

In all that we do, we should continuously examine our motives and allow the Holy Spirit to purify our intentions. David's prayer in Psalm 139:23–24 should be our constant plea: "Search me, God, and know my heart; test me and know my anxious thoughts. See if there is any offensive way in me, and lead me in the way everlasting." Only God can truly reveal the hidden motives of our hearts. As we seek Him with humility and openness, He refines us, aligning our desires with His will.

Let us pursue a deep, authentic, and Spirit-filled relationship with the Lord, knowing that the rewards we receive are merely a reflection of the love and faithfulness we have shown Him in this life.

Story Time: With Daniel

Daniel was a man who, from the outside, seemed to be everything a faithful Christian should be. His life was a whirlwind of ministry, service, and religious activity. He was always in church, leading prayer groups, organizing community events, and giving generously to those in need. People admired him and often said, "If anyone has a special place in Heaven, it's Daniel." They saw him as a spiritual giant, always striving for the Kingdom of God.

But deep within, Daniel harbored a secret struggle—a battle with his own pride and self-centeredness. As a young boy, Daniel had truly accepted Christ with an innocent and sincere heart. That decision was genuine, and it sealed his eternity. But as he grew older, something shifted. The love that had once motivated his walk with Christ began to be overshadowed by a desire for recognition, influence, and personal gain.

Daniel found himself increasingly driven by the approval of others. He enjoyed being seen as the "go-to" person for anything spiritual. Over time, his service became more about building his own reputation and less about glorifying God. He was meticulous in his works, striving to perfect every project, every sermon, every act of kindness—not because he sought to honor the Lord, but because he craved the applause of those around him.

In his mind, he justified it all. After all, wasn't he doing good things? Wasn't he helping people? Surely, the praise he received was just a reflection of how well he was serving God—or so he told himself. Yet deep down, Daniel knew something was missing. His prayers became routine, his Bible reading felt dry, and he couldn't shake the emptiness that gnawed at him. But instead of turning back to the sincere devotion he once knew, Daniel pushed harder, doing more, striving more, and seeking validation in the outward successes of his "ministry" life.

Then, the day came when Daniel's earthly journey ended. He stepped out of time and into eternity, confident that his works would be counted as treasures stored up in Heaven. As he approached the gates of Heaven, the light of God's presence shone with an intensity he had never imagined. Everything was exposed in that holy light—his thoughts, his motives, and the true nature of his works.

Daniel's heart swelled with anticipation as he imagined the rewards he was sure awaited him: crowns, jewels, and recognition in the Kingdom. But what happened next was not what he expected. As his life was laid bare before the throne of God, all his grand acts of service, his ministries, and charitable deeds were revealed—not as shining gold or precious jewels but as wood, hay, and straw. In an instant, they were consumed by the fire of God's truth, leaving only ashes behind.

The weight of realization hit Daniel like a crashing wave. His life's work, which had seemed so impressive on earth, was revealed for what it truly was—empty of eternal value. The applause, the recognition, the influence he had craved so deeply on earth amounted to nothing in the light of God's judgment. But then, a voice—gentle, yet filled with authority—spoke: "Daniel, you are My child, and you are welcome here. But your works were for yourself, not for Me. You sought your own glory rather than Mine. Your place in My Kingdom is secure because you are redeemed, but your rewards are lost, burned away by the fire of truth."

The words pierced Daniel's heart. He had spent his life working tirelessly but for the wrong reasons. He was entering Heaven—not because of anything he had done, but because of that one simple decision he had made as a child to accept Christ. That was his salvation, the unshakable foundation that nothing could take away. Yet, he felt the deep sorrow of knowing that he had missed out on the fullness of what could have been. The treasures he might have laid at Jesus's feet were gone, consumed by his pride and selfish ambition.

As Daniel looked around, he saw others—people who had lived quiet, humble lives on earth, unnoticed by most. Their crowns shone with a brilliance that took his breath away, filled with jewels and rewards they had earned through lives lived in simple obedience and love for God. These were people who had never sought recognition, who had served faithfully in obscurity, content to be known only by the Lord. Their joy was radiant, their faces aglow with the satisfaction of having lived for an audience of One.

Daniel felt both joy and deep regret. Joy because he was in the presence of his Savior, secure in his eternal home. Regret because he realized how much he had focused on his own desires instead of surrendering fully to God's will. The rewards he had imagined were nowhere to be found; his life, though busy and outwardly successful, had been spent chasing fleeting recognition rather than storing up treasures in Heaven.

In that moment, Daniel understood what had been missing all along—a heart that was truly surrendered to God, motivated by love for the Lord and others rather than by personal ambition. He would spend eternity in Heaven, but the rewards he might have gained were lost forever. He saw with clarity what really mattered: not the quantity of his works but the quality of his heart, the purity of his motives, and the depth of his love for Jesus.

As Daniel entered his eternal home, he was met with the overwhelming love of Christ—a love that had never wavered, even in the face of his misguided pursuits. Jesus embraced him, not with disappointment, but with a compassion that broke Daniel's heart even more. "You are Mine," Jesus said gently, "and I have loved you from the beginning. But if only you had known the joy of living for Me alone, how much more your life would have meant, both here and on earth."

Daniel would live in the joy of God's presence for eternity, but the knowledge of what could have been would remain with him. He realized now that the greatest reward was not the recognition of men or the accumulation of earthly accolades but the deep satisfaction of knowing that every act, every word, and every deed had been done out of pure love for God. And though he was saved, he was saved "as one escaping through the flames" (1 Cor. 3:15), with nothing left to show for his life but the love of a Savior who had never let him go.

Daniel's story became a reminder to all who followed: that while salvation is a gift given freely through faith, the rewards of Heaven are a reflection of a life lived in true devotion to God. The crowns we receive are not for our own glory but to be laid at the feet of Jesus in humble adoration. In the end, it is the heart that matters most—whether it beats for the applause of others or beats in rhythm with the love of Christ. For Daniel, the joy of Heaven was tinged with the bittersweet knowledge of how much more fulfilling his journey could have been if only he had lived with a heart fully surrendered to the One who gave everything for him.

Understanding how to live an unshakable and abundant life is essential because it aligns us with God's true character and eternal perspective. By clarifying misconceptions and shedding light on the myths, we grasp the significance of storing treasures in Heaven and embracing an unshakable redemption. As we align our lives with eternal values for God's Kingdom, we gain the clarity to walk in unshakable eternity with the right focus. These principles are not only for our own spiritual enrichment but also to reflect God's love, righteousness, and generosity on earth—ensuring our lives bear lasting fruit both now and in eternity.

Where have I been? I had *no idea.* When I started to really study what eternity means, I was dumbfounded. Some of you may have already grasped this, but for me, all I knew was, "I'm going to Heaven, and it'll be good." That was it. But why don't we teach more about this? Why aren't we talking about the fact that *right now*—in this very moment—we're shaping our eternal destiny? Living life just for the sake of saving for retirement? Are you serious? Is that really the best we've been offered? "Oh yay, once you hit 65, you can finally do some volunteering for the church." *That* was my life for 20 years in investment management—helping people plan for such a shallow life purpose, thinking that the golden years were the ultimate goal.

But now, after understanding Heaven and the *real* work that awaits us there, I can't contain my excitement! My spirit literally *thrills* at the thought of eternity. Honestly, I'm excited to die—not because I want to leave this life, but because I now understand that this life is just the beginning of a much greater journey! The only thing that holds me here is that I want to be on this earth as long as possible, doing *God's work*—building treasures for eternity. This is the only chance I'll ever get to do that. When Jesus said, "Store up your treasures in Heaven, not on earth," He wasn't kidding! It's so *clear*—so what are we doing about it?

What's your strategy? How are you intentionally storing treasures in Heaven? If you're not already thinking about this every day, it's time to start. We need to be talking about eternity with our friends, our families, our coworkers— *everyone.* Can you imagine what it would look like if everyone around you were working toward the same goal, the goal of eternity, instead of a couple of decades of retirement? What a difference that would make.

What are you going to do about it?

CHAPTER 27

Living a Great Life on Earth

How Does God Want to Give Us Wealth and Blessings on Earth?

Life as a believer is exhilarating when we grasp the promise of heavenly rewards. However, the reality of living in a world where the enemy still has influence is a daunting challenge. If you're like me, the thought of storing up treasures in Heaven fires you up, yet balancing that excitement with the demands of this earthly life isn't easy. We juggle providing for our families, raising kids, loving people, and revealing Christ—all while surviving in a world that often seems determined to wear us down.

So, what does God really want for us on this earth? Are we called to a life of sacrifice, or does He want us to live abundantly, showcasing what He can do through a life fully surrendered to Him? It's tempting to think that abundance isn't biblical, but the truth is, there are so many examples of God's people—like David, Solomon, and Abraham—who lived with incredible wealth and influence. Were they exceptions? Or is there something we're missing? Didn't God promise us that he was going to bless us in the covenants?

It's easy to spend years praying for God to prosper us, to pull us out of our struggles, and to bring us into a place of great wealth and comfort, only to feel like those prayers go unanswered. I know this struggle well. I used to pray endlessly for God's miracle-working power, hoping for quick fixes and sudden blessings, but nothing ever changed. Eventually, I realized I was asking for the power but not the wisdom. I wanted God to drop a miracle in my lap, but I wasn't asking Him to guide me through the minefield the enemy had set up—those traps meant to frustrate me and make me lose hope.

It isn't about choosing between sacrifice and abundance; it's about understanding that God wants to walk us through both with His wisdom. It's about trusting His direction more than just longing for His miracles. When we seek His heart, guidance, and timing, we begin to see the path He's laid out, even in the middle of life's challenges. So, is it sacrifice or abundance? Maybe it's both, depending on the season and His purpose for our lives.

God provides guidance step by step rather than revealing everything at once (Ps. 119:105). He doesn't function as a spotlight showing the entire path but as a lamp, illuminating the next step. He tells us step by step if we are looking for what we are to be doing to create the wealth that He has set aside for us. He typically does not drop millions of dollars in our bank accounts (although He may in some circumstances); He wants to journey with us, telling us where to go and what to do to give us the land and cattle (figuratively) that He promises.

God's Role in Our Abundance

God will bless abundant crops and livestock—We are still planting the crops and taking care of the livestock, but then God does His work. Nothing happens to the ground if we don't plant seeds. We cannot just sit and pray for crops and be annoyed at God for not miraculously popping a corn stalk out of the ground. He wants to work in partnership with us, telling us when to plant, what to plant and where to plant. Sometimes, it rains at the right time, and we see it and praise God for His abundant blessings. Sometimes, it keeps the insects away, and we don't even realize what He did. That's why it's so important to thank God for all we have all the time. He is always working on bringing us blessings, whether or not we see it and understand it.

This principle of partnership with God is illustrated throughout scripture. In the book of Genesis,

- **Genesis 8:22**—After they emerged from the ark, God made a covenant with Noah and his family, ensuring the continued cycle of seasons for planting and harvesting. Noah still had to till the land and plant the seeds.

- **Genesis 26:12–13**—Isaac obeyed God's direction during a time of famine and sowed in the land, and the Lord blessed him with a hundredfold harvest.

- **Proverbs 12:24**—God's blessings flow through our obedience and diligence as He partners with us to bring the increase. God does not say, "Pray, and I will give you what you need." (Although we know He does that sometimes). We need to know what God is telling us to do, and we need to do it. God said He is the light unto our feet, not the spotlight, showing the entire path with explanations and directions. He will show us step by step what we are to do, and we must believe that when God puts His hand of blessing on our obedience, the blessings will come.

Trusting God's Wisdom

God might simply say you need to plant beans or squash one year because He knows it will be a wet year. But the next year, He might tell you to plant corn because He knows it won't be as wet. We don't know why He would be telling us to plant corn when we did so well the year before with squash, but if we trust Him, He will bless us. If we don't understand and do our own thing, we won't receive the blessings He is trying to give us. If you miss a blessing, however, don't worry; He is always trying to give us blessings as He promised.

Trusting God with our abundance requires a deep reliance on His wisdom, even when it challenges our understanding (Prov. 3:5–6). When we choose to trust Him and give Him control over our resources, He multiplies them in ways we could never foresee. And even when we make mistakes or don't see immediate results, God's grace remains. His provision is not limited by our understanding but fueled by His endless abundance and desire to bless His children (Phil. 4:19).

The Power of Obedience: God's Comprehensive Blessings

Obeying God's commands leads to blessings that impact every area of our lives (Deut. 28:1–2). These blessings aren't confined to one aspect of life; they extend to family, health, finances, and spiritual well-being. For example, the story of Joseph in Genesis illustrates how his obedience to God, even in challenging circumstances, brought him favor in Potiphar's house, in prison, and ultimately, over all of Egypt. Likewise, when we align our actions with God's Word, we invite His favor in ways that go beyond material success, touching relationships, peace of mind, and spiritual growth.

Psalm 1:1–3 describes the one who delights in God's law as "a tree planted by streams of water, which yields its fruit in season and whose leaf does not wither—whatever they do prospers." Obedience opens the door to God's promises of protection, provision, and guidance, ensuring we experience His blessings in our daily lives. Even when challenges arise, God's hand remains over those who follow His will, ensuring that His blessings cover all aspects of their existence.

In the Old Testament covenant between God and the Israelites, specific blessings promised to the Israelites through Moses are listed (Deut. 28:1–14):

- Blessings in the city and in the country

- Blessings of abundant crops and livestock

- Blessings of fertility and prosperity among the people

- Blessings in their basket and kneading bowl (i.e., in their food provisions)

- Blessings in their coming in and going out (i.e., in all their activities)

These blessings encompass various aspects of life, ensuring prosperity and well-being in both urban and rural settings. They imply safety, protection, and provision in all areas of life.

It's clear that God wants us to live amazing lives on earth while doing His will. He provides everything we need; we just need to walk in His provisions. Giving His children a great, loving, and spectacular life is part of His nature. Understanding His nature helps us comprehend His gifts to us.

Story Time: Alex's Amazement

Once there was a man named Alex, a believer who always tried to walk the straight and narrow, but life didn't always match the promises he read in scripture. He had a good heart, always praying, asking for blessings, and seeking

God's favor. But somehow, no matter how many prayers he whispered or hours he spent in devotion, the miracles seemed to skip over his life. Bills piled up, work was draining, and the promises of abundance felt distant—until the day everything changed.

Alex had been reading about God's covenants with His people—stories of David, Solomon, and Abraham—and something caught his eye. These men didn't just live lives of faith; they lived with wealth, influence, and abundance. Could it be that he was missing something? Was there more to this life of faith than just waiting for God to drop blessings from Heaven?

One afternoon, after another long, exhausting day at work, Alex found himself praying again—this time, with more determination than before. "God, what am I missing? Your Word says You have plans to prosper us, to bless us with abundance, but I'm not seeing it. Show me what I need to do."

The next day, something miraculous happened. It wasn't a sudden influx of money or a job promotion but something even more powerful—wisdom. Alex felt a deep stirring in his spirit, like a divine whisper, saying, "You've been waiting for a miracle, but I've been waiting for you to walk with Me step by step. I want to show you how to live the abundant life I promised."

That whisper lit a fire in Alex. He dove back into scripture, this time with a hunger to understand God's partnership in the process of blessing. He came across Deuteronomy 28, where God promises blessings in the city and in the field, in the work of your hands and the fruit of your labor. Alex realized something stunning—it wasn't about sitting back and waiting for miracles; it was about working *with* God, planting seeds in faith, and trusting Him to bring the increase.

He suddenly understood why his prayers seemed unanswered. It wasn't that God hadn't been listening—it was that Alex had been praying for the result without seeking the guidance to get there. He had asked for blessings without asking for the *wisdom* to walk in them.

That day, Alex made a decision. He was going to stop just asking for abundance and start walking in God's step-by-step guidance. He asked God, "What do You want me to do today?" And slowly but surely, the answers came. Some days, it was as simple as making a small investment, talking to a neighbor, or helping a coworker. Other days, God nudged him to step out in faith, take a risk, or plant a new seed in his career.

Months passed, and though his bank account didn't instantly swell, something far more exciting was happening—*fruit*. God was multiplying Alex's efforts. A new job opportunity opened up, an unexpected bonus arrived, and new friendships blossomed—all blessings Alex never saw coming. The more Alex obeyed, the more doors God opened. It wasn't just about wealth; it was about seeing God's hand move in every area of his life.

One rainy afternoon, as Alex reflected on this journey, he couldn't help but laugh in amazement. *It works!* God's way worked! He had stopped striving, stopped trying to force God's hand, and instead walked hand in hand with Him, trusting His timing and His wisdom.

Just like Isaac sowed in famine and reaped a hundredfold, Alex had sown in faith and seen his life transformed. God wasn't just a miracle worker dropping blessings from the sky—He was a *partner*, leading Alex step by step into the abundant life He had promised.

Looking out over his small but flourishing garden, Alex realized this was just the beginning. The blessings weren't just financial—his heart was fuller, his relationships deeper, and his sense of purpose stronger. God had not only met his needs but had exceeded his wildest expectations, bringing him into a life he never thought possible.

And so, Alex stood there, grateful and awestruck, realizing that living a great life on Earth wasn't just a lofty dream. It was real. It was available. And it was all about trusting God's wisdom, planting in faith, and letting Him bring the harvest.

With a heart full of excitement, Alex couldn't wait for what tomorrow would bring because he knew one thing for sure—when you walk with God, the best is always yet to come.

Living an unshakable and abundant life is about aligning ourselves with God's true character and understanding the covenant He has established with us. It's not just about heavenly rewards but experiencing the fullness of His blessings here on earth as well. When we shed misconceptions and walk in the truth of who God is—our provider, guide, and source of wisdom—we unlock the abundant life He has promised. This includes both spiritual and material blessings, but it requires faith, obedience, and partnership with God. By trusting in His step-by-step guidance and embracing His wisdom, we experience the unshakable redemption that reflects His glory in every area of our lives, both now and in eternity.

CHAPTER 28

Who is God?

Understanding God's Character through Scripture

Knowing God's character is paramount for anyone striving to live according to His will, follow His guidance, and trust in Him fully. When we understand who God truly is—His unwavering love, infinite wisdom, boundless grace, and steadfast faithfulness—we can confidently place our trust in Him, even in the face of life's uncertainties. This deep knowledge of God's nature—through scripture—strengthens our faith, enabling us to align our actions with His will and embrace His promises.

Our God is always good, always just, and always present, providing the foundation we need to walk in obedience, live with purpose, and find peace in His plans for our lives. God's character is a tapestry of greatness, strength, majesty, goodness, loyalty, joy, grace, love, purity, hope, and deliverance. Each attribute is a beacon of His unending love and care for us.

Many scriptures are directed toward the Israelites, but we are included. When we believe in Jesus, we are grafted and adopted into His family. "For there is no difference between Jew and Gentile—the same Lord is Lord of all and richly blesses all who call on him" (Rom. 10:12). These verses speak to all who believe.

To truly grasp the person of God, His character, and how the Bible describes Him, we must go beyond simply reading scripture—we need to delve into the profound truths embedded within. Is He good? Can we trust Him if we surrender our will to His instead of trying to force our way? The Bible overwhelmingly answers "Yes" by revealing God as a trustworthy, just, and loving Father who deserves our confidence and devotion.

The Greatness and Majesty of God

God is sovereign over all creation—nothing happens without His authority. He possesses all strength, power, and honor (1 Chron. 29:10–12). When we surrender to His will, we are placing our trust in the One who controls all things. God's ways are not just powerful—they are perfect and just (Deut. 32:1–4). He does no wrong, and His actions are always rooted in justice. We can trust Him completely. When life's uncertainties weigh us down, understanding God's unchanging nature becomes a source of deep comfort.

God's Strength and Power

Psalm 29 shows us how "The voice of the Lord is powerful; the voice of the Lord is majestic." The imagery used here likens God's voice to a mighty force that can break cedars, shake deserts, and bring peace. The passage culminates with, "The Lord gives strength to His people; the Lord blesses His people with peace." When we submit to His will, we're not relinquishing control to weakness but to a God who is infinitely strong and who imparts that strength and peace to us.

The Excellence and Wisdom of God

In Daniel 5:10–12, even a pagan queen recognizes the divine wisdom in Daniel, who was guided by God's Spirit. She acknowledges the "insight and intelligence and wisdom like that of the gods" in him. God's wisdom surpasses human understanding and is freely available to those who seek Him. This wisdom is not meant just to solve our problems but to guide us into deeper trust in His purposes.

The Goodness of God

God is approachable, forgiving, and good (Ps. 65). And His goodness isn't contingent upon our behavior—He is good because it's His nature. The Bible repeatedly shows that God's goodness is a reason for praise and trust (Ps. 135:3).

God's Covenant Loyalty and Faithfulness

God's covenant love and loyalty are unwavering (Ps. 100:5). Even when circumstances seem uncertain, His promises remain true (Ps. 111). God's enduring faithfulness is the foundation upon which we can securely place our trust.

The Joy, Grace, and Love of God

Joy comes from being in the presence of God and being part of His redemptive plan. He promises a future where there is no more weeping or crying—a reflection of His loving heart toward us (Isa. 65:17–19). Through Jesus, we receive grace upon grace—undeserved favor and love (Rev. 1:3–6; John 1:14–18). This grace reveals a God who isn't distant but who has drawn near to us, offering salvation and reconciliation. God's love is not merely an abstract concept but was demonstrated when He sent Jesus to be the atoning sacrifice for our sins. The love God shows is sacrificial, unconditional, and eternal (John 4:7–11).

The Hope We Have in God

Psalm 62:5–7 offers a deep well of hope: "Yes, my soul, find rest in God; my hope comes from Him. Truly, He is my rock and my salvation; He is my fortress; I will not be shaken." When we surrender to God's will, He fills our lives with hope that goes beyond mere optimism—it's a living hope rooted in His faithfulness (Rom. 15:13).

The Bible overwhelmingly reveals God as good, just, faithful, and loving. When we surrender our will to His, we're entrusting ourselves to a perfect, powerful, and compassionate God. He doesn't call us to blind faith; He reveals His nature and character through His Word, inviting us into a relationship built on trust. To surrender to God's will is not to lose control—it's to hand control over to the One who is infinitely capable, endlessly loving, and utterly trustworthy. This understanding transforms our faith from mere belief into a deep, abiding trust in the goodness and greatness of our God.

As we immerse ourselves in these scriptures, we see the abundant and unwavering goodness of God's nature. He desires nothing less than the best for His children. Do we believe this? Do we embrace this truth for ourselves? It applies to us if we love Him and walk in His kingdom as He calls us to do. Let these scriptures energize your faith and deepen your understanding of the incredible God we serve. More importantly, don't just read what I say here. I put all the scripture references here so you can read the scriptures yourself and talk to God about his character. See what else he has to say to you, specifically about who He is and how He feels about you.

CHAPTER 29

Why So Much Bad When God Is Good?

Do I Have to Believe This Blindly When I Don't Always See It?

If you're like most people, reading this might stir up a mix of emotions. If God is truly sovereign, loving, and all-powerful, why is the world in such a state? It's understandable why some might conclude that this is evidence that God isn't who we claim He is, and that everything we believe is just a comforting lie. I know God is sovereign, just, loving, and merciful—He created and sustains everything—yet I often feel lost trying to comprehend His ways (Ps. 103:19; Dan. 4:35). If He's in control, why is there so much suffering? I know sin has broken the world, but if God is both good and powerful, why doesn't He just put an end to it?

I hear people say that suffering has a purpose, like strengthening our faith or revealing God's glory, but that doesn't make it any easier to grasp. When life gets confusing and hard, we're told to trust that God's ways are higher and that He's working everything for good. But how do you hold onto that when everything around you feels upside down? Why don't I always feel His love, joy, or peace the way I'm supposed to? Sometimes, it feels like He's so distant, like the promises in scripture are true for everyone else but not for me. Still, I cling to the hope that one day, God will wipe away every tear and make all things new—but until then, I'm stuck wrestling with these questions.

When my family and I faced our darkest days, these were the exact questions that gripped our hearts. It felt like we were barely hanging on, desperately trying to understand how a loving God could allow such pain. Yet, in those moments of doubt and despair, God met each of us in unique and personal ways, gradually revealing His character and faithfulness in ways we could never have anticipated. The journey wasn't quick or easy, but it was in those raw, tear-filled moments that we caught glimpses of His sovereignty and purpose.

The Reality of a Fallen World

In Genesis 1–2, we see that God created everything "very good" (Gen. 1:31). There was no suffering, no death, and no pain. However, when sin entered the world through Adam and Eve's disobedience (Gen. 3), it brought about the brokenness we experience today—pain, evil, and suffering became part of human existence. Creation itself was subjected to frustration, and it groans as it waits for redemption (Rom. 8:20–22). The bad we experience isn't a reflection of God's character; it's a consequence of humanity's rebellion against God's design.

God's Sovereignty Over Evil

Even though evil exists, God's sovereignty is not diminished. The Bible is clear that God can and does work through even the darkest situations to bring about His ultimate purposes. Joseph's story in Genesis is a prime example. After being sold into slavery by his brothers and enduring years of hardship, Joseph says to them, "You intended to harm me, but God intended it for good" (Gen. 50:20). God didn't cause the evil, but He used it for a greater purpose.

Similarly, the crucifixion of Jesus was the most unjust act in history—the sinless Son of God was brutally executed. Yet through that act of evil, God brought about the greatest good: the redemption of humanity "by God's deliberate plan and foreknowledge" (Acts 2:23). Even when evil seems overwhelming, God is still at work, turning what the enemy intends for harm into something that can ultimately bring about His glory and our good.

Another powerful example is found in the story of Esther. When Haman plotted to destroy all the Jews in the Persian Empire, it seemed as though evil would triumph. However, through God's providence, Esther was placed in a position of influence as queen. Her courage to approach the king and intercede for her people led to the downfall of Haman and the salvation of the Jewish nation (Est. 7:9–10). What began as a wicked plot against God's people ended with their deliverance and Haman's own demise.

And there's Job. Though he was righteous, Satan was allowed to test him, bringing about immense suffering and loss for Job. While his friends believed that his trials were a result of sin, the story shows that God permitted the suffering not as punishment but as a way to refine Job's faith. In the end, God restored Job's fortunes, giving him twice as much as he had before (Job 42:10).

Trusting God in Suffering

One of the hardest aspects of faith is learning to trust God when life is painful, or we don't understand what He is doing. The Bible addresses this tension with honesty and hope.

1. God's Ways Are Higher: Reminds us that God's ways and thoughts are higher than ours. We are finite, limited in our understanding, while God's wisdom is infinite. He sees the full picture, while we often only see fragments (Isa. 55:8–9).

2. God's Presence in Our Suffering: Jesus said we would have trouble in this world (John 16:33). But He also promised that He would be with us through it. God doesn't always remove the pain, but He does walk with us through it, offering comfort, strength, and hope.

3. The Purpose of Trials: Trials develop perseverance and mature our faith (James 1:2–4), and suffering produces perseverance, character, and hope (Rom. 5:3–5). God can use our hardships to refine us, to draw us closer to Him, and to shape us more into the likeness of Christ.

4. The Ultimate Hope: Evil, pain, and suffering are not the end of the story. In the end, God will make all things right (Rev. 21:4).

5. Why Don't We Always Feel God's Love, Joy, and Peace?: It's normal to have seasons when we don't feel close to God or experience His love, joy, and peace as much as we would like.

There can be several reasons for this:

a. The Reality of Spiritual Warfare: We wrestle not against flesh and blood but against spiritual forces of evil (Eph. 6:12). Sometimes, the lack of joy or peace is due to spiritual attacks that seek to shake our faith and trust in God.

b. Our Emotional State and Circumstances: Human emotions fluctuate. Sometimes, our feelings don't align with the truth. That's why it's important to anchor our faith not in how we feel but in what God's Word says.

c. Seasons of Testing and Growth: Just as gold is refined in fire, our faith is often tested and purified through difficult seasons. During these times, God may seem distant, but He is working in ways we cannot see (Job 23:8–10).

d. Invitation to Deeper Trust: When we don't feel God's presence, it's often an invitation to grow in deeper trust and faith. God desires that we seek Him even when we don't feel Him because faith is the assurance of things hoped for, not just things seen or felt (Heb. 11:1).

Reconciling God's Character with Suffering

The presence of evil and suffering doesn't negate God's goodness or power—it's a part of the broken world we live in, but it's also a world God is actively redeeming. God's character remains consistent: He is just, loving, merciful, and sovereign. Though we may not always understand His ways, the Bible calls us to trust Him because He is faithful.

Christian faith is built not on a God who is distant from our pain but on a God who entered into it. Jesus, the Son of God, suffered, died, and rose again to defeat sin, death, and evil. Our hope isn't that life will be easy but that in the middle of a broken world, God is with us, for us, and ultimately working all things for good (Rom. 8:28).

CHAPTER 30

God's Plan for Us to Live a Grand Life

While the world is full of darkness and challenges, God's desire for us transcends merely surviving in it. He wants us to flourish within His plan, which is full of physical and spiritual blessings. His desire for us is not just to experience abundance in terms of wealth or success but to live a fulfilling life in deep relationship with Him. This full life is the richness of living in harmony with God's purpose, where every need is met according to His will (John 10:10). God has blessed us with "every spiritual blessing in Christ," demonstrating that our inheritance is vast and all encompassing, both here on earth and in eternity (Eph. 1:3).

God's plan isn't random or careless; it's carefully orchestrated to lead us into a life of both joy and purpose. His Holy Spirit is our constant companion, whispering His will and guiding our every step (Isaiah 30:21). When we submit to His leadership, the abundance He desires for us becomes evident—not just in tangible blessings but in the peace, joy, and spiritual richness that flow from His presence.

It's important to remember that abundance doesn't always look like what the world defines as success. Sometimes it's the simple, yet profound, peace in the midst of trials, the love we experience in relationships, or the joy found in small blessings. God knows exactly what we need to live a "grand" life in alignment with His purpose. As we trust His wisdom and follow His plan, we experience a life that is truly abundant in every way, reflecting the glory of His kingdom and drawing others into that same fullness. In this way, God's blessings are both physical and spiritual, touching every aspect of our lives when we walk in obedience and trust in His perfect timing and plan.

How the Covenant Applies to Us Today

We talked in depth about the Abrahamic and Mosaic Covenants in Chapter 17. Through Christ, we are heirs of the New Covenant, which brings both spiritual and earthly abundance. God's desire is not only to bless us in eternity but to bless us here on earth as we live in alignment with His will. When we live in relationship with Him and follow His guidance, we reflect His goodness and power to the world around us.

Through Christ, we are heirs of the New Covenant, which brings both spiritual and earthly abundance. God's desire is not only to bless us in eternity but to bless us here on earth as we live in alignment with His will. When we live in relationship with Him and follow His guidance, we reflect His goodness and power to the world around us.

1. Spiritual and Earthly Prosperity: The New Covenant gives us the Holy Spirit, who leads us into truth, peace, joy, and wisdom. This prosperity isn't just spiritual; it extends to our relationships, work, and every area of life. God equips us to live with purpose and to show what it looks like to walk in His favor.

2. Freedom and Victory: In Christ, we are set free from the burden of sin and guilt, allowing us to live confidently, knowing that God is for us and that He empowers us to overcome life's challenges.

3. Living as a Reflection of God's Kingdom: As we walk in victory, we become living examples of what a life in Christ can look like, living in such a way that others see His blessing in our lives. As we live in faith, unity, wisdom, and love, we demonstrate what it means to be aligned with God's purpose, showing the beauty of following the Father's will.

4. God's Provision and Favor: God provides for our needs, both spiritual and physical. As we trust in Him, we experience His blessings in our health, finances, relationships, and work.

5. Flourishing in Every Area of Life: When we follow God's plan, we see His hand in every part of our lives, where we are thriving spiritually, emotionally, and materially.

How God Expresses His Desire To Walk in Covenant with Us

- Psalm 111:5–9 God's faithfulness to His people and His covenant is unwavering.

- Deuteronomy 7:6–9 God chose Israel, not because of its size, but out of His enduring faithfulness to His promises, ensuring that His promises are upheld through generations.

- Deuteronomy 6:10–13 God promised a land of prosperity, warning us not to forget Him amid blessings.

- Deuteronomy 28:12 God will bless the work of our hands and provide for our needs, emphasizing the importance of obedience.

- John 10:10 Jesus came to give life in abundance, surpassing all expectations.

- Deuteronomy 30:9–10 God promises success and prosperity when we wholeheartedly follow His commands.

- Ephesians 3:20–21 God's power within us is immeasurable, far exceeding our dreams and desires.

- Psalm 65:5–13 God's provision and nurturing care for the land is lavish, symbolizing the abundance and joy God offers His people.

- Ezekiel 36:33–36 God can turn desolate lands into fruitful gardens, much like the Garden of Eden.

- Psalm 20 God is the true source of victory and support.

- Zechariah 8:11–15 God promises renewed prosperity and restoration, urging God's people to be strong and trust in His plan.

- Isaiah 51:1–5 God will transform wastelands into joyful paradises, demonstrating His continual restoration in our lives.

- John 14:26 The Holy Spirit teaches us all things and helps us recall Jesus's teachings.

- Romans 8:14 Being led by the Spirit confirms our identity as children of God.

- Galatians 5:22–23 The fruit of the Spirit shapes us to live abundantly, reflecting God's grace. Through the Holy Spirit, we gain wisdom, discernment, and direction for living a life aligned with God's will.

Kingdom Principles for Covenant Living and Receiving Abundance and Purpose

God offers the New Covenant as a free gift to all who believe and accept adoption into His kingdom. Ephesians 2:8–9 highlights that salvation comes by grace through faith, not by our works. Living in the fullness of this gift requires active participation. Simply hearing God's Word isn't enough; we must live it out (James 1:22). Our actions are not about earning salvation but are a response to the grace that God has freely provided.

Live in Abundance, Empowered by Grace

God's grace not only saves us but empowers us to live in accordance with His will. It is God who works in us to fulfill His purpose (Phil. 2:13). By aligning ourselves with His guidance, we position ourselves to experience His blessings and the abundant life He promises. As we follow His guidance and trust in His promises, we can live out the grand and abundant life He has prepared for us, both now and in eternity.

Walk by Faith, Not by Sight

Living by faith means trusting God even when we can't see the outcome. Hebrews 11:1 teaches that faith is the assurance of what we hope for and the conviction of things unseen. Trusting God through uncertainty deepens our relationship with Him. Even when we struggle with doubt, this faith draws us closer to God and allows Him to work in ways beyond our understanding.

Be Led by the Spirit

The Holy Spirit is our guide, leading us into truth and away from the desires of the flesh (Gal. 5:16). Walking in step with the Spirit allows us to experience the fullness of the life God has prepared for us, as He provides wisdom and direction in every situation.

Begin with Praise

Starting each day with praise sets the tone for our walk with God. The Psalms show us that praising God opens our hearts to His presence, reminding us of His love and provision, and aligning us with His guidance for the day ahead.

Seek, Draw Near, and Call on Him

When we seek God with all our heart, we will find Him (Jer. 29:12–13). This assurance encourages us to pursue God through prayer, worship, and meditation, trusting that He is always ready to respond and draw us closer to Him.

Strive for Excellence

God desires us to pursue excellence in everything we do. Colossians 3:23–24 teaches us to work with all our heart, as though serving the Lord. Expecting greatness from ourselves, because we serve a great God, honors Him and positions us to receive His best.

Pursue Truth

Truth aligns us with God's will. Jesus declared that He is the way, the truth, and the life (John 14:6). As we seek God's truth in every situation, we allow Him to guide us and reveal His wisdom, helping us grow in our walk with Him.

Live with Hope and Expectation

God's plans for us are filled with hope and a future (Jer. 29:11). Living with expectation rooted in God's promises keeps us grounded and strong through life's challenges. Biblical hope, unlike the world's version, is a confident expectation in God's unchanging faithfulness.

Hear and Receive Wisdom

Proverbs 2:6 reminds us that wisdom comes from God. Seeking His guidance ensures we walk according to His will. Listening and applying His wisdom leads to a life aligned with His purpose.

Obey and Follow

Obedience is key to experiencing the life God promises. Jesus said, "If you love me, keep my commands" (John 14:15). Obeying God's instructions brings blessings and keeps us on His path of purpose and fulfillment.

Possess the Promises

God has given us promises, but we must take possession of them, as the Israelites were commanded to do with the Promised Land (Deut. 1:8). By claiming and living in these promises, we experience the fullness of His blessings.

Trust and Prove What is Excellent

Romans 12:2 encourages us to be transformed by renewing our minds so we can discern and prove God's perfect will. Trusting God's excellence leads us to recognize and live out His good and pleasing plan for our lives.

Give Freely to Others

Jesus instructed, "Freely you have received; freely give" (Matt. 10:8). Sharing God's blessings with others expands His kingdom and allows us to be conduits of His grace and love.

By following these principles—seeking God first, walking by faith, embracing His Word, and sharing His blessings—we align ourselves with God's divine plan and experience the abundant life He has promised.

The Elusiveness of Abundance

I don't know about you, but the abundant life has often felt elusive for me—like trying to catch a greased pig or, as I attempted just last night, picking up a slippery ice cube off the kitchen floor. If God promises an abundant life here on earth, why does it feel so hard to grasp?

For years, I searched for wisdom in all the wrong places. Maybe you've done the same. After earning my theology degree, I went to college to learn how to make money, run a business, and invest. I went to seminars and conferences and read countless books. I sought out mentors, became a mentor, and built a career around the pursuit of abundance. I became an "expert" in worldly success, but deep down, something was still missing.

The Truth Behind Worldly Wisdom

Then, in a moment of painful clarity, I realized that all the answers I had sought were smoke and mirrors. The world's wisdom, as impressive as it seemed, wasn't real wisdom at all. And even though I thought I was doing what God wanted—building security and wealth for my family—it all came crashing down. I felt like God had let it fall apart. But now, with hindsight and grace, I see it so clearly: God's abundance was always around me. I was just looking for it in one dimension—wealth and security.

Story Time: Town of Change

In a town that was once like any other, a divine transformation began taking place that would make Heaven and earth rejoice. The community became a living testimony of what happens when people fully embrace the covenant God offers—a life marked by unity, love, wealth, and abundance beyond what they ever imagined. The more they stepped into the fullness of what Jesus had made available through His sacrifice, the more they saw not just individual lives changed but an entire town transformed. This was the place where the promises of God collided with the faith of His people, and the result was nothing short of miraculous.

It all began with a few believers who dared to take God at His word. They had heard of abundant life, but now they were determined to live it. Sarah, the single mother, was one of the first. She had lived in scarcity and fear for so long, but something deep within her stirred when she read Philippians 4:19: "And my God will meet all your needs according to the riches of his glory in Christ Jesus." For the first time, she began to believe that those riches weren't just for someone else—they were for her, too. As she stepped out in faith, trusting that God's covenant was real and that she was included in it, her life began to change. Her children noticed it first—the peace that replaced her worry, the joy that filled their home. It was as if a weight had been lifted, and in its place was a sense of overflowing provision.

Sarah's newfound faith became contagious. She shared her story with a small group, and soon, others began to catch the vision. Mark, the businessman who once felt empty despite his wealth, was drawn in. He had always felt like something was missing, even as he achieved success by the world's standards. But when he heard about the Kingdom life—a life where God's blessings are given not because of our striving but because of our position as His children— he knew he had found what he was searching for. Mark started using his business as a platform to bless others. He began giving generously, helping those in need, funding community projects, and investing in people instead of just profits. The more he gave, the more God poured back into his life, confirming the truth of Luke 6:38: "Give, and it will be given to you. A good measure, pressed down, shaken together and running over, will be poured into your lap."

As more people experienced this Kingdom abundance, the excitement in the town grew. Families that had been struggling financially found that as they gave, even when it didn't make sense, God was faithful to meet their needs. Neighbors began sharing their resources freely, confident that in God's Kingdom, there is always more than enough. The enemy's plans to sow fear and division were continually frustrated. Every time he tried to stir up anxiety or lack, the people responded with faith and generosity. They had learned that in unity, God commands a blessing (Psalm 133:1-3), and they were determined to protect that unity at all costs.

The movement wasn't limited to adults. Young people caught the fire of what was happening and began to believe that God could use them, too. A group of teenagers started meeting in a park to worship, pray, and dream about how they could bring Heaven to earth in their schools and neighborhoods. They weren't content with just hearing about miracles—they wanted to see them. And they did. They laid hands on the sick, and people were healed. They prayed for struggling classmates, and hope was restored. They spoke life into situations that seemed dead, and things began to turn around. The enemy tried to bring confusion and conflict among them, but their love for each other was stronger than any of his schemes. They lived out the truth of John 13:35: "By this everyone will know that you are my disciples, if you love one another." Their unity became a powerful testimony to everyone around them.

As this unity and abundance spread throughout the town, God's joy over His people was palpable. It was as if Heaven was celebrating with them, excited to see what would happen next. The Father's heart was delighted to see His children living in the fullness of His covenant, thriving together in love and purpose. Zephaniah 3:17 came alive: "The Lord your God is with you, the Mighty Warrior who saves. He will take great delight in you; in his love, he will no longer rebuke you, but will rejoice over you with singing." God was singing over this town, rejoicing in the way they reflected His Kingdom.

The ripple effects of this revival couldn't be contained. People from neighboring towns heard about what was happening and came to see for themselves. They encountered a community where love was the currency, where generosity was a way of life, and where miracles were everyday occurrences. As they witnessed what God was doing, many of them gave their lives to Christ, wanting to be part of this Kingdom life. They saw that this wasn't just about individual blessings—it was about creating a culture where everyone flourished together. The enemy, once so effective in sowing division and despair, was utterly powerless in the face of such unity and faith.

The more the people gave, the more God gave back to them. They couldn't out-give Him, no matter how hard they tried. Homes were filled with joy and laughter, businesses prospered, and relationships deepened. The town became a picture of what Jesus prayed for in John 17:21: "That all of them may be one, Father, just as you are in me and I am in you. May they also be in us so that the world may believe that you have sent me." Their unity and love were so powerful that even those who were skeptical couldn't help but be drawn in.

The long-term impact was extraordinary. Generations later, the town was still living in the overflow of the seeds planted by those first believers. The principles of Kingdom living—unity, generosity, faith, and love—became a foundation that endured. As children grew up witnessing the abundance of God's provision and the joy of giving, they carried those values into their own lives, marriages, and businesses. The enemy's frustration only increased as he saw that the legacy of faith and unity was being passed down, making it even harder for him to find a foothold.

And then there were the heavenly rewards. Those who had sown faithfully into God's Kingdom discovered that their sacrifices on earth were not only multiplied back to them in this life but also stored up treasures in Heaven (Matthew 6:20). When they entered eternity, they were welcomed into a place where the rewards were beyond anything they could have imagined. They saw how every act of obedience, every gift given, and every choice to walk in love had contributed to God's eternal glory. They couldn't out-give God, and they rejoiced in the eternal impact their lives had made.

This town became a beacon of light in a dark world, a picture of what happens when people live in God's unity and under His covenant. They showed the world what Heaven looks like: a place where love is abundant, needs are met, and joy overflows. Their story was one of excitement, miracles, and faith, where God's presence was tangible and His blessings were evident. The enemy's work was continually thwarted because this community had tapped into the power of living in unity with God and each other. They revealed God's heart to the world, and in doing so, they left a legacy that glorified Him both now and for all eternity.

This is a story of a town where Heaven met Earth, where the Kingdom of God was not just a future hope but a present reality. It was a place where the excitement of what God was doing couldn't be contained, where lives were changed forever, and where the enemy's plans crumbled under the weight of God's truth. The community's unity and abundant life were a testimony to the world of what happens when believers live fully in the covenant promises of God—when they walk in love, give generously, and trust in the One who delights in pouring out His blessings.

God's Abundance Is More Than Wealth

God's abundance is so much more than that. He's always been there, guiding me, offering me His path, but I was too busy chasing my version of abundance to see His. The truth is, He didn't deny me wealth—He just wanted me to walk with Him, step by step, in trust. Now, I'm more blessed than ever, but it's not just about money or success. It's about peace, fulfillment, purpose. It's about being blessed to be a blessing to others. He's leading me in multiple businesses, ministries, friendships, and family—all of it, step by step. And here's what I've learned: abundance isn't a destination. It's a journey. We'll never "arrive" because we're always walking with God through both the good times and the hard ones.

The Truth That Changed Everything

But the truth that changed my life can change your life too: God loves you deeply, specifically, and uniquely. He has a path designed just for you—a path that takes into account everything about you, your likes, dislikes, dreams, and fears. And He's waiting, with His hand extended, ready to walk you down that path. Yes, it might include suffering and challenges, but that doesn't mean it's not good. I trust Him now, fully. Do you?

Think for a moment: What if God has been waiting for you to see how much more He has for you? What if His promises are far bigger than you've allowed yourself to believe?

This is your personal invitation to step into the life God has always intended for you, a life full of abundance—real abundance: wealth, peace, purpose, and power that extend far beyond the limits of this world. This is about you living the full, grand life God promises, right here, right now, while preparing for a future so glorious it defies imagination.

Story Time: Living Like Journey 3 Describes

In the serene yet bustling town of Solace Hill, a group of friends were on the brink of a transformation that would shake their lives to the core, opening their eyes to a truth they had only skimmed the surface of. These weren't just casual acquaintances; they were bound together by shared struggles, deep faith, and an insatiable hunger for more—a hunger to see the fullness of God's promises in their lives. They had heard about living in abundance, read scriptures that promised wealth, peace, and joy, but for some reason, those promises seemed like distant stars, beautiful but unreachable.

The friends included Michael, a businessman who had been dragging the heavy weight of debt and the suffocating pressure of providing for his family. Life had squeezed the joy out of him, and the abundance God promised felt like a distant dream. Sarah, full of faith but haunted by the wreckage of a painful divorce, had lost her sense of purpose and joy despite years of prayers for healing. Ethan, the youngest, carried a fire of ambition but felt an emptiness in his pursuits of success, unsure if he was truly walking in God's will. Olivia, strong-willed and compassionate, gave everything to others but found it impossible to allow herself to receive. And then there were three more friends, each carrying a crucial piece of the puzzle that would unlock the door to their destiny.

Lydia had lived with a heart shackled by unforgiveness for years. She held onto past hurts like a badge of honor, not realizing the prison she had built around her own soul. Joshua, a successful entrepreneur with wealth beyond his wildest dreams, wrestled with the gnawing feeling that his money wasn't enough—it couldn't buy him peace or a sense of God's approval. He had heard about tithing but never really bought into the idea. And Caleb, passionate and driven, felt the pull of eternity, knowing deep down that life was about more than temporary achievements. He wanted to make a real, lasting difference but wasn't sure how to translate that desire into reality.

One fateful evening, as they gathered around the fire pit in Michael's backyard, everything began to shift. Sarah was the first to break the silence. "Do you ever feel like we're missing something? Like, we've heard about God's promises for abundance, but we're not *living* it. Why does life feel so heavy?"

Her words struck a chord with every single one of them. Michael spoke next, his voice low but firm. "I think we're missing something big. We're asking for blessings, but we're not asking for *wisdom*. Maybe we're focused too much on what we want and not enough on listening to what God's trying to tell us."

Ethan, eyes wide with excitement, leaned in. "Are you saying... that abundance isn't just about receiving blessings? It's about walking with God every step of the way, trusting Him in the process?"

The fire crackled as the words settled in. Olivia, usually the one to keep her emotions in check, wiped a tear from her cheek. "What if it's more than that? What if we're not only meant to give to others but to *receive* God's blessings for ourselves, too? I've been pouring out so much, I've forgotten that I'm allowed to receive."

The atmosphere around them shifted. It was like God Himself was sitting with them, pressing on their hearts to dig deeper. They began pouring over scripture together, devouring stories of Abraham, Isaac, Joseph, and others who walked in covenant with God—men and women who experienced not just spiritual blessings but real, tangible wealth, peace, and joy on earth. They weren't special exceptions. They were ordinary people who partnered with an extraordinary God.

As the weeks passed, their prayers transformed. No longer were they just asking for miracles; they were asking for God's guidance, His wisdom, and His step-by-step instructions. And as they did, their lives began to change in ways they never expected.

Michael, the businessman, felt a strong pull to make a bold move in his company—something that, in the natural, didn't make sense. But he trusted that it was God's nudge, and he obeyed. Within weeks, new clients flooded in, and opportunities he hadn't even considered began to pour out of nowhere. He was floored. God's blessings weren't just about miracles—they were about following the path God was laying out, one obedient step at a time. "This is what I've been waiting for," Michael told the group, breathless with excitement. "It's not about striving for success—it's about *trusting* in God's provision."

Olivia, for the first time in years, let herself receive. She realized that abundance wasn't just meant to be given away but lived out. God wasn't calling her to self-sacrifice without reward; He wanted to bless her, too. She started to notice God's gifts in small things: deeper friendships, unexpected financial blessings, and a peace that she hadn't felt in years. "I've been blocking myself from receiving His goodness," she said one evening, glowing with joy. "But now I see that God's abundance is meant for *me* too."

Sarah's transformation was just as remarkable. She had prayed for years for healing, but it wasn't until she stepped into God's joy that her heart began to heal. She launched a ministry for women going through heartbreak, and it grew faster than she could have ever imagined. "This is the abundant life," she said through tears. "God turned my pain into something beautiful. I thought I was too broken to be used, but now I see He had a plan all along."

Ethan found his place in God's Kingdom, too. His ambition wasn't wrong—it just needed to be redirected. He launched a nonprofit to help young adults find their God-given calling, and the fruit was undeniable. "Success isn't about me," he said, shaking his head in amazement. "It's about how many people I can bring with me into the life God has for them."

Then there was Lydia. Her journey with unforgiveness had been long and painful, but one day, during a prayer meeting with the group, she finally let it go. She confessed how the bitterness had stolen her joy for years, but as she released it, she felt like chains were breaking off her heart. "Forgiveness was the key," Lydia said, beaming through her tears. "It was like I had locked myself in a cage, and I didn't even know it. Now, the blessings have been pouring in— my relationships, my career, my joy—it's all being restored."

Joshua's breakthrough came through tithing. For years, he had given generously but had never fully embraced the idea of giving God his first fruits. After reading Malachi 3:10 and feeling the Spirit's conviction, he decided to trust God with his finances in a new way. He tithed faithfully, even when it didn't make sense. And just like God promised, the floodgates opened. His business soared to new heights, and more importantly, his heart felt secure in God's provision. "Tithing wasn't about money—it was about trust. I had no idea how much I needed to let God be in control until I finally did."

Caleb, ever the visionary, found his focus sharpened by eternity. He had always been driven to achieve, but now he realized that true success was about leaving a legacy that mattered in Heaven, not just on Earth. He started mentoring others to live with an eternal perspective, challenging them to see beyond the temporary and into the forever. "We're not just building for today," Caleb told the group one evening. "We're building for eternity. Everything we do here has eternal value. This life—it's just the beginning."

As they sat together around the fire one evening, watching the sun dip below the horizon, the group realized something profound: they weren't the same people who had gathered there months ago, full of questions and uncertainties. They were living proof of God's abundance—each one of them transformed by His promises, His guidance, and His unshakable love.

Their excitement was palpable. They couldn't wait to tell everyone what they had discovered—that living in abundance wasn't just possible; it was what God *desired* for His children. They wanted to shout it from the rooftops, to tell everyone who would listen that they didn't have to settle for a life of struggle and survival. *God's abundance was here, now,* and they were walking in it.

Michael, with a grin on his face, said it best, "We've tasted it. We've *seen* what life can be like when you live with God at the center. And let me tell you— there's no going back. The best is yet to come."

The others laughed, tears of joy brimming in their eyes. Lydia stood, raising her arms to the sky. "We're living in the overflow!" she shouted, and the group erupted in cheers.

This wasn't just about them anymore. They had unlocked something life- changing, something so powerful and transformative that they couldn't keep it to themselves. They had discovered the secret to an unshakable, abundant life—and they knew that anyone who dared to trust God with their whole heart could experience the same.

The fire crackled as they shared stories of how God had moved in their lives, each one more miraculous than the last. And as they sat there, in the warm glow of the fire, hearts overflowing with gratitude and excitement, they knew this was only the beginning.

They were living in abundance. They were walking in God's promises. And they couldn't wait to see what God would do next. Because with God, the adventure never ends.

So here's the challenge, and it's personal: Do you believe that God's promises are for you personally? Do you believe that He has a specific plan of abundance for your life? And are you willing to trust Him, even if that path includes some pain and difficulty, knowing that His way is the best for you—not just now but for eternity? This is the question. Will you step into that trust? Will you let go of the world's wisdom and embrace the journey God has set before you? Because on the other side of that trust is a life richer, deeper, and more abundant than you could ever imagine. Ask Him for help to believe if you are struggling.

I'm calling you to step out in faith and let God show you how much bigger His plans are for you. This is your moment. Trust Him. Trust that He's ready to lead you into a life more rewarding, and more abundant than you've ever dared to believe. God's promises for you are real, they are rich, and they are right now. Will you embrace them? Will you step boldly into this grand, eternal life God has waiting for you? Because He's waiting—for you.

Walking With God on His Path for Your Life

Imagine this: You're living your life, seeking God, but only through other people. You rely on what your pastor says in church, what your spiritually strong friends share, what popular podcasts or radio hosts declare. It feels like you're connecting to God, but are you? Or are you living a second-tier relationship—one where you're hearing about God, but not hearing from Him yourself?

Many of us Christians fall into this trap, believing that certain people—pastors, mentors, friends—have some kind of VIP access to God that we don't. So we keep going back, leaning on their spiritual connection instead of building our own. And yes, they might have great insights, but what if you're missing out on the most powerful relationship you could ever have? The one that is waiting just for you, directly from God.

This was exactly what happened to the Israelites at Mount Sinai. God invited all of them to come near, to hear His voice directly and be part of the covenant He was making with them. But they were overwhelmed with fear. Instead of stepping into the relationship God wanted, they chose to send Moses in their place. They said, "You speak to us, and we will listen. But do not let God speak to us, or we will die" (Ex. 20:19). So Moses went up alone, while the rest of the people missed out on the deeper connection God had prepared for them.

Now, think about this: If you're married, how would your spouse feel if you only spoke to their friends, coworkers, or family members to figure out what's going on in their heart? You're asking everyone else, "What do they want? What should I do for them? What do they love? How are they feeling?" You'd hear secondhand stories, advice, and suggestions, but you'd be missing out on the deepest connection of all: speaking to them directly. And you'd miss out on the joy, love, and depth of that relationship.

That's what so many of us are doing with God! We try to piece together a picture of who God is based on what others say. Imagine how that feels to God, who is waiting with His arms open, ready to talk to you, to love you, to share the deepest truths of life with you directly.

Here's the truth you need to hear: God loves YOU, and He desperately wants to speak to YOU. Not through someone else but to you one-on-one. He has things to say to you that no one else can tell you. He wants you to know the plans He has for your life, plans that are drenched in blessing and purpose. He wants to whisper in your ear how proud He is of you, how much He believes in you, and how excited He is to walk with you every step of the way. But that can only happen if you choose to listen for yourself.

Yes, the people you seek out for wisdom—pastors, friends, podcasts—can be helpful, but they can never take the place of God's direct voice in your life. If you want a life overflowing with abundance, joy, and purpose, you need to stop relying on others to tell you what God is saying. You need to step into the first-tier relationship that God has been waiting for, just like He waited for the Israelites at Mount Sinai. The invitation is open. Will you choose to accept it?

Journey 4 is your guide to that adventure. It's here to help you break free from the second-tier life and step boldly into a one-on-one relationship with the Creator of the universe. The One who knows you better than anyone. The One who designed a life for you that is far greater than you can imagine—a life dripping with blessings, purpose, and an intimate relationship with Him.

Imagine the shift in your life when you no longer need to ask others what God is saying about your future, your career, your relationships, and your decisions—because you hear from Him yourself. He is waiting. He's been waiting, full of love and excitement, for you to turn to Him directly. The question is: will you choose the second-tier life, or will you step into the fullness of the first-tier relationship He's offering?

This is your moment. Choose the first tier. Let this book show you how to unlock the direct, powerful, life-changing relationship with God that you've been longing for. It's time. Step into the abundant, personal connection that is waiting just for you. God Himself is waiting to speak to YOU. Will you listen?

CHAPTER 31

Does God Really Talk to Me?

God's Desire to Speak to You Directly

God doesn't just want a distant, formal relationship with us—He desires to speak to us directly, guiding us in every area of our lives. Jesus reassures us that "My sheep hear my voice, and I know them, and they follow me" (John 10:27). This means that as His followers, we are able and *invited* to hear His voice. Imagine the Creator of the universe, the One who holds all wisdom and knowledge, desiring to speak to you personally! He knows you deeply, and He wants to guide you through life with His loving voice. In Jeremiah 33:3, God makes an incredible promise: "Call to me and I will answer you and tell you great and unsearchable things you do not know." This isn't just a promise only for prophets or the exceptionally holy—it's for all of us. God is saying, "Come to Me, and I will reveal the mysteries and plans I have for your life."

Hearing God's Voice in the Bible and in Life

Throughout the Bible, we see countless examples of God speaking to His people in profound, life-changing ways. Moses had face-to-face conversations with God (Ex. 33:11), and Elijah experienced God speaking in a "gentle whisper" during his darkest hour (1 Kings 19:12). Maybe you're waiting for God to speak to you in some dramatic fashion, but what if He's already whispering to you, inviting you to listen? God is actively guiding us (Isa. 30:21). Think of it as a personal GPS system for your life—God's guidance is always available if we're tuned in.

Everyday Stories of Hearing God's Voice

There are countless modern-day examples of people hearing from God in powerful, personal ways. Take the story of a man who was unsure about a major career change. He prayed for guidance, and during a time of worship, he felt an overwhelming sense of peace and the distinct words, "Trust me and move forward." That simple, quiet nudge changed the course of his life. Or consider the woman who, during a routine morning prayer, felt God prompting her to call a friend she hadn't spoken to in months. When she called, she discovered that her friend was going through a deep personal struggle and was on the verge of giving up. That call—prompted by God's voice—saved her friend from despair. These aren't isolated incidents; God is constantly speaking to us, giving us wisdom, direction, and encouragement.

Leaning Into God's Voice

God's desire to speak to you is not limited to moments of crisis or major life decisions. In every situation—big or small—God is ready to give you the wisdom you need (James 1:5). Whether it's choosing the right path for your career, navigating a tough relationship, or even deciding how to spend your day, God is eager to lead you step by step. He may not always reveal the entire roadmap of your life, but He will faithfully show you the next step. Learning to hear His voice is like tuning a radio—you have to dial in and practice listening regularly through prayer, scripture, and moments of stillness.

How to Start Hearing God's Voice

If you're wondering how to hear God's voice, the answer is simple: Ask. Just as God invites us to seek Him in prayer, He also promises to respond. Through Jesus, we have access to direct communication with God (Heb. 1:1–2). Start by setting aside time to be still before God, asking Him to speak to you. Open His Word and read with an expectation that He will reveal His heart to you. Many people also find that journaling is a powerful way to hear from God, writing down what they sense Him saying and reflecting on it over time. The more you practice, the more clearly you'll recognize His voice in the everyday moments of life.

The Life-Changing Power of Hearing God's Voice

When you hear God's voice, it changes everything. Think about it—what would your life look like if you had constant access to the wisdom of God

Himself? If you could ask Him for direction in your marriage, your career, and your friendships and hear His response? Hearing from God isn't just about gaining insight for the future; it's about walking in the fullness of the relationship He desires with you right now. One of the most exciting truths is that God speaks to us in every season of life. Whether you're in a season of joy or struggle, abundance or lack, God is right there, ready to speak into your situation. Jesus promised the Holy Spirit would guide us into all truth (John 16:13). This means that you are never left to navigate life on your own—God is present, and His voice is always available. Trust that, like Moses, you can have intimate conversations with God. Believe that, like Elijah, God can speak to you in a whisper when life feels overwhelming. And remember that, like Jeremiah, you can call out to God in any situation, and He will answer.

Story Time: Finding His Truth Yourself

Maggie sat in the back of the church, her heart heavy with questions. She had listened to the pastor preach about God's love, His guidance, His plan for each person's life—but none of it felt real to her. She admired the pastor's wisdom and felt grateful for his teachings, but something was missing. Every week, she left the church with the same aching thought: *Why doesn't God speak to me the way He speaks to them?*

She looked around at the congregation, watching people nod in agreement, taking notes, smiling as if every word was meant just for them. But not for her. Maggie had convinced herself long ago that she wasn't spiritual enough, holy enough, or worthy enough to have that kind of relationship with God.

I'm not like them, she thought. God speaks to people like that pastor, or my friend Jenny, or the Bible study leader, but not me.

And so, she went through the motions. She listened to the sermons, read her Bible when she could, and turned to Jenny for guidance whenever life felt overwhelming. Jenny always seemed to have the answers—always had the right scripture, the right prayer. Maggie admired her faith, but secretly, she resented it too. Why did God seem so close to Jenny while He felt so distant from her?

One afternoon, after another coffee meeting where Maggie poured out her heart to Jenny, seeking advice on everything from her job to her faith, Jenny said something that shook Maggie to her core.

"Maggie, I think you've been looking in the wrong places. You keep asking me what God is saying, but have you asked Him yourself? God doesn't just speak to pastors or spiritual leaders. He wants to speak to *you*. You're His daughter, too."

Maggie's chest tightened. The idea that God might want to speak directly to her, with all her doubts and insecurities—felt impossible. But what if Jenny was right? What if all this time, she had been missing out on the very relationship she longed for because she was too afraid to believe it was possible?

Tears brimmed in her eyes as Jenny continued, "God loves you. Not in a general, He-loves-everyone kind of way, but *you*, specifically. He's been waiting for you to talk to Him, to listen, to open your heart. I can give you advice, sure, but that's not enough. God wants *you*. He wants your trust, your time, your heart."

It felt like a dam had broken inside of Maggie. She had spent years waiting for someone else to tell her what God was saying. She had spent so much time admiring other people's relationships with God, never realizing that He was calling her into her own.

Meanwhile, on the other side of town, Alex was sitting in his car, staring blankly at the steering wheel. He had just left his parents' house after another long conversation with his dad. His father, a man who had always seemed to have a deep, unshakeable faith, had once again offered Alex advice on what he should do with his life. But for some reason, it didn't sit well this time.

Alex had always gone to his dad for guidance. His father was a spiritual giant in his eyes—always knowing the right path, always hearing God's voice. But as Alex sat in his car, a thought he'd never had before crept into his mind: *Why am I always asking my dad what God is saying? Why don't I ask God myself?*

He had relied on his father's faith for so long that it never occurred to him that God might want a direct relationship with him, too. Could it be that God was just as eager to speak to Alex as He was to his dad?

Alex closed his eyes and took a deep breath. "God," he whispered, "I don't know if You'll answer, but ... I want to hear from You. I want to know what You want for my life. Help me listen."

In that quiet moment, something shifted in Alex. It wasn't that he suddenly had all the answers, but for the first time in his life, he believed—truly believed—that God wanted to speak to him personally. He didn't need to rely on someone else's relationship with God. His own was waiting.

And then there was Beth.

Beth had spent her whole life chasing spiritual wisdom from every possible source. She went to church every Sunday, attended three different Bible studies, and followed at least ten Christian podcasts religiously. But the more she consumed, the emptier she felt. She was always searching for someone else to tell her what God was saying, as if she could gather enough knowledge to finally feel close to Him. But every new sermon, every new book, left her feeling more disconnected.

One evening, after listening to yet another podcast, Beth found herself staring at the ceiling, feeling utterly lost. "God," she whispered, her voice shaking, "I don't understand. Why can't I feel You? Why can't I hear You like they do?"

For a moment, there was only silence. And then, as clear as anything, Beth felt a stirring in her spirit—a small, quiet voice that made her heart pound.

"I've been here all along, Beth. You've been searching everywhere but with Me. I've been waiting for you."

Tears streamed down her face as she realized the truth. God wasn't far away. He wasn't reserved for the pastors and podcasters she admired. He was right there, waiting for her to stop looking for Him through other people and start looking for Him directly.

That night, for the first time, Beth stopped listening to other voices and opened her heart to hear God's. It was the most powerful moment of her life.

Maggie, Alex, and Beth all came to the same realization in different ways. They had spent their lives believing they had to go through someone else to reach God, thinking that others had a deeper connection to Him. But the truth was that God had been waiting for them all along—longing for a direct, personal relationship with each of them.

It's Time to Lean In

Now is the time to lean into God's voice with expectation. The God who spoke to prophets, kings, and disciples is the same God who wants to speak directly to *you* today. Whether it's through His Word, in prayer, or through that still small voice in your spirit, God is ready to guide you into the abundant life He has promised. Imagine what life would be like if you could confidently hear His voice every day, receiving His wisdom, love, and direction for your life. You don't have to wonder if God will speak—you can know that He already is. Lean in, listen, and watch how hearing God's voice will transform your life from the inside out. This is the invitation of a lifetime, and the best part is, it's for you!

You don't need to rely on others to hear from God. You don't need to keep asking everyone else what He's saying, hoping that maybe, just maybe, some of that wisdom will trickle down to you. God is waiting for *you*. He loves *you*. He knows *you*. He is speaking to *you*—if only you would listen.

Will you keep living a second-tier life, depending on others to tell you what God wants? Or will you step into the fullness of the first-tier relationship that has been waiting for you all along?

The choice is yours. God is calling *your* name. Will you answer?

He's waiting, and He's never stopped loving you—right where you are.

CHAPTER 32

The Trinity

Introduction to Understanding the Trinity

To be led step by step into God's will for your life, it's essential to know and understand the Holy Spirit. The Holy Spirit is not just a guide; He is your Comforter, Teacher, and constant Companion on this journey. He reveals God's will to you, bringing clarity and direction when things seem uncertain. This is why it's crucial to grasp the depth and power of the Trinity—Father, Son, and Holy Spirit. Each part of the Trinity plays a unique role in your life, but the Holy Spirit is the one who actively walks with you every day, teaching you everything you need to know. Through Him, you will find comfort in your hardest moments and wisdom for every decision. It's through this deep relationship with the Holy Spirit that you will not only hear God's voice but be empowered to follow His perfect will for your life, one step at a time.

The Trinity Is God Existing as Three Persons in One Essence

This doctrine, while not explicitly stated in a single verse in the Bible, is derived from a synthesis of various scriptural passages. The Trinity describes God as one Being in three persons: God the Father, God the Son (Jesus Christ), and God the Holy Spirit. Each person of the Trinity is fully and completely God, sharing the same divine essence, but they are distinct in their persons.

Scripture emphasizes the oneness of God in verses such as Deuteronomy 6:4, "Hear, O Israel: The Lord our God, the Lord is one," and Isaiah 44:6, "Thus says the Lord, the King of Israel and his Redeemer, the Lord of hosts: 'I am the first and I am the last; besides me there is no god.'" The New Testament reaffirms this in James 2:19, "You believe that God is one; you do well. Even the demons believe—and shudder!"

God the Father is recognized as the source of all things, as stated in 1 Corinthians 8:6, "Yet for us there is one God, the Father, from whom are all things and for whom we exist, and one Lord, Jesus Christ, through whom are all things and through whom we exist." Jesus, God the Son, is fully divine, as seen in John 1:1–3, "In the beginning was the Word, and the Word was with God, and the Word was God. He was in the beginning with God. All things were made through him, and without him was not anything made that was made." Jesus's divinity is further affirmed in John 10:30, "I and the Father are one," and Colossians 2:9, "For in him the whole fullness of deity dwells bodily."

The Holy Spirit is also fully God, as illustrated in Acts 5:3–4, where lying to the Holy Spirit is equated with lying to God. Jesus promises the Holy Spirit's guidance in John 14:26, "But the Helper, the Holy Spirit, whom the Father will send in my name, he will teach you all things and bring to your remembrance all that I have said to you."

The unity of the three persons in one God is encapsulated in the Great Commission in Matthew 28:19, "Go therefore and make disciples of all nations, baptizing them in the name of the Father and of the Son and of the Holy Spirit," and in the apostolic blessing in 2 Corinthians 13:14, "The grace of the Lord Jesus Christ and the love of God and the fellowship of the Holy Spirit be with you all."

The Trinity works through distinct persons who are co-equal and co-eternal, sharing the same divine nature, power, and attributes. They have always existed together without beginning or end, united in essence or substance. While analogies like the three states of water or the three parts of an egg can help illustrate the Trinity, they ultimately fall short because God's nature is beyond full human comprehension. The doctrine of the Trinity underscores the complexity and majesty of God, highlighting the relational aspect of God's nature and the harmonious work of the Father, Son, and Holy Spirit in creation, redemption, and sustaining the world.

The Holy Spirit is the third person of the Trinity, co-equal with God the Father and God the Son.

- He is not a vague force or impersonal power but a distinct person who plays a crucial role in the Godhead. The Holy Spirit has been active from the beginning of creation, hovering over the waters (Gen. 1:2) and participating in the divine plan of redemption. As part of the Trinity, He shares in the divine essence, working in perfect harmony with the Father and the Son.

- The Holy Spirit is a person with intellect, emotions, and will. He teaches (John 14:26), intercedes (Rom. 8:26), and can be grieved (Eph. 4:30). As a person, He engages with us in a personal and intimate manner. He is not a force to be harnessed but a divine person to be known and loved. His presence in our lives signifies a deep, ongoing relationship with God.

- Jesus promised the Holy Spirit would be with us forever (John 14:16). The Holy Spirit dwells within believers, making our bodies His temple (1 Cor. 6:19), a permanent residency that begins when we believe in Jesus and continues throughout our lives.

- The Holy Spirit leads us into all truth, revealing God's will and helping us understand His Word (John 16:13). He teaches us and reminds us of everything Jesus said (John 14:26), ensuring we have the wisdom and knowledge to follow God's path.

- The Holy Spirit empowers us to live out God's will, giving us spiritual gifts to build up the church and advance God's Kingdom (1 Cor. 12:4–11).

- The Spirit convicts us of sin, righteousness, and judgment (John 16:8), leading us to repentance and a transformed life, making us more like Christ. The Holy Spirit produces the fruit of the Spirit in us, cultivating Christlike character (Gal. 5:22–23).

- The Holy Spirit is given to believers when they accept Jesus Christ as their Savior. The Holy Spirit comes to reside in us at the moment of our salvation, marking us as God's own (Eph. 1:13–14).

- As the Comforter, the Holy Spirit provides peace and reassurance, especially in challenging times (John 14:26–27). He helps us overcome fear with power, love, and a sound mind (2 Tim. 1:7), enabling us to face life's difficulties with confidence and faith.

- The Holy Spirit replaces fear with power, love, and a sound mind (2 Tim. 1:7). He empowers us to live boldly, witnessing and living out our faith with courage (Acts 4:31). The Spirit fills us with God's love, enabling us to love others as Christ loved us (Rom. 5:5). He grants us wisdom and self-control, guiding our thoughts and decisions and helping us maintain mental and emotional well-being (1 Cor. 2:16).

- The Holy Spirit is a deposit guaranteeing our inheritance until the redemption of all those who are God's possession (Eph. 1:13–14). This guarantee connects us to our eternal destiny, ensuring we are sealed for the day of redemption. The Spirit's work in us is a foretaste of the eternal life we will fully experience in Heaven. He transforms us into the likeness of Christ, preparing us for our eternal home (2 Cor. 3:18).

Living in the Kingdom Now

Though the Kingdom of God is not fully realized on earth, we can participate in it through the Holy Spirit. Jesus declared that the Kingdom of God is within us (Luke 17:21), and the Spirit enables us to live out kingdom values here. Our union with Christ brings us into a new life, where the Holy Spirit makes this union real by living in us and connecting us with the Father and the Son (Rom. 6:5–11). The church, as the body of Christ (meaning all the believers and not the building on the corner), is a manifestation of God's Kingdom on earth, living out these kingdom values and advancing God's purposes in the world.

CHAPTER 33

Choosing to Walk with the Holy Spirit

The Holy Spirit: A Gift at Salvation

Choosing to walk with the Holy Spirit involves a conscious and ongoing decision to invite His guidance, presence, and power into our daily lives. However, experiencing the fullness of the Holy Spirit's work in our lives requires active engagement and cooperation with Him. Jesus emphasized the importance of asking for the Holy Spirit's presence (Luke 11:13). While the Holy Spirit is given at salvation, believers are encouraged to continually seek His presence and filling.

Walking by the Spirit

To walk with the Holy Spirit, we must consciously choose to live by His guidance. Galatians 5:16 instructs, "So I say, walk by the Spirit, and you will not gratify the desires of the flesh." Walking by the Spirit means allowing Him to lead us in our thoughts, actions, and decisions. This involves daily surrendering our will to God's will, seeking to align our desires with His, and being sensitive to His promptings and convictions. Practically, this can be done by starting each day with prayer, inviting the Holy Spirit to guide and fill us.

Consider the scripture: "Do not get drunk on wine, which leads to debauchery. Instead, be filled with the Spirit" (Eph. 5:18). The Greek term used here for "be filled" implies an ongoing action, suggesting that we need to continually seek the Spirit's filling. This ongoing process involves regular prayer, reading and meditating on scripture, and being attentive to the Spirit's voice in our hearts. Additionally, the Holy Spirit speaks to us through God's Word. By immersing ourselves in the Bible, we open ourselves to the Holy Spirit's teaching and reminders of Jesus's words, which help us navigate life's challenges and make godly decisions (John 14:26).

Cultivating Sensitivity to the Holy Spirit

Engaging with the Holy Spirit also involves cultivating a sensitivity to His presence and promptings. Romans 8:14 says, "For those who are led by the Spirit of God are the children of God." To be led by the Spirit, we must develop an awareness of His nudges, whether they come through a sense of peace, a conviction about a particular action, or a sudden clarity in decision-making. This awareness can be cultivated through quiet times of reflection, journaling our spiritual experiences, and seeking the counsel of mature believers who can help us discern the Spirit's voice.

Producing the Fruit of the Spirit

Moreover, walking with the Holy Spirit means allowing Him to produce His fruit in us. Gal. 5:22–23 describes the fruit of the Spirit, as we have discussed in detail, as "love, joy, peace, forbearance, kindness, goodness, faithfulness, gentleness, and self-control." As we yield to the Holy Spirit, these characteristics become increasingly evident in our lives, transforming our relationships and interactions with others.

By living in the Spirit, we participate in God's Kingdom on earth, experiencing the realities of Heaven now and looking forward to the fullness of our eternal home with God. Through the Holy Spirit, we have a personal and permanent connection with the divine, transforming our lives and equipping us for the journey of faith.

Story Time: John, Peter, and the Holy Spirit

The Tale of Two Lives

In a small, close-knit town, two friends, John and Peter, grew up together, both accepting Jesus as their Savior and believing in His sacrifice for their sins. Yet, their spiritual journeys diverged significantly. John embraced the Holy Spirit wholeheartedly, believing in His indwelling presence and guidance. Peter, however, was skeptical about the Holy Spirit's active role in daily life. He acknowledged Jesus's sacrifice but viewed the Holy Spirit as more abstract, distant, and less relevant to his everyday experiences.

John's life became a dynamic journey of faith and discovery. Each morning, he started his day with prayer, inviting the Holy Spirit to guide him. This practice filled John with a profound sense of peace and purpose, leading him to serve others selflessly. There was a contagious joy in his heart, even during the most challenging times. Friends and family often marveled at his wisdom and compassion, attributes that seemed beyond his years and circumstances.

Peter's life, in contrast, felt more burdensome. Though he believed in Jesus, his faith lacked the vibrancy and depth that John experienced. His prayers felt like rituals rather than heartfelt conversations with God. Without the Holy Spirit's guidance, Peter struggled with decisions, often feeling anxious and uncertain. His faith seemed more like a set of rules than a living relationship. He sought solace in familiar routines, but his life lacked the profound sense of purpose and joy that radiated from John.

John's days were marked by remarkable encounters. One day, he met a homeless man named Sam. The Holy Spirit nudged him to help, and John responded with enthusiasm. He didn't just give Sam money; he befriended him, helped him find a job, and introduced him to a supportive community. John's actions transformed Sam's life, and Sam, in turn, became a beacon of hope for others in similar situations. The Holy Spirit's power of love and compassion flowed through John, impacting everyone around him in ways that were both tangible and deeply spiritual.

Peter often felt overwhelmed by the needs around him. He wanted to help but didn't know where to start. Without the Spirit's guidance, he felt his efforts were insignificant, and his heart was heavy with unmet desires to make a difference. He donated to charities but never saw the faces of those he helped, leaving him feeling disconnected and unfulfilled. His life seemed to lack the deep relationships and transformative encounters that characterized John's journey.

John faced numerous trials, but the Holy Spirit provided him with remarkable strength. When his mother fell seriously ill, John prayed fervently, seeking the Spirit's comfort and healing. The Holy Spirit gave him emotional strength and practical wisdom, helping him navigate the medical system efficiently. Throughout the ordeal, John remained calm and hopeful, his unwavering faith a source of strength for his family. The experience deepened his reliance on the Holy Spirit and reinforced the power of divine presence in his life.

Peter faced similar challenges when his father lost his job, plunging the family into financial uncertainty. Without the Holy Spirit's comfort and wisdom, Peter felt stressed and overwhelmed. He tried to solve everything on his own, which led to frustration and burnout. His faith felt distant and inadequate, unable to provide the support he desperately needed. The weight of responsibility without divine guidance made his journey more arduous and lonelier.

John's church was a vibrant community fueled by the Holy Spirit. He participated actively, leading Bible studies and encouraging others in their faith. The Holy Spirit often guided his words, providing insights that helped others grow spiritually. His church was like a second family, united by the Spirit's love and power, creating a haven of support and growth for all its members.

Peter attended church regularly but felt like an outsider. Without the Holy Spirit's indwelling, his faith lacked the warmth and intimacy he saw in others. He admired John but felt a gulf between their experiences. His church participation was more about duty than joy, and he struggled to form meaningful connections. The lack of spiritual vibrancy left him feeling isolated and yearning for more.

As John and Peter grew older, their lives bore the marks of their choices. John's life was a testament to the transformative power of the Holy Spirit. He had touched countless lives, leading many to Christ and deepening the faith of others. His life was filled with love, joy, and a profound sense of fulfillment. The Holy Spirit's presence in John's life was undeniable, making every moment significant and eternally impactful.

Peter, despite his belief in Jesus, felt a nagging emptiness. He often wondered why his faith didn't bring the same joy and purpose he saw in John. His life was good but lacked the supernatural touch of the Holy Spirit. He had achieved success by worldly standards but felt something essential was missing.

The absence of the Spirit's active presence left a void that nothing else could fill.

When John and Peter passed away, their journeys to Heaven revealed the full impact of their earthly lives. John experienced a glorious welcome, surrounded by the lives he had touched. Each person testified to the power of the Holy Spirit working through him, showing how his faith had transformed and inspired countless others. His eternal rewards were abundant, reflecting the depth of his relationship with God and his faithful service on earth. John found himself in a place of honor, his life of obedience and partnership with the Holy Spirit richly rewarded. His standing in Heaven was elevated, with a sense of eternal purpose and joy that mirrored his earthly walk with the Spirit.

Peter also entered Heaven, welcomed by Jesus's love. However, he realized the depth of what he had missed on earth. His faith had saved him, but his lack of engagement with the Holy Spirit had limited his earthly experience and eternal rewards. He saw the vibrant life he could have lived, filled with the Spirit's power, love, and wisdom. The realization brought a mix of gratitude for his salvation and regret for not fully embracing the Holy Spirit's role. Peter's eternal rewards were fewer, and his standing in Heaven, though secure, reflected the lesser impact his life had on earth. He saw the missed opportunities for deeper fellowship and greater service.

The stories of John and Peter illustrate the profound difference the Holy Spirit makes in a believer's life. The Holy Spirit is a person, a constant companion who dwells within us, guiding, empowering, and transforming us. His presence brings a fullness of life, a deep sense of purpose, and an eternal perspective. John's life was a testament to living in the Spirit, experiencing God's Kingdom on earth, and impacting lives for eternity. Peter's life, though saved by faith, lacked the fullness that comes from walking step by step with the Holy Spirit. The Holy Spirit invites every believer into a deeper, more dynamic relationship, promising a life of power, love, and a sound mind. Through the Holy Spirit, we participate in God's Kingdom now and prepare for the eternal joys and rewards to come.

CHAPTER 34

Finding God's Will

My Personal Journey

For a long time, I believed that since God had given me a brain, whatever decisions I made must have been in line with His will. I thought that if I was heading in the wrong direction, God would make things fall apart. Sometimes, I didn't even think about God in my day-to-day life—I just did what made sense. Then, there were those moments when I prayed, and something came to mind, and I figured it must be from God. But the truth is, I had no idea what I was doing.

I often sought advice from others, but I found that most people were just as uncertain as I was, even though they had plenty of answers. Some gave spiritual-sounding advice, like: "Throw out a fleece, and God will show you," or "Just pray about it." They made it seem like there was a guaranteed way to ensure you were on the right track, as if following a specific formula would lead to hearing God's voice clearly.

But hearing God's voice and walking in His path isn't about following a formula at all. It's not like you can just do the same things that worked last year and expect everything to fall into place. Relationships don't work like that— whether it's with a spouse, a friend, or with God. Relationships are dynamic; they grow, they change, and they require ongoing attention and care.

What God really desires is a relationship with us—a relationship like the one He had with Adam in the Garden of Eden. Now, I know we're not living in the Garden, and it's not always easy to feel that close to God in our daily lives. But here's what I've learned and what scripture has taught me: walking side by side with God isn't just possible—it's something He desires to do with us. It's actually easier than we often make it out to be because God is already guiding us, even when we're not fully aware of it.

This realization has been a turning point for me. I'm learning to let go of the need to figure everything out on my own or to rely on what has worked in the past. Instead, I'm focusing on building that relationship with God, trusting that He's with me in every step. It's less about getting everything "right" and more about simply being with Him, walking and talking with Him in a relationship that grows deeper over time.

This journey of understanding has shown me that it's not about having all the answers but about embracing the relationship God wants to have with us. It's freeing to realize that the pressure is off and that walking with God is more about being present with Him than following a set of rules or formulas. This is the path I'm on now, and it's one of trust, relationship, and discovering what it truly means to walk side by side with God. This is what it means to truly walk with God, not chasing after what He can give, but simply being with Him and following His lead every step of the way.

Finding God's Will for Your Life

Understanding and embracing God's will for our lives is key to experiencing His best. While free will allows us to pursue any path that seems appealing, the most fulfilling and fruitful path will always be the one aligned with His divine plan. Romans 12:1–2 speaks powerfully to this truth: it urges us to present our bodies as a living sacrifice, holy and pleasing to God, as an act of worship. By renewing our minds and resisting the pull of worldly standards, we open ourselves to discerning His good, pleasing, and perfect will. Transformation through the Holy Spirit empowers us to see life through God's lens and to embrace the unique calling He has set before us.

Ephesians 2:10 further reinforces this by reminding us that we are God's handiwork, created in Christ Jesus to do good works that He prepared in advance for us. These good works are not just random acts of kindness; they are specific tasks designed uniquely for each of us, aligned with God's purpose and plan. When we seek and follow His will, we find ourselves in harmony with the life He intended—one that brings glory to Him and abundant joy and purpose to us.

Our responsibility is to seek His will daily, to ask for guidance in every step, and to remain open to His leading. God's will is not always a mystery; it often unfolds through prayer, scripture, and the leading of the Holy Spirit. As we trust Him and commit our ways to Him, He faithfully directs our paths, leading us toward the good works He has set aside for us and into a life that reflects His glory.

Faithfulness and Responsibility

In 1 Corinthians 3:8, Paul explains that everyone has different roles in God's work. Each person's contribution is valuable, and God rewards us based on our faithfulness in performing our individual tasks. Colossians 3:23–24 encourages believers to work diligently and wholeheartedly as if serving Christ directly. This mindset ensures that our efforts are directed toward God's glory, securing eternal rewards.

Rewards and Kindness

In Luke 12:47–48, Jesus teaches that greater knowledge of God's will brings greater responsibility. Failure to act accordingly results in more severe consequences, while ignorance results in lesser punishment. This highlights the importance of obedience to God's revealed will. Paul reflects in 2 Timothy 4:7–8 on his life of faithfulness and obedience, confident of receiving the crown of righteousness. This reward is promised to all who live in anticipation of Christ's return and strive to fulfill God's will. Even the smallest acts of kindness done in His name are noticed and rewarded by God (Matt. 10:42). No act of service is too insignificant in the Kingdom of God. Mark 9:41 encourages believers to seize every opportunity to serve.

Abiding in Jesus with the Holy Spirit as our Helper

The Trinity in John 15

John 15 is a perfect representation of how the Trinity works together as one, illustrating the harmonious and interconnected roles of God the Father, Jesus the Son, and the Holy Spirit. God the Father, as the vinedresser, meticulously tends to the branches, ensuring they are healthy and fruitful, organizing the great master plan. Jesus, the vine, serves as the central source of life and sustenance, connecting the branches to the divine. The Holy Spirit, flowing like sap through the vine into the branches, empowers and fuels the development of spiritual fruit. This divine synergy demonstrates the unity and distinct roles within the Trinity, showing how believers flourish by staying connected to Jesus and allowing the Holy Spirit to work through them under the guidance of God the Father.

Jesus Is the True Vine

Jesus begins by declaring, "I am the true vine, and my Father is the gardener" (John 15:1). The concept of abiding in the vine is a dynamic and powerful illustration of the relationship between Jesus, God the Father, the Holy Spirit, and His followers. In John 15:1–8, Jesus paints a vivid picture of spiritual life and growth, emphasizing the necessity of staying closely connected to Him for a fruitful and fulfilling existence.

God the Father is the vinedresser, Jesus is the vine, and we are the branches. God's role is to tend the vine, ensuring every branch is healthy and productive. Our role, however, is simpler yet crucial—to stay connected to Jesus, the vine. Jesus underscores the importance of maintaining a close, continuous relationship with Him. Just as a branch draws life-giving sustenance from the vine, we must remain in Jesus to bear spiritual fruit (John 15:4).

Jesus intensifies this metaphor in John 15:5: "I am the vine; you are the branches. Whoever abides in me and I in him, he it is that bears much fruit, for apart from me, you can do nothing." This highlights our absolute dependence on Jesus for spiritual growth and fruitful living. Without this vital connection, our efforts are in vain.

Moreover, the Holy Spirit acts as the life-giving sap that flows through Jesus, the vine, into us, the branches. It's the Holy Spirit who fuels the development of the fruit. Our job isn't to focus on producing fruit; it's to stay connected to Jesus. When we do, the Holy Spirit naturally works through us, developing the fruit in our lives. But Jesus also gives a stern warning: staying rooted in Christ is essential to avoid spiritual decay and separation from God (John 15:6).

The Blessings of Abiding

When we remain in Jesus, our prayers align with His will, and we glorify God by living fruitful lives that reflect genuine discipleship. It's God the Father, the vinedresser, who picks the fruit from our branches and distributes it as He sees fit (John 15:7–8).

The Choice: to remain, to abide. This means to stay, to tarry, not to depart, to continually be present. **Apart from Christ, we can do nothing.** Repeat this: **Apart from abiding, we can do nothing.** It's a choice we must make; abiding is something we decide to live out every day. To have a vital, fruitful spiritual life, we must learn to abide. Abiding is not passive; it's an intentional decision to stay connected to Christ, to listen, and let His life flow through us. I'm here to show you how to abide and guide you on the unique path the Father has for you. Let's start this journey together, learning to remain in Him and watching the fruit of that choice transform your life.

Simply put, the vibrant metaphor of abiding in the vine in John 15 highlights the critical importance of staying intimately connected to Jesus. God the Father is the master gardener, Jesus is the vine, and we are the branches. Our sole job is to remain attached to the vine and allow the Holy Spirit, the life-giving sap, to flow through us, fueling the development of spiritual fruit. We don't focus on producing fruit; we focus on staying connected to Jesus. God, the vinedresser, takes care of the rest, picking and distributing the fruit as He deems fit. This powerful relationship brings blessings, answered prayers, and a life that glorifies God through faithful, obedient living.

CHAPTER 35

Abiding Training

Based on content and teaching from Abide Ministry (www.abide ministries.com), I recommend that you visit this site for teachings and training videos after completing this book. You will find it helpful.

But what does "abiding" look like, and how do we really live like that day to day?

What does it mean to abide? We will understand the foundation of staying connected to Jesus and submitting to him for everything. Trusting that his plan is best.

How to Abide: A Deeper Approach to Reading the Bible

If you are like me, sometimes you read the Bible to get it done. I read three chapters today. Hurray! This is not what we are going for. We want to read the Bible so God can speak to us and we can understand it. If you don't fully and completely understand something you're reading, ask God for the wisdom to understand. He will guide you on a journey sometime through the scriptures to give you an understanding you never had before. Other times, he might guide you through your thoughts, which you can verify through the scriptures. He might guide you through your journal, where you are keeping track of your questions and answers. The one thing you can be confident in is that He will speak to you.

The practice of reading God's Word should be done slowly and thoughtfully, with the goal of truly absorbing and meditating on what is being read—not merely rushing through a passage to check it off the list. This approach involves reading with a focus on understanding why each word is placed there by God.

As you read, if a word or phrase is unclear or seems significant, pause and ask God to reveal its meaning. Take time to explore other parts of the Bible or examine the Hebrew or Greek origins of the word, allowing yourself to meditate on that portion of scripture. When you find yourself wondering about something, recognize that the Holy Spirit may be guiding you toward a deeper understanding of who God is.

Remember, the Holy Spirit is actively involved, guiding you toward deeper understanding when you find yourself wondering about something, that curiosity could be the Spirit leading you to a richer knowledge of God. The practice of reading this way—intentional, meditative, and open to God's guidance—will deepen your relationship with Him.

God speaks directly to us through His Word, offering guidance and life. Jesus declares in Matthew 4:4, "Man shall not live by bread alone, but by every word that comes from the mouth of God," and in John 6:63b, "The words that I have spoken to you are spirit and life." The Holy Spirit takes the written Word (Logos) and makes it personal (Rhema), revealing what God has prepared in advance for us.

As our Shepherd, Christ calls us to hear His voice and follow Him. John 10:3b says, "The sheep hear his voice, and he calls his own sheep by name and leads them out." He knows us intimately, as John 10:14 confirms: "I know my own, and my own know me." Learning to recognize His voice allows Him to guide us personally.

The Holy Spirit, sent as our Helper, continues the intimate relationship Jesus had with His disciples. John 14:25–26 teaches that the Spirit "will teach you all things and bring to your remembrance all that I have said to you." This is not a distant connection but a personal, Spirit-led relationship where God reveals His truth and wisdom to us.

Our sinful nature often resists this connection, as shown in Genesis 3:1–7, where self-centeredness led to humanity's fall. Even believers can live carnally if they fail to abide in Christ. Walking with God daily is a choice we must make to live in His fullness.

We also face an enemy who seeks to harm us, but Jesus promises abundant life in John 10:10: "I came that they may have life and have it abundantly." By abiding in Him, we can live victorious, grand lives despite the brokenness around us.

Jesus modeled perfect obedience and reliance on God. In John 8:38b, He says, "I do nothing on my own authority, but speak just as the Father taught me." Even Jesus depended on the Father's voice, showing us the importance of abiding by God's guidance.

The fruit of abiding includes forgiveness, unity, joy, and transformation. Romans 8:1–2 reminds us to forgive ourselves and others, as forgiveness frees us from condemnation. Unity, celebrated in Psalm 133:3, invites God's blessings, while disagreements call for discernment and alignment with His will.

Joy flows from abiding, as Psalm 128 says, "Blessed is everyone who fears the Lord." Abiding brings daily joy and fulfillment to our work and relationships. This process also transforms our character into Christ's likeness, producing the fruit of the Spirit listed in Galatians 5:22–23: "love, joy, peace, patience, kindness, goodness, faithfulness, gentleness, self-control."

Answered prayer is another result of abiding. John 15:7–8 promises, "If you abide in me and my words abide in you, ask whatever you wish, and it will be done for you." Prayer aligns us with God's will, and His promises are always "Yes" in Christ, as 2 Corinthians 1:18–22 affirms.

Finally, abiding opens our minds to God's truth. Luke 24:45 says, "Then he opened their minds to understand the scriptures." The Spirit teaches us all things, as 1 John 2:27 assures: "His anointing teaches you about everything." By relying on the Spirit, we gain insights we could never achieve on our own.

Abiding connects us deeply with God, allowing Him to transform our lives, fulfill His promises, and lead us into the grand life He designed. Stay connected to Him, and experience the joy, guidance, and fruit of His Spirit.

The Mystery Revealed Through Abiding in God's Word

1 Corinthians 2:9-16 "Eye has not seen, nor ear heard, nor have entered into the heart of man the things which God has prepared for those who love Him." (v. 9)

This verse reminds us that God's plans for us are beyond human comprehension. You cannot grasp them through intellect or human effort; they are revealed only through the Holy Spirit. Verse 10 tells us that "God has revealed them to us through His Spirit. For the Spirit searches all things, yes, the deep things of God." Abiding in God's Word requires that we approach it as receivers, relying fully on the Holy Spirit to unveil truth to us personally.

It's not about working harder to "get it." Instead, we stay open to the Spirit's revelation. Verse 12 confirms this: "Now we have received, not the spirit of the world, but the Spirit who is from God, that we might know the things that have been freely given to us by God." Let go of the pressure to understand everything instantly. God's Spirit gives revelation freely as you abide.

Verse 14 warns that approaching scripture intellectually or through the flesh will lead to frustration: "The natural man does not receive the things of the Spirit of God, for they are foolishness to him." When scripture doesn't seem to make sense, ask the Spirit to show you how it's true. This process can be joyful, a journey of discovery as God unfolds His truths to you.

Verse 16 assures us that "we have the mind of Christ." With His Spirit in us, we can discern and receive His revelations step by step.

2 Corinthians 3:4-6, 16-18 Our ability to abide and receive revelation doesn't depend on our own skill or maturity but on God. "Not that we are sufficient of ourselves, but our sufficiency is from God." (v. 5). This means anyone— new believers and seasoned saints alike—can receive God's truth.

The Spirit gives life, while reading scripture as mere law or intellect brings death: "The letter kills, but the Spirit gives life." (v. 6). Abiding stirs life within you—it energizes, brings hope, and quickens your spirit. When abiding feels life-giving, you know you're in alignment with God's Spirit.

Verses 16-18 reveal that abiding removes veils from our understanding. When we turn to the Lord, "the veil is taken away." This process transforms us "from glory to glory" into His image. Like a caterpillar becoming a butterfly, once transformed, we cannot return to our old nature. Abiding isn't about managing sin; it's about real transformation as we walk with God and experience freedom along the journey.

John 6:63; 6:68; 17:3 "It is the Spirit who gives life; the flesh profits nothing. The words that I speak to you are spirit, and they are life." (John 6:63)

Abiding in scripture is not just an intellectual exercise. Jesus' words themselves are Spirit and life, working powerfully in us to transform and guide us. Peter affirms this in verse 68: "Lord, to whom shall we go? You have the words of eternal life."

Eternal life isn't just a future reality in Heaven. Jesus defines it in John 17:3: "This is eternal life, that they may know You, the only true God, and Jesus Christ whom You have sent." Eternal life begins now through an intimate, personal relationship with God—a relationship deepened as you abide in His Word.

Mark 4:13-20 Jesus' parable of the sower reveals that the Word of God produces fruit depending on the condition of our hearts. Good soil—those who "hear the word, accept it, and bear fruit" (v. 20)—results in abundant harvests. But this takes time and perseverance.

Like a kernel of corn planted in soil, the Word begins to work unseen before a breakthrough happens. If a farmer gives up because he doesn't see immediate results, he misses the harvest. Similarly, many Christians quit abiding too soon—either because they see no immediate impact or because they experience a small breakthrough and assume the process is complete. But true fruit requires ongoing nourishment.

The Word will work in your soul even when you see no visible signs. Trust the process. Abiding is necessary until the promises are fully fulfilled or the transformation is complete.

Enjoying Abiding: Building an Intimate Relationship with God

Abiding isn't a duty, task, or goal to achieve. It's about cultivating a relationship with God—learning to enjoy intimacy with Him, hearing His voice, and being fulfilled by His presence. This process allows us to process His Word, understand His heart, and live out His truth with joy.

Luke 10:38–42 "Martha, Martha, you are worried and troubled about many things. But one thing is needed, and Mary has chosen that good part, which will not be taken away from her." (vv. 41–42)

Martha thought her service for Jesus was the priority, but Jesus revealed that Mary had chosen the better way—sitting at His feet and listening to Him. This is the essence of abiding: entering into a dialogue with Jesus, not just studying or performing tasks. Set aside time daily, even 20 minutes at the start of your day, to be in His presence and enjoy the sweetness of fellowship. It's a choice to focus on Him above distractions.

Proverbs 4:1–7, 20–23 "Give attention to my words; incline your ear to my sayings. Do not let them depart from your eyes; keep them in the midst of your heart." (vv. 20–21)

Abiding begins by receiving God's words and allowing them to sink deeply into your heart. Pay attention to what the Spirit highlights—whether through themes, a verse that stirs your heart, or something you feel drawn to explore. Abiding involves "camping out" in these words through memorization, journaling, asking questions, and listening for His responses. Stay with His words until they transform your heart and build your faith in His promises.

Proverbs 22:17–21 "Incline your ear and hear the words of the wise, and apply your heart to my knowledge. For it is a pleasant thing if you keep them within you." (vv. 17–18)

Scripture memory and journaling allow God's Word to take root in your heart. When His truth is in you, it will flow from your lips, deepening your trust in Him and bringing transformation. Anyone, regardless of maturity, can receive revelation because it's God's work. Your role is simply to have a willing heart and remain faithful in abiding.

Jeremiah 15:16 "Your words were found, and I ate them, and Your word was to me the joy and rejoicing of my heart."

Abiding in God's Word brings joy and life to your soul. It's a process of meditating, pondering, and processing His truths. Even correction through His Word is life-giving, as it leads to encouragement and guidance. God uses His Word to invite you to walk with Him, offering power and revelation to sustain and transform you.

Luke 2:42–52 "After three days they found Him in the temple, sitting in the midst of the teachers, both listening to them and asking them questions." (v. 46)

Even at 12 years old, Jesus modeled abiding by listening, asking questions, and sharing His understanding. Use this approach in your journaling—ask questions like "What does this mean?" or "How does this work?" Write down your thoughts, express your understanding, and confirm truths with God. This process of dialogue and discernment deepens your relationship with Him.

Practical Steps for Abiding

Set aside time daily – Start your day with 20 minutes in His presence.

Listen and receive – Pay attention to what God highlights in scripture.

Memorize scripture – Let His words take root in your heart.

Journal – Write down questions, personal thoughts, and what you hear from God.

Pray scripture – Speak His promises back to Him.

Share – Discuss your journey with a trusted friend or mentor for encouragement and accountability.

Abiding is a joyful journey of hearing God's voice, receiving His truth, and living in His promises. Let the Word transform you as you walk closely with Him.

Abiding in the Word: A Practical Guide

Abiding in God's Word is an active, Spirit-led journey where you engage deeply with scripture, allowing it to transform your heart and life. Here's a step-by-step approach to help you grow in this process:

1. Pursue Your Interest: Pay attention to what the Spirit is piquing your interest in—those topics or scriptures that resonate deeply or address something God has been laying on your heart. Let your abiding begin with this personal connection.

2. Write Out the scriptures: Take time to write down specific scriptures that stand out to you. Use a reliable cross-reference study Bible like the **NKJV (Spirit-Filled Life Bible)**, **NASB**, **NEV**, or **Amplified Bible**. Avoid paraphrased translations as your primary source, though they can be helpful supplements.

- Use online tools like **www.biblegateway.com** or **www.crosswalk.com** to compare translations.

- Read the verse in its full context by studying the surrounding paragraph or chapter.

- Spend time understanding the background of the book where the verse is found.

3. Cross-Reference and Word Studies: Use your study Bible or online resources to find cross-references that expand on the verse's truth. As you explore related scriptures:

- Be sensitive to the Spirit's "quickening" (when a verse strikes your heart or brings clarity).

- If a verse resonates, spend more time processing it. If not, move on to other verses or references.

- Perform word studies using tools like **www.studylight.org** to explore the Greek or Hebrew meanings of keywords.

4. Reflect on God's Character and Promises: Write down your reflections, focusing on:

a. What does the passage reveal about God's character?
b. What God has done, is doing, or promises to do.
c. Any conditions attached to His promises (e.g., "If...then").
d. Your responsibilities or responses to His Word.

5. Explore Deeper Meaning:s Dive deeper into specific words using tools like **www.studylight.org**. The Interlinear Bible feature allows you to:

- Click on individual words to uncover their Greek or Hebrew definitions.

- Explore word origins for additional insights into their meaning.

6. Memorize the Word: Commit key verses to memory. Write them on 3x5 cards and carry them with you to review throughout the day.

7. Journal Your Journey: Take time to write out your thoughts and wrestle with the Word:

a. Do you truly believe what the Word says? Why or why not?
b. What struggles or life experiences might be working against your ability to receive this truth?
c. How does this scripture apply to your situation?
d. How is God calling you to adjust your life to align with His will?
e. Ask questions, seek clarity, and write down what you believe God is saying to you.

8. Pray the Promises: Turn the scriptures into prayers, asking God to fulfill the promises He's spoken to you.

9. Share with a Trusted Friend or Spouse: Engage with someone for accountability. Share your journal entries and discuss:

a. What God is saying to you and why it's important.
b. Insights, feelings, and how the scriptures resonate with each other.
c. Pray the scriptures together for encouragement and growth.

Next Steps Day-by-Day with Others

Follow the same instructions. Write out the scriptures, reflect on their meaning, and record what God speaks to you. Once completed, reach out to review your journey together, whether in person or by phone.

This process will deepen your relationship with God, allowing His Word to take root in your heart and transform your life.

Faith and Abiding: Receiving and Living God's Promises

Abiding in the Word is about staying with the scriptures. God is speaking to you until faith is given and transformation or fulfillment occurs. Faith is the key to receiving God's promises—it is not merely learning about joy, peace, or His will but actually experiencing them through faith. Let's explore this together.

HEBREWS 11:1–3: "Now faith is the substance of things hoped for, the evidence of things not seen." (v. 1)

Faith is certainty about what we do not yet see. How do we gain this certainty? Verse 3 explains: through what God speaks. Just as God created the world by His Word, He can speak into your life and change your circumstances. Faith begins with hearing what God has spoken and trusting it before it is visible.

The example of the Israelites crossing the Red Sea illustrates this. God promised the Promised Land, but while Joshua and Caleb trusted God's Word (faith), the others doubted and refused to believe. Faith requires being persuaded of the certainty of what God speaks, just like trusting a friend to meet you when they say they will. Faith is not about striving—it's about believing what He has already spoken.

HEBREWS 11:6: "But without faith it is impossible to please Him, for he who comes to God must believe that He is, and that He is a rewarder of those who diligently seek Him."

Faith pleases God. To walk with Him, we must believe not only that He exists but that He is "I AM"—able to fulfill every word He speaks and handle every circumstance. God rewards those who diligently seek Him, and His greatest reward is faith itself. As you abide, God gives you the faith you need to trust Him fully.

HEBREWS 12:1–2 "Looking unto Jesus, the author and finisher of our faith." (v. 2)

Faith begins and ends with Jesus. He authors faith by speaking His Word into your life, and He finishes it by bringing you to the certainty of His promise. Your role is to lay aside distractions and sin and to run the unique race He sets before you. Abiding is about staying connected to the Vine, hearing His voice, and letting Him complete the work of faith in you.

ROMANS 10:17: "So then faith comes by hearing, and hearing by the word of God."

Faith comes through hearing God's Word. Abiding is about staying with what He is speaking until faith comes. Don't rush through devotions or jump from topic to topic. Camp out in the scriptures He is highlighting for you until you have the certainty of faith.

HEBREWS 3:15–19: "Today, if you will hear His voice, do not harden your hearts as in the rebellion." (v. 15)

The Israelites refused to believe God's promise of the Promised Land and wandered for 40 years. Though God provided for their needs, they never entered His rest because of their unbelief—not struggling belief, but outright refusal to be persuaded by His Word. Abiding is a choice. If we refuse to trust what God speaks, we can miss His best for us. But if we abide, His will—grand and full of promise—becomes our reality.

ROMANS 4:17–21: "He did not waver at the promise of God through unbelief, but was strengthened in faith, giving glory to God, and being fully convinced that what He had promised He was also able to perform." (vv. 20–21)

Abraham's journey shows that faith grows through abiding. Though he failed at times, he ultimately became fully persuaded of God's promises. He trusted God to fulfill His Word, even when asked to sacrifice Isaac. Faith came as he walked with God, trusting Him through the process.

Your Next Steps

1. **Abide in His Word** – Begin with scriptures the Spirit highlights for you. Write them out, reflect on them, and stay with them until faith is given.

2. **Journal Your Journey** – Write down your thoughts, questions, and what God is saying to you. Allow this to be a dialogue with the Father.

3. **Memorize His Word** – Carry key verses with you and meditate on them throughout your day.

4. **Pray His Promises** – Speak His Word back to Him, asking Him to fulfill what He has spoken.

5. **Share with a Friend or Mentor** – Discuss what you're learning, how it applies to your life, and what God is saying to you.

Launching Your Abiding Journey

As you continue, use what you've learned to deepen your abiding practice. Begin with scriptures related to your life, questions, or spiritual needs. Write them out, process them through journaling, and reflect on their meaning. Stay with them until faith comes and transformation occurs.

Remember, your role is to diligently seek Him and abide. God is the author and finisher of your faith. Trust Him, and enjoy the journey as He brings His promises to life in you.

Practical Steps to Get Started

Abiding Exercise

I've had the joy of teaching many people how to truly abide in God's presence and experience the overwhelming love He longs to share with them, and I'm inviting you to take a moment to do the same! This exercise is simple but deeply impactful. It's all about setting aside intentional time with God, where you can open your heart and really listen.

Start by finding a quiet spot where you can be alone with your Bible, free from distractions. Then, simply invite God to speak—ask Him, "Lord, what do You want to share with me today?" This small step opens the door to something beautiful.

To really set the tone, pray through Psalm 143:8–10: "Let me hear in the morning of Your steadfast love, for in You I trust. Make me know the way I should go, for to You I lift up my soul. Deliver me from my enemies, O Lord!

I have fled to You for refuge. Teach me to do Your will, for You are my God! Let Your good Spirit lead me on level ground."

After praying, take a few minutes to simply sit in His presence and listen. Don't rush—let His peace fill you. Write down any thoughts, scriptures, or feelings that come up, knowing that God desires to meet you at this time. This is where the fun happens! Trust that He's ready to pour out His love, wisdom, and guidance as you spend time abiding with Him. Get ready—you're about to experience God's voice in a way that will fill you with joy, peace, and excitement!

Preparation for your Exercise

1. Have a cross-reference Bible that includes notes that guide readers to related verses on the same topic, theme, or event, connecting different parts of scripture. These references help deepen understanding by showing how various passages are interrelated, making it a valuable tool for comprehensive Bible study.

2. Read the Verse: Start with the verse or passage you're studying.

3. Find Cross-Reference Notations: Look for small letters or numbers next to words in the verse.

4. Locate the Cross-References: Check the margin, center column, or footnotes for related verses.

   a. Read Related Verses: Look up and read the cross-referenced verses.

   b. Compare and Connect: Reflect on how the verses relate and deepen your understanding.

5. Have a journal to write in. For this exercise, any notebook will work, but if you make this a daily habit, you might want to have a dedicated notebook or journal to keep track of your time with God.

6. Have a pen or, if you want to get fancy, a few pens. (I use a black pen for all my thoughts, a green pen for my prayers, a blue pen for the

scriptures I am writing down and a red pen when I know that God is speaking to me. I do this so that when I go back through my journal, it is easier for me to see what God is leading me through.)

Start your Exercise with Ezekiel

1. You really can start anywhere, but if you need a place to start by reading through Ezekiel 34:11–30 (twenty-one promises of God) and identify one verse that jumps out to you. Let the Spirit impress upon you the one that He wants to speak to you today. Or choose the verse you are hoping God would speak to you about today.

2. Write out the verse from Ezekiel 34 in your journal word for word.

3. Underline any of the parts that seem especially important or valuable to you.

4. Next, write what this promise means to you and why the Lord might be promising it to you. How do you feel about it? Don't be shy. This is your journal. Speak to God as you would in prayer. Gratitude, anger, whatever you feel going through this. Just be honest.

5. Underline everything that you write out that seems to be especially important or relevant.

6. Next, Look up each of the cross-references related to that verse that the Holy Spirit prioritizes for you (and the verses around them for context). Which one(s) of them do you feel God is also promising to you or highlighting for you as important in your research?

7. Write out the cross-reference verses you feel are important and that you feel God is promising to you also. Then write what this means to you as you continue through the cross-reference.

8. Underline everything you feel is especially important that you wrote down.

9. Next, look up each of the cross-references from each of the verses you just cross-referenced from and do the same thing.

10. Write out all the verses that stood out to you. Which one(s) of them do you feel God is also speaking to you?

11. Underline everything you feel is especially important.

You can keep going on, bouncing from cross-reference to cross-reference. It is amazing how the Lord continues to speak. If you go back through your underlining and just read that, you will find themes speaking directly to you. You know that He is speaking to you because you see things repeated over and over again. (Typically, three times means a lot to me). I then go back and underline it all in red. I then summarize what I feel that God is saying in red as well. It is an amazing experience to go back through your journal and read the red. (Just like a red-letter Bible.) What direction is He taking you? Remember to trust in faith that God wants to speak to you. If you don't feel He is talking to you, keep asking Him and seeking Him.

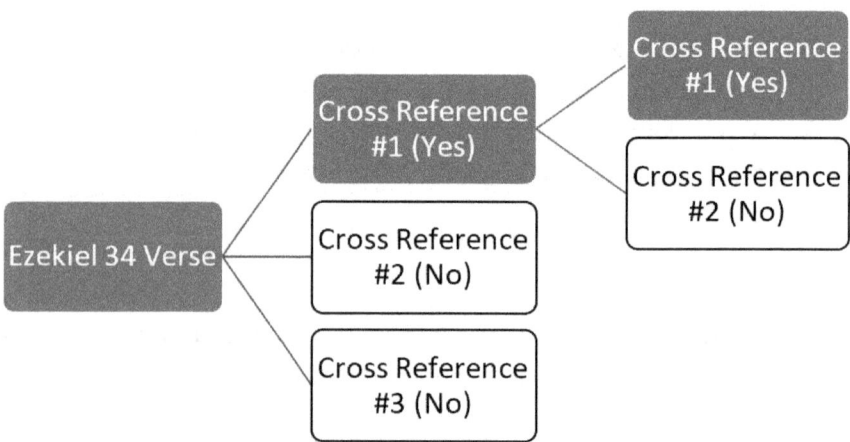

More thoughts on journaling:

- Write it out—longhand is important

- What is the verse saying? It should prompt questions. Write them down.

- Have a "parking lot" in your journal where you keep future ideas or topics to focus your abiding on. This allows you to focus on what He is speaking to you about, and not follow bunny trails. After God is finished with one subject with you, you have other things to study in the future that interest you.

Abiding in the Word

Knowing God's will for your life is truly about knowing God Himself and walking in close relationship with Him. The journey isn't about finding a hidden plan; it's about abiding in His presence and letting His Word shape your life. This abiding isn't merely about reading scripture but about letting His Word dwell richly within you, creating a vibrant, living connection to His heart.

Think about how we get to know someone well: we read what they write, listen to their words, and spend time with them. God has given us His Word, His breath, to reveal who He is (2 Tim. 3:16). The more time we spend reading and understanding what He's written, the more we grow in intimacy with Him. And if we ever find the scriptures difficult to understand, the Holy Spirit is right there, ready to guide us.

If you make a commitment to abide every day for just one month—spending time in the Word, listening, and journaling your experiences—you'll notice God's voice in new ways. You won't want to stop abiding. His guidance will become clearer, but even more, you'll feel His overwhelming love and appreciation for your pursuit of Him. James 4:8 promises, "Draw near to God, and He will draw near to you." As you seek Him, He won't hide from you. In fact, Jeremiah 29:13 assures us, "You will seek Me and find Me when you seek Me with all your heart." God's greatest desire is for you to be close to Him, to know His heart, and to experience the fullness of His love.

Tips and Tricks for Pursuing a Life of Abiding

1. Go to abideministries.com and watch the videos about abiding and a myriad of other topics.

2. Pursue your interest: What interesting word or thought has the Spirit been piquing your interest; what do you already know God is laying on your heart?

3. Write out the specific scriptures: I recommend a good cross-reference study Bible with help and concordance: NKJV (*Spirit Filled Life Bible* is particularly good, as it includes translations of Greek and Hebrew words); NASB; NEV; Amplified—and don't use paraphrase as primary Bible, only as some additional help. You can go to www.Biblegateway.com or www.crosswalk.com for different translations. Spend some time understanding the context of the specific Bible book from which the verse is taken. Also, don't read just the specific verse, but read the entire paragraph for context.

4. Cross-reference specific verses, which will take you to another truth about that particular revelation; perform Word studies using the concordance at the back of your Bible or www.Biblegateway.com or www.crosswalk.com. As you spend time in the cross-referenced or word study verses, let the "quickening" of the Spirit lead you regarding whether this is something He is speaking to you, and only then spend time further processing. If it does not strike your heart much, don't spend any further time on it, and continue to cross-reference other verses that strike your heart, or go to another verse from your Word study.

5. Write out your thoughts about:

   a. What does this say about the character of God?

   b. What has God done, is He doing, or promising to do?

   c. Are there any conditions to what God promises? (If ... then)

   d. What are my responsibilities or responses?

6. Go deeper into Hebrew and Greek meanings of the Words He is speaking to you:

   a. Go to www.crosswalk.com

   b. Click on "Bible Study Tools" at the top of the website, center-right

   c. On the next screen, click on "Interlinear Bible."

d. Key in a word or verses

e. When the verses come up along with the Greek & Hebrew on the next screen

f. Click on your chosen word

g. From the next screen, print the Hebrew or Greek word meanings

h. Memorize the verses (word for word) – carry 3-by-5 cards with you.

7. Journal your thoughts:

a. Do I believe this in my heart? (Is it settled?)

b. Why or why not? (What do I struggle with & what experiences in my life work against what I am receiving in the Word?)

c. How do these words apply to my situation and to me?

d. How is God calling me to adjust my life to Him and His will?

e. What thoughts come to me about all this?

8. Dialogue with the Father your thoughts. Ask for clarity, understanding, wisdom, and faith.

9. Pray the promises: Ask God to fulfill what He has said to you.

10. Commit time with your friend or spouse, sharing your journal and what God is saying to you.

a. Discuss feelings, reactions, insights, and why it is important to you.

b. Study specific verses that each participant is sharing.

c. Pray verses together.

Abiding and Culture

In today's world, cultural questions and arguments are more complex and divisive than ever before. Society seems to be constantly redefining what it means to live, love, and belong. We see people questioning their own identities, asking, "What gender am I?" and witnessing fierce debates over whether it's unloving or hateful to address someone based on their appearance. Conversations around abortion are equally charged, with passionate discussions about the right to choose versus protecting life. Confusion abounds about marriage and divorce—who should be married when divorce is acceptable, and what it even means to commit to love in this day and age. And then there are the environmental issues, where the world is split on what's true and what action should be taken. In this whirlwind of conflicting ideas, even basic principles like free speech, religious freedom, and justice are being called into question.

Here's the thing: you don't need another opinion. The world doesn't need one more voice saying what's right or wrong, biblical or not. What we truly need is to seek the source of all truth—God Himself. In James 1:5, we're told, "If any of you lacks wisdom, let him ask of God, who gives to all liberally and without reproach, and it will be given to him." The answers you seek aren't found in another news article or opinion piece; they're found in your time spent with the Father.

Abiding in Him means going to Him with neutrality, being open to hearing His voice and letting Him show you the truth through His Word. John 15:4 reminds us, "Abide in Me, and I in you. As the branch cannot bear fruit of itself, unless it abides in the vine, neither can you, unless you abide in Me." Your role is to stay connected to the vine—Jesus—so that He can reveal to you what's real and what's right. And when He speaks, your next step is to ask, "Lord, what do You want me to do with this?" Whether He leads you to share it with others or keep it between you and Him, your job is simply to follow. Don't rush ahead or lag behind. Remember, His timing is perfect, and He's always working on all sides of the situation.

You also need to know that God might not give you an answer right away—and that's intentional. He might want to first show you how deeply He loves you before diving into cultural topics. Maybe He needs to bring healing to an area of your life or work on forgiveness or generosity in your heart before He addresses what's happening in the world. Psalm 27:14 says, "Wait on the Lord; be of good courage, and He shall strengthen your heart; wait, I say, on the Lord!" Sometimes, God just wants to spend quiet, loving time with you. Trust that He knows what's best and that His timing is perfect.

So, here's the challenge: let God be the Lord of your relationship with Him. Let Him lead the conversation. Let Him reveal the truth to you in His perfect time and guide you in how to respond. Proverbs 3:5–6 encourages us, "Trust in the Lord with all your heart, and lean not on your own understanding; in all your ways acknowledge Him, and He shall direct your paths." When you live this way—abiding in Him daily, seeking His truth, and moving at His pace— you'll not only find answers, but you'll walk in the fullness of what He has planned for your life. Trust that His path is greater, and His answers are worth the wait!

Abiding in Christ is not following in blind faith; it's a confident, expectant faith rooted in the knowledge that God is for you and loves you beyond measure.

When you choose to abide in Christ, you are choosing to live in the fullness of His promises. You are choosing to be transformed by the renewing of your mind, to embrace the purpose He created you for, and to experience the abundance that comes from a life lived in partnership with God.

Will you take that step today? Will you commit to making abiding your highest priority? The life you desire—the life God has for you—is within reach, but it begins with a decision to abide. Set aside the distractions, silence the noise, and dedicate time to being in His presence. As you do, you will find that God is not only ready to meet you but to exceed your expectations with a life overflowing with His goodness, grace, and glory.

Eternal Welcome:
Stepping Into God's Reward

CHAPTER 36

Embracing the Fulfillment of a Life Well Lived

After completing the final journey of this book, I had a vivid dream—a rare occurrence for me, but it stayed with me long enough to write it down. I quickly asked God what He wanted me to do with it, and His response was clear: "You've already highlighted the importance of living with an eternal perspective. Now, I want you to finish this book by pointing all of My children toward the grand, eternal life I have in store for them." So, I changed the ending and integrated this story. Though not everything in the story was part of the dream, the framework was laid out in those vivid moments.

This story can't even begin to capture the incredible life God has already prepared for each of us—a life full of love and abundance. Whether you believe it or not, God has written an amazing and wonderful plan for your life, a journey beyond anything you can imagine, if you choose to accept it.

As I write this final journey, I want to remind you that while I've shared my story, God has already written yours. It's a unique story filled with His love, purpose, and abundance, just waiting for you to step into it. Though I've written from my perspective, the reality is that God has already crafted a version for you—one that is magnificent beyond words. Only you can choose to live it out, filling in the details as you walk with Him.

Your story is part of His grand design, and it's far more beautiful and impactful than anything you could plan on your own. Will you accept the incredible journey He has already laid out for you? The choice is yours.

As you read this, imagine yourself stepping into Heaven for the first time, seeing God face-to-face, and feeling His overwhelming joy as He welcomes you with open arms. Picture His eyes, filled with love, as He looks at you—proud of the faith you carried, the life you lived, and the times you served Him. But also, consider the moments He might gently show you—the opportunities missed because fear held you back from sharing His message or stepping fully into your purpose.

Think about the reunions you'll have with family and friends in Heaven, but also reflect on who might not be there. Will there be someone you missed reaching, someone who never heard the message of redemption? This is a moment for you to think deeply about the legacy you want to leave behind and the lives you can still impact.

This story, though written from my perspective, is yours too. What will your story look like? How will you feel standing before God, face-to-face? There is still time to shape your story.

Story Time: The Life of Brad—A Journey of Faith, Wealth, and Eternal Perspective

Brad grew up in a middle-class family where faith and hard work were the cornerstones of their lives. From a young age, Brad was determined to achieve greatness, driven by ambition and an unyielding faith in God. His dedication earned him degrees in theology, business, and finance. His faith was the foundation of his life, guiding every decision, while his ambition propelled him to grow businesses and build wealth. He married Latisha, a wonderful and supportive woman who was his rock and confidante. Together, they raised four children: Chelsea, David, Benjamin, and Brittany. Their home was a haven of love and laughter, filled with the joy of Sunday church services, children's sports games, Great friends and memorable family trips.

Brad's journey was filled with thrilling highs and heart-wrenching lows, but all of it led him to the most extraordinary experience—his arrival at the gates of Heaven.

As Brad stood before the massive gates, he felt his heart swell with anticipation. The gates were unlike anything he had ever seen, towering high and shimmering with an indescribable light. They seemed to pulse with life, almost as if they were breathing in rhythm with Heaven itself. Brad stood before the grand gates of Heaven, their immense size and shimmering glow like nothing he had ever imagined. As they slowly swung open, a melody filled the air, a sound that seemed to invite him into something far beyond his earthly understanding. It sounded more like music than movement, and as Brad stepped through, he felt an overwhelming sense of peace. The light pouring through the gates wasn't just bright—it was alive. Every ray seemed to carry warmth, love, and welcome.

Brad felt a presence beside him, and turning, he saw Jesus, smiling at him with a warmth that made every worry, every fear vanish in an instant.

"Are you ready, Brad?" Jesus asked, His voice tender and filled with love.

"I don't know what to say," Brad replied, his voice trembling with emotion.

"Come," Jesus said. "It's time."

As Brad stepped forward, he was filled with awe. The streets beyond the gate were made of pure, translucent gold, so clear it was like walking on a solid, glowing light. The golden streets stretched out before him in a vast expanse, shimmering with a brilliance that almost looked like liquid yet was perfectly solid underfoot. He could see in every direction, far beyond what the human eye could normally perceive. There were no limits; his vision spanned miles, from the smallest details to the grandest structures.

He was home. And then, before him, stood God the Father, in all His glory. Brad fell to his knees, overwhelmed by the sheer presence of the Almighty.

God's voice was both powerful and gentle, filling the air with love. "Brad, my son, welcome home."

Brad felt tears stream down his face as he looked up at God, feeling the weight of his life before him. In an instant, his entire life played out like a story before his eyes. The joys, the triumphs, the struggles, and yes—the missed opportunities. Brad saw moments where he could have done more, where he hadn't fully followed God's will, where fear or doubt had held him back. He saw the faces of people he had known, some whom he had led to Christ, and others with whom he had missed the chance to share the good news. His heart ached for what could have been.

"I could have done more," Brad whispered, his voice breaking. "I missed so much. I didn't always follow Your will, and I left out some blessings. I'm so sorry."

God's eyes, full of infinite love and grace, softened as He looked at Brad. "Yes, there were moments you missed, Brad, but you are still my son, and you have done well. You have loved, and you have followed me, and for that, I rejoice."

As Brad stood before the presence of God, he gazed into God's eyes and was engulfed in a depth of love so profound it felt like the essence of existence. It was an all-encompassing love—open, welcoming, and infinitely patient. In that moment, Brad felt fully known and completely accepted, as if the weight of his entire life had been leading up to this single encounter. The power in God's gaze was beyond anything Brad had ever experienced, yet it was gentle and intimate. Then, God spoke. His voice was booming, resonating with unimaginable strength, yet it was soft, like the whisper of a mighty wind.

"Brad," God said, "Well done, my good and faithful servant. I have been looking forward to this time all your life. You have been faithful in the little things; now, I will place you where you can be faithful in much more. I am so proud of you and the person you have become. You have found your way, and you have finished the race I placed before you faithfully. Enter into your eternal reward." As God spoke, Brad's heart overflowed with joy and peace. He knew, in the deepest part of his soul, that this was what he had been longing for all along—to hear those words, to be embraced by the endless love of his Creator, and to step into the eternity God had prepared for him.

Tears continued to flow as Brad felt both the weight of his regrets and the joy of God's acceptance. God extended His hand and gave Brad the fruit of the Tree of Life. As Brad took it, he felt a surge of life, peace, and joy so profound it filled his entire being. In that moment, Heaven erupted in celebration. All around him, voices of angels and saints filled the air with praises. "Well done, well done!" they shouted as they rejoiced in Brad's homecoming. He was overwhelmed by the sound of joy, love, and acceptance.

God smiled and said, "This is the eternal joy that awaits all who follow me. Eat, and be filled with life forever."

As Brad took a bite of the fruit, he felt the pure essence of Heaven surge through him, transforming his very being. He was filled with indescribable peace, joy, and love.

And standing there, waiting for him, was Jesus.

"Brad," Jesus said, His eyes full of warmth, love, and a deep sense of knowing. "Welcome home."

As Brad stood beside Jesus, still in awe of the wonders of Heaven, Jesus smiled and spoke with a tone both gentle and powerful. "Brad, you have been faithful in much, and now I give you even greater responsibility. Just as I serve and love, so will you. I am entrusting you with overseeing a part of My heavenly kingdom, where you will serve others, guide them in love, and reflect My heart in everything you do. This is a part of your rewards that I have accumulated and stored for you. As I have asked other faithful servants to rule and reign with Me, you too will have the honor of leading with kindness, humility, and grace. Your task is not to wield power but to love, to serve, and to uplift. Here in My kingdom, those who lead do so by serving, just as I have served you. Love others with the same love I have poured into you." Brad's heart swelled with joy at this profound calling, knowing that his eternal purpose would be to reign with Jesus, not for his own glory, but to reflect the endless love and service of his King. Jesus then said, Brad, I so look forward to giving you many more rewards that you have earned by loving me and loving others very soon.

Brad's heart swelled. He didn't know what to say—words failed him as he stood in the presence of the One who had guided him throughout his life. The One he had prayed to, trusted, and hoped in for so many years. Tears streamed down his face as he knelt before Him.

"Come with me," Jesus said gently, offering His hand. Brad took it, and they began to walk together through the golden streets of Heaven.

Jesus's eyes filled with love and joy, ready to show Brad everything his heart could barely contain. The streets beneath them shimmered with opalescent gold—so pure, they were nearly transparent. There was no haze, no barrier to his vision. Wherever Brad looked, he could see the farthest reaches of the kingdom. Everything was clear, perfect, and dazzling in its purity.

Jesus smiled; His voice filled with warmth. "Here, Brad, there are no limits. You can see as far as you wish. Everything is laid bare, nothing is hidden, and every corner of creation is yours to explore."

Brad's eyes widened with excitement. "You mean, I can see across all of Heaven. Instantly?"

Jesus nodded, His grin widening. "And you can go anywhere. Watch." Jesus demonstrated, thinking of a place. In the blink of an eye, they were there—on the steps of an enormous building filled with vibrant light. Brad laughed in amazement.

"Let's try walking," Brad suggested. And so, they did. As they walked through the city, the gold under their feet sparkled like the sun, yet it felt soft, as though the ground itself welcomed them. They passed lush gardens where flowers in colors Brad had never seen bloomed in radiant perfection. Every moment felt like pure joy, a song of eternal praise echoing in his soul.

But what caught Brad's breath was the peace—the undeniable, unshakable peace that seemed to unite every being. There was no jealousy, no sorrow, no pain. Just pure, unbroken joy.

As they walked, Brad could hardly take in the magnificence around him. Everywhere he looked, Heaven seemed to pulse with life and beauty beyond comprehension. The air was filled with music—songs that resonated deep within his soul. Flowers of every imaginable color lined the streets, their fragrance so sweet it brought tears to Brad's eyes. Buildings towered above them, their walls shimmering with light, like they were alive. Every structure seemed perfectly designed, full of intricate detail, yet without any flaws.

"I have much to show you," Jesus said, His voice full of excitement.

As they walked, Jesus explained that Heaven was not just a place but a living, vibrant kingdom where everyone was united in perfect peace, love, and joy. Brad felt it all around him—there was no emptiness, no envy, no struggling. The air itself seemed alive with joy and unity. Everyone they passed greeted them with warmth and love, and Brad could feel their hearts were full of peace, the likes of which he had never known on earth.

As they continued their tour, Jesus took Brad to the city center. There, worship was happening in the most awe-inspiring way Brad had ever seen. The music, the voices—they lifted into the sky like a living cloud of praise. Truly as if it was alive, and in the center of it all was Jesus, rising with the waves of worship, flipping and floating in pure joy, delighting in the love of His people. As the worship got even louder and more intense, Jesus rose even higher, and he joyfully flipped around. Brad had never seen anything like it. Jesus's joy was contagious—everyone around them was caught up in the beauty and unity of worship.

The love among the people was palpable—there was no division, no misunderstanding, only perfect harmony. Everyone was together, yet each person was fully seen and known. And as Brad worshiped alongside them, he felt as if he was part of something far greater than himself—he was woven into the very fabric of Heaven.

Suddenly, Brad noticed something remarkable—though Jesus was right beside him, interacting with him, He was also with everyone else at the same time. It was as though Jesus could be with everyone, fully present, fully engaged, without ever neglecting a single soul. It was a mystery that filled Brad with wonder. How could Jesus be so close to him while also being with millions of others? But in Heaven, it made perfect sense. There was no distance, no lack. It was pure love, always present, always available.

"You're with me, and yet, you're with everyone else too," Brad said, astonished.

Jesus smiled. "Here, there is no limitation of time or space. I am always with you, just as I am with each person. My love knows no boundaries."

They walked in silence for a while, Brad simply marveling at everything. But then, as they passed a massive library, Jesus smiled and motioned for them to enter. "This is a very special place," He said.

The library was unlike anything Brad had ever seen—endless rows of books, each one glowing with its own unique light. There were shelves that seemed to stretch into eternity, filled with countless volumes. Jesus led Brad down one of the aisles, pulling out a book that radiated warmth. It had Brad's name on the cover.

"This," Jesus said, handing the book to Brad, "is the story of your life. But more than that, it is the plan I had for you—full blueprints of every detail and every plan. The will of the Father."

Brad's hands trembled as he opened the book. Inside, he saw every moment of his life, written in a way that made every experience—even the painful ones—radiate with purpose. He could see the missed opportunities, moments where fear had held him back, and it saddened him. But just as clearly, he saw the love and grace of God weaving through every page, never leaving his side.

"I could have done more," Brad whispered, his heart heavy.

Jesus placed a hand on Brad's shoulder. "Yes, there were moments you missed, but nothing was wasted. You followed me, you trusted me, and you loved well. And for that, I rejoice."

Tears filled Brad's eyes again, not out of sadness but out of gratitude. "Thank You, Lord."

They spent what felt like hours in the library, and yet time didn't seem to pass in the way it did on earth. Brad felt no rush, no pressure, only the peace of being fully known and loved. Jesus showed him the books of others, too—lives that Brad had touched, people he had helped lead to the Father. Brad saw names he recognized and others he had forgotten, and still others he did not even know about, but all of them were part of the grand story God had written.

As they left the library, Jesus led Brad toward a grand hall, where the sounds of worship again filled the air. "I want you to meet some more people," Jesus said, and together they walked into the Hall. It was like a party of worship.

The atmosphere was electric with joy. Excitement filled the air, and Brad watched again in awe as Jesus walked among the people, rising and floating again with the waves of praise. The worship itself continued to lift Him higher, and Brad could feel the joy radiating from Jesus—His delight in His people's love. Brad's heart swelled as he joined in the worship. The love, the unity, the peace—it was beyond anything he could have imagined. It was a pure, unfiltered celebration.

As he looked around, he saw people he had known on earth, people whose lives he had touched, standing beside him, lifting their voices in worship. They smiled at him, their faces glowing with gratitude and love.

"Brad," one of them said, "thank you for helping me find Jesus. Your life changed mine."

Brad was speechless. He hadn't realized the impact his life had on others. Tears filled his eyes as he embraced them, feeling the deep connection that Heaven had created between them. It was then that Brad realized the full scope of his life's work—not the businesses, not the earthly successes, but the souls he had touched. This was the true legacy he had left behind.

They began to meet the people who had lived lives of great faith. Brad met Paul, the missionary who had endured persecution to spread the gospel. "On earth, my work was hard, but now I see the harvest," Paul said, his face glowing with joy. "Every sacrifice was worth it."

Brad embraced Paul, filled with gratitude for the work he had done to share the gospel. "Your story encouraged so many," Brad said, his voice full of emotion.

Next, they met Grace, a woman who had dedicated her life to caring for the sick and the elderly. Her joy was radiant as she spoke. "I never realized the impact of my small acts of love," Grace said. "But here, I see the ripples. Every person I cared for, every moment of compassion, it all mattered."

Brad marveled at the deep connections that existed here. There was no distance, no separation. Everyone seemed intertwined, their stories part of a greater whole.

As they continued, Brad felt an overwhelming sense of unity and love everywhere they went. And then, after what felt like both an eternity and no time at all, Jesus led Brad to a quiet place, away from the crowds. His family— Latisha, Chelsea, David, Benjamin, and Brittany- were waiting for him. Each of them stood glowing with the light of Heaven, their faces filled with joy and love.

"Dad!" Chelsea called out, running into his arms. David, Benjamin, and Brittany followed, and soon Brad was embraced by his beloved family. Latisha smiled through her tears as Brad pulled her close. The kids' spouses—Jonah, Paige, Kayla, and Jarrod—joined in, tears of joy streaming down their faces. There were grandkids and even great-grandkids all around, playing and jumping. There seemed to be hundreds of people in his family. Everyone, full of excitement, surrounded them. And in the midst of it all, Jesus held everyone close.

"I can't believe this," Brad whispered, overwhelmed with emotion. "We're here. We're really here."

"We're together, forever," Latisha said, her voice trembling with joy.

Jesus stood beside them, watching with a smile as they embraced and reunited. "This is just the beginning," Jesus said. "There is so much more for you to experience together."

And then, with a joyful laugh, He invited them all to the grand banquet. "Come," He said, His eyes twinkling. "There is a feast prepared, and it's time to celebrate."

As they continued their journey, Brad, Jesus, and his family entered a grand celebration hall. It was unlike anything they had ever seen. The tables stretched for miles, laden with food that shimmered with an almost unearthly glow. The aromas were beyond anything they had ever smelled on earth. Every bite he took was a revelation—flavors that danced on their tongues, tastes that words could never describe. The food was endless, yet it wasn't about filling hunger. It was about pure enjoyment, celebration, and communion. They all sat together, laughing, eating, and sharing stories of their lives, knowing that this joy would never end.

Even though all of Brad's family was all together, Brad marveled at how connected they were even when apart. It was as though they didn't need to be physically together to be present with one another. They could see each other, communicate effortlessly, and feel the love that bound them in a way that transcended earthly limits.

After the feast, Jesus took Brad on a tour of Heaven's wonders. Together, they traveled faster than the blink of an eye, moving from one place to another simply by thinking of where they wanted to go. Jesus showed Brad the vast expanse of the universe, galaxies spinning in perfect harmony. They explored planets, stars and places of unimaginable beauty. The universe was their playground, a vast expanse of beauty and wonder, and they reveled in the joy of discovering God's creation.

And through it all, Brad felt the presence of his family, even though they were off experiencing their own joys.

After the feast, Jesus led Brad to one of the immense living complexes. The living complex in Heaven was one of the largest and most breathtaking structures Brad had ever seen, stretching far beyond anything he could have imagined. It wasn't like houses or apartments on Earth; instead, it was an extraordinary design that radiated beauty and unity, with each dwelling seamlessly interconnected yet offering complete individuality. It was so beautiful and so massive, yet everyone was operating in a community. The architecture was unlike anything Brad had encountered before. It was alive with light, colors, and intricate details; it pulsed with the joy and peace of Heaven itself. It was a place where people lived in perfect harmony, helping and loving one another. There was no loneliness, no competition—only unity. The work they did wasn't burdensome; it was filled with purpose and joy. Every task was a joy, every moment filled with the satisfaction of contributing to the lives of others.

"Here, we help each other, we love each other, and we live in perfect peace," Jesus said. "This is how life was always meant to be."

Jesus continued, "You see, Brad, every life is a masterpiece, a work of art. Even the trials, the struggles—they all play a part in the beauty of the story. Nothing is wasted, nothing is forgotten."

Jesus and Brad walked as Brad marveled at the beauty of the buildings—each one unique, each one more magnificent than the last. The architecture seemed to breathe, alive with light and color, and Brad couldn't help but feel a deep sense of peace and belonging.

"Brad," Jesus said, "this is your eternal home. A place where love, joy, and peace never end. Here, you will continue to learn, grow, and explore. There is no end to the wonders of Heaven."

They walked through more gardens filled with flowers of every imaginable color. Waterfalls cascaded from great heights everywhere, and the air was filled with the sound of laughter, song, and the constant hum of life. Everywhere they went, Brad met people—each with their own story of faith, perseverance, and love. And with each story, Brad felt more connected to the grand tapestry of Heaven.

Brad and Jesus walked, floated, and thought their way through different parts of the kingdom—one moment on the edge of a galaxy, the next moment back in the city center, meeting more people, hearing their stories. Each person they encountered had lived a unique journey, but all shared one thing in common: they had all been led by the hand of God. Whether their earthly life was filled with wealth, service, or trials, they had all arrived at this same destination— eternal joy.

"You see, Brad," Jesus said with a smile, "this is what I've prepared for all who love me. This is the inheritance I have promised. And there is always more beauty, more joy, more to discover. "You will always be learning here.

As they continued to walk, Brad met more people—each with their own story of faithfulness. He met Joshua, a man who had spent countless hours in prayer on earth, often without recognition. "I never realized how powerful my prayers were," Joshua said, his voice filled with awe. "But here, I see the lives that were changed because of them."

He met Anna, a woman who had cared for the forgotten and downtrodden. "On earth, my work seemed small," Anna said, smiling. "But here, I see the fruit. Every act of kindness, every moment of love—it all led to this."

As they continued to journey, they met more and more people—each with their own story of faith, perseverance, and love. Brad listened as they shared their experiences from earth, their struggles, and how they had overcome through the love and guidance of Jesus. And in every story, Brad saw the same thread—the unfailing love of God, woven through every life, every journey.

Each conversation left Brad amazed more and more. Heaven was not just a place of rest—it was a place of purpose, where every life was celebrated, and every act of love was remembered.

As they continued their journey through Heaven, He continued to marvel at the beauty of everything around them. Jesus told Brad that beauty never gets old. They explored gardens filled with colors he had never seen before, waterfalls that sparkled like diamonds dropping into vast lakes, and skies that shifted in hues beyond earthly comprehension. The streams seem to sound like that precious sound of children laughing. Every moment was filled with joy, every step an adventure.

Finally, Jesus took Brad back to the city center, where worship was still happening. The air was alive with praise, and Jesus once again rose with the waves of worship, floating with joy. And as Brad stood there, watching the beauty of Heaven unfold before him, he knew that this was where he was meant to be.

Forever.

No more pain, no more sorrow—just endless joy, peace, and love. Brad looked at Jesus, at his family, at the multitudes of people gathered in worship, and his heart was filled with gratitude. This was the fulfillment of everything, and it was far more than he could have ever imagined.

And the best part? It would never end. The love, the joy, the unity—it was eternal.

This was our destination. This was the home Jesus had prepared for all of us—a place where joy, love, and unity never end. And as Brad continued his journey through Heaven, he couldn't help but think, *Why did I worry about the world when we know what awaits us in eternity?* This was the ultimate reality, and it was offered to every person if only they chose to accept it.

In Heaven, every soul was welcomed, every story was celebrated, and every life was a masterpiece of God's love. And Brad knew, with absolute certainty, that this was where he was meant to be, and it was where everyone was invited. This was the joy of Heaven—eternal, unshakable, and available to all who believe.

Heaven was his home. And it was perfect.

Step Boldly into the Eternal Life You Were Created For—Right Here, Right Now

Imagine standing on the edge of something extraordinary—an abundant life filled with joy, purpose, and victory that stretches beyond anything you could ever imagine. But here's the twist—this life isn't just something that begins one day in Heaven. Your eternity has already begun.

Right now, here on earth, you are living in the beginning of eternity. God has already promised that you will never truly die. Yes, your body will pass away and be replaced with a glorified one, but your soul—who you are—will continue. You will walk into Heaven as the same person you are today. The question is: will your life here on earth reflect that eternal reality?

You see, this life isn't just a waiting room for Heaven. It's not about merely surviving until we get to eternity. This life is our opportunity to live in such deep intimacy with God that when we step into Heaven, it's a seamless transition. We're meant to live hand in hand with Him now, just as we will in eternity. Let's not let it be a drastic change when we get there. Instead, let's live fully aligned with His will, so our lives here and our lives in Heaven are simply different chapters of the same eternal story.

Let's not forget about our rewards. We are still in the season of our ninety-year-long job interview, the only chance in all of eternity where we can show God our obedience, follow His statutes, love those around us, and store up treasures in Heaven. The enemy is constantly trying to pull you into the traps of this world, and while he may not be able to keep you out of Heaven (although you know he will do everything he possibly can to do so), he will work extremely hard to keep you in a state of mediocrity, distracted by earthly concerns. This is your one opportunity to truly live out God's commands and build your eternal rewards. Don't get caught up in the noise of this world—maximize your chance to make an impact, to walk faithfully, and to store up treasures that will last for eternity.

A Story of Almost Giving Up: From Doubt to Eternal Breakthrough

I once met a man who was at the point of giving up. He was devoted to God, committed to his faith, and he knew all the right things to believe. But deep down, he was frustrated. He had tried to live out the promises of God, but nothing seemed to change. He started to believe that maybe these promises were true for others but not for him.

One day, he sat down in defeat and told God, "I've done everything, but nothing seems to work."

But then a quiet question rose in his heart: "Have you really trusted Me? Have you truly believed My promises, or have you just hoped they might be true?"

That question hit the man like a bolt of lightning. He realized he had been treating God's promises as a last resort—a backup plan if nothing else worked. He had prayed, but he hadn't fully surrendered his fears, his doubts, and his need to control.

Maybe you're feeling a familiar hesitation right now. You might be thinking, "I've heard this before. I've tried to live this way. I've prayed, I've hoped, but nothing changed. It just didn't work for me." If so, I get it. It's easy to feel like you've already tried what's been laid out in this book—like you've dipped your toe in the water and didn't see the results you were hoping for.

But here's the honest question: Have you really tried it, or have you just thought about it? Have you merely tested the waters, or have you taken the full plunge into trusting and believing in God's promises with unwavering faith? There's a difference between considering God's promises and fully believing in them, and that difference changes everything.

This was the turning point for the man. He chose to go all in, to truly trust and believe in God's promises as his eternal truth. He realized that life on earth is more than just a temporary struggle; it's the first chapter of his eternal walk with God. He began to live with an eternal mindset—making decisions not just for today but for eternity. His faith grew stronger, his trust deepened, and soon, his life started to reflect the abundance God had promised all along.

Challenges still came, but now he faced them with an unshakable confidence that this life is just the beginning of a much grander, eternal journey with God.

The Call to Action: Live in God's Abundance, Starting Now

So, let's bring this back to you. You've read the book, seen the principles, and heard the promises. But what happens next? Will this just be another inspiring read that fades as life returns to normal, or will this be the moment everything changes? This is your call to action—to choose to live as if eternity has already begun. Because it has. You're already living in eternity, and what you do right now echoes into forever. Every act of obedience, every step of faith, every decision to trust God—none of it is wasted. It matters, and it shapes your eternity.

God isn't calling you to wait for someday—He's calling you to live in His abundance *now*. The life you've dreamed of, filled with purpose, faith, and fulfillment, is not just a future hope—it's here, ready for you.

But having that kind of life requires a decision. Will you choose to live as if eternity is already underway? Will you trust that God's promises are real, that His Word is your truth, and that the path He's given you leads to abundance both today and forever?

This is your moment. Don't hold back. Don't let doubt or past disappointments stop you. Step into the life God has prepared for you—an eternal, abundant, purpose-filled life that starts *right now*. God has laid the path before you. All you need to do is walk it, hand in hand with Him, knowing that your decisions today shape you forever.

The choice is yours. Will you live in His abundance today and step into eternity with boldness? It's time. Your journey starts now.

What Happens When You Choose to Live in God's Abundance Today and for Eternity?

When you make the decision to fully embrace this truth—everything changes. Imagine waking up every day knowing that the choices you make now aren't just for this moment but for eternity. You're no longer bound to the temporary—you're living with an eternal perspective that reshapes your priorities, your relationships, and your purpose. Suddenly, your life is overflowing with meaning. Every step you take is aligned with God's abundant plan, and His provision flows into your life in ways that are beyond what you could have imagined.

Challenges won't disappear, but they will no longer overwhelm you. When you view your struggles through the lens of eternity, they become stepping stones toward the greater life God is preparing for you. This life isn't just a battle—it's your training ground for the eternal roles and rewards God has waiting for you. Every act of obedience, every leap of faith, is an investment in the eternal life you'll live. When you stand before God, your faithfulness here will show that you are ready to be trusted with greater and mightier things in the life to come.

Your life will radiate with the light of God's eternal promises. You will become a living testimony of what it means to walk in His abundance—here and forever. As you walk this path, you're not just living for today; you're storing up treasures in Heaven, rewards that will last for all eternity. And these treasures won't just be yours—they will be your gift to Jesus, a way to honor Him forever for all He has done for you.

Now, you can sit there and say, "This is wrong. This is not what I've been taught before. This doesn't make sense in the world I live in." You can reject this truth in any way the enemy convinces you to. But understand this: no matter how you try to reason it away, it won't change what will happen for eternity. The truth of God's Word is unshakable, and the path He has laid out is real.

You can say *yes*. You can dive into the Bible, stirring up those verses that reveal the truth of what this book is showing you. Let God's Word fill your heart and mind so that when the enemy's lies try to pull you back, you are armed with scripture—a powerful sword to fight off every deception. You don't have to live in doubt or lack anymore. God's abundance is *real*, and it is available for you to walk in and enjoy today.

The enemy will try to convince you otherwise, but the truth is right there in front of you. Will you embrace it? Will you let the Word of God guide your steps, bringing you into the fullness of life He has planned for you? You can choose to live in God's abundance now and for eternity. It's real. It's for you. And it's time to step into it.

As we come to the conclusion of this journey, Hebrews 12:28 stands as a final, triumphant declaration of the unshakable kingdom we have received through God's grace: "Therefore, since we are receiving a kingdom that cannot be shaken, let us be thankful, and so worship God acceptably with reverence and awe" (NIV). This kingdom is not a distant promise but a present reality, one that anchors us in the middle of life's storms. It is a kingdom founded on God's unwavering promises, His eternal covenant, and His abundant blessings.

With this understanding, we are called to respond with hearts overflowing in gratitude, not just for the blessings we receive but for the unshakable foundation we stand upon. Our lives, therefore, become a reflection of our worship—worship that is grounded in reverence, awe, and an unbreakable connection to the Creator.

This is your moment to embrace a life hand in hand with God, making decisions that reflect the eternity you've already entered. Your journey starts now, and it's a journey that will last forever.

###